INDUSTRIAL POLICY AND ECONOMIC TRANSFORMATION IN AFRICA

INITIATIVE FOR POLICY DIALOGUE AT COLUMBIA

INDUSTRIAL POLICY AND ECONOMIC TRANSFORMATION IN AFRICA

EDITED BY

Akbar Noman
and Joseph E. Stiglitz

COLUMBIA UNIVERSITY PRESS

NEW YORK

Columbia University Press
Publishers Since 1893
New York   Chichester, West Sussex

Copyright © 2015 Columbia University Press
All rights reserved

Library of Congress Cataloging-in-Publication Data

Industrial policy and economic transformation in Africa /
edited by Akbar Noman and Joseph E. Stiglitz.
pages cm
Includes bibliographical references and index.
ISBN 978-0-231-17518-0 (cloth: alk. paper) —
ISBN 978-0-231-54077-3 (ebook)
1. Industrial policy—Africa. 2. Industrial promotion—Africa.
3. Africa—Economic policy. 4. Economic development—Africa.
5. Learning—Economic aspects—Africa. I. Noman, Akbar,
editor of compilation, writer of introduction.
II. Stiglitz, Joseph E., editor of compilation, writer of introduction.
HD3616.A3513153 2015
338.96—dc23
2015005507

Columbia University Press books are printed on permanent and
durable acid-free paper.

This book is printed on paper with recycled content.

Printed in the United States of America
c 10 9 8 7 6 5 4 3 2 1

*Cover image: Left: ©Getty/Independent Picture Service,
Right: ©Getty/Bloomberg
Cover design: Jordan Wannemacher*

References to Internet Web sites (URLs) were accurate at the time
of writing. Neither the author nor Columbia University Press
is responsible for URLs that may have expired or changed since
the manuscript was prepared.

INITIATIVE FOR POLICY DIALOGUE AT COLUMBIA

JOSÉ ANTONIO OCAMPO AND JOSEPH E. STIGLITZ, SERIES EDITORS

The Initiative for Policy Dialogue (IPD) at Columbia University brings together academics, policymakers, and practitioners from developed and developing countries to address the most pressing issues in economic policy today. IPD is an important part of Columbia's broad program on development and globalization. The Initiative for Policy Dialogue at Columbia: Challenges in Development and Globalization book series presents the latest academic thinking on a wide range of development topics and lays out alternative policy options and trade-offs. Written in a language accessible to policymakers and students alike, this series is unique in that it both shapes the academic research agenda and furthers the economic policy debate, facilitating a more democratic discussion of development policies.

The revival of economic growth in Sub-Saharan Africa in the twenty-first century is all the more welcome for having followed one of the worst economic disasters since the Industrial Revolution. During Africa's "lost quarter century," per capita income, which had starting falling towards the end of the 1970s, did not recover to its previous peak level until after the turn of the century. In an impressive turnaround from what was arguably the longest and deepest economic decline anywhere, six of the world's fastest-growing economies in the first decade or so of the 2000s were African. But with the exception of Ethiopia and Rwanda they were the beneficiaries of discoveries and rising prices of oil.

Some of the causes of the revival of growth in the region are controversial and examined in the opening chapter. That it has been heavily dependent on the commodity boom, though, is incontrovertible. Africa's deindustrialization is yet to be reversed. As a leading African think-tank, ACET, says: "To ensure that growth is sustainable and continues to improve the lives of the many, countries now need to vigorously promote economic transformation." How to go about doing so is the main theme of this volume. We focus, in particular, on the vital role that industrial policies can play. We use the term *industrial policy* in a broad sense: it is not confined to industry but refers also to policies aimed at other sectors, notably modern services like finance or information technology as well as agriculture. These are more accurately described as learning, industrial, and technology policies.

The essays in this volume mainly focus on successes with such policies in Africa or of relevance to Africa elsewhere. Like most policies these carry both risks and rewards. We draw lessons for getting the risk-reward ratio right in the pursuit of sustaining, accelerating, and improving the quality of economic performance in Africa, south of the Sahara. Much of it is also of general relevance to countries elsewhere, especially the low-income ones.

For more information about IPD and its upcoming books, visit www .policydialogue.org.

CONTENTS

ACET	African Center for Economic Transformation
AfDB	African Development Bank
AGF	African Guarantee Fund
APSTCH	Chilean Association of Salmon and Trout Producers (today SalmónChile)
ASEAN	Association of South East Asian Nations
BIS	Bank for International Settlements
BITs	Bilateral Investment Treaties
BNDES	Brazilian Development Bank
BOI	Board of Investment
BOP	Balance of Payments
CD	Capacity Development
CKD	Completely Knock Down
CPIA	Country Policy and Institutional Assessment (of the World Bank)
CSA	Central Statistical Agency
DBE	Development Bank of Ethiopia
DFI	Development Finance Institution
DNTTAH	Do Not Try This At Home
DRC	Democratic Republic of the Congo
EAL	Ethiopian Airlines
ECBP	Engineering Capacity Building Program
EDB	Economic Development Board
EHDA	Ethiopian Horticulture Development Agency
EHPEA	Ethiopian Horticulture Producers and Exporters Association
ELIA	Ethiopian Leather Industries Association

EMBRAPA	Brazilian Agricultural Research Corporation
EMBRATER	Brazilian Enterprise for Technical Assistance and Rural Extension
EPZ	Export Processing Zone
ETB	Ethiopian Birr
FDI	Foreign Direct Investment
FDRE	Federal Democratic Republic of Ethiopia
FTA	Free Trade Agreements
GDP	Gross Domestic Product
GPT	General Purpose Technologies
GTP	Growth and Transformation Plan
ICT	Information and Communications Technology
IDS	Industry Development Strategy
IEs	Industrial Estates
IFOP	Fishery Promotion Institute
IMF	International Monetary Fund
IPRs	Intellectual Property Rights
ISI	Import Substitution Industrialization
JBIC	Japan Bank for International Cooperation
JICA	Japan International Cooperation Agency
L/C	Letter of Credit
LDCs	Least Developed Countries
LCR	Local Contents Requirement
LGED	Local Government Engineering Department
LICs	Low-Income Countries
LIDI	Leather Industry Development Institute
LIT	Learning, Industrial, and Technology [Policies]
LLPTI	Leather and Leather Products Technology Institute
MDGs	Millennium Development Goals
MFN	Most-Favored Nation
MNCs	Multinational Corporations
MoI	Ministry of Industry
MoTI	Ministry of Trade and Industry
MoUDC	Ministry of Urban Development and Construction
MVA	Manufacturing Value Added
NPB	National Productivity Board
NSE	New Structural Economics
ODA	Official Development Assistance
OECD	Organization for Economic Co-operation and Development

OECF	Overseas Economic Cooperation Fund (now JICA)
OLS	Ordinary Least Squares
PADAP	Program of Guided Settlement of Alto Paranaiba
PASDEP	Plan for Accelerated and Sustained Development to End Poverty
PRODECER	Japan-Brazil Cooperation Program for Cerrados Development
R&D	Research and Development
SERNAPESCA	National Fishery Services
SME or SMEs	Small and Medium Enterprises
SPDP	Singapore Productivity Development Project
SPRING	Standards, Productivity, and Innovation Board
SSA	Sub-Saharan Africa
TNCs	Transnational Corporations
TRIMS	Trade-Related Investment Measures
TRIPS	Trade-Related Intellectual Property Rights
UNGA	United Nations General Assembly
UNIDO	United Nations Industrial Development Organization
WC	Washington Consensus
WTO	World Trade Organization

ACKNOWLEDGMENTS

This book is the outcome of the work of the Africa Task Force of the Initiative for Policy Dialogue (IPD) directed by Akbar Noman and Joseph Stiglitz, in collaboration with Japan International Cooperation Agency (JICA). In addition to financial support, JICA staff contributed to the work of the Task Force. Two of them—Akio Hosono and Go Shimada—wrote papers published in this volume and others participated in the meetings, including notably Hiroshi Kato.

In addition to them and contributing authors, we gratefully acknowledge the comments of a long list of colleagues who participated in the discussions of the Task Force (without of course committing them to our analysis or conclusions) and in particular to: K.Y. Amoako, Yaw Ansu, Sakiko Fukuda-Parr, Ato Newai Gebre-Ab, Paul Jourdan, Ravi Kanbur, Hiroshi Kato, Justin Lin, Celestin Monga, Deepak Nayyar, Leonce Ndikumana, Jose Antonio Ocampo, John Page, Martin Rama, Shari Spiegel and Ippei Tsuruga. We are very grateful to the two anonymous referees who provided insightful comments on the manuscript. This work would not have been possible without the professional dedication of IPD's former and current Program Managers, Mildred Menos and Jiaming Ju, who helped arrange the Africa Task Force's meetings and coordinate the production process of the book. We also owe a large debt of gratitude the hard and excellent work of Rahel Diro as note taker at the meetings and of Kristen Grennan for her invaluable contributions to the copyediting and coordination of the later stages of the production of this volume. We are also very gratefully indebted to Bridget Flannery-McCoy at Columbia University Press for her superb help, guidance, flexibility and patience.

Finally, we are most grateful to JICA for for funding the work of the task force and hosting a meeting in Japan on the side of the fifth Tokyo International Conference on African Development (TICAD V).

INDUSTRIAL POLICY AND ECONOMIC TRANSFORMATION IN AFRICA

CHAPTER 1

Introduction and Overview

ECONOMIC TRANSFORMATION AND LEARNING, INDUSTRIAL,
AND TECHNOLOGY POLICIES IN AFRICA

Akbar Noman and Joseph E. Stiglitz

The revival of reasonably rapid growth in Sub-Saharan Africa of about 5 percent per year for over a decade is all the more welcome for having followed a "lost quarter century": per capita income for the region, which had started falling toward the end of the 1970s, did not recover to its previous peak level until after the turn of the century. This is an impressive turnaround from what was arguably the longest and deepest economic decline anywhere. In the 2000s, six of the world's fastest-growing economies were in Sub-Saharan Africa (which we refer to simply as Africa): over about a decade, annual growth averaged more than 7.5 percent in Angola, Chad, Ethiopia, Mozambique, Nigeria, and Rwanda.

There is much promise in the turnaround in Africa. Some talk of "Africa Rising," a perspective highlighted by the online debate held by *The Economist* in 2013 titled "Africa's Rise: How Real Is the Rise of Africa?" Particularly notable are Ethiopia and Rwanda, whose growth has not been based on a natural resource boom. In contrast, oil lubricated the rapid growth of Angola, Nigeria, Mozambique, and Chad.[1] Indeed much of the revival of growth in the region is attributable to a commodity boom.

As we will discuss, while it is difficult to parse the relative roles of different causes of improved growth and there is some controversy on the role of better policies (and which particular ones), there is a consensus that booming commodity prices and mineral discoveries—especially oil—have played a vital role. There is also widespread agreement that improved macroeconomic management—at least avoidance of serious inflation and volatility—and debt relief made significant contributions.

Nonetheless, African countries typically have made little or no progress in transforming their economies, notably with respect to reversing deindustrialization that began in the late 1970s. The share of manufacturing in 2012 barely reached the level of the mid-1970s. Related to this lack of transformation is the woeful inadequacy of generating "decent" jobs, forcing large proportions of the rapidly expanding labor force into very low-productivity agriculture and the informal sector, which arguably disguise at least as much unemployment as the jobs they reveal.

In the words of an impressive and wide-ranging report of the African Center for Economic Transformation (ACET), one of Africa's leading think-tanks, "the recent economic growth, while welcome, will not by itself sustain development on the continent. To ensure that growth is sustainable and continues to improve the lives of the many, countries now *need to vigorously promote economic transformation*" (ACET 2014, 1, italics added).

The main objective of the contributions in this volume is to shed light on how to go about doing so. They emphasize the vital role of industrial policies. It is perhaps noteworthy that the two economies among the fastest-growing in Africa in this century did not rely on an oil boom: Ethiopia and Rwanda pursued to varying degrees deliberate policies of government interventions of the type we label industrial policies. These two countries were consciously and explicitly influenced by the successful experiences with industrial policies of the most successful East Asian countries (see World Bank 1993; Stiglitz and Uy 1996).

We provide a quick overview of Africa's development experience in the next three short sections in order to provide a context for the two longer ones concerning the main themes of this volume. "Static Efficiency vs. Dynamic Gains: Learning, Industrial, and Technology Policies" examines the need and possibilities of learning, industrial, and technology policies in the region, and the last section provides an overview of the other chapters in this volume and how they contribute to that aim.

AFRICA'S DEVELOPMENT EXPERIENCE

Africa's "lost quarter century," along with the economic meltdown of the former Soviet Union and Eastern Europe in the transition to a market economy, possibly ranks as among the worst economic disasters since the Industrial Revolution.[2] The lost quarter century was a period not just of deindustrialization but also of declining per capita income. After stagnating in the late 1970s, average per capita income fell steadily from 1980 to 1995 and did not recover to its 1974 level until 2004. The share of manufacturing in GDP shrank to such an extent that in 2012 it was lower than what it had been in 1965.

In a region as large and diverse as Africa, averages conceal much. Even before the recent acceleration of growth, there were several successes in the region on assorted dimensions of development in different periods, including GDP growth and managing the resource curse. Some natural resource–abundant economies such as Côte d'Ivoire, Mozambique, and, above all, Botswana (the fastest-growing economy in the world from 1960 to 2000) have experienced significant periods of fairly good growth. Even more impressive was the achievement of growth exceeding 5 percent per year for substantial periods in countries such as Ethiopia, Ghana (pre-oil), Tanzania, Rwanda, and Mauritius, which are not blessed/cursed by natural resource wealth.

As noted earlier, much of the growth in Africa since the turn of the century is attributable to booming commodity prices and hydrocarbon discoveries.[3] But there are many instances in various parts of the world of resource-rich countries mismanaging their wealth, demonstrating that an abundance of resources and booming prices are no guarantee of success.

We turn now to the following questions: Why did the region go through such a prolonged period of economic decline? What caused the decline in per capita incomes, the failure not only to make the economic transformation that was going on, say, in East Asia, but to move in the opposite direction, to deindustrialize? What are the lessons for future policy that emerge from this review of these past failures?

The period of Africa's severest economic decline, from 1980 to 1995, was an era of a multitude of reform programs reflecting external advice and conditionalities based on a brand of economics that came to be labeled the "Washington Consensus" (WC).[4] These policies reflected what became the dominant orthodoxy in economics: neo-liberalism. In our other writings (Noman and Stiglitz 2012 and forthcoming), we have explained the fallacies and failures of those policies and their contribution to the lost quarter century in Africa. But for the unabashed proponents of the Washington Consensus, the problem was not that the policies were mistaken but that they needed to be intensified and implemented better.

The failures of policies also gave rise to a search for other ingredients of successful development, going *beyond* the Washington Consensus— including notably a focus on "governance." Governance is, of course, important. But as we have argued elsewhere, it was mistaken to attribute the failure of the Washington Consensus policies simply to governance: Africa's experience reveals the limitations of arbitrary and generalized explanations, especially when they confuse cause and effect, and ends and means (Noman and Stiglitz 2014).

Policies have to be designed to be able to be administered by governments with particular competencies. The failure to do so was certainly central to the failure of the WC policies. But policies should also have aimed to strengthen competencies; instead, many of the WC policies actually worked in the opposite direction.

Of course, as we also wrote elsewhere, economics does not have much to offer as solutions to states that are failed or mired in armed conflict; but it is too simple to blame economic failure on political failure. The former also contributes to the latter (Noman and Stiglitz 2014). At any rate, we exclude from our purview here the rather different set of issues raised by the research on states embroiled in severe conflicts or that have failed.

Just as there is controversy surrounding the causes of the lost quarter century, there is controversy about the causes and sustainability of Africa's growth resurgence in the twenty-first century.

Perhaps predictably, advocates of the WC policies believe that Africa's recovery is due to those policies and is sustainable—if only the countries persist in their adherence to the WC policies. That interpretation ascribes relatively little weight to the boom in commodity prices and mineral discoveries and to the success of countries like Ethiopia, Botswana, and Rwanda that, while adopting *some* of the WC consensus policies, resisted others. It glosses over the deindustrialization that accompanied the WC policies and the fact that outside of the natural resource sector, foreign direct investment (FDI) has remained anemic. It ignores too the particular failures of some of the critical reforms in some of the countries in such areas as agriculture and finance.

The continuing controversies arise in part from the difficulties of establishing indisputable causal links between economic policies and outcomes. Reform programs may fail because of their inherent weaknesses (bad policies, or at least policies inappropriate to the circumstances of the economy), because they are not adequately implemented, or because of unanticipated exogenous shocks, and it is often difficult to parse out the relative role played by each of these. Still we can examine whether there are reforms in the reform programs that can enhance the likelihood of success.

Consider the issue of implementation: advocates of the WC policies often attribute disappointing results to failures in implementation. Earlier we noted that part of the explanation for the problems of implementation is that the "programs" were not designed to take into account the strengths and limitations of those who were supposed to implement them.

PACING AND SEQUENCING OF REFORMS

Aside from such implementation issues, there were often even more fundamental weaknesses in the reform programs, stemming from insufficient attention to the pacing and sequencing of reforms.

Sequencing is especially important because economic reforms to remove distortions confront the problem of the second best: eliminating some of many distortions may make matters worse. This is clearly demonstrated by Africa's experience with, for example, the financial sector, agricultural pricing, and trade policy reforms. The competitive marketplace that the reform advocates hoped would arise spontaneously did not emerge—partly because some of the reforms that would have enabled the emergence had not yet been put into place. While this argues for comprehensiveness in reforms, limitations in the capacity for implementing reforms point to the vital importance of prioritization and sequencing.

Thus one lesson of the failed programs in Africa is that reforms need to be mindful not just of the second-best dilemma but also of the absorptive capacity of the country—not only governmental capacity but also the ability of agents to digest and respond to a myriad of changes. Any particular reform program has transaction costs and opportunity costs. Information about reforms and their implications is neither costless nor instantaneously and universally available.

Moreover, no set of reforms is ever perfect. Any successful implementation process must entail learning about both what is working and what is not. Successful reform programs thus must create institutional frameworks for learning and adaptation.

In addition, to be sustainable, reforms have to have "political buy-in." They cannot be seen to be imposed by outsiders, especially when those outsiders lack legitimacy as a result of a conflict of economic interests or a colonial heritage. Conditionality was, as a result, often counterproductive.

This does not constitute a general argument for always going slowly: there may be threshold effects that require decisive, critical, minimum efforts. Thus, for example, when Ethiopia launched its reform program in the early 1990s, it moved rapidly on selected fronts: establishing macro-economic stability, dismantling collectivized agriculture, and establishing a system of famine prevention. But Ethiopia's reforms have been much more measured and gradual in other areas, such as financial liberalization. While some have suggested that in some areas Ethiopia could have moved faster (for example, in telecommunications[5]), its mixture of speediness and gradualism has served the country well overall, with its economy growing at a rate in the vicinity of 10 percent per year for nearly a decade before the global crisis of 2008. Even after the crisis, its economy maintained much of the growth momentum. One welcome consequence was that the proportion of the population living below the poverty line of $1.25 per day—in purchasing power parity terms—fell from 56 percent in 2000 to 31 percent in 2011.[6]

Further afield, perhaps the most notable case of combining fast and slow reforms is that of China; its success stands in marked contrast with the "shock therapy" of the former Soviet Union (see Stiglitz 1999). In China the initial focus was predominantly if not exclusively on agriculture, and subsequently on two-track price reforms and creating Township and Village Enterprises. Only later did it engage in large-scale privatizations. As another example: it first invited foreign firms only in joint ventures; much later, it allowed foreign financial firms to enter, and then only with extensive restrictions, and it still has not fully liberalized its capital accounts. In the case of the other mega country, India, a different sort of gradualism may have worked (see Ahluwalia 2002).

The issue is thus not one of how fast or how slow, but one of priorities and sequencing given the country's capacities for implementation, the transactions and opportunity costs of any set of policy measures, and the country's ability to assimilate information about the successes and failures of each policy measure and to adapt the policies in response. An approach that allows for experimentation and flexibility with successes scaled up and failures quickly abandoned is an important ingredient of success.

To take the example of financial sector reforms, liberalization of interest rates to make them market-determined typically faced the problem of financial markets that were at best thin and highly imperfect or at worst non-existent. The all-too-frequent result was exceptionally high real interest rates (a range of 12 to 15 percent was not uncommon) and the absence of long-term credit for investment. Even the United States and Europe learned in 2008 that financial sector "reforms" could be taken too far; strong regulations are necessary to maintain an efficient, competitive, and stable financial system. This is even more so in developing countries.

Privatization, trade policy, and related reforms compounded the problems posed by the "reformed" financial sector. While there was much to be said for rationalizing and liberalizing the trade regimes and public sector enterprises, the structure, pacing, and sequencing of reforms in these areas led to the deindustrialization of Africa instead of the emergence of a more competitive and vibrant sector and one that attracted foreign investment in non-extractive activities. Domestic firms faced strong competition from abroad—competitors who had better access to finance at attractive rates. Not surprisingly, many did not survive. Trade policies were one sided: the advanced countries did not simultaneously liberalize their markets. Escalating tariffs were designed to keep poor African countries supplying raw materials and to prevent them from entering into higher value-added activities. A lack of investment in infrastructure meant that even were firms able to produce something that might be desired in developed countries, the "internal barriers" to trade remained significant. (Aid for trade did not enter seriously into the trade agenda until 2005.)

INSTITUTIONS AND GOVERNANCE

The question of why the neo-liberal reforms did not work as expected led to a renewed interest in institutions. As Thandika Mkandawire (2012) states, the failure of the "good policies" of "getting prices right" prompted those multilateral institutions and aid donors advocating such policies to turn their attention to an institutional agenda.

There is a large literature on the *development state* emphasizing the role of the state in successful development, not just in the East Asian "miracle" economies, but also in many of the now-developed countries elsewhere.[7] This literature notes the important role the state played in creating institutional mechanisms for interventions that accelerated development.

What constitutes good institutions, how they are created, and how institutional deficiencies are addressed are vital for developmental success, but there are no easy answers. The 2008 crisis exposed fundamental institutional weaknesses in the United States (including in some of its most venerable institutions; for example, the Federal Reserve). But here too the neo-liberal WC reforms served Africa poorly. Some of the policies weakened or eliminated state institutions that instead needed refining and strengthening.

Belatedly, as the failure of the WC policies became evident, blame was shifted to deficiencies in public governance. These concerns led to the emergence of a particular agenda of institutional reforms in Africa under the label of "good governance" (GG). This agenda was based on a particular view of the relative roles of the state and markets. It assigned what Meles Zenawi (2012) refers to as a "night-watchman" role for the state, confining it to what is required to make markets work better. (Even then, the agenda was excessively narrow, paying, for instance, too little attention to the importance of financial regulation.) In Mushtaq Khan's words, this so-called good governance agenda is more accurately referred to as an agenda of "market-enhancing governance" that emphasizes what Thandika Mkandawire calls "restraining" as opposed to "transformative" institutions in Africa (see Zenawi 2012, Khan 2012, and Mkandawire 2012). The focus of GG is on public governance pertaining to bureaucratic hurdles, corruption, feeble enforcement of contracts and other laws, and generally poor implementation of policy initiatives.

No doubt, corruption and lack of competence of state institutions can lead to poor economic outcomes. But the GG agenda has been used to promote a particular view of which institutions are important for development and how they should be designed: a view that is embedded in neo-liberalism and its precepts on the relative roles of the state and markets, and a view that gives short shrift to other institutional arrangements, such as the role of cooperatives and other not-for-profit institutions.[8]

This view is profoundly ahistorical. It sees flawed public institutions as hindrances to markets performing in the way neo-liberalism presumes them to. It neglects attention to institutions that improve on or substitute for markets (for example, by addressing market failures).

An influential argument for the importance of the standard GG agenda is based on astatistical relationships between growth and governance as measured by the standard indicators. But as Mushtaq Khan has shown within developing countries and emerging markets, there is no such meaningful statistical relationship. More precisely, developing countries can be divided into high-growth "converging" economies and low-growth "diverging" economies, and within each group there is no relationship between growth and the measures of governance employed.

The GG agenda encapsulates intrinsically desirable ends that may well be good for and in turn be an outcome of development. For the most part, they embody worthy ends that are to be valued and pursued in their own rights. But the GG reform agenda that has emerged is neither necessary nor sufficient for economic success. We noted earlier the importance of setting priorities and sequencing reforms. The critical questions, typically not addressed by the advocates of the GG agenda, are as follows: Which of the GG reforms be given priority? and How should the prioritization and sequencing of these reforms be meshed with other economic reforms? Arguably, no country has ever implemented the GG agenda first and then developed—neither the now-advanced economies in the past nor the rapidly transforming ones of East Asia today. This may be partly because poverty and stagnation provide a context that is inimical to a full-fledged GG agenda.

What is needed is not a simplistic one-size-fits-all GG agenda, but a pragmatic one that is tailored to the particular stage of development, the key issues confronting economic management at that stage, and the particular circumstances of the country. The so-called developmental states of East Asia, as well as those in which development occurred before World War II, intervened successfully in ways that required governance capacities other than simply those adumbrated under the GG agenda.

The growth-enhancing governance reforms that we advocate here prioritize those capabilities that facilitate *learning*, in particular via industrial policies in the sense and of the type we outline further on. Africa's experience highlights the importance of *not* neglecting such policies.

Markets on their own typically do not manage structural transformations well.[9] This is true even in developed countries, but even more so in developing countries. What is needed are industrial and trade policies that promote learning, the subject to which we now turn.

STATIC EFFICIENCY VS. DYNAMIC GAINS: LEARNING, INDUSTRIAL, AND TECHNOLOGY POLICIES

Industrial policy in the broad sense in which the term has come to be used refers to any action that aims to alter the allocation of resources (or the choice of technology) from what the market, left to itself, would bring about. In this broad sense, industrial policy is not confined to industry; it also refers to policies aimed at other sectors, notably modern services like finance or information technology and agriculture. Indeed the green revolution in South Asia can be said to be a prime example of successful industrial policy.[10] Languishing African agriculture has had little or no such policy support.

In one sense, industrial policies are unavoidable: all countries have industrial policies whether they know it or not. Public expenditure (for example, the location of highways and the design of the education system) and regulatory and legal regimes (for example, bankruptcy law) affect the utilization of resources. Our concern here, however, is narrower: we are concerned with the deliberate actions intended to promote particular kinds of activities, especially those that have come to be referred to as learning, industrial, and technology (LIT) policies (we will use that term interchangeably with the more familiar "industrial policy").

Such policies are directed at improving the dynamic capacities of the economy. Allocating a given amount of resources at a point in time in a way that is consistent with *static* efficiency, as desirable as it may seem, may actually impede development and growth. These phenomena and the associated societal transformation depend on *learning* in all of its forms—including closing the knowledge gap that separates developing and developed countries.

But there may be a conflict between policies that enhance static efficiency and those that contribute to learning (see Greenwald and Stiglitz 2006 and 2014a, b, and c). Striking the right balance is at the core of success in achieving growth and development. The neo-liberal WC policies paid no attention to learning, seemingly unaware of the potential conflict, and thus failed to strike the right balance.

Patent laws illustrate the trade-off: they restrict the availability of knowledge, a public good, and confer monopoly power, thus entailing static inefficiency, but the rationale for these "distortions" is that the resulting loss in static efficiency will be more than offset by the dynamic gains from investment in new technologies that they encourage.[11] Patents also, of course, give rise to rents—a potent demonstration that rents can be channeled in ways that promote economic progress.[12] Building governance capabilities to ensure that rent seeking is so directed ought to be a vital aim of reforms that serve to move the economy to a sustained higher development and growth path.

The proponents of the Washington Consensus focused on the risks and failures of attempts to promote learning with industrial policies. They suggested that such policies were inevitably costly and invariably doomed to failure. Indeed "industrial policy" acquired such bad connotations that it could be said to have become unmentionable in polite company. Countries embarking on such policies have struggled to find other names.

But recent years have provided a strong theoretical basis for such policies in the market failures inevitably associated with learning and structural transformation. Moreover, there have been notable historical successes of such policies—not only in East Asia, but even in the United States. Africa's experience shows the enormous price of neglecting the pursuit of these policies (see Lin and Stiglitz 2014).

LIT policies are multidimensional and take many different forms across and within countries. The most famous examples are those of the so-called East Asian developmental state economies, especially Korea, Taiwan, Singapore, and an earlier-era Japan. Japan is by no means the only developed country that pursued LIT policies: they were central to almost all countries that "caught up" with the technological frontier and became developed. (Ha-Joon Chang documents this insightfully and comprehensively.[13])

There are, of course, good theoretical reasons why LIT policies are desirable. They focus on learning, especially by infant industries and economies (which are so prototypical in Africa); they address externalities, knowledge spillovers, coordination failures, and deficiencies in risk and capital markets.

They are *not* or at any rate need not be about picking winners and losers, as the issue is often misleadingly phrased. Of course, properly designed LIT policies aim to minimize the risks of picking "losers," of state capture, and of industrial policies shifting away from their catalytic role in development and addressing deficiencies in markets.

One of the major risks of LIT policies that its critics have emphasized is that such policies are vulnerable to capture and corruption. But such risks are by no means the preserve of LIT policies, as illustrated by the fact that central banks in the advanced industrial country were "captured" by the financial sector they were supposed to regulate.

Indeed the agenda of liberalization and privatization in Africa, as elsewhere, that was argued for on the basis that it would limit the scope for capture and corruption, was actually "captured" and became the source of enormous corruption in many countries, both in the developed and the developing worlds.[14] Frameworks that were created gave rise to enormous rents (both in dealings with government—in buying public assets at below fair market values and selling the government goods and services at inflated prices—and in exploiting workers and consumers through, for instance, the greater scope they provided for anticompetitive practices and market manipulation).

Indeed liberalization and privatization have arguably been a major source of corruption; major contributors to the high level of inequality that marks many African countries and a major impediment to development and growth. Mineral rights have been sold to foreign firms in processes that have given rise to corruption and have been totally divorced from any benefits of learning, technology acquisition, or spillovers that might have emanated from the development of these resources.[15]

The fact that there have been some "failures" in industrial policies is no more a reason for eschewing such policies than the failures in macro, monetary, and financial policies that were so evident in the run-up to the 2008 crisis are an argument against having macro, monetary, and financial policies. In the aftermath of the 2008 crisis, we have sought to learn from those failures. So, too, should we seek to learn from the failures of industrial policies. Whilst LIT policies have risks, they also have rewards. Indeed there are few successful economies in which governments have not pursued such policies. Arguably, Africa has paid a high price for foregoing the rewards of LIT policies.

Limitations in state capacity (deficiencies in governance) may, of course, affect the form that industrial policies take. Several African countries—Ethiopia, Kenya, Mauritius, South Africa, and Rwanda—have shown to varying degrees that they can manage industrial policies and use them to enhance growth. The success stories highlighted in several of the contributions to this volume show the potential for industrial policies in Africa (for example, the contributions of Abebe and Schaefer, Hosono, Primi, and Shimada).

The availability of finance on appropriate terms is a key element of success with LIT policies and indeed more generally is necessary to promote growth. The financial crisis of 2008 and the ensuing recession have drawn attention to the issue of making finance serve the economy rather than the other way round. In Africa, the reforms of the financial sector combined with macroeconomic stability served to do away with the highly negative real interest rates that had become common in Africa.[16]

But financial liberalization largely failed in Africa not just because it led in some cases to instability, but more often than not because it saddled Africa with very high real interest rates and a dearth of long-term credit. At the same time, the banking sector has tended to have excess liquidity, preferring short-term government securities to lending.

Perhaps in no other area did the reform programs of Africa's lost quarter century ignore the lessons of success in development, especially of

East Asia, more extensively than in finance. The analysis of the extraordinary success of East Asian economies has shown the vital role played by interventions by the state in finance (see, for example, World Bank 1993). Stiglitz and Uy (1996) brought out the role of financial restraint (or mild financial repression) that held real interest rates low and enhanced access to and confidence in the financial system. The East Asian countries employed a variety of forms of intervention that enhanced the stability of the financial system and thereby savers' confidence in it, and that lowered transactions costs. These were highly effective in mobilizing savings—more so than would have been the case had there been unregulated financial markets with high real interest rates.

Ensuring access to long-term credit at moderate real rates, sometimes through development banks, promoted long-term investments that are so essential to sustainable growth. Development banks in East Asia and elsewhere have played an important role in encouraging the kind of economic transformation based on learning and the LIT policies that we discussed previously. Development banks have made important contributions in other regions at different stages: in South Asia, especially India and Pakistan in the 1950s and 1960s, as well as Latin America, including notably Brazil, Chile, and Colombia, not just then but also more recently.

Stephany-Griffith Jones with Ewa Karwowski's contribution to this volume emphasizes the importance of development banks. An African example is the highly positive role played by a development bank in recent years in one of the very few economies in Africa that still has such a bank: Ethiopia, where financing by the development bank was crucial to the impressive success with industrial policies that promoted the development of horticulture and manufactured leather exports, as the case studies by Girum Abebe and Florian Schaefer in this volume bring out.

While there have been failures (though nothing to match the scope and breadth of the failures associated with America's banking system), there have been notable successes and considerable learning by the most successful of such banks on how to increase the odds of success.[17] We now have a much better understanding of these lessons than we did in the era of a naïve faith in state interventions that neglected the risks of government failure. Clearly the answer is not to replace that faith with naïve belief in unfettered markets that neglects the pervasive market failures by ignoring the limitations of markets, for example in providing long-term credit or credit to SMEs. (Even the United States, with its well-developed financial markets, has found it desirable to have active state provision of credit: the Small Business Administration plays a major role in the provision of small business loans, the Export-Import Bank is a major provider of lending support, especially for exporters like Boeing, and, in recent years, more than 90 percent of all mortgages have been underwritten by the federal government.)[18]

The presumption of the neo-liberal economists was that development banks, being public institutions, *couldn't* work. (There was a certain irony in this: many of the strongest critics of the development banks were economists in the World Bank and other multilateral *development banks* and from the IMF—all public institutions.) They ignored the successes and focused on the failures. Not surprisingly, the response of the WC reform program was not to reform development banks to improve their efficiency and efficacy but to dismantle them.

As with all areas of reform and good economic management, the issue is one of learning the lessons of successes and failures. Development banking raises governance issues that underline the salience of the "growth-enhancing governance" that we have emphasized. Of course, as in any area, there are downsides. But there is also enormous upside potential. This stance against development banks—like the more general WC stance against industrial policies—made Africa pay the price of foregoing the rewards of development banks. The countries could have designed their development banks—including structuring their governance and scaling them appropriately—to get the risk-reward ratio right. The costs of not having a development bank have been particularly high for those countries that have demonstrated a capacity to implement effective industrial policies. Countries that can do so might be expected to have the capacity to run an effective development bank.

THE CONTRIBUTIONS OF THIS VOLUME

As Africa seeks economic transformation for sustained growth, its policymakers need to reverse the tendencies of WC reforms, which, on the one hand pay too little attention to the benefits of learning, to critical issues of pacing, sequencing, and to the development of state capacity, including the capacity to implement reforms; and on the other hand place too much faith in markets as efficient, stable, and developmentally transformative.

Given the failure of the structural adjustment policies, it was natural that the reform agenda be broadened. Proper governance—both in the public and private sectors—is important for good economic performance, but we have argued that what we referred to as the good governance agenda—the governance agenda that was pushed by the international institutions—is in some respects too narrow. It focuses on restraining the role of government and limiting its role to "enabling" the private sector, rather than developing state capacities that have marked the development state and have played such an important role in many of the most successful countries. But it is also too ambitious: just like the economic policy agenda ignored issues of sequencing and pacing, so too for the governance agenda. We have argued, for instance, that industrial policies, including development banks, have played a critical role in many countries, including Africa, and could in the future play an even more important role. Several of the contributions to this volume buttress that case.

We have illustrated these ideas looking at several concrete issues, in particular industrial policy and the reform of financial markets. But each area of policy can be viewed from the perspective of a *development transformation.* Consider, for instance, exchange rate policy. In natural resource–rich economies, without appropriate interventions, the exchange rate will be too high, inhibiting both export- and import-competing industries, a major contributor to the "resource curse." In Africa, this common problem is compounded in some heavily aid-dependent economies by aid inflows. But there are notable examples of both countries that are resource rich (Malaysia and Chile) and those that are not (like China) that have managed their exchange rates in ways that have promoted growth and a developmental transformation.

Today is a particularly opportune time for a change in Africa's development strategy in these directions. There are major changes occurring in the global economic landscape. China provides a very large and rapidly growing market for African exports, and not just for its natural resources. Moreover, wages in China are rising. As Danny Leipziger and Shahid Yusuf's chapter points out, there will be "space" in world markets for labor-intensive, simple manufacturers that Africa could easily occupy and, eventually, for less labor-intensive and more complex manufacturers as well. To the extent such a window opens, it might not be for long: other low-income economies could fill the void rapidly. This consideration enhances the urgency of the sort of trade, industrial, and financial policy reforms that we suggest should be high on the agenda of policy reforms in the region.

Several of the chapters in this volume make the general case for industrial policies.[19] Differences in emphasis and nuances enrich our understanding of these policies, the sources of their successes, and their limitations. Hence we prefer to allow the different authors to present their views, even at the cost of some repetition, rather than impose a uniform view confined to this chapter.

In chapter 2, Ha-Joon Chang elaborates on the case for industrial policies in Africa and emphasizes its feasibility. In doing so he addresses what is often cited as a special constraint on success with industrial policies in Africa: its alleged institutional, political economy and "structural" peculiarities. He notes the important role that industrial policies played not only in the "miracle economies" of East Asia but also in the development of the now-developed countries, including notably in the United Kingdom and the United States, as well as many developing countries across all regions.

Chang then proceeds to demolish "Afro-pessimism," which holds that some peculiarly African structural factors of climate, geography, culture, and history act against success with industrial policies in the region. Chang notes the heterogeneity of Africa and compares African countries with other countries at similar stages of development, including today's rich countries, and finds these constraints to be much exaggerated.[20] For example, he notes that the fact that many, if not most, of today's rich countries faced similar constraints. They are not insurmountable. On climate, Chang points out that having a cold one also has its disadvantages and quotes Aristotle, who expounds the view that northern European countries were handicapped by their cold climates, reflected in their people being "full in spirit but lacking in intelligence and skills." Chang also provides some splendid examples of how people in more developed countries held similar prejudices against the less developed countries, including the English toward the Germans in the mid-nineteenth century and Australians, Americans, and the British variously toward Japan and Korea in the early twentieth century.

In sum, Chang emphasizes that many of these so-called structural arguments *confuse the symptoms of underdevelopment with their causes.* So do many other arguments relating to institutions, political economy, the resource curse, bureaucratic capabilities, and so forth. He notes the importance of learning by doing in managing industrial and other development policies, akin to such learning in production, and that these capacities can be built up reasonably quickly.

Much of Ha-Joon Chang's chapter is devoted to the nexus of political economy, rent seeking, and state capabilities. He notes that the tendency to assume that the alleged constraints on African development—including those reflected in "Afro-pessimism"—make industrial policies particularly likely to fail has little basis. As he points out, "Industrial policies are not necessarily more demanding in institutional or political economy terms than many other types of policies."

Chang's setting of the stage is followed in the next four chapters by a series of case studies. These are followed by contributions on the financial sector, growth and development strategies, and finally on assessment of overall policy regimes, in particular a critical examination of the World Bank's Country Policy and Institutional Assessment (CPIA).

Chapter 3 by Akio Hosono examines the lessons for Africa from what it deems to be five "outstanding cases" of success with industrial policies. These cases are highly varied both in terms of the type of sectors as well as country contexts. Hosono looks at (1) automobiles in Thailand; (2) the "Cerrado" in Brazil (which was transformed from a huge tract of barren land to high-productivity agriculture); (3) the garment industry in Bangladesh; (4) salmon in Chile; and (5) Singapore's upgrading of its industrial sector from a labor-intensive sector to a knowledge-intensive one.

Hosono seeks to extract insights from these rich case studies on how the various considerations that go into the making of industrial policy interact in practice in successful cases. He focuses in particular on the acquisition of capabilities, the creation of a learning society, using and altering factor endowments to move from static to dynamic comparative advantage, compensation for the positive externalities generated by the costs of discovery by pioneer firms, and the management of the pressures generated by globalization and the ideology and interests of "free-marketers."

Hosono's five case studies illustrate how the general principles of good industrial policy vary in their translations into different contexts. But they also illustrate the mutual causality between industrial development and economic transformation on the one hand, and the "constant development of capabilities and knowledge through learning" on the other. In the case of Singapore in particular, Hosono emphasizes the crucial role of "learning to learn." These cases also serve to bring out that reasonably good institutional "islands" created for specific purposes, as distinct from an overhaul of the entire institutional structure, can be highly effective. In this, it nicely complements Ha-Joon Chang's contention that inadequacies of bureaucratic and associated capabilities do not present an insurmountable barrier to success of industrial policies in low-income countries or Africa. Hosono's chapter also highlights the important role that the development of physical infrastructure plays as an instrument of industrial policy.

The next two chapters focus on Ethiopia, probably the most notable case of successful industrial policy in Africa. Ethiopia has particularly relevant and important lessons for the region. In this overview of the contents of the volume, we assess the Ethiopian cases in particular detail. Its late prime minister Meles Zanawi (2012) articulated an explicit and sophisticated case for Africa to learn from East Asian successes, particularly in the area of industrial policies (and those policies have been endorsed and continued by the government formed by his successor).

Go Shimada's case study of Ethiopia aims, inter alia, to illustrate the importance of disaggregating learning. He notes the prominence given to acquisition of technology (technological knowledge) and skills in the relevant literature on Africa and the neglect of other types of knowledge, especially knowledge related to policy formulation and implementation and to managerial skills. He examines the case of a program in Ethiopia to support productivity and quality enhancement by providing basic management skills and improving management practices at the factory floor level. This approach labeled *kaizen* requires very modest capital investment and focuses instead on a regular process of improving management and organizational capabilities within a firm in a participatory manner, that is, involving both managers and workers (kaizen was introduced in Japan in 1955).

A pilot project covering twenty-eight firms in five sectors—agroprocessing, chemicals, metals, leather, and textiles—had quite a remarkable impact in as short a time as six months. With no additional investment, the average benefit for a firm was around 500,000 Ethiopian Birr (USD 30,000) over the period. This was equivalent to almost USD 75 per employee, roughly equal to the prevailing gross monthly wage. The other aspect of this project pertained to improving bureaucratic capability, especially in policy coordination and implementation, the results of which are not so easily assessed (especially given the short time period of six months covered in the evaluation). Go Shimada argues for a comprehensive approach to learning, which disaggregates different elements of learning and devises suitable instruments for each of them. He holds that "managerial" and "policy" learning are important and deserve far more attention than they have tended to receive.

Girum Abebe and Florian Schaefer narrow the focus to two sectors in Ethiopia, at the same time widening it by examining a greater range of industrial policy instruments. We summarize their chapter in some detail as it raises, like Hosono's contribution, a wide range of issues concerning industrial policy, and it does so in an exclusively African context. These sectors were an important part of Ethiopia's success over the past decade. Ethiopia's GDP grew at 10.6 percent per year between 2004 and 2011 compared to the average of 5.2 percent for Sub-Saharan Africa.[21] (As we noted, much of that region's growth reflected a commodity boom, especially new discoveries of oil amid soaring prices of oil. By contrast, Ethiopia is a resource-poor country.)

Their focus is on floriculture and leather processing. These are sectors that have developed rapidly, with significant overall impact on the economy. Exports of floriculture rose from a paltry USD 0.15 million in 1997 to USD 210 million in 2011. Promotion and export of leather goods was a more gradual process. After initially rising slowly from USD $67 million in 2004/05 to USD $104 million in 2010/11, leather goods are now taking off dramatically, with a major Chinese shoe producer, Hujian, having established a huge plant in Ethiopia. This came about after a meeting with the late prime minister Meles Zenawi on his visit to China in 2011. Presumably the capabilities built up in the sector also influenced the decision to invest in Ethiopia. The company has already begun to produce some 2,000 pairs of shoes per day for designer labels and to employ some 1,600 workers. Hujian plans to expand its production rapidly, with the aim of generating USD $4 billion worth of exports per year within a decade.

The growth in these two sectors alone represents a significant transformation of the Ethiopian economy, whose total exports in 2012 amounted to about USD $3 billion. This is akin to the role of garments in Bangladesh, but the "transformation" is less likely to be confined to one sector, as Ethiopia seems to be pursuing more broad-based and deliberate industrial policies, as also suggested in Go Shimada's contribution in this volume.

One of the key issues of LIT policies concerns how learning comes about. Similar to the case of Bangladesh garment exports that Hosono discusses, Hujian is sending local employees for training to its parent company, with some 130 Ethiopian university graduates already sent to China by 2012/2013 and another batch of about 300 to follow.

According to Abebe and Schaefer, it was easy to pick these sectors for support as they have "production organizations and technological intensities that suit the labor-abundant-capital-scarce nature of the Ethiopian economy." Both sectors benefitted from a wide gamut of activist industrial policies, and Abebe and Schaefer's study brings out both the commonalities in policy measures and also how policies were tailored to the specific requirements of each sector.

The common elements in the industrial policy support of both sectors of particular importance were (1) access to finance on reasonably attractive terms through the Development Bank of Ethiopia;[22] (2) close government-business consultations; and (3) flexibility in altering forms and degrees of support.

On the differences in approaches in the two sectors and the tailoring of policies to deal with sector-specific challenges, the following are noteworthy: The leather sector was characterized by the need to overcome coordination failures that required several problems along the value chain to be tackled simultaneously to achieve global competitiveness. The dominant challenges in the floriculture sector on the other hand, pertained to logistics, land acquisition, and initial capital (that needed to be financed at terms that were not too short term and costly for such investments).

In the leather sector, the government aggressively promoted acquisition of technological capabilities, including establishing a leather training institute that organized several training programs often involving foreign experts, and also subsidized their employment by domestic firms. The government also provided land and semi-constructed factories as well as basic infrastructural facilities in industrial zones. Tax and regulatory policies were also employed to encourage upgrading. These included a ban on exports of raw hides and skins, followed in subsequent years by export taxes on minimally processed, low value-added, leather products. Such preannounced actions helped push "more innovative and efficient producers up the value chain," as Abebe and Schaefer put it.

In the case of cut flowers, industrial policies were tailored to provide land at reasonable prices and in proximity of the airport and reliable, low-cost airfreight services including air-conditioned transport to the airport and coordination with Ethiopian Airlines so that its flight timetables got the flowers to overseas markets, especially Amsterdam, at the right time.

The last of the set of case studies is the chapter by Annalisa Primi that seeks to answer the question of what lessons Africa can learn from the experiences in Latin America. She argues that whilst the "success" of East

Asia with industrial policies is often contrasted with the "failure" of Latin America, the latter has accumulated considerable experience in the design and implementation of industrial policies that have relevance for Africa. While recognizing the context specificity of appropriate policies, Primi holds that the Latin American experience, particularly in the past decade or so that has witnessed a revival of industrial policy in the region, can be utilized to derive useful lessons for Africa.

Her starting point is the changing global landscapes that African as well as Latin American countries face in pursuing economic transformation today. Primi points to a "new geography" of growth, production, trade, and innovation as a result of the rise of emerging economies, especially of China. By 2010, China had a larger share in the world's manufacturing value added than any other country: 18.9 percent compared to 18.2 percent for the United States. While Africa has been deindustrializing, the share of non-OECD countries, even excluding China, in world manufacturing has been rising: from around 14 percent in 1990 to about 20 percent in 2010. China, India, and Brazil have been growing in importance as Africa's trade partners—and sources of FDI—with the share of China alone in Africa's exports growing from roughly 5 percent in 2000 to around 19 percent by 2010. Primi contends that these changes present new opportunities for transfers of technology and learning.

Industrial policies are becoming more widespread, not only in Latin America but also in OECD countries with newer varieties of form, nuance, and emphasis, differing in important ways from the "classical" East Asian policies of the type pursued in Korea and Taiwan, for example. Understanding these policies could offer more learning opportunities for Africa.

In Latin America, as in Africa, the WC policies led to a dismantling of industrial policies. In recent years, the region has faced the challenge of rebuilding the capabilities for designing and implementing industrial policy—what she refers to as the "planning function" of the state—after their evisceration during the heyday of the Washington Consensus. As such, Latin America and Africa can learn from each other. Among the lessons for Africa from the recent revival of industrial policies in Latin America that Primi outlines are those that relate to:

(1) The strategic management of FDI to enhance technology transfers, and backward and forward linkages;
(2) Building capabilities for learning in the management of public procurement;

(3) Setting up government programs to promote the creation of start-ups;

(4) Development banks for channeling finance to production, development, and innovation (also see Griffith-Jones with Karwowski's contribution in this volume);

(5) New forms of partnerships with the private sector to match funds and encourage innovation and production;

(6) Channeling natural resource rents toward economic transformation (in particular through the creation of public funds for innovation and transformation);

(7) Investing in strengthening relevant state capabilities, recognizing that the sequence of first getting the institutions and then the policies "right" does not make much sense because they co-evolve.

The next chapter, by Stephany Griffith-Jones and Ewa Karwowski, focuses on the financial sector in Africa. Like Primi, they emphasize the important role that development banks can play—the more so because of very limited outside financing for investment by firms in Africa, with firms relying heavily on internally generated funds. This obviously constrains investment and thereby economic transformation. They point to the need for more research on development banks to learn from the failures and successes of the past.

Griffith-Jones and Karwowski begin by examining the implications of the financial crisis of 2008 and its aftermath for financial sector policies in Africa. Their contribution includes an excellent, pithy review of the recent literature on the relationship between finance and growth. One upshot of the literature that they emphasize is the inverted U-shaped relationship between finance and growth. Up to a point financial depth is good for growth, but beyond that expansion of the financial sector seems to impede growth. They suggest one possible hypothesis for explaining this: that decreasing returns to financial depth reach a point at which the increased volatility that accompanies the expansion of the financial sector more than offsets the gains from it.

While investment or long-term financing is very limited in Africa, there has been rapid growth of essentially short-term credit in several African countries in the later part of the 2000s. This has occurred in the context of limited regulatory and supervisory capacity, especially in some of them. Griffith-Jones and Karwowski note that there is general agreement in the light of the 2008 crisis and its aftermath that regulations need to be both countercyclical and comprehensive to minimize systemic risks. They argue for caution and prudence in financial liberalization in Africa, especially of cross-border capital flows. Their contribution also notes the special attention needed in the region to shape a financial sector that does a good job of serving the real economy for sustainable and inclusive growth, including notably lending to SMEs. This is, of course, of particular importance for industrial policies aimed at economic transformation. That the financial sectors in the region tend to be small in relation to the economy may facilitate shaping it appropriately. They also argue for substantially greater involvement of African and other low-income countries in discussions on financial regulations in international fora, such as the IMF, the Bank for International Settlements (BIS), and the Financial Stability Board (FSB).

The next chapter by Danny Leipziger and Shahid Yusuf delves into a very wide range of policy issues and controversies in making what it terms "policy observations" for growth strategies for Africa. In doing so it places a great deal of emphasis on a changing global context, rather similar to what Annalisa Primi's chapter does, but touching on many more issues, including the changing nature of technological trends, climate change, democratization, and the prospects for export-led manufacturing growth (which in its view are not particularly bright).

To some degree this contribution can be said to add a rather different viewpoint (or at least emphasis) to that which underlies the preceding ones. Leipziger and Yusuf's support for industrial policies is more tepid and qualified both in itself and, at least to some degree, implicitly because of the relative importance they attribute to other policies for accelerated growth and transformation. While they are in broad agreement with Griffith-Jones and Karwowski on the dangers of excessive financial liberalization, they worry that regulations and restraints on finance can hamper growth.

There are other areas of emphasis and nuance that are not entirely in consonance with the thrust of the rest of the volume. They are, for instance, more sympathetic with the good governance agenda to which we referred earlier in this introduction. Leipziger and Yusuf demonstrate that the debate over what will contribute to Africa's growth and development is alive and well and has varied hues.

Julia Cagé's chapter brings the volume to an appropriate closure. We noted earlier that the Washington Consensus provided a well-articulated view of what was required for successful development. Even when the policies *seemed* to fail, the response was less to change the policy but more to broaden the agenda to include the institutional reforms that we labeled as the good governance agenda. She subjects the different measures of "policy performance" that are being used by international organizations to rank countries on the "goodness" of their policies to critical analysis.

Cagé begins by noting the high-profile criticism by China regarding its ranking on the "Doing Business" indicators that the World Bank churns out and that are so influential in measures of country policy performance. They are supposed to assess the quality of the country's environment for doing business. The implication is that countries with good scores on the "Doing Business" indicators will have a stronger private sector and will grow more robustly. While these indicators have rightly been criticized for seeming to suggest that having poor labor conditions and an unbalanced tax regime—favoring corporations—is good for business and for the economy, the problems are deeper: China, the outstanding case of growth and transformation that is having such a profound influence on the world economy—as Leipziger and Yusuf and Primi emphasize in this volume—ranks ninety-first out of 185 countries in 2013 (India does worse and Vietnam is close to China in "Doing Business" in recent years).

Julia Cagé focuses in particular on the World Bank's Country Policy and Institutional Assessment (CPIA) measures, probably the most influential of these composite measures. Her chapter begins with some anecdotal evidence on how the CPIA performs as a predictor of growth. She then employs a yearly panel data set of more than 140 developing countries covering the period from 1977 to 2008. Both her anecdotal and econometric evidence find that CPIA is not a good predictor of future economic growth. Julia Cagé argues for other, new measures of policy performance and for more weight to be given to the role and capacities of governments. She emphasizes the importance of measuring the quality of industrial policy, especially of export promotion strategies.

Her chapter provides strong empirical verification of many of the claims made earlier in this introduction and elsewhere in the book: the policies advocated by the Washington Consensus do not lead to strong economic growth, development, and economic transformation. This book highlights the importance of an alternative set of policies that has demonstrably broad success, at least in a number of cases.

NOTES

1. Chad's growth was concentrated in the first half of the 2000s and tapered off sharply in recent years with a drop in oil production and related foreign investment.

2. For a more detailed discussion of the issues in this and the next section, see Noman and Stiglitz (2012) and Noman and Stiglitz (forthcoming). The discussion here draws heavily on these essays.

3. There is some controversy on the relative roles of commodity booms and improved policies, but that the former have been very important is beyond dispute.

4. John Williamson coined the term *Washington Consensus*, describing the consensus of policies surrounding the reforms advocated by the Washington-based institutions in Latin America. But the term has come to refer to a broader set of policies, advocated not only in Latin America but also in other developing countries. See Williamson (1989, 2008) and Stiglitz (2008b, 2008c).

5. Though even here it was arguably wise to resist the policies of selling off licenses to foreign firms, instead focusing on procuring particular services from foreign providers. Moreover, in the presence of fast-changing technologies, there are distinct advantages from maintaining flexibility.

6. World Bank (2015).

7. On East Asia, see, for example, Amsden (1989, 2001), Wade (1990), and World Bank (1993). Ha-Joon Chang (2002) covers both East Asia as well as the developed countries of North America and Europe.

8. Bangladesh provides what is arguably the most striking example of the important role that such institutions can play as exemplified by BRAC and the Grameen Bank.

9. This is partly because of capital market imperfections: the new sectors typically have difficulties raising funds to finance new enterprises, and individuals have difficulties raising funds to finance the new human capital required in the new sectors (see Delli Gatti et al. 2012a and b). It is also because learning is central to transformation, and there are numerous market failures associated with learning. See Greenwald and Stiglitz (2014c).

10. In both India and Pakistan the green revolution was facilitated by policies of price support setting a floor on output prices, as well as input subsidies, including notably for electricity, that enhanced the profitability of tube-well irrigation.

11. What constitutes a good patent law is another matter. The details of design make some entail more static losses and/or less dynamic gains than others. See, for example, Dosi and Stiglitz (2014) and Stiglitz (2008c).

12. Arguably, the East Asian countries did this very successfully. See references cited in previous endnote.

13. Ha-Joon Chang (2003).

14. Stiglitz (2002a) described the process of privatization in many countries as one of "briberization." Much of the inequality in wealth and income that has become such a subject of concern in recent years, which Stiglitz (2012) has argued has had significant adverse effects on growth and economic performance, arose out of these poorly designed privatizations.

15. See Jourdan (2014) for an excellent discussion on how the development of natural resources can be the basis of broader-based growth through the design of appropriate industrial policies.

16. Note that the real interest rate in the United States and Europe in recent years has been negative. Hellmann, Murdock, and Stiglitz (1997 and 1998) distinguish between the potentially beneficial effects of mild financial restraint (often associated with slightly negative real interest rates) and financial repression (marked by highly negative real interest rates).

17. In Africa, the failures often stemmed from some combination of poor governance of such banks, with loans often given on the basis of political influence rather than the merit of the project, and an economic environment characterized by macroeconomic instability and other policy failings, especially of trade and exchange rate policies.

18. Emran and Stiglitz (2009) provide a theoretical explanation for why, without government intervention, there will be an undersupply of loans to small businesses.

19. For more elaborate discussions of the case for industrial policies in recent years, see Greenwald and Stiglitz (2014a, b, and c); Lin (2012); Aghion (2014); Cimoli, Dosi, and Stiglitz (2009); and Stiglitz, Lin, and Patel (2014). There are also of course the classic works of Alice Amsden (1989, 2001) and Robert Wade (1990).

20. For a more elaborate and detailed case along similar lines, see the contributions of Akbar Noman and Joseph Stiglitz, Thandika Mkandawire, Mushtaq Khan, and Meles Zenawi in Noman et al. (2012).

21. Also for comparison: Bangladesh's annual economic growth during the period was 6.2 percent.

22. Ethiopia is rare in Africa in still having a development bank after the wave of financial liberalization that closed down such banks not only in Africa but in many other developing countries.

REFERENCES

African Center for Economic Transformation (ACET). 2014. *African Transformation Report: Growth with Depth*. Washington, DC: ACET.

Aghion, Philippe. 2014. "Afterword: Rethinking Industrial Policy." In *Creating a Learning Society: A New Approach to Growth, Development, and Social Progress*, ed. Bruce C. Greenwald and Joseph E. Stiglitz, 509–521. New York: Columbia University Press.

Ahluwalia, Montek S. 2002. "Economic Reforms in India Since 1991: Has Gradualism Worked?" *Journal of Economic Perspectives* 16 (3): 67–88.

Amsden, Alice. 1989. *Asia's Next Giant: South Korea and Late Industrialization*. New York: Oxford University Press.

——. 2001. *The Rise of "The Rest": Challenges to the West from Late-Industrializing Economies*. Oxford: Oxford University Press.

Chang, Ha-Joon. 2002. *Kicking Away the Ladder: Development Strategy in Historical Perspective*. London: Anthem Press.

Charlton, Andrew, and Joseph E. Stiglitz. 2012. *The Right to Trade: A Report for the Commonwealth Secretariat on Aid for Trade*. London: Commonwealth Secretariat.

Cimoli, Mario, Giovanni Dosi, and Joseph Stiglitz, eds. 2009. *Industrial Policy and Development*. New York: Oxford University Press.

Commission on Growth and Development. 2008. "The Growth Report: Strategies for Sustained Growth and Inclusive Development." Washington, DC: World Bank. https://openknowledge.worldbank.org/handle/10986/6507.

Delli Gatti, D., M. Gallegati, B. C. Greenwald, A. Russo, and J. E. Stiglitz. 2012a. "Sectoral Imbalances and Long Run Crises." In *The Global Macro Economy and Finance*, ed. F. Allen, M. Aoki, J.-P. Fitoussi, N. Kiyotaki, R. Gordon, and J. E. Stiglitz, IEA Conference Volume No. 150-III, 61–97. Houndmills, U.K.: Palgrave Macmillan.

———. 2012b. "Mobility Constraints, Productivity Trends, and Extended Crises." *Journal of Economic Behavior & Organization* 83 (3): 375–393.

Dosi, Giovanni, and Joseph E. Stiglitz. 2014. "The Role of Intellectual Property Rights in the Development Process, with Some Lessons from Developed Countries: An Introduction." In *Intellectual Property Rights: Legal and Economic Challenges for Development*, ed. Mario Cimoli, Giovanni Dosi, Keith E. Maskus, Ruth L. Okediji, Jerome H. Reichman, and Joseph E. Stiglitz, 1–53. Oxford: Oxford University Press.

Economist, The. 2013. "Africa's Rise: How Real Is the Rise of Africa?" March 20. www.economist.com/debate/days/view/956.

Emran, Shahe, and Joseph E. Stiglitz. 2009. "Financial Liberalization, Financial Restraint, and Entrepreneurial Development." Working paper, Columbia University, January.

Gerschenkron, Alexander. 1962. *Economic Development in Historical Perspective: A Book of Essays*. Cambridge, Mass.: Harvard University Press.

Godoy, Sergio, and Joseph Stiglitz. 2006. "Growth, Initial Conditions, Law and Speed of Privatization in Transition Countries: 11 Years Later." NBER Working Paper No. 11992, January.

Greenwald, Bruce C., and Joseph E. Stiglitz. 2006. "Helping Infant Economies Grow: Foundations of Trade Policies for Developing Countries." *American Economic Review: AEA Papers and Proceedings* 96 (2): 141–146.

———. 2014a. "Industrial Policies, the Creation of a Learning Society, and Economic Development." In *The Industrial Policy Revolution I: The Role of Government Beyond Ideology*, ed. Joseph E. Stiglitz and Justin Yifu Lin, 43–71. New York: Palgrave Macmillan.

———. 2014b. "Learning and Industrial Policy: Implications for Africa." In *The Industrial Policy Revolution II: Africa in the 21st Century*, ed. Joseph E. Stiglitz, Justin Yifu Lin, and Ebrahim Patel, 25–29. New York: Palgrave Macmillan.

———. 2014c. *Creating a Learning Society: A New Approach to Growth, Development, and Social Progress*. New York: Columbia University Press.

Hellmann, Thomas, Kevin Murdock, and Joseph E. Stiglitz. 1997. "Financial Restraint: Toward a New Paradigm." In *The Role of Government in East Asian Economic Development*, ed. M. Aoki, H. Kim, and M. Okuna-Fujiwara, 163–207. Oxford: Clarendon Press.

———. 1998. "Financial Restraint and the Market Enhancing View." In *The Institutional Foundations of East Asian Economic Development*, ed. Y. Hayami and M. Aoki, 255–284. London: MacMillan.

Jomo, K. S., and R. von Arnim. 2012. "Economic Liberalization and Constraints to Growth in Sub-Saharan Africa." In Noman et al. (2012), 499–535.

Jourdan, P., 2014. "Toward a Resource-based African Industrialisation Strategy." In *The Industrial Policy Revolution II: Africa in the 21st Century*, ed. Joseph E. Stiglitz, Justin Yifu Lin, and Ebrahim Patel, 364–385. Houndmills, U.K.: Palgrave Macmillan.

Kennedy, David, and Joseph Stiglitz. 2013. "Introduction." In *Law and Economic Development with Chinese Characteristics: Institutions for the 21st Century*, ed. D. Kennedy and J. E. Stiglitz, 1–16. New York: Oxford University Press.

Keynes, John M. [2007] 1936. *The General Theory of Employment, Interest and Money*. London: Macmillan.

Khan, Mushtaq. 2012. "Governance and Growth: Challenges for Africa." In *Good Growth and Governance in Africa: Rethinking Development Strategies*, ed. Akbar Noman, Kwesi Botchwey, Howard Stein, and Joseph Stiglitz, 51–79. New York: Oxford University Press.

Lin, Justin Yifu. 2012. *New Structural Economics: A Framework for Rethinking Development and Policy*. Washington, DC: World Bank.

Lin, Justin Yifu, and Joseph E. Stiglitz, eds. 2014. *The Industrial Policy Revolution: The Role of Government Beyond Ideology*. New York: Palgrave Macmillan.

Mazzucato, Mariana. 2013. *The Entrepreneurial State: Debunking Public vs. Private Sector Myths*. London: Anthem Press.

Mbom, Lambert. 2013. "World Bank: 'Structural Adjustments Programmes Worked in Africa.' (Interview with Shantayanan Devarajan)." *Think Africa Press*, May 7. http://thinkafricapress.com/development/world-bank-devarajan.

Mkandawire, Thandika. 2012. "Institutional Monocropping and Monotasking in Africa." In *Good Growth and Governance in Africa: Rethinking Development Strategies*, ed. Akbar Noman, Kwesi Botchwey, Howard Stein, and Joseph Stiglitz, 80–113. New York: Oxford University Press.

Noman, Akbar, Kwesi Botchwey, Howard Stein, and Joseph Stiglitz, eds. 2012. *Good Growth and Governance in Africa: Rethinking Development Strategies*. New York: Oxford University Press.

Noman, Akbar, and Joseph E. Stiglitz. 2012. "Strategies for African Development." In *Good Growth and Governance in Africa: Rethinking Development Strategies*, ed. Akbar Noman, Kwesi Botchwey, Howard Stein, and Joseph Stiglitz, 3–47. New York: Oxford University Press.

——. forthcoming. "Economics and Policy: Some Lessons from Africa's Experience." In *Oxford Handbook of Africa and Economics*, ed. Celestin Monga and Justin Yifu Lin. Oxford: Oxford University Press.

Stiglitz, Joseph. 1996. "Some Lessons from the East Asian Miracle." *World Bank Research Observer* 11 (2): 151–177.

——. 1999. "Quis custodiet ipsos custodes? Corporate Governance Failures in the Transition." *Challenge* 42(6): 26–67.

——. 2002a. *Globalization and Its Discontents*. New York: W. W. Norton.

——. 2002b. "New Perspectives on the Role of the State." In *Editing Economics: Essays in Honour of Mark Perlman*, ed. H. Lim, Ungsuh K. Park, and G. C. Harcourt, 216–217. New York: Routledge.

———. 2008a. "The Economic Foundations of Intellectual Property," sixth annual Frey Lecture in Intellectual Property, Duke University, February 16, 2007. *Duke Law Journal* 57 (6): 1693–1724.

———. 2008b. "Introduction: From the Washington Consensus Towards a New Global Governance." In *The Washington Consensus Reconsidered: Towards a New Global Governance*, ed. N. Serra and J. E. Stiglitz, 3–13. New York: Oxford University Press.

———. 2008c. "Is There a Post-Washington Consensus Consensus?" In *The Washington Consensus Reconsidered: Towards a New Global Governance*, ed. Narcis Serra and Joseph E. Stiglitz, 41–56. New York: Oxford University Press.

———. 2010. "Interpreting the Causes of the Great Recession of 2008." In *Financial System and Macroeconomic Resilience: Revisited*, BIS Paper 53: 4–19. Volume prepared for BIS conference, Basel, June 25–26, 2009.

———. 2012. *The Price of Inequality: How Today's Divided Society Endangers Our Future.* New York: W. W. Norton.

Stiglitz, Joseph E., Justin Yifu Lin, and Ebrahim Patel, eds. 2014. *The Industrial Policy Revolution II: Africa in the 21st Century.* London: Palgrave Macmillan.

Stiglitz, Joseph E., and M. Uy. 1996. "Financial Markets, Public Policy and the East Asian Miracle." *World Bank Research Observer* 11 (2): 249–276.

Wade, Robert. 1990. *Governing the Market: Economic Theory and the Role of the Government in East Asian Industrialization.* Princeton: Princeton University Press.

Williamson, John. 1989. "What Washington Means by Policy Reform." In *Latin American Adjustment: How Much has Happened*, ed. John Williamson, 5–24. Washington: Institute for International Economics.

———. 2008. "A Short History of the Washington Consensus." In *The Washington Consensus Reconsidered: Towards a New Global Governance*, ed. Narcis Serra and Joseph E. Stiglitz, 41–56. New York: Oxford University Press.

World Bank. 1993. *The East Asian Miracle: Economic Growth and Public Policy.* Oxford: Oxford University Press.

———. 2015. *Ethiopia: Poverty Assessment 2014* (Report No. AUS6744). Washington, DC: World Bank.

Zenawi, Meles. 2012. "States and Markets: Neoliberal Limitations and the Case for Developmental State." In *Good Growth and Governance in Africa: Rethinking Development Strategies*, ed. Akbar Noman, Kwesi Botchwey, Howard Stein, and Joseph Stiglitz, 140–174. New York: Oxford University Press.

CHAPTER 2

Is Industrial Policy Necessary and Feasible in Africa?

THEORETICAL CONSIDERATIONS AND HISTORICAL LESSONS

Ha-Joon Chang

RISING INTEREST IN INDUSTRIAL POLICY SIDESTEPS AFRICA

Industrial policy has been one of the most controversial issues in economics, especially in development economics (for a review of the industrial policy debate since the 1980s, see Chang 2011). Particularly surrounding its role in the development success of East Asia, there was a fierce debate that came to a head in the late 1980s and the early 1990s (Amsden 1989; Wade 1990; World Bank 1987, 1991, and 1993; Stiglitz 1996).

Fortunately, during the last decade or so there have been a number of developments in academia and in the real world that have made industrial policy more acceptable and thus the debate surrounding it less ideologically charged and more pragmatic and nuanced.

At the theoretical level, the market fundamentalist view that there are very few theoretical justifications for industrial policy has lost its dominance. On top of that, the infant industry argument has been refined in a number of ways (Chang 2002; Shaffaedin 2005; Greenwald and Stiglitz 2006; Dosi, Cimoli, and Stiglitz 2009). An increasing number of more orthodox economists accept that there are many types of market failures that need to be addressed through industrial policy—not just the more conventional "externalities" problem, but also economies of agglomeration and coordination failures (see Lin's interventions in Lin and Chang 2009; Lin and Monga 2012).

The interpretation of the evidence on industrial policy has also evolved. It is increasingly recognized that industrial policy is not some highly idiosyncratic practice found only in East Asian "miracle" economies (Japan,

South Korea, Taiwan, and Singapore), but what most of today's rich countries used when they were catch-up economies themselves (Bairoch 1993; Chang 2002 and 2007; Reinert 2007). Some econometric studies have even identified a positive correlation between protectionism and economic growth in the late nineteenth and early twentieth centuries (O'Rourke 2000; Vamvakidis 2002; Clemens and Williamson 2001). Irwin (2002) provides a criticism of these studies, which is then countered by Lehmann and O'Rourke (2008). In particular, the increasing recognition of Britain and the United States—the supposed homes of free market and free trade policies—as the pioneers of infant industry promotion through protectionism and other forms of industrial policy has added a whole new complexity to the history of capitalist development. Recent studies, especially Chang (2002) and Reinert (2007), have revealed that the practice of infant industry promotion was first systematically applied by Robert Walpole, the British prime minister from 1721 to 1742, and the theory of it was first invented by Alexander Hamilton, the first U.S. treasury secretary, in his report to the U.S. Congress in 1791 (see Chang [2002] for further details; see Hamilton [1791] for his original report).

The import substitution industrialization (ISI) experience in the developing world before the 1980s has also been subject to a more nuanced interpretation. The role of industrial policy in the significant economic development achieved by many Latin American countries between the 1930s and the 1980s is increasingly accepted, as well as the success of earlier protectionism in the continent in the late nineteenth and the early twentieth centuries (on the latter, see Clemens and Williamson [2004]). Even the typical depiction of industrial policy in Africa, especially Sub-Saharan Africa, in the 1960s and the 1970s as an unmitigated disaster has been questioned (Jerven 2011).

More recently, the 2008 global financial crisis has enhanced the legitimacy of industrial policy. First, the crisis prompted some major industrial policy actions—both defensive and proactive—by the rich countries that used to preach against industrial policy (for example, bailout of U.S. automakers and an increase in "green" subsidies in many developed countries, including the United States). Second, the crisis has prompted countries like the United States, and especially Britain, to accept that their financial sector had been overdeveloped and therefore that there is a need to rebalance their economies by reviving the manufacturing sector, through industrial policy if necessary. Third, since the crisis, the continued rise of China (and to a lesser extent Brazil) and the solid performance of Germany, all of which have actively used industrial policy, have also made people reassess the importance of industrial policy.

This general shift in the mood in favor of industrial policy has not, however, extended to the African countries. However effective the policy may have been in Japan, Korea, or China (or even the United States in the nineteenth century), it is argued, it simply cannot work in those African countries. A wider range of reasons is given—such as excessive natural resource endowments (the so-called resource curse thesis), pathological politics, the lack of bureaucratic capabilities, and the changes in the global economic rules—but the implication is that the African countries would be better off sticking to their natural resource advantages rather than trying to develop manufacturing industries through industrial policy.

ARE AFRICA'S DEVELOPMENT FAILURES STRUCTURAL? CLIMATE, GEOGRAPHY, CULTURE, AND HISTORY

In this section, I discuss those factors that are supposed to make industrial policy inapplicable to Africa, but, before doing that, I first need to critically review those arguments that Africa is doomed to development failure because of its climate, geography, culture, and history—a group of arguments known as "Afro-pessimism" (the most prominent examples include Easterly and Levine [1997]; Bloom and Sachs [1998]; Collier and Gunning [1999]; Sachs and Warner [2001]; and Acemoglu, Johnson, and Robinson [2001]).

Now, in discussing these arguments, we should bear in mind that there is a huge problem in talking of Africa as if it is homogeneous. After all, it is a continent of nearly sixty countries (the exact number depends on your attitude toward entities like Western Sahara) with very varied natural and human conditions. If most African economies look rather similar to each other economically, it is not because they are in the same continent, but because all economies—in whichever continent they are—at low levels of development look rather similar to each other due to the lack of specialization and diversification in the production structure, which then leads to high degrees of homogeneity in occupational structures, social organizations, and lifestyles. Bearing this important point in mind, let us see how those arguments that emphasize structural factors, like climate, geography, culture, and history, explain African development experiences.

THE ARGUMENTS

According to the argument emphasizing the climate factors, being close to the equator, the African countries suffer from tropical diseases such as malaria. These diseases become burdens on economic development, as they reduce worker productivity and raise health care costs. Some also point out that tropical soil is of poor quality, reducing agricultural productivity.

The geography argument points out that many African countries are landlocked and thus are disadvantaged in integrating into the global economy through international trade. Many of them are also in "bad neighborhoods" in the sense that they are surrounded by other poor countries that have small markets (that restrict their trading opportunities) and, frequently, violent conflicts (that often spill over into neighboring countries).

Two aspects are highlighted by those arguments emphasizing the historical factors: ethnic diversity and colonialism. The high ethnic diversity of many African nations makes their people distrust each other, raising transaction costs. Ethnic diversity, it is pointed out, is likely to encourage violent conflicts, especially if there are a few groups of similar strengths (rather than many small groups, which are more difficult to organize). Africa's colonial history is argued to have produced low-quality institutions in most African countries, as the colonizers did not want to settle in countries with too many tropical diseases (so there is an interaction between climate and institutions) and thus only installed low-quality institutions that were needed for resource extraction ("extractive institutions" of Acemoglu, Johnson, and Robinson [2001]).

The cultural argument is usually presented in rather convoluted ways to avoid the accusation of racism, but it is essentially that African culture is bad for economic development: Africans do not work hard, do not plan for the future, and cannot cooperate with each other. In explaining the economic divergence between South Korea and Ghana, two countries that were at similar levels of economic development in the 1960s, Samuel Huntington of *The Clash of Civilizations* fame argues: "Undoubtedly, many factors played a role, but . . . culture had to be a large part of the explanation. South Koreans valued thrift, investment, hard work, education, organisation, and discipline. Ghanaians had different values. In short, cultures count" (2000, xi). Daniel Etounga-Manguelle (2000), a Cameroonian engineer and writer, notes: "The African, anchored in his ancestral culture, is so convinced that the past can only repeat itself that he worries only superficially about the future. However, without a dynamic perception of the future, there is no planning, no foresight, no scenario building; in other words, no policy to affect the course of events" (69). And then he goes on to say that "African societies are like a football team in which, as a result of personal rivalries and a lack of team spirit, one player will not pass the ball to another out of fear that the latter might score a goal" (75).

THE CRITICISMS

All the factors highlighted by the "structural" arguments discussed earlier are relevant, to one degree or another. However, that a factor is given by nature or history does not mean that the outcome is predetermined. Indeed the fact that most of today's rich countries have also suffered from similar "structural" handicaps suggests that all those structural factors are not insurmountable (Chang 2009a, 2009b, and 2010).

CLIMATE

In relation to the climate argument, I should first note that many of today's rich countries used to have malaria and other tropical diseases, at least during the summer—not just Singapore, which is right in the middle of the tropics, but also southern Italy, the southern United States, South Korea, and Japan. These diseases have largely (although not entirely) disappeared in those countries not because their climates have somehow changed, but because they have better sanitation (that has vastly reduced their incidences) and better medical facilities (that allow them to effectively deal with the few cases that still occur) thanks to economic development.

Moreover, it should be pointed out that not just tropical climates but also frigid and arctic climates (affecting a number of rich countries, such as Finland, Sweden, Norway, Canada, and parts of the United States) impose economic burdens—machines seize up, fuel costs skyrocket, and transportation is blocked by snow and ice. The Scandinavian countries used to be effectively landlocked for half of the year until the advent of the ice-breaking ship in the late nineteenth century. Once again, the cold climate doesn't appear to hold those rich countries back because they have acquired the money and the technologies to deal with it (the same as in the case of Singapore's tropical climate).

When you think about it, there is no a priori reason to believe that a cold climate is better than a hot climate for economic development. Indeed in *Politics* (Book VII, chapter 7), Aristotle argued that the European societies are not very developed because their climate is too cold, which makes their people, well, stupid. He said: "Those who live in a cold climate and in Europe are full of spirit, but wanting in intelligence and skill; and therefore they retain comparative freedom, but have no political organization, and are incapable of ruling over others. Whereas the natives of Asia are intelligent and inventive, but they are wanting in spirit, and therefore they are always in a state of subjugation and slavery. But the Hellenic race, which is situated between them, is likewise intermediate in character, being high-spirited and also intelligent. Hence it continues free, and is the best governed of any nation, and if it could be formed into one state, would be able to rule the world" (Aristotle 2001, 1286).

Therefore to blame Africa's underdevelopment on climate is to confuse the cause of underdevelopment with its symptoms—poor climate does not cause underdevelopment; a country's inability to overcome the constraints imposed by its poor climate is a symptom of underdevelopment.

GEOGRAPHY

Much has been made out of the landlocked status of many African countries. Landlockedness does impose economic burdens, but then how do we explain the economic successes of Switzerland and Austria? These are two of the richest economies in the world, but they are both landlocked. Some people would respond to this point by saying that those countries could develop because they had good river transport, but many landlocked African countries are *potentially* in the same position: for example, Burkina Faso (the Volta), Mali and Niger (the Niger), Zimbabwe (the Limpopo), and Zambia (the Zambezi). So once again the argument is based on confusion between the cause and the symptom—it is the lack of investment in the river transport system, rather than the geography itself, that is the problem.

Being in a "bad neighborhood" may not be as disadvantageous as it may seem. India has grown very fast in the last couple of decades despite being in the poorest region in the world (poorer than Sub-Saharan Africa), with its share of conflicts (the long history of military conflicts between India and Pakistan, the Maoist Naxalite guerillas in India, Hindu-Muslim violence in India, the Tamil-Sinhalese ethnic war in Sri Lanka, and so on).

HISTORY

It would be silly to deny that ethnic divisions can hamper growth. However, their effects should not be exaggerated. Ethnic diversity is the norm elsewhere too. Even ignoring ethnic diversities in immigration-based societies like the United States, Canada, and Australia, many of today's rich countries in Europe have suffered from linguistic, religious, and ideological divides—especially of the "medium degree" (that is, a few, rather than numerous, groups) that is supposed to be most conducive to violent conflicts. Belgium has two (and a bit, if you count the tiny German-speaking minority) ethnic groups. Switzerland has four languages and two religions, and has experienced a number of mainly religion-based civil wars. Spain has serious minority problems with the Catalans and the Basques, which have even involved terrorism. Due to its 560-year rule over Finland (1249 to 1809, when it was ceded to Russia), Sweden has a significant Finnish minority (around 5 percent of the population); likewise, in Finland there is a Swedish minority of similar proportion. The examples can go on.

The East Asian countries, often believed to have exceptionally benefited from their ethnic homogeneities, also have serious internal divisions. You may think Taiwan is ethnically homogeneous, as its citizens are all "Chinese." However, to begin with, there is actually a tiny native population of Polynesian origin (the so-called Kaoshan people). Moreover, even the "Chinese" population consists of two (or four, if you divide them up more finely) linguistic groups (the mainlanders vs. the Taiwanese) that are hostile to each other. Japan has serious minority problems with the Koreans, the Okinawans, the Ainus, and the Burakumins. South Korea may be one of the most ethno-linguistically homogeneous countries in the world, but that has not prevented my fellow countrymen from hating each other. For example, there are two regions in South Korea that particularly hate each other (southeast and southwest), so much so that some people from those regions would not allow their children to get married to anyone from "the other place." In this regard, it is very telling that Rwanda is nearly as homogeneous in ethno-linguistic terms as Korea but that the homogeneity did not prevent the ethnic cleansing of the formerly dominant minority Tutsis by the majority Hutus—this is an example that proves that "ethnicity" is a political, rather than a natural, construction.

The previous examples show that rich countries do not suffer from ethnic heterogeneity not because they do not have it, but because they have succeeded in nation building (which, I should note, was often an unpleasant and even violent process). Indeed despite being genetically the most heterogeneous country in the world, Tanzania has been very successful in nation building, and it has not had any serious ethnicity-based conflicts.

Finally, the argument that bad institutions are holding Africa back (and often they are) should be tempered by the fact that, when they were at similar levels of material development to those we find in Africa currently, the institutions of today's rich countries were in a far worse state than what we find in Africa today (Chang 2002, ch. 3). These rich countries built the good institutions largely after, or at least in tandem with, their economic development. In other words, high-quality institutions are as much outcomes as they are the causes of economic development.

CULTURE

Many people who believe that "bad" cultures are holding Africa back do not usually realize that all of the descriptions of those "negative" cultural traits of Africa heard today used to be hurled at many rich countries when they were poor (Chang 2007, ch. 9).

Before the start of German economic development in the mid-nineteenth century, the British would frequently say that the Germans were too stupid, too individualistic, and too emotional for economic development—the exact opposite of the stereotypical image that they have of the Germans today and exactly the sort of things that people now say about the Africans. For example, John Russell, an early-nineteenth-century British traveler in Germany, remarked: The Germans are a "plodding, easily contented people . . . endowed neither with great acuteness of perception nor quickness of feeling. . . . It is long before [a German] can be brought to comprehend the bearings of what is new to him, and it is difficult to rouse him to ardour in its pursuit" (Russell 1828, 394). When traveling in Germany, Mary Shelley, the author of *Frankenstein*, complained that "the Germans never hurry" (Shelley 1843, 276).

Until the early twentieth century, Australians and Americans would go to Japan and say the Japanese were lazy. Having toured lots of factories in Japan, an Australian engineer remarked in 1915: "My impression as to your cheap labour was soon disillusioned when I saw your people at work. No doubt they are lowly paid, but the return is equally so; to see your men at work made me feel that you are a very satisfied easy-going race who reckon time is no object. When I spoke to some managers they informed me that it was impossible to change the habits of national heritage" (*Japan Times*). Even Sidney Gulick, an American missionary who lived in Japan for twenty-five years and later became a champion of Asian American human rights back in the United States, had to admit that many Japanese "give an impression . . . of being lazy and utterly indifferent to the passage of time" (Gulick 1903, 117).

The Koreans were held in even lower esteem. In 1912, they were condemned as "12 millions of dirty, degraded, sullen, lazy and religionless savages who slouch about in dirty white garments of the most inept kind and who live in filthy mudhuts." That comment came from a leading female socialist intellectual at the time, that is, Beatrice Webb of the Fabian movement (Webb and Webb 1978, 375), so one can imagine what a regular European male conservative would have said about the Koreans had he visited the country.

Of course, the cultures of Germany, Japan, and Korea today are completely different from what was previously described. Those transformations happened mainly because of economic development, which created societies in which people have to behave in more disciplined, calculating, and cooperative ways than in agrarian societies. These historical examples show that culture is more of an outcome, rather than a cause, of economic development. Given this, it is wrong to blame Africa's (or any region's or any country's) underdevelopment on its culture.

NATURAL RESOURCE ABUNDANCE AND INDUSTRIAL POLICY

In relation to industrial policy more specifically, the natural resource abundance of Africa is often cited as the reason why industrial policy is unwise and/or unworkable. First, it is argued that the African countries have relative abundance (and therefore comparative advantage) in natural resources. Given this, trying to industrialize, especially "artificially" through industrial policy, would be bad for their economies. Second, countries with natural resource abundance, it is argued, suffer from perverse politics in the forms of corruption and violent conflicts (a form of "resource curse"). Trying to graft industrial policy onto that political economy, it is pointed out, will mean that it will only be abused, even if it worked elsewhere.

NATURAL RESOURCE ABUNDANCE AND COMPARATIVE ADVANTAGE

Many people take it for granted that the African countries are well endowed with natural resources, but in fact few of them are (see Chang 2006 for further details). Fewer than a dozen African countries have any significant mineral deposits. Only South Africa and the Democratic Republic of the Congo (DRC) are exceptionally well endowed with more than one mineral resource. Most African countries may have low population density and thus a lot of land, but only a handful of them are exceptionally well endowed with arable land (Niger, Liberia, DRC, Chad, Senegal, Sierra Leone, and the Central African Republic). Most African countries look abundantly endowed with natural resources only because they have so few manmade resources, such as machines, infrastructure, and skilled labor. Moreover, even in the case of countries that have exceptionally abundant natural resource endowments, exploiting them without any clear long-term industrial policy is unlikely to lead to long-term economic development.

Except for a few small oil-rich countries like Brunei, Kuwait, and Qatar, no country—not even the United States, Australia, or Canada, the three countries that are best endowed in the world with natural resources—has been blessed by nature to such an extent that it could become rich only by doing things that came "naturally." Australia has the smallest manufacturing sector (in per capita terms) by far among the rich countries (it is one-third smaller than the next smallest ones) owing to its abundant natural resource endowments, but even it produces, at $2,422, manufacturing value added (MVA) per capita that is 35 times greater than relatively more industrialized Senegal ($69) and 220 times greater than the least industrialized Niger ($11) (all figures are as of 2005, in 2000 dollars; UNIDO 2009, 129, table 1). Given that Senegal's and Niger's natural resource endowments are not even remotely as abundant as that of Australia, they will have to industrialize much more than Australia has done if one day they are to have living standards that are comparable to that of Australia's today.

We should also note that few countries actually do "natural" things. Even many "primary" commodities are not natural but products of colonialism. For example, many African countries export cocoa and tea, which were brought from, respectively, Central America and China to Africa by the imperialists. When it comes to high-productivity activities whose existence determines whether a country is economically developed or not, countries become good at something only because they deliberately decide to become so—there is really no "natural" reason for the Japanese to be good at building cars, the Finns at making mobile phones, and the Koreans at making steel.

If we left things to the market, high-productivity industries simply would not get established in developing countries, as there are already superior producers from the more advanced countries. If they want to develop those industries, they have to protect and nurture those industries through tariffs, subsidies, and other means of industrial policy—this is, of course, the logic of infant industry promotion, which I discussed earlier. If the African countries are to develop their economies, they will have to deploy an industrial policy that will eventually make their "natural advantage" industries unimportant by developing higher-productivity activities.

By saying this, I am not trying to argue that the African countries should ignore their natural resource–based industries. There are at least two reasons. First, it takes a lot of time to develop new industries. For example, it took forty years for the Japanese car makers (established in the early 1930s) to break into the world market, while it took seventeen years for Nokia electronics (founded in 1960) to make any profit. Therefore before the new industries fully develop, the natural resource–based sectors need to provide the output, jobs, and, above all, export earnings that will finance the imports of machinery and technologies for the new industries. Second, natural resource–based industries can be, and should be, upgraded (on how to upgrade out of the natural resources sectors, see discussions in Chang [2008, section III]). Despite having very little land (the fifth highest population density in the world, excluding island- and city-states), the Netherlands is the third largest agricultural exporter in the world, as it has upgraded its agriculture.

In the long run, however, successful upgrading of natural resource–based industries requires successful industrialization. The Netherlands has a high-productivity agricultural sector only because it has "industrialized" the sector, using its strengths in industries like electronics (for example, computer-controlled feeding) and chemicals (for example, fertilizers and pesticides). In the end, the African countries will have to get into many industries that today *no one* would think they can succeed in if they are going to become economically developed. And, as I argued earlier, that requires systematic industrial policy.

NATURAL RESOURCE ABUNDANCE AND PERVERSE POLITICS

In relation to the argument that natural resource abundance in Africa is bound to create a perverse pattern of politics (corruption and violent conflicts) that leads to abuse of industrial policy, even if it were true, it would apply to only a handful of African countries, as most African countries are not that particularly well endowed with natural resources in the first place, as I have pointed out earlier.

Moreover, there is no inevitable relationship between a country's natural resource endowment and its politics. If natural resource abundance inevitably led to perverse politics, we could explain how many countries— not just super well-endowed United States, Canada, and Australia, but also the Scandinavian countries—have not developed perverse forms of politics despite (or in many cases because of) their abundant natural resource endowments (see Wright and Czelusta [2004, 2007] on the role of natural resources in the economic development of the United States). In addition, in the late nineteenth and early twentieth centuries, the fastest growing regions of the world were resource-rich areas like North America, Latin America, and Scandinavia, which shows that the "resource curse" is not something that is inescapable.

POLITICAL ECONOMY CONSIDERATIONS: LEADERSHIP, STATE COHERENCE, AND STATE-SOCIETY RELATIONSHIP

Even ignoring perverse politics due to natural resource abundance, there is a general concern that the political economy of most African countries makes effective implementation of industrial policy impossible. Many people characterize politics in most African countries as "neopatrimonial," which undermines economic rationality in favor of "Big Man" politics (for a comprehensive critique of this literature, see Mkandawire [2013]). Given this political economy, it is believed that any policy that suspends market discipline will be hijacked and abused, unlike in East Asia or Europe.

This argument is partly in line with one key conclusion of the industrial policy debate, which is that a key difference between success stories and failure stories of industrial policy is in the differences in their political economy (Toye 1987; Amsden 1989; Chang 1994; Evans 1995). There are three aspects to this.

First, political leadership is considered important in determining the nature of industrial policy. Even if we ignore some extreme cases in which the leaders are interested only in personal aggrandizement, the leaders may have a "wrong" vision. They may be looking backward, rather than forward, as Thomas Jefferson did when he opposed Hamilton's infant industry protection. Or they may be hostile to private sector development, as many African countries' leaders were in the 1960s and the 1970s. Or, as many nineteenth-century liberal politicians did, they may think that doing nothing, other than protecting private property, is really the best industrial policy.

Second, even if the political leaders have the "right" vision, they should be able to impose that vision on the rest of the state apparatus. While in theory the state is a hierarchical organization, in practice the wish at the top does not always percolate through the hierarchy. There will be some degree of self-seeking by government bureaucrats, although not as much as it is assumed in the public choice theory. There will also be problems arising from clashing visions (for example, the bureaucrats may be more conservative than the political leaders), turf wars within the bureaucracy, "tunnel vision" that specialized organizations are wont to develop, internal coordination failures (coming from poor organizational design inside the government or the emergence of new issues that cut across the existing organizational structure), and many other reasons.

Third, even if the leadership has the right vision and even if the state apparatus is coherent, the state still should be able to impose its will on other agents in the society. In some extreme cases, the state may not even have full control of its claimed territories. In some countries, the state cannot implement policies effectively due to manpower and resource shortages. Even when the state has enough enforcement capabilities, there will be attempts by some private sector agents to neutralize or even pervert policies through lobbying and bribing.

The tendency is to assume that these types of political economy problems are uniquely serious in the African countries, but this assumption lacks empirical foundations (Mkandawire 2013). In addition, the advanced economies all suffered from these problems in the past (and some of them still do to an extent). In fact, when they were at levels of economic development comparable to today's African countries, the developed countries were actually much worse in terms of suppression of democracy, corruption, state capture, incoherence of the state machinery, nepotism, and other "pathological" forms of politics (Chang 2002, ch. 3).

Whatever we think of African countries' political economy problems, we should not let the best be the enemy of the good. The existence of those problems should not make us believe that African countries have to wait for a perfect state to emerge before doing anything. In the real world, successful countries are those that have managed to find "good enough" solutions to their political economy problems and gone on to implement industrial (and other) policies rather than sitting around bemoaning the imperfect nature of their political systems.

In fact, quite a few of the successful "industrial policy states" themselves overcame political obstacles to effective statecraft in situations that did not instill much hope. For example, between the fall of Napoleon and the end of World War II, the French state was notoriously laissez-faire, ineffectual, and conservative. However, this was completely changed after the war, with the rise of *Gaullisme*, the establishment of the planning commission, and the foundation of the École Nationale d'Administration (ENA), the famous school for elite bureaucrats (Cohen 1977; Kuisel 1981). For another example, the Kuomintang (Nationalist Party) bureaucracy was arguably one of the most corrupt and inefficient in modern history when it ruled mainland China. However, after being forced to migrate to Taiwan following defeat by the communists in 1949, it was transformed into a highly efficient and relatively clean bureaucracy. This was done through a gradual but deliberate process of building "islands of competence" and then giving them greater responsibilities as they succeeded and increased their legitimacy and status within the bureaucracy, finally replacing much of the old bureaucracy with the new one (Wade 1990).

"DO NOT TRY THIS AT HOME": THE QUESTION OF BUREAUCRATIC CAPABILITIES

Whatever the political intention and power of the top leadership may be, policies are likely to fail if the government officials implementing them are not capable. They have to make difficult decisions with limited information and fundamental uncertainty, often under political pressure from inside and outside the country. Dealing with all of this requires competent decision makers. On this ground, it has been argued that "difficult" policies like (selective) industrial policy should not be tried by countries with limited bureaucratic capabilities, especially the African countries (World Bank [1993] is the best example).

In other words, this is the policy world equivalent of the "do not try this at home" (DNTTAH) warning that accompanies the demonstration of difficult and dangerous stunt acts in TV shows. However, there are numerous problems with this argument.

First, the assumption is that industrial policy is exceptionally difficult. However, this assumption is made without any theoretical reasoning or empirical evidence. For example, World Bank (1993) assumes that policies getting the "fundamentals"—such as human capital, agriculture, and macroeconomic stability—right are easier than industrial policy, but there can be no such presumption. Different governments have competences in different areas—the Japanese government was good at industrial policy but messed up macroeconomic policies in the 1990s. The ease of a policy will also partly depend on its scale. For example, promoting a few industries through industrial policy may be a lot easier than organizing a mass education program. It will also depend on the number of agents involved in the policy. Trying to coordinate investments among a few large firms may be easier than organizing a country-wide distribution of subsidized fertilizer that involves millions of small farmers who are not organized into cooperatives and are scattered all over the country.

Second, another (implicit) assumption behind the DNTTAH argument is that industrial policy requires sophisticated knowledge of economics—as exemplified by the comment by Alan Winters, the former head of the research department at the Bank and the former chief economist of the U.K. government's Department of International Development (DfID), that "the application of second-best economics needs first-best economists, not its usual complement of third- and fourth-raters" (Winters 2003, 66). But is this true? An important fact in this regard is that the East Asian economic bureaucrats were *not* "first best economists." While they were smart people, most of them were not even economists. The majority of the Japanese economic officials that engineered the country's "miracle" were graduates from the law department of Tokyo University. Until the 1980s, what little economics they knew were mostly of the "wrong" kind—the economics of Karl Marx and Friedrich List, rather than neoclassical economics. In Taiwan, most key economic bureaucrats were engineers and scientists, as is the case in China today. Korea also had a high proportion of lawyers in its economic bureaucracy until the 1970s, while the brains behind the famous heavy and chemical industrialization (HCI) program in the 1970s, Oh Won-Chul, was an engineer by training. Both Taiwan and Korea had rather strong, albeit officially unacknowledged, communist influence in their economic thinking until the 1970s.[1]

Third, many advocates of the DNTTAH argument believe that high-quality bureaucracies are very difficult to build and that the East Asian countries were exceptionally lucky to have inherited them from history. However, a high-quality bureaucracy can be built pretty quickly, as shown by the examples of Korea and Taiwan themselves. Contrary to the popular myth, Korea and Taiwan did *not* start their economic "miracles" with high-quality bureaucracies. For example, until the late 1960s, Korea used to send its bureaucrats for extra training to—of all places—Pakistan and the Philippines. Taiwan also had a similar problem of generally low bureaucratic capabilities in the 1950s and most of the 1960s. These countries could construct a high-quality bureaucracy only because they invested in training, organizational reform, and improvement in incentive systems. In addition, there was also a lot of "learning by doing." By trying out relatively easy industrial policy from early on, the East Asian bureaucrats could build up the capabilities they needed to effectively run more sophisticated industrial policy later. In other words, there has to be *some* trying at home if you aspire to become good enough to appear on TV with your own stunt act.

Last but not least, the fact that something is difficult cannot be a reason not to try it. When it comes to personal advancement, we actually go to the other extreme and encourage our youngsters to aspire to become the best of the best, when most of them are going to end up as production line workers or shop assistants rather than prime ministers or business tycoons. Even when it comes to countries, developing countries are routinely told to adopt "best practice" or "global standard" institutions used by the richest countries when many of them clearly do not have the capabilities to effectively run the American patent law or Scandinavian welfare system. However, when it comes to industrial policy, countries are told to aim low and not to try at all, or at best to try to learn from the Southeast Asian countries, which used more market-conforming (and therefore presumably easier) industrial policy than did the East Asian countries (this is the position taken by World Bank [1993]). I am all for people warning against the risks involved in aiming too high, but why should countries aim low only when it comes to industrial policy?

The problems of low bureaucratic capabilities are real in most African countries. However, they should not be exaggerated. They are not unique to industrial policy, nor are they unique to Africa. And there can be no presumption that industrial policy is necessarily more demanding in terms of bureaucratic capabilities than other policies are. More importantly, in the longer run, bureaucratic capabilities may be enhanced (and relatively quickly at that) with appropriate investments and "learning by doing" so their poverty at the present moment cannot be an excuse for not using industrial policy ever in the future.

CHANGING RULES OF THE GLOBAL ECONOMY

The changes in global rules of trade and investment since the 1990s—through the World Trade Organization (WTO), bilateral and regional Free Trade Agreements (FTAs), and bilateral investment treaties (BITs)—have made use of many of the classic tools of industrial policy either banned or significantly circumscribed. Given this, it is argued that developing countries, including the ones in Africa, should not waste their time thinking about policies that cannot be used anyway.

The most important changes have been brought about by the launch of the WTO in 1995. Quantitative restrictions (for example, quotas) have been banned altogether. Tariffs have been reduced and "bound" (that is, tariff ceilings have been set). Export subsidies are banned. Most other subsidies (except those frequently used by the rich countries, such as those for agriculture, research and development [R&D], and regional equalization) have become open to countervailing duties and other retaliatory measures. New issues, like regulations on foreign direct investment (FDI) and intellectual property rights (IPRs), have been brought under the jurisdiction of the WTO, making it difficult for countries to "borrow" foreign technologies for free by violating IPRs or put performance requirements (regarding things like local contents) on the transnational corporations (TNCs) that make FDI.

While the WTO has certainly made industrial policy more difficult to implement, the constraints imposed by it should not be exaggerated.

To begin with, even on paper the WTO by no means obliges countries to abolish all tariffs—only to bind them. Although the middle-income developing countries were forced to bind most of their tariffs, the least developed countries (LDCs), including most countries in Africa, were exempt from tariff binding. Even though some low-income countries chose to bind some tariffs, the extent of such binding is small and the ceiling is quite high. So the "policy space" for using tariffs is still considerable for the LDCs.[2]

Second, the use of emergency tariff increases ("import surcharges") is allowed on two grounds. The first is a sudden surge in sectoral imports, which a number of countries have already used. The second is the overall balance of payments (BOP) problem, for which almost all developing countries, including the African ones, would qualify, and which quite a few countries have also used. Because countries have discretion over the coverage and the levels of emergency tariffs that are meant to lessen the BOP problem, they can target particular industries through this provision.

Third, not all subsidies are "illegal" for everyone. For example, the LDCs are allowed to use export subsidies. Given the enormous benefits that exports generate for developing countries—by enabling them to import better technologies, by exposing them to international quality standards, and by making it easier for them to measure performance of the recipients of industrial policy supports—this is a very valuable policy tool that many African countries can utilize. Also, subsidies for agriculture, regional development, basic R&D, and environment-related technology upgrading are at least de facto allowed.[3] Even though some of these subsidies are not relevant for most African economies (for example, R&D subsidies), others (for example, agricultural subsidies) are, so they should use them proactively. Moreover, the subsidy restrictions only cover "trade-related" subsidies, which means that "domestic" ones can be used (for example, subsidies on equipment investments, subsidies for investment in particular skills).

Fourth, the trade-related intellectual property rights (TRIPS) agreement has certainly made technology absorption more expensive for developing countries (Chang 2001). However, this mainly affects the middle-income countries. The technologies that most African countries need are often the ones that are too old to be protected by patents.

Fifth, the trade-related investment measures (TRIMS) agreement has banned certain policy measures that had been successfully used by both the developed and the developing countries in the past (Kumar 2005) (for example, local contents requirements and trade balancing requirements), but other measures are still allowed. These include conditions regarding the hiring of local labor (a good way to create technological spillover effects), technology transfer, and the conduct of R&D in the host country. They can also provide targeted subsidies, directed credits, and tailor-made infrastructure (measures that Singapore and Ireland have used to attract FDI into "targeted" industries; Chang 2004), insofar as these do not violate the most-favored nation (MFN) provision (Thrasher and Gallagher 2008). Many of these measures are relevant for the African countries.

Even though the WTO rules allow quite a lot of industrial policy measures, especially for the LDCs and other poor economies, this policy space is in practice highly constrained by other international factors. First, the conditions attached to bilateral and multilateral aids and loans, on which they are quite dependent, significantly constrain their industrial policy space. Second, many developing countries are also parties to bilateral and regional trade and investment agreements, which tend to be even more restrictive than the WTO agreements (Thrasher and Gallagher 2008).

So all in all the range of industrial policy measures that developing countries can use has become considerably smaller compared to the 1960s and the 1970s. However, there is still room for maneuver for countries that are clever and determined enough, especially for the poorest economies, many of which are African, that are subject to less systemic restrictions (especially in relation to tariffs and subsidies).

Moreover, the new global rules of trade and investment are not some unalterable laws of nature. They can be, and should be, changed if they are found wanting. The modification of the TRIPS agreement in relation to HIV/AIDS drugs is a good, if a relatively small, example.

CONCLUDING REMARKS

In this chapter, I have critically examined a number of arguments suggesting that the African countries cannot learn from other experiences because they possess uniquely disadvantageous conditions against any attempt to develop their economies through deliberate measures.

I first criticized the more general arguments espousing "Afro-pessimism" on the bases of "structural" factors like climate, geography, history, and culture. Then I critically examined four types of arguments skeptical of the applicability of industrial policy to the African context—natural resource abundance, political economy, bureaucratic capabilities, and the changes in global economic rules. I maintained that, while all these arguments contain some germs of truths (some more than others), they are all highly biased and partial.

The African countries—even the exceptionally well-endowed and most industrialized South Africa—still need huge amounts of industrial development. Such developments require substantial degrees of industrial policy. Given this, getting industrial policy right and getting the conditions for its successful implementation right are not matters of choice but imperatives for the African countries. In this chapter, I tried to show how the existing possibilities may be exploited and the constraints overcome in all sorts of areas—ranging from landlockedness to bureaucratic capabilities—through an appropriate mix of vision, realism, institutional reform, and investments.

NOTES

This is a modified version of "Industrial Policy: Can Africa Do It?," a paper presented at IEA/World Bank Roundtable on Industrial Policy in Africa, Pretoria, South Africa, July 3–4, 2012. I thank for their helpful comments especially, in alphabetical order, Mario Cimoli, Akbar Noman, Simon Roberts, and Joseph Stiglitz.

1. The Nationalist Party's constitution was a copy of the Soviet Communist Party's constitution. Taiwan's second president, Chiang Ching-Kuo, who succeeded his father Chiang Kai-Shek, was a communist as a young man and studied in the Soviet Communist Party School in Moscow with future leaders of the Chinese Communist Party, including Deng Xiaoping. Korea also had its share of communist influence. General Park Chung-hee, who masterminded the Korean economic miracle, was a communist in his younger days. He was sentenced to death in 1949 for his involvement in a communist mutiny in the South Korean army but earned amnesty by publicly denouncing communism. Many of his lieutenants were also communist in their younger days.

2. Of course, if the rich countries have their way in the current nonagricultural market access (NAMA) negotiations of the Doha Round in the WTO, industrial tariffs in the developing countries are, at 5 to 10 percent, likely to fall to the lowest level since the days of colonialism and unequal treaties (Chang 2005, 4). However, this is yet to happen.

3. These subsidies were explicitly allowed ("non-actionable" in WTO parlance) until 1999. Even though the first three have become "actionable" since 2000, not a single case has been brought to the dispute settlement mechanism since then, suggesting that there is an implicit agreement that they are still acceptable.

REFERENCES

Acemoglu, D., S. Johnson, and J. Robinson. 2001. "The Colonial Origins of Comparative Development: An Empirical Investigation." *American Economic Review* 91 (5): 1369–1401.

Amsden, A. 1989. *Asia's Next Giant: South Korea and Late Industrialization*. New York: Oxford University Press.

Aristotle. 2001. *Politics*. In *The Basic Works of Aristotle*, ed. Richard McKeon. New York: Random House.

Bairoch, P. 1993. *Economics and World History—Myths and Paradoxes*. Brighton: Wheatsheaf.

Bloom, D., and J. Sachs. 1998. "Geography, Demography and Economic Growth in Africa." *Brookings Papers on Economic Activity* 2 (2): 207–295.

Chang, H-J. 1994. *The Political Economy of Industrial Policy*. London: Macmillan.

———. 2001. "Intellectual Property Rights and Economic Development—Historical Lessons and Emerging Issues." *Journal of Human Development* 2 (2): 1–36.

———. 2002. *Kicking Away the Ladder: Development Strategy in Historical Perspective*. London: Anthem Press.

———. 2004. "Regulation of Foreign Investment in Historical Perspective." *European Journal of Development Research* 16 (3): 687–715.

———. 2005. *Why Developing Countries Need Tariffs—How WTO NAMA Negotiations Could Deny Developing Countries' Right to a Future*. Oxford: Oxfam International.

———. 2006. "How Important Were the 'Initial Conditions' for Economic Development—East Asia vs. Sub-Saharan Africa." In *The East Asian Development Experience: The Miracle, the Crisis, and the Future*, ed. H-J Chang, 143–179. London: Chang Zed Press.

———. 2007. *Bad Samaritans*. New York: Bloomsbury.

———. 2008. "State-owned Enterprise Reform in UNDESA." In *National Development Strategies—Policy Notes*, ed. United Nations Department of Economic and Social Affairs. New York: United Nations.

———. 2009a. "Under-explored Treasure Troves of Development Lessons—Lessons from the Histories of Small Rich European Countries (SRECs)." In *Doing Good or Doing Better—Development Policies in a Globalising World*, ed. M. Kremer, P. van Lieshout, and R. Went. Amsterdam: Amsterdam University Press.

———. 2009b. "Economic History of the Developed World: Lessons for Africa." In *Eminent Speakers Series Volume II—Sharing Visions of Africa's Development*, ed. S. Tapsoba and G. Oluremi Archer-Davis. Tunis: African Development Bank. http://www.econ.cam.ac.uk/faculty/chang/pubs/ChangAfDBlecturetext.pdf.

———. 2010. *23 Things They Don't Tell You About Capitalism*. London: Allen Lane.

———. 2011. "Industrial Policy: Can We Go Beyond an Unproductive Confrontation?" In *Annual World Bank Conference on Development Economics 2010, Global: Lessons from East Asia and the Global Financial Crisis*, ed. J. Lin and B. Pleskovic, 83–110. Washington, DC: World Bank.

Clemens, M., and J. Williamson. 2001. "A Tariff-Growth Paradox?—Protection's Impact the World Around 1875–1997." NBER Working Paper No. 8459 : 1–26.

———. 2004. "Closed Jaguar, Open Dragon: Comparing Tariffs in Latin America and Asia." NBER Working Paper No. 9401: 1–33.

Cohen, S. 1977. *Modern Capitalist Planning: The French Model*. 2nd ed. Berkeley: University of California Press.

Collier, P., and W. Gunning. 1999. "Why Has Africa Grown Slowly?" *Journal of Economic Perspectives* 13 (3): 3–22.

Dosi, G., M. Cimoli, and J. Stiglitz, eds. 2009. *Industrial Policy and Development: The Political Economy of Capabilities Accumulation*. Oxford: Oxford University Press.

Easterly, W., and R. Levine. 1997. "Africa's Growth Tragedy: Policies and Ethnic Divisions." *Quarterly Journal of Economics* 112 (4): 1–39.

Etounga-Manguelle, D. 2000. "Does Africa Need a Cultural Adjustment Program?" In *Culture Matters—How Values Shape Human Progress*, ed. L. Harrison and S. Huntington, 65–78. New York: Basic.

Evans, P. 1995. *Embedded Autonomy*. Princeton: Princeton University Press.

Greenwald, B., and J. Stiglitz. 2006. "Helping Infant Economies Grow: Foundations of Trade Policies for Developing Countries." *American Economic Review* 96 (2): 141–146.

Gulick, S. 1903. *Evolution of the Japanese*. New York: Fleming H. Revell.

Hamilton, A. 1791 [2001]. *Report on the Subject of Manufactures, 5 December 1791*, as reprinted in *Alexander Hamilton—Writings*. New York: The Library Classics of the United States.

Huntington, S. 2000. "Foreword: Cultures Count." In *Culture Matters—How Values Shape Human Progress*, ed. L. Harrison and S. Huntington, xiii–xvi. New York: Basic.

Irwin, D. 2002. "Interpreting the Tariff-Growth Correlation of the Late 19th Century." *American Economic Review* 92 (2): 165–169.

Japan Times. August 18, 1915.

Jerven, M. 2011. "The Quest for the African Dummy: Explaining African Post-colonial Economic Performance Revisited." *Journal of International Development* 23 (2): 288–307.

Kuisel, R. 1981. *Capitalism and the State in Modern France*. Cambridge: Cambridge University Press.

Kumar, N. 2005. "Performance Requirements as Tools of Development Policy: Lessons from Developed and Developing Countries." In *Putting Development First*, ed. K. Gallagher. London: Zed.

Lehmann, S., and K. O'Rourke. 2008. "The Structure of Protection and Growth in the Late 19th Century." NBER Working Paper No. 14493 (November): 1–44.

Lin, J., and H-J Chang. 2009. "Should Industrial Policy in Developing Countries Conform to Comparative Advantage or Defy It?—A Debate between Justin Lin and Ha-Joon Chang." *Development Policy Review* 27 (5): 483–502.

Lin, J., and C. Monga. 2012. "Comparative Advantage—The Silver Bullet of Industrial Policy." Paper presented at the Roundtable on New Thinking on Industrial Policy, International Economic Association (IEA) and the World Bank, May 22–23, Washington, DC.

Mkandawire, T. 2013. "Neopatrimonialism and the Political Economy of Economic Performance in Africa: Critical Reflections." Working paper, Institute for Future Studies.

O'Rourke, K. 2000. "Tariffs and Growth in the Late 19th Century." *Economic Journal* 110 (4): 456–483.

Reinert, E. 2007. *How Rich Countries Got Rich and Why Poor Countries Stay Poor.* London: Constable.

Russell, J. 1828. *A Tour in Germany.* Vol. 1. Edinburgh: Archibald Constable & Co.

Sachs, J., and A. Warner. 2001. "The Curse of Natural Resources." *European Economic Review* 45: 827–838.

Shaffaedin, M. 2005. *Trade Policy at Crossroads—The Recent Experiences of Developing Countries.* London: Palgrave Macmillan.

Shelley, M. 1843. *Rambles in Germany and Italy.* Vol. 1. London: Edward Monkton.

Stiglitz, J. 1996. "Some Lessons from the East Asian Miracle." *World Bank Research Observer* 11 (2): 151–177.

Thrasher, R., and K. Gallagher. 2008. "21st Century Trade Agreements: Implications for Long-Run Development Policy." *The Pardee Papers* 2 (September): 1–58.

Toye, J. 1987. *Dilemmas of Development.* Oxford: Blackwell.

United Nations Industrial Development Organization (UNIDO). 2009. *Industrial Development Report 2009.* Vienna: UNIDO.

Vamvakidis, A. 2002. "How Robust Is the Growth-Openness Connection?—Historical Evidence." *Journal of Economic Growth* 7 (1): 57–80.

Wade, R. 1990. *Governing the Market: Economic Theory and the Role of the Government in East Asian Industrialization.* Princeton: Princeton University Press.

Webb, S., and B. Webb. 1978. *The Letters of Sidney and Beatrice Webb.* Edited by N. MacKenzie and J. MacKenzie. Cambridge: Cambridge University Press.

Winters, A. 2003. "Trade Policy as Development Policy." In *Trade and Development— Directions for the Twenty-first Century*, ed. J. Toye, 62–81. Cheltenham: Edward Elgar.

World Bank. 1987. *World Development Report 1987.* New York: Oxford University Press.

——. 1991. *World Development Report 1991.* New York: Oxford University Press.

——. 1993. *The East Asian Miracle.* New York: Oxford University Press.

Wright, G., and J. Czelusta. 2004. "The Myth of the Resource Curse." *Challenge* 47 (2): 6–38.

——. 2007. "Resource-based Growth, Past and Present." In *Natural Resources: Neither Curse nor Destiny*, ed. D. Lederman and F. Maloney, 183–212. Stanford: Stanford University.

CHAPTER 3

Industrial Strategy and Economic Transformation

LESSONS FROM FIVE OUTSTANDING CASES

Akio Hosono

Industrial policy and economic transformation have been attracting renewed attention of late. Thus several studies in the past decade or so have focused on industrial development, especially industrial structure upgrading and diversification, as a basis for sustained economic growth and development.

These studies have emphasized such aspects as the accumulation of knowledge and capabilities and the creation of a learning society (Cimoli, Dosi, and Stiglitz 2009; Greenwald and Stiglitz 2012); the exploiting and changing factor endowments and comparative advantage (Lin 2012); the need to compensate for the information externalities generated by pioneer firms (Rodrik 2007); and pragmatic policymaking for developing countries that must cope with the strong pressures of market orientation and globalization in our times (Ohno 2013).

The main objective of this chapter is to obtain insights into how these crucial factors interact in practice, focusing on five outstanding cases of what we call "industrial strategy" that resulted in a remarkable economic transformation in a country or in regions of a country. These five cases are: (1) the automobile industry in Thailand; (2) the transformation of the "Cerrado" in Brazil from barren lands to a source of high-productivity agriculture; (3) the garment industry in Bangladesh; (4) salmon farming and processing industry in Chile; and (5) the upgrading of Singapore's industrial sector from labor to knowledge intensive. These case studies that are the main contribution of this chapter are in the section titled "Case Studies."

As these five cases suggest, we use the terms "industry" and "industrial sector" very broadly to refer not only to the manufacturing sector but also to agro-business, modern agriculture, aquaculture, transport, logistics, tourism, and any other activities that produce nontraditional or "modern" goods and services that require significant human and/or physical capital. Similarly, "industrial strategy" refers not only to narrowly defined "industrial policy" targeted at manufacturing but also to others such as education policy, fiscal policy, financial policy, trade policy, and labor policy, which encourage the development of the aforementioned productive activities.[1]

The next section briefly reviews the major findings of some recent studies related to industrial policy and economic transformation and sketches the analytical perspective of this chapter. This is followed by the case studies. Finally, the concluding section attempts to extract lessons that could be derived from these cases.

AN ANALYTICAL PERSPECTIVE

MAJOR FINDINGS OF SOME RECENT STUDIES RELATED TO INDUSTRIAL STRATEGY AND ECONOMIC TRANSFORMATION

LEARNING AND ACCUMULATION OF KNOWLEDGE AND CAPABILITIES

Noman and Stiglitz (2012) emphasize that "long-term success rests on societies' 'learning'—new technologies, new ways of doing business, new ways of managing the economy, new ways of dealing with other countries" (7). Related to this notion of a "learning society" is Cimoli, Dosi, and Stiglitz's (2009) view that great industrial transformation "entails a major process of accumulation of *knowledge* and *capabilities*, at the level of both *individuals* and *organizations*" (2; italics in original). We find a lot of similarities between this view and the capacity development (CD) approach in which the capacity refers to individuals', organizations', and society's (or the country's) capacity as a whole. Knowledge and learning in a CD process have increasingly been a feature of recent discussions (Hosono et al. 2011, 180–181).

Cimoli, Dosi, and Stiglitz (2009) contend that "capabilities have to do with the problem-solving knowledge embodied in organizations—concerning, for example, production technologies, marketing, labor relations, as well as the 'dynamic capabilities' of search and learning" (2). Here again we find similarities between their ideas and the concepts of

CD. The problem-solving knowledge could be considered a core capacity in terms of CD, which could include problem-identifying and problem-solving capacities (Hosono et al. 2011, 180).

Regarding this aspect, Greenwald and Stiglitz (2012) further elaborate: "The discussion so far has focused on 'learning,' but even more important is 'learning to learn.' Industrial and trade policy can enhance an economy's learning capacities, its underlying 'capabilities,' and development strategies need to be focused on that, especially in an era with fast-changing technologies, where specific knowledge learned at one moment risks rapid obsolescence" (18).[2] In the management field, this fundamental capacity for individual workers and an enterprise as a whole to "learn to learn" could be enhanced through continuous improvement activities (also called *kaizen* activities) aimed at improving quality and productivity by, among others, modifications to the organization, work flow, and so on—with the participation of workers—rather than via significant physical investment. These activities, which go far beyond simple improvements in productivity, enable the enhancement of both workers' and enterprises' capabilities to "learn to learn."[3] This chapter will highlight this fundamental aspect of learning when we discuss the Singapore case later.

CHANGE OF ENDOWMENTS AND COMPARATIVE ADVANTAGE

According to Noman and Stiglitz (2012), the "old" policies focused on improving economic efficiency *within a static framework*: "But the essence of development is dynamic. What matters, for instance, is not comparative advantage as of today, but dynamic comparative advantage" (7).

Justin Lin (2012) discusses changing comparative advantage: "The more effective route for their learning and development is to exploit the advantages of backwardness and upgrade and diversify into new industries according to the changing comparative advantages determined by the changes in their endowment structure" (73). Lin goes on to explain, "Conceptually, it is useful to add infrastructure as one more component in an economy's endowments. Infrastructure includes hard infrastructure and soft infrastructure" (22). The new structural economics, which he advocates, "considers human capital to be one component of a country's endowment" (36). And several components, among others infrastructure and human capital, which determine changing comparative advantage, are endogenous.

The concepts of accumulation of knowledge and capabilities, and the creation of a learning society, especially for "learning to learn" or for core capacity, as discussed earlier, are intimately related to the "soft infrastructure" (or human capital) that, together with "hard infrastructure," constitutes an important part of a country's endowment.

However, we should emphasize the fundamental differences between "hard infrastructure" and "soft infrastructure" in this context. First, while the former (roads, ports, airports, energy plants, and so on) could be realized through intensive investments in a relatively short period, the latter is achieved only through a longer-term, incremental process, and is essentially path dependent. Second, investments in learning are high risk, and risk markets are absent (especially in developing countries), which also discourages such investments (Greenwald and Stiglitz 2012, 6), while the feasibility and rate of return of investments in hard infrastructure can be measured. Both knowledge and hard infrastructure tend to have a public good dimension but, as Greenwald and Stiglitz mention, "markets by themselves are never efficient in the production and utilization of public goods" (5).

JICA and JBIC (2008, 48–55) review some cases of the industrial development of Asian countries through "developing new comparative advantage." Diverse, specific cases are discussed: the development of ICT industry through higher education; investment in climate enhancements through the establishment of special economic zones; strategic human resource development and support for overseas employment; and establishment of a development corridor. In this study, both "soft" and "hard" infrastructures are included.

LEADING INDUSTRIES, ECONOMIC TRANSFORMATION, AND ROLE OF GOVERNMENT AND INSTITUTIONS

Now two basic questions need to be answered in this context: How and under what conditions do countries change endowments? How and under what conditions do countries take advantage of a changing comparative advantage to develop new industries? Endowments could be changed dynamically. As soft and hard infrastructures—important components of endowments of a country—are endogenous and essentially public goods, and as the market is often not efficient in the production and utilization of public goods, government and/or public and private institutions have to play an important role in the dynamic change of endowments.

The Commission on Growth and Development's report (2008) studied the experience of thirteen countries that achieved annual growth rates of 7 percent or more for at least twenty-five years. The report identified "committed, credible, and capable governments" as one of five characteristics of high-performing countries. These governments, except for that of Hong Kong, were more hands-on, intervening with tax breaks, subsidized credit, directed lending, and other such measures. These interventions may have helped them to discover their comparative advantage (Noman and Stiglitz 2012, 12).

Their finding drew on the experience of twelve high-performing countries throughout the world. However, the role of governments referred to by the Growth Commission's report is related basically to the static comparative advantage of countries. Rodrik's (2007) view on "self-discovery" can be said to also bear mainly on static comparative advantage. As the dynamic change of endowments that transforms long-term comparative advantage is endogenous, the governments also have an important role to play in relation to dynamic comparative advantage. Noman and Stiglitz (2012, 12 and note 15) refer to this point. In short, the government's role is twofold: (1) facilitating "self-discovery" of static comparative advantage and (2) investing in soft and hard infrastructures that are endogenous components of endowments for dynamic (long-term) comparative advantage.

This chapter's objective is to get insights into both of these aspects, but with special reference to the second aspect, based on case studies of countries that realized outstanding economic transformation rather than just high performance in terms of growth. We will focus on (1) how factor endowments dynamically changed in terms of hard and soft infrastructures; (2) how investment in hard infrastructure was made and how learning as well as the accumulation of knowledge and capabilities were achieved; (3) how the transformation was triggered (initiated) with the change of endowments; (4) what kind of drivers (driving forces) kept the momentum of transformation; and (5) what kind of strategy/vision was behind the process and what policies and institutions promoted it.

The World Bank (2012, 218) summarizes the current discussion on "industrial policy," highlighting three schools of thought: (1) new structural economics; (2) an approach that emphasizes the policy process and especially a public-private partnership; and (3) a school of thought that stresses spillovers of productive knowledge—mastering ways of doing things. The document cites views of opponents regarding, among others, the practicality of implementing such a policy, doubting especially whether the public sector has the capacity to identify industries with potentially sizable knowledge spillovers and dynamic scale economies.

This chapter's analysis of these five aspects, in addition to addressing basic questions of the "industrial strategy and economic transformation agenda" discussed in this section, will also offer insights into several aspects of the controversy among the three schools of thought and those opposing them.

TYPOLOGY OF INDUSTRIAL DEVELOPMENT AND TRANSFORMATION CHALLENGES

Challenges facing countries are different as they move along the development path and as endowments change. Industrial development strategies could be different depending on the challenges countries face. They could have different focuses on infrastructure, human resource development, technological innovation, and so on. In some countries, industrial challenges are shaped by special circumstances affecting particular groups such as resource-rich countries, small countries, and post-conflict countries.[4]

A typological approach could be useful to address these diversities. JICA and JBIC (2008) distinguish, first of all, resource-rich countries and resource-poor countries. The World Bank (2012) identifies eight categories of "job challenge," including resource-rich countries, urbanizing countries, and conflict-affected countries.

From the point of view of the "economic transformation agenda," meaningful categorization could be accomplished according to the endowments of almost-fixed or exogenous factors such as mineral and energy resources on the one hand and to the endowment of endogenous factors such as hard and soft infrastructure on the other. In this sense, with regard to the former line of typology, we need to introduce the two categories of resource-rich countries and resource-poor countries. For the latter we need to take into account the development phases reflecting human resource development as well as physical infrastructure endowment such as (1) agrarian countries, (2) urbanizing and early industrializing countries dependent on labor-intensive sectors, (3) industrializing countries with higher skills and technology, and (4) countries with high-level technological and innovative capabilities.

These categories are not mutually exclusive and might not cover all types of divergence among countries. Having this endowments-based categorization in mind, we selected for our analysis three resource-poor Asian countries in different phases of development: Bangladesh, Thailand, and Singapore. From Latin America, two resource-rich countries were also included: Brazil and Chile. All of them have been at least fairly high-performing countries for roughly two decades.

RESEARCH QUESTIONS FOR CASE STUDIES

The most important research questions to be answered in case studies of selected countries are how economic transformation was achieved with endowment changes, and how such endowment changes were attained. More concretely, the case studies examine how learning and accumulation of knowledge and capabilities took place, how hard infrastructure was constructed, and what kinds of policies and institutions enabled the process of change and transformation. These practical aspects need to be analyzed in order to get insights into successful industrial strategies with impacts on economic transformation.

As mentioned earlier, how the transformation process was triggered (initiated) with the change of endowments and what kind of drivers (driving forces) maintained the momentum of transformation are important research questions as well.

CASE STUDIES

Case 1: Thailand's Automobile Industry

In 1995, Thailand's annual automobile exports were less than half a billion U.S. dollars, well below exports from India and Malaysia. By 2008, exports approached twenty-eight billion U.S. dollars, making Thailand the largest automobile exporter in the Association of South East Asian Nations (ASEAN) region, the third largest in Asia, after Japan and South Korea, and the seventh largest exporter in the world. Production reached 1 million cars in 2005 and 2.5 million cars in 2012. Automobile assembly and autoparts industries account for more than 10 percent of the GDP of the country and employ approximately 1 million people.

It is estimated that as of 2010 there were about 690 first-tier parts makers, 30 percent of them Thai majority joint venture companies, 23 percent of them pure Thai companies, and 1,700 second- and third-tier parts makers, most of them locally owned small and medium enterprises (SMEs) supporting the automobile industry in Thailand (Natsuda and Thoburn 2011, 8). As such, "Thailand is not a country where carmakers assemble their products. Most parts come from local companies. At more than 80 percent, the country has the highest localization in South East Asia. . . . Thailand also exports parts worth about $5 billion" (T.J. 2013). At present, the automobile industry is the principal engine for growth in Thailand's economy. "The Detroit of Asia" envisaged once by the Thai government is now a reality, and the "automobile belt" has been established from Ayutthaya to the Eastern Seaboard.

Accumulation of Knowledge and Capabilities, Prerequisite for Development of an Automobile Industry

As Athukorala and Kohpaiboon (2011) mention, "The automobile industry has been the target of industrial development in many countries as a growth driver—a source of employment, technological expertise, and a stimulus to other sectors through backward linkages. . . . But only a handful of developing countries have managed to develop an internationally competitive automobile industry."[5]

Development of an automobile industry requires skilled labor and supporting industries to provide twenty thousand to thirty thousand parts and components. Supporting industries and automobile assembly plants are closely related and provide externality to each other. Accordingly, in many countries, the lack of supporting industries made the installation of automobile assembly plants difficult, while supporting industries were constrained by the demand of parts and components of assembling plants. Their relationship is like that of the chicken and egg. Furthermore, the development of supporting industries for automobile industries takes years because they need a prolonged process of accumulation of knowledge and capabilities, especially the formation of human resources and learning about technology.

Among several policy measures, a series of initiatives by the Thai government to incrementally enhance the localization of parts production was important for the accumulation of knowledge and capabilities of supporting industries. In the 1960s, the board of investment (BOI) introduced the Industrial Investment Promotion Act, and six major foreign automobile joint venture companies were established with Thai capital by the end of the decade. However, the production of vehicles remained very limited, accounting for only 18.5 percent of the total sales of automobiles in the country in 1969, and the process heavily depended on assembly operations using imported completely knock down (CKD) kits that created a serious imbalance of trade and payment deficits (Natsuda and Thoburn 2011, 13).

The specific policies for the automobile industry, introduced for the first time in 1971, established, among others, a local contents requirement (LCR) of 25 percent, which became effective in 1973, and conditions for new market entry of over 0.2 million baht for investment (except for land) and production capacity of 30 units per day in order to achieve economies of scale, which is essential for competitive development in the automobile industry.[6] The LCR encouraged car assemblers to produce locally or to purchase parts from local companies. This was not easy because supporting industries in Thailand did not exist. Assembling companies had to start the process of localization from scratch. Following this, the LCR was raised incrementally through 1994 up to 60 percent for pickup trucks with gasoline engines and 72 percent for those with diesel engines. The LCR was abolished in 2000 in consideration of WTO rules.[7]

Techakanont (2008) considers that "the most important policy of the Thai state was the implementation of the LCR" (8). In order to comply with the LCR, automobile assembly companies in Thailand had to increase the local content of components that they produced themselves, ask their component suppliers in their countries of origin to invest in Thailand, or support local Thai firms to produce components with the required quality standards. Based on his extensive field research, Yamashita (2004) concludes that "the process of adapting to the LCR enabled the accumulation of a very wide range of automobile parts industries and the training of skilled technicians and engineers, both of which are indispensable for the development of the automobile industry" (5).[8] Through this process, assembly companies have offered continuous technological support to local supporting industries.

In this context, it should be emphasized that "most of the policies in the early 1980s were deliberated in a formal public-private cooperation committee (PPCC) before they were officially declared as government policy" (Techakanont 2008, 12). Doner (1991) explains: "The policy makers were quite flexible for assemblers to choose how to produce parts: either produce them locally or assemble components from imported parts."[9] Assembly companies asked the Thai government to revise the LCR policy when they reached the 54 percent level because any further increase of the LCR percentage would make it difficult to assure the safety of the cars and further reduce the cost of production. Responding to this request, the government switched its policy from the LCR to one requiring the local production of specific important components such as engines (Techakanont 2008, 9).

Formation of Automobile Clusters and Industrial Estates

The government facilitated the formation of industrial clusters by establishing the infrastructure for manufacturing activities, especially automobile assembly and parts production. Automakers and their components suppliers enhanced their competitiveness when they were agglomerated as a cluster with articulated value chains.

For this purpose, the Industrial Estate Authority of Thailand (IEAT) was established in 1972 and many industrial estates (IEs) were constructed, firstly around Bangkok and later on the Eastern Seaboard and its vicinities. The agglomeration of assemblers and part makers in IEs began in the 1970s. The establishment of IEs, leading to cluster formations, has been an important instrument through which the Thai government attracts foreign investors by providing infrastructure and tax incentives (Lecler 2002, 802).

Eastern Seaboard: Infrastructure that Triggered the Rapid Expansion of Thailand's Automobile Industry

The automobile industry requires efficient ports and logistics facilities in order to be competitive in the export market. From this perspective, the most important milestone for Thailand's automobile industry was the construction of infrastructure on the Eastern Seaboard.

The Eastern Seaboard infrastructure created an export hub and the center for technology-intensive industries: 14 industrial estates, 360,000 workers, 1,300 factories, and 516 automobile-related factories. The explosive emergence and concentration of new machinery and metal and non-metal industries with FDI inflows in the early 1990s, which occurred around Leam Chabang, became possible only through the completion of such large-sized infrastructure as the Eastern Seaboard Development Plan, which became a synergetic production nexus and a hub for the shipment of products (Shimomura and Mieno 2008, 14–16).

The Eastern Seaboard Development Plan is a leading large-scale development scheme that the Thai government implemented in the 1980s with assistance from Japan and the World Bank. It had a twofold purpose of boosting international strength and inviting direct overseas investment in export-oriented industrial fields, and easing the over-concentration of economic activity in Bangkok. The large-scale project, which extends over three provinces in the coastal area southeast of Bangkok, consists of a composite industrial site formed by two deep sea ports, Leam Chabang and Map Ta Put, supported by harbors, roads, railways, dams, service pipelines, and other facilities.[10]

Today, Leam Chabang, Thailand's largest port, plays a significant part in increasing trade in Thailand and is home to a heavy concentration of Thailand's automobile industry, with many automakers' and parts manufacturers' operations set up in the area. The Eastern Seaboard region accounted for 16 percent of Thailand's GDP, making it, along with the Bangkok metropolitan area, a key source of the country's economic strength (*The Japan Journal* 2014, 7). Figure 3.1 illustrates how these activities have moved into the Eastern Seaboard and demonstrates that this infrastructure produced a major change in the endowments structure in Thailand and played a crucial role in this country becoming the "Detroit of Asia."

"Detroit of Asia" Vision

The Thai automobile industry experienced different phases of development, namely the introduction of the localization policy (1971–1977),

the strengthening of localization capacity (1978–1990), and liberalization (1991–1999) (Natsuda and Thoburn 2011, 13–20). A new phase
started after the Thai government abolished the LCR in 2000 and
introduced the New Automobile Investment Policy in 2002, which
aimed to develop Thailand into a regional center of the automobile
industry in Southeast Asia. Two years later, a further automobile development plan was introduced, the so-called Detroit of Asia plan, which
was later renamed the "Production of Asia" plan (22). However, the
government's first "product champion," the pickup truck, was not considered enough to meet the targets of this plan by 2016. To attract additional foreign investment from automobile producers, the "Eco Car"
project was introduced as the second "product champion" in 2007 (23).
At the same time, a policy to strengthen supporting industries through
the promotion of SMEs was established: the SMEs promotion law of
2000 and the Master Plan of SMEs promotion of 2003. In addition,
the Automotive Human Resource Development Project (AHRDP) was
launched in 2006.

Institutions That Facilitated Changes of Endowments

Among others, there are two public institutions that have contributed to the development of Thailand's automobile industry. One is
the Automobile Development Committee and the other is the Eastern
Seaboard Development Committee (ESDC), a cabinet-level national
committee chaired by the prime minister together with the Office of
ESDC (OESD).

The Automobile Development Committee provided an effective
institutional setting for mid-level and senior officials to formulate policies in consultation with firms and business organizations. Interference
by political leaders and top-level policymakers was virtually absent in
the decision-making process (Athukorala and Kohpaiboon 2011, 12). Thai
authorities adopted a consensual and pragmatic approach to setting
the LCR target in consultation with automakers, as mentioned earlier.
Athukorala and Kohpaiboon highlight that the consensual approach
to policymaking and the absence of abrupt policy shifts created stable
expectations and confidence in the overall business environment.

Evaluating the Eastern Seaboard, JICA/JBIC (2008, 51) states:

> The reasons behind the success of the Thai government's plans for the Eastern Seaboard Development are 1) the consistent skill level of the technocrats and their independence from politics; 2) the unique check and balance structure in Thailand (several players sharing influence meant that mutual checks were continuous); 3) the development-centered orientation of the Prem administration; and 4) "the unintended transparent and open political process" created by the intervention of the media.[11]

Other Factors

In addition to the factors that enabled the outstanding development of the automobile industry of Thailand, we should mention others such as the advancement of economic integration among ASEAN countries via the ASEAN Free Trade Area (AFTA), ASEAN Industrial Cooperation (AICO) and others, and the size of the country's automobile market (the largest among ASEAN countries).

Summary of the Industrial Development Process

Figure 3.1 roughly illustrates the development of the automobile industry in Thailand. It details investments by global automobile companies in chronological order indicating the year of each company's investment. Characteristics of different phases of the development process are shown together with relevant policies of each phase (left-hand side). The construction of infrastructure in the Eastern Seaboard, the establishment of ASEAN Free Trade Area (AFTA), and other initiatives triggered investments in the Eastern Seaboard and other zones outside of Bangkok, further accelerating the development process.

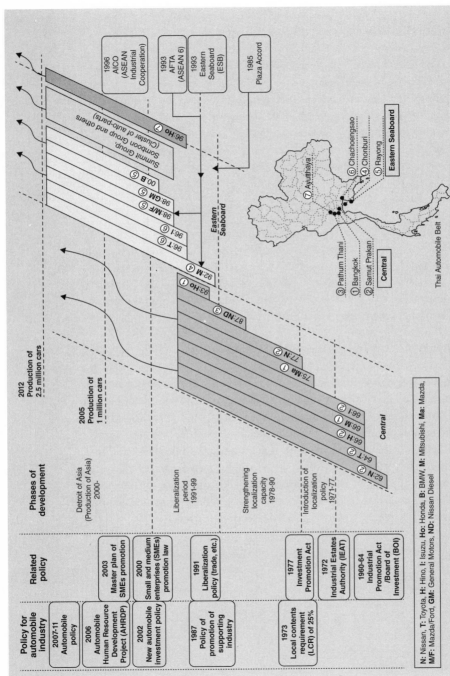

Figure 3.1 Development of the automobile industry in Thailand

Source: Prepared by the author, based on Lecler (2002), Table 2.4, and Natsuda and Thoburn (2011).

N: Nissan, T: Toyota, H: Hino, I: Isuzu, Ho: Honda, B: BMW, M: Mitsubishi, Ma: Mazda, M/F: Mazda/Ford, GM: General Motors, ND: Nissan Diesel

Case 2: Cerrado Miracle

Starting in the mid-1970s, the tropical savanna of Brazil, called the Cerrado, was transformed into one of the world's most productive grain-growing regions in just a quarter of a century, realizing modern upland farming in a tropical region for the first time in human history.[12] This remarkable transformation has become known throughout the world as the Cerrado Miracle (*Economist* 2010). Today, Brazil is one of world's major grain-producing countries, and in 2012 it exported the world's largest volume of soybeans. Dr. Norman E. Borlaug, who received the Nobel Peace Prize for his work related to the green revolution, rated the development of agriculture in the Cerrado as one of the great achievements of agricultural science in the twentieth century. The World Food Prize founded by Borlaug was awarded in 2006 to two Brazilians who contributed to the Cerrado Miracle. This agricultural transformation not only increased the production of competitive commodities such as soybeans, corn, coffee, sugar, and cotton, but also enabled the development of food value chains both inside and outside the Cerrado region. While the production of broiler chicken and pork had been growing steadily in the 1990s, this growth accelerated at the end of the decade and a sharp increase in meat exports was seen.

The Portuguese word *cerrado* refers to "closed" land, or land that was for many years regarded as unfit for agriculture. The total area of this vast region is about 240 million hectares, or 5.5 times the land area of Japan. This land was considered to be unsuitable for agriculture because the soil has extremely high acidity, lacks potassium and phosphoric acid, and contains large amounts of aluminum, all of which hinder crop growth.

Change of Endowment by Technological Innovation, Achieving "a New Comparative Advantage"

For the development of Cerrado agriculture, three technological aspects appear to have been essential. First, soil improvement and the development of new crop varieties suited to the tropical zone were crucial. These constituted the core technological innovations needed to launch Cerrado agriculture from a base of practically zero. Second, the effective dissemination of new technologies and practices to an increasing number of farmers who were the main actors in Cerrado agriculture was necessary. This was because this new industry was undertaken by a large number of farmers and enterprises instead of a limited number of companies, as is the case in some manufacturing industries. Third, a solid and highly effective system was indispensable to continue achieving the technological innovations required for Cerrado agriculture.

The vast land of the Cerrado had a drastic value change, which produced a "new comparative advantage" in terms of the JICA and JBIC study (2008). Here technological innovation was crucial, but the inland transport infrastructure constructed before and after the transfer of the national capital from Rio de Janeiro to Brasilia could have been another factor.

The Brazilian government "invested in learning," to borrow a term from Noman and Stiglitz (2012). But as emphasized earlier, investments in learning are highly risky, and risk markets are normally absent in developing countries. Therefore such investments are discouraged (Noman and Stiglitz 2012, 6). For Cerrado agricultural development, the government took the initiative. The Brazilian Agricultural Research Corporation (EMBRAPA) and its Cerrado Agricultural Research Center (CPAC) were established in 1973 and 1974, respectively, and did in fact achieve a lot of innovations: recent discussions on the Cerrado point out that EMBRAPA's greatest contributions were soil improvement in the Cerrado and breeding improvements in soybeans and other crops. In particular the success in developing new varieties of soybeans that were fit for the tropical climate was a significant technological breakthrough.

Soybeans, a crop suited to temperate regions, bloom and sprout by sensing differences in day length (photoperiod), and soybean cultivation was therefore difficult in the tropical region. Cultivation is even more difficult in lower-latitude areas in the Cerrado because the day length is nearly constant year-round. Dr. Plínio Itamar de Mello de Souza developed the revolutionary varieties of soybeans suited to the tropical region. Dr. de Mello collected three thousand soybean varieties from the southern United States, the Philippines, Japan, and other parts of the world, selected those with low sensitivity to changes in day length, then selected those that grow tall in tropical regions and crossbred them with varieties with high yields. Finally, in 1980, the first soybean variety was completed for cultivation in the Cerrado.

Soybean varieties adapted to tropical zones were essential not only as a new crop but also for soil improvement in the Cerrado. Soybeans fix nitrogen in the soil through root nodule bacteria and facilitate the soil to absorb fertilizers. Therefore soybeans played the role of a precursor among the plants introduced to the Cerrado.

Accumulation of Knowledge and Capabilities

Although the technology for Cerrado had been developed from scratch, there had been years of effort to establish Cerrado agriculture even before the establishment of EMBRAPA. Initiatives of farmers with experience in the southern region outside of the Cerrado were crucial as well. They undertook pioneering experimental work in the Minas Gerais Cerrado region. Drawing on their experience, the Program of Guided Settlement of Alto Paranaiba (PADAP) was implemented by the state of Minas Gerais together with the Cooperative Cotia. It was the first structured program to prove the feasibility (for business development) of Cerrado agriculture. The starting point was São Gotardo, in the state of Minas Gerais, in 1974.

On the basis of the successful PADAP experience, the Japan-Brazil Cooperation Program for Cerrados Development (PRODECER) was launched to extend Cerrado agriculture to other areas of Minas Gerais. The pilot projects of the first phase of PRODECER fully demonstrated the feasibility and high potential of Cerrado agriculture. The second phase of PRODECER carried out full-fledged projects in Minas Gerais as well as in the states of Goiás and Mato Grosso do Sul. At the same time, PRODECER also started pilot projects in the states of Bahia and Mato Grosso. The third phase of PRODECER covered the states of Tocantins and Maranhão. In this way, PRODECER was scaled up from the core regions to the frontier regions of the Cerrado. In this process, there has been continuous learning and the accumulation of knowledge and capabilities for both the researchers and farmers. How did these groundbreaking technologies developed by EMBRAPA spread? How did the pioneers of Cerrado agriculture improve their technological capabilities after they settled in the Cerrado, once believed to be sterile, and strove tirelessly to establish agricultural land? As noted by Dr. Eliseu Alves (2012), who is known as the father of EMBRAPA, many of the farmers who migrated to the Cerrado from southern Brazil had experience in agricultural production and were proactive about adopting new technologies. Cooperatives such as Cotia contributed greatly to the process of technological dissemination. The Brazilian Enterprise for Technical Assistance and Rural Extension (EMBRATER) was initially in charge of disseminating technologies developed mainly by EMBRAPA. EMBRATER was dissolved as a part of administrative reform and deregulation policies in 1992. A recent study by the Inter-American Development Bank (2010, 320) points out that after the organization was liquidated, producers utilized technological innovations through cooperatives and other organizations. In PRODECER, the growth pole strategy was adopted at Cerrado frontiers. Cotia and other cooperatives provided detailed technological consultations for individual farmers, contributing greatly to raising their technological capabilities.

Institutions that Facilitated Changes of the Endowment

The single most important institution that enabled the amazing change in the Cerrado and the establishment of Cerrado agriculture is considered to be EMBRAPA. The research begun by EMBRAPA in 1973 progressed steadily, making it one of the largest agricultural research institutes in the southern hemisphere and one of the largest tropical agricultural research institutes in the world. As of 2010, there were over 8,637 people working with the institute, 2,116 of whom were researchers, 1,622 holding doctorates. Only three researchers with doctorates were with the institute at its founding in 1973. Since then, EMBRAPA has dispatched three thousand people to advanced countries to study, and it now has forty-three affiliated research centers. EMBRAPA is today highly appreciated overseas for its distinguished research. Analyzing the factors behind its success reveals some clues on how to develop institutions capable of research and development activities suited to a country's conditions, which at the same time generate technological innovations, cultivate human resources, and produce "miracles" similar to that in the Cerrado.

EMBRAPA set the development of Cerrado agriculture as its core mission, achieved success, and therefore established its eminent position, thus succeeding in steadily securing its research budget while maintaining political neutrality; consequently, further research results were obtained, which further reinforced its position. Alves's (2012) view could be thusly summarized: What solidified the position of EMBRAPA was the achievement of transforming the Cerrado into a modern agricultural region. EMBRAPA's contributions are at the core of Cerrado agriculture, and society recognized that its involvement is vitally important for the region's success.

In addition, Alves and other authors emphasize other factors that made the EMBRAPA model successful: close relations between researchers and farmers, meritocratic incentive system and structure, transparency, and so on.

Summary of Agricultural Development Process

Figure 3.2 roughly illustrates the development process of the Cerrado agriculture in Brazil. It shows how experiences from the pioneering efforts of PADAP were scaled up to the first phase of PRODECER in Minas Gerais (MG) state, which was successfully expanded to the full-fledged projects in other zones of MG and the neighboring Goias (GO) and Mato Grosso do Sul (MS) states, and ultimately extended to other states of Cerrado (Mato Grosso, MT; Bahia, BA; Tocantins, TO; and Maranao, MA). In this process, technological development and dissemination by EMBRAPA, established in 1973 and continuously strengthened in the whole process, has been crucial. The Cerrado Development Program (Polocentro) carried out since 1975 by the government of Brazil contributed a lot to the Cerrado agriculture at its preparatory and establishment periods.

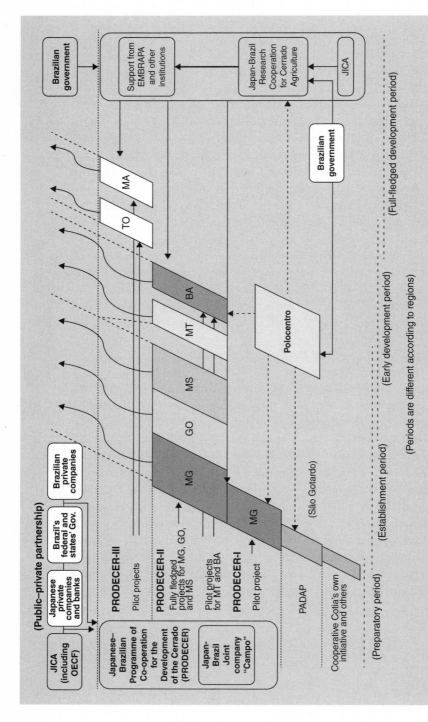

Figure 3.2 Development of Cerrado agriculture

Source: Prepared by the author, based on Hongo and Hosono (2012).

Case 3: Bangladesh Garment Industry

In 1981, ten years after Bangladesh achieved independence, raw jute and jute goods made up 68 percent of the country's total exports. In 2011, garments and textiles constituted 85 percent of total exports, of which 76 percent corresponded to garments. These industries' business entities amounted to 50 percent of all manufacturing establishments in the country (UNCTAD 2012, 11). Today, the garment industry has five to six thousand factories with seven to eight million workers using the assembly line method of production. The wages of the workers in these industries are around 35 percent higher than the national average (11). Exports as a percentage of GDP tripled between 1990 and 2010, with much of the increase in the thriving ready-made garment industry, which is largely comprised of female labor (World Bank 2012). This Bangladesh success story is remarkable because, as a recent World Bank study highlighted, "the country was often held out in the development literature as a hopeless case" (197).

Learning, Accumulation of Knowledge, and Capabilities

Rhee (1990) undertook extensive research on how this country's garment industry started. In 1978 Daewoo of Korea proposed to the government of Bangladesh an ambitious joint venture involving the development and operation of tire, leather goods, cement, and garment factories. As it turned out, the Bangladesh government actually put the garment industry first. Although the public and private sectors were particularly interested in the garment industry, Bangladesh was not exporting garments because of a total lack of domestic production technology and marketing knowhow, and had no apparent means of acquiring them from overseas (336). In this context, Noorul Quader, who had been introduced to the foreign business world as a senior official in the previous government, founded the Desh Garment Company and expressed the desire to collaborate with Daewoo in a new garment venture in the country (336). Quader and Daewoo signed an agreement to collaborate in the areas of technical training, purchase of machinery and fabric, plant start-ups, and marketing. Desh recruited 130 workers for training at Daewoo's Busan plant, where over seven months in 1979 "they received some of the most intensive on-the-job training in garment production ever seen in the history of developing countries" (337).

In addition to receiving in-depth, excellent skills training, Desh workers were also given a wide-ranging, high-quality education involving a look at the entire operations of a highly successful, multifaceted international company and the corporate culture that created and supported its superior performance, which Rhee emphasized as one of the most outstanding features of this training (338). The 115 Daewoo-trained workers who left Desh in the latter half of 1981 proved a very powerful medium for transferring knowhow throughout the whole garment sector and for significantly improving garment exports. In 1985, there were more than seven hundred garment export manufacturing factories in Bangladesh, compared with only a few such factories in 1979. Rhee mentions that many new garment firms have been able to handle production and marketing without involving expatriates or foreign companies because they have been staffed by former Desh workers who had fully mastered production and marketing (342). However, he also recognizes the continuous need for many of these new factories to collaborate to some degree with foreigners in the areas of marketing and technology (342).

Another noteworthy feature of Daewoo's training was that there were fourteen women among the trainees. Rhee explains, "Muslim tradition had precluded females from working in factories in Bangladesh. However, Quader had been so impressed by the efficiency and sheer numbers of women at Daewoo and other garment factories in Korea that he persuaded the Bangladesh government to support female trainees" (337).

Easterly (2002, 149) comments on the Desh-Daewoo collaboration from the standpoint of learning and knowledge creation: "Creating knowledge does not necessarily mean inventing new technologies from scratch. Some aspects of garment manufacturing technology were probably several centuries old." Bangladesh has the legacy of Dhaka Muslin. "The relevant technological ideas might be out there floating in the ether, but only those who apply them can really learn them and teach them to others"(149). In this regard, Mostafa and Klepper (2010, 3) emphasize that tacit knowledge seeding was essential for the initial establishment and subsequent expansion of the Bangladesh garment industry. They contend that key to the explosive growth of the industry were knowledgeable workers leaving Desh, and then other successful firms, to set up the production processes of later entrants. These workers organized an assembly line production process, trained workers, and supervised production, effectively diffusing vital tacit knowledge to new garment producers. Despite having limited literacy, Bangladesh had a sufficient number of educated entrepreneurs with some prior business experience who could gather the relevant resources and establish garment factories (29).

The process of learning and the accumulation of capabilities continued after this impressive transfer of technology from Korea. Mottaleb and Sonobe (2011, 4–5) conjectured that highly educated entrepreneurs have been attracted to the garment industry by high profitability, which was boosted initially by the Desh-Daewoo infusion of Korean skills and knowhow. Their analysis indicated that the high-level education of manufacturers and enterprise performance were closely associated. This is because manufacturers have to continuously upgrade their skills and knowhow in order to survive the intense competition in the world garment market and because high levels of general human capital are necessary for the entrepreneur to manage an increasing number of managers and experts (20–21).

Change of Endowments: Rural Development and Mobilization of Female Workers with Low Opportunity Cost

World Bank (2012, 197–199) classifies Bangladesh as an urbanizing country. Indeed the changes in rural society in this country have been profound and are closely related to the massive mobilization of female workers by the garment industry located mainly in two big cities: Dhaka and Chittagong. Generally speaking, urbanizing countries are endowed with abundant unskilled labor, and these countries' integration into the world economy can lead to the development of light manufacturing industries. In the case of Bangladesh, several factors interacted in order for this change to take place. Among the major factors that changed the rural society of Bangladesh were the modernization of agriculture based on technology that enabled farmers to shift from low-yield, single-crop, deep-water rice to the double cropping of short maturity, high-yield rice and the well-known rapid spread of microfinance and construction of rural infrastructure (197). More specifically, rural roads, irrigation, market facilities, and other rural infrastructure, microcredit, school education, and so forth provided by NGOs, central and local governments, and donors, all together enabled the remarkable agricultural and rural development of Bangladesh in the last three decades. In this process, the rural development programs of the government and donors were implemented effectively by the Local Government Engineering Department (LGED), which played a critical role in the provision of rural infrastructure.[13] Microcredit and related services were also effectively extended by NGOs including BRAC and Grameen Bank.

This process enhanced the mobility and readiness of low-opportunity cost labor in rural Bangladesh and changed gradually, but steadily, the endowments of the country. We should remember that a pessimistic appraisal was common regarding women's roles in the labor market in Bangladesh, which caused pessimism about the country's growth, due in part to the fact that most East Asian countries had the advantage of a high initial female labor force participation rate at the start of the growth process. As Hossain, Sen, and Sawada (2012, 29) emphasize, none of the predictions could anticipate that women would offer the secret ingredients of the success that was achieved in Bangladesh, from exports to schooling to microcredit use. The dramatic nature of the increase in female participation in the growth of ready-made garment (RMG) workers is a case in point.

The mobilization of this labor was triggered by the Desh-Daewoo garment project. Rhee (1990) explains, "Development is a dynamic process in which self-generating mechanisms may emerge once action is initiated. . . . To start on the path of development in an outward-oriented direction, a first spark must be created" (45). That spark was the collaborative effort of a domestic catalyst (Desh) that mobilized the necessary local resources and a foreign catalyst (Daewoo). It was a process of self-discovery of the changing comparative advantage of the country.

As such, the self-generating dynamic process of the garment industry was possible due to the changing comparative advantage with the mobility and readiness of low-opportunity cost labor, particularly female, in rural Bangladesh. At the same time, the positive externalities the garment industry brought to the economy in terms of the empowerment of women, their increased schooling, use of microcredit, and so on cannot be overemphasized.

Hossain, Sen, and Sawada (2012) contend that in the predominant agricultural economy with high population density and high population growth, the critical challenge is to reduce the burden of surplus labor in agriculture. "This challenge can be met through sustained sectoral and social policies and attendant institutional changes *commensurate to each stage of development* to support productivity/growth-enhancing relocation of 'surplus' farm labor to non-farm and non-agricultural jobs" (5; italics in original).

Change of Endowments: Connectivity and Logistics Upgrading by Infrastructure

When Desh started its business in 1980, its factory was located in Chittagong, the country's main port. The first export processing zone (EPZ) was also constructed in 1983 in this port city. Exports from Dhaka, which does not have an efficient port facility nearby, had a serious bottleneck due to the lack of bridges spanning the rivers that cross Highway No. 1, which connects the capital city with Chittagong. As trucks had to use ferries, the transport between Dhaka and Chittagong was constrained by time and unpredictability. This handicap affected the competitiveness of the garment industry in Dhaka. It was overcome by the construction of the Meghna Bridge in 1991 and the Meghna-Gumti Bridge in 1995. The Dhaka EPZ was constructed in 1993.

The Jamuna multipurpose bridge, inaugurated in 1998 as the largest construction in Bangladesh history, has been a major channel for integrating the lagging western region of the country with the leading eastern region, enabling cheaper transportation of gas, electricity, and telecommunications, and enhancing the labor mobility of the western region (Hossain, Sen, and Sawada 2012, 11).

Institutions that Facilitated Garment Industry Development

Initial conditions in Bangladesh, when the garment industry started with the Desh-Daewoo initiative, were affected by high levels of policy distortions and weak institutions. However, in spite of the rigidity of the government's response in terms of the adaptability of the ideas coming from private entrepreneurs, which is very common in developing countries, Yunus and Yamagata (2012, 5) mention that in the case of Bangladesh, the innovative ideas and strategies from the entrepreneurs were well accommodated by the government policymakers. A back-to-back letter of credit (L/C) system[14] and special bonded warehouse facilities were two of the most important features and were formulated based on the prescription of the leading entrepreneurs.

The special bonded warehouses were critical to the initiation of garment export production. According to Rhee (1990), "It appears that Daewoo's intimate knowledge of the nuts and bolts of the successful bonded warehouse system in Korea, its ability to transmit that knowledge to Desh staff, and the advice that Desh's senior manager gave to administration officials on the new system were instrumental in the design and implementation of the special bonded warehouse system" (339). Although the government did not provide any import financing facility, it did allow the back-to-back L/C, which was a very effective instrument given the system of strict foreign exchange controls in the country at that time. Here again Daewoo and Desh's influence on the public agencies was instrumental (340).

The consequent accelerated development of the garment industry was enabled by learning and the accumulation of the capabilities as mentioned earlier. The government facilitated its development through infrastructure investment, construction of export processing zones, policies for the free importation of machines, bonded warehouses, and back-to-back L/C, followed by other general policies such as the new industrial policy (1982), revised industrial policy (1986), and credit facilities (1991). At the same time, the multifiber agreement (1985) and its quotas as well as preferential access to the EU market have been important factors.

On the other hand, a comprehensive set of labor market and social policies need to be introduced, as a recent study by the International Labor Organization (ILO) Research Department (2013) warns. A garment factory fire in November 2011, which killed 117 workers, and the April 2012 collapse of a building housing several factories on the outskirts of Dhaka, in which 1,129 workers were tragically killed and another 2,500 were injured, brought the issue of occupational safety of the Bangladesh garment industry to the world's attention.

Summary of the Industrial Development Process

Figure 3.3 roughly illustrates the development of the garment industry in Bangladesh. It shows the evolution of a number of garment factories from the 1980s to today, together with the introduction of industrial policies and international framework related to the garment industry, such as the multifiber agreement and its expiration (the right-hand side of the figure). The process has also been facilitated by infrastructure investments such as bridges and export processing zones (left-hand side of the figure). The figure also refers to incremental changes of endowments such as the accumulation of capabilities by small business owners, the mobility and readiness of female workers, changes in rural society, and so on.

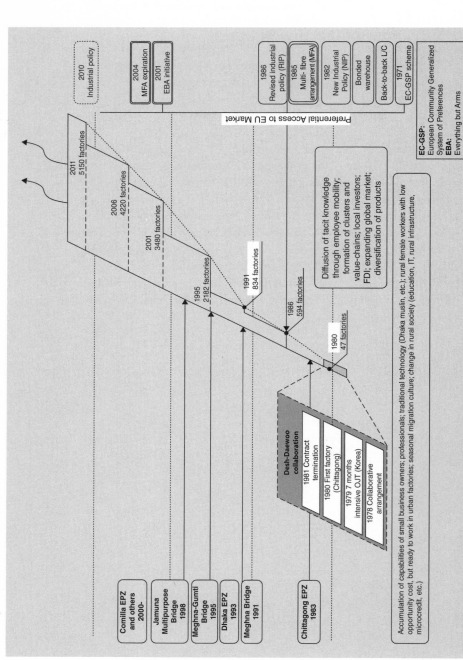

Figure 3.3 Development of Bangladesh garment industry

Source: Prepared by the author, based on BGMEA (2013), ILO (1993), Islam and Mukhtar (2011), Rhee (1990), and Yunus and Yamagata (2012)

Case 4: Chile's Salmon Industry [15]

Aquaculture is growing globally and makes up almost 50 percent of the global fish harvest in what is called the "blue revolution" (drawing a comparison with agriculture's green revolution) (OECD 2008, 85). One of the most impressive cases of the blue revolution is Chile's salmon farming and processing industry.

Salmon did not exist in Chile four decades ago. Now Chile is one of the world's top salmon-exporting countries, producing approximately 40 percent of the world's farmed salmon, and is ranked on par with Norway. It is no exaggeration to describe this as a miracle. Moreover, Chile is a resource-rich country highly dependent on copper exports, faced with the challenge of diversifying its exports. In 2011, exports of mineral ores and their refined products corresponded to more than 60 percent of total exports, 52 percent of which were copper ore and refined copper. The ensuing export revenue from rich resources leads to strong real exchange rate appreciation and deterioration in competitiveness in sectors exposed to international competition (World Bank 2012, 199). Today, salmon is the second largest export sector of Chile after copper, and its export value amounted to USD 3,517 million in 2013. The sector employs more than sixty thousand people in four southern regions of the country.[16]

Change of Endowment by Technological Adaptation/Innovation

Chile's comparative advantage in salmon sea farming was definitely confirmed when the Chile Foundation's subsidiary, Salmones Antártica, demonstrated the commercial feasibility of salmon aquaculture at a scale of one thousand tons per year in 1988. The Chile Foundation (Fundación Chile in Spanish) is a public-private corporation that aims at developing technologies for establishing new industries, setting up businesses, and selling successful ones for profit. This unique organization, which has no equivalent elsewhere in Latin America, was created through compensation consultations that the Chilean government had been having in the mid-1970s with an American multinational corporation that was nationalized by the previous government.

In general, for a new industry to be established so that it grows in a self-sustaining manner, the industry must demonstrate its feasibility and international competitiveness as a sustainable profit-making business. This requires, as a precondition, technology development, which in turn calls for sizable investment. Many venture businesses invest in the development of such technologies and new products. Although technology development itself carries the risk of failure, the guarantee that the founder's profit will be secured under the protection of patent rights provides a substantial incentive for creating a new industry. This is not to say, however, that the founder's profits in a new industry are always protected by patents or other means, and there are in fact many cases to the contrary.

In developing countries trying to catch up with developed countries, for example, entrepreneurs aiming to develop a new industry with the help of technology transfer from other countries usually find it difficult to protect the technologies gained through such transfer, as they will not be protected by patent. As a result, as soon as a company succeeds in a technology transfer, others will soon follow in the successful company's footsteps. This will intensify competition. In this case, the profit the pioneer deserves may not be guaranteed. Or worse still, the investment may not be recouped. Therefore Rodrik (2007, 117) argues that the costs of "self-discovery" of pioneers should be subsidized.

This may be described as a case of market failure in that open access to the information in question discourages investment. Specifically, this is known as market failure associated with "information externalities." In the case of Chile in the 1970s and 1980s, the government did not take an interventionist policy of directly supporting the development of industries. However, it is clear that the Chilean salmon industry was not developed as a result of the private sector making voluntary investments from the outset. In this context, noting that the major export items for Chile include copper, grapes, fish, and lumber/wood, Rodrik stresses that the diversification of export products from copper had not been achieved in a laissez-faire market (109).

In the case of the Chilean salmon industry, market failure was averted by the Chile Foundation and Japan-Chile salmon project. The Chile Foundation, a newly created, semi-governmental foundation, made an investment large enough to support salmon production through sea farming on a major scale and successfully recouped this investment. The foundation thus demonstrated the commercial profitability of sea farming on that scale. In addition to proving the profitability of the venture, the Chile Foundation provided as a public good information on salmon farming for free or for a fee so as to allow many companies to invest in the salmon farming industry without having to make a sizable investment in research and development.

Two private companies had started salmon sea farming before the Chile Foundation started its salmon initiative. In 1978, Nichiro Fisheries of Japan, which had already accumulated salmon sea farming technologies in Japan, set up Nichiro Chile, which in 1979 launched salmon sea farming near the city of Puerto Montt, the first of its kind in the country. This was a groundbreaking event that astounded fisheries experts at home and abroad who were familiar with the situation. Following Nichiro's groundbreaking success in salmon farming, the Chile Foundation acquired the facilities that Domsea Pesquera—a company under the umbrella of Campbell Soup of the United States—had owned in Chiloé Island and elsewhere. This represented the starting point for the Chile Foundation to enter the salmon industry in earnest.

Nichiro's success in pioneering mariculture and its commercialization in Chile had a great impact on the success of the semi-governmental Chile Foundation. Nichiro's corporate history says: "The Chile Foundation of the Republic of Chile had been keeping an eye on our progress in coho salmon seafarming. Upon learning about our success, the foundation wasted no time in launching feasibility studies on sea farming" (Maruha-Nichiro Salmon Museum). Though it was a latecomer to the industry, following the trailblazing Nichiro and Mytilus (latter-day "Mares Australes"), the second entrant into the market, Chile Foundation's Salmones Antártica successfully put larger-scale salmon mariculture on track. What factors lay behind this success? In short, the Chile Foundation was a semi-governmental corporation capable of mobilizing ample risk capital. Originally designed to encourage venture businesses, the Chile Foundation was in a better position to promote salmon farming than private companies in general.

The Chile Foundation, following the successful achievement of the one-thousand-ton program, decided to sell the venture to a private company. This led to an international bidding contest in 1988, in which many companies participated. Nippon Suisan Kaisha (today

Nissui), one of the major fisheries in Japan that operated in Chile at that time, won the bid. As a result, Salmones Antártica became wholly owned by Nippon Suisan Kaisha, which had been conducting salmon and trout businesses in the north Pacific Ocean since before World War II and had acquired advanced technical capabilities.

The Chile Foundation unexpectedly came up with the idea of offering corporate consulting services, started by the broadcasting in 1986 of a TV program featuring salmon farming in cooperation with Salmones Antártica. Many Chilean entrepreneurs who watched the program made inquiries to the TV station; some of them later ventured into the salmon industry. In the mid-1980s, the Chile Foundation supported projects by seven private companies.

Learning and Accumulation of Capabilities and Knowledge

In the case of the Chilean salmon industry, the natural conditions, capital, and labor were generally favorable. With technological adaptation and development, the value of these endowments changed, enabling Chile to attain a new comparative advantage. However, R&D professionals and trained industrial personnel were still scarce. Introducing and developing technology with high-level professionals is not an easy task for the private sector. Industrial personnel cannot be trained overnight, and such training is expensive for the private sector. In the preparatory phase of the Chilean salmon industry, these circumstances made it difficult for private companies to develop technologies and train industrial personnel by themselves.

This gap was filled by the Japan-Chile Salmon Project, which was implemented for twenty years, beginning in 1969, by Japan International Cooperation Agency (JICA) and its counterparts, National Fishery Services (SERNAPESCA) and Fishery Promotion Institute (IFOP), under an agreement between the Japanese and Chilean governments. Because the Japan-Chile Salmon Project was under the auspices of these two governments, technologies developed and personnel trained by the project were public goods and were available to what was to later become the salmon industry in Chile. This allowed salmon firms to save on the cost of investment in industrial personnel training. The Chile Foundation also played a similar role.

Between 1969 and 1989, twenty-eight Chileans received training in Japan under the salmon project, which was implemented by JICA and its counterpart organizations in the Chilean government: firstly SERNAPESCA, including its predecessor Agriculture and Livestock Service (SAG), and secondly IFOP. The training participants to be dispatched to Japan were selected from Chilean professionals who had been assigned to the project based on an order of priority that took their assignments into consideration. What the Chilean participants learned in Japan, where the technology of seed production and fry farming was advanced, as well as in the joint project, later translated into their own specialty, which in turn proved to be of great help in establishing and developing the salmon farming industry in Chile. The Chilean fishery journal *AQUA* attracted the attention of people who had been involved in salmon farming in Chile when it issued a twentieth anniversary special issue in December of 2007. The article on the aquaculture pioneers in Chile carried pictures of familiar faces who had worked in the industry for more than two decades. In all, six out of the eleven pioneers in salmon farming in Chile had received training in Japan. Of the six, five played a central role in the Japan-Chile Salmon Project over a long period.

Institutions that Facilitated the Development of the Chilean Salmon Industry

As explained earlier, in order to establish the Chilean salmon industry it was important to demonstrate that the salmon business was promising and commercially viable. This was accomplished through feasibility studies and investments in the salmon business by the Chile Foundation. In addition, the Chile Foundation's feasibility studies were partly supported by the Japan-Chile Salmon Project. Together with technology development, industrial personnel training was an important activity in this establishment phase.

It was not until the full-fledged development phase that salmon industry clusters increased their importance as an innovation system. It is worth noting here that the nascent form of that innovation system was already emerging in the establishment phase and that the Chile

Foundation and the Japan-Chile Salmon Project contributed to the process. Although industrial clusters in a wider sense include research institutes and universities, Chilean universities did little in the role as components of such clusters at the beginning. The scale-up of salmon production resulted in the deepening of the division of labor, the expansion of the value chain, and the development of salmon industry clusters involving a wide range of components, including salmon farming companies and their affiliated firms, government agencies, universities, and research institutes. One of the organizations that played an important role in this context was the Chilean Association of Salmon and Trout Producers (APSTCH, today SalmónChile). The Chile Foundation again made a significant contribution here, supporting the establishment of APSTCH.

The Chilean government, through its specialized entities SERNAPESCA and IFOP, and the Japan-Chile Salmon Project also served as a catalyst and played a facilitating role contributing to technological development in the area of national salmon eggs production, fish diseases, and fry farming. Furthermore, the Japan-Chile Salmon Project contributed a great deal to the establishment and enforcement of relevant laws and regulations. The Office of the Undersecretary of Fisheries of the Ministry of Economy, Development and Tourism, established in 1978, played a pivotal role in establishing relevant laws and regulations, while SERNAPESCA assumed the responsibility for their enforcement.

Each of these two organizations served as the counterpart organization of JICA. SERNAPESCA, the Chilean counterpart organization for the Japan-Chile Salmon Project until 1987, has put many of the project's outcomes to good use in establishing laws and regulations concerning the aquaculture industry in Chile. For example, technical cooperation in the area of fishery disease control has resulted in the development of regulations on the prevention of infectious disease epidemics associated with salmon and trout farming. Likewise, a Chilean Ministry of Economy ordinance issued in 1985 has imposed control on imported salmon eggs. The ordinance has also provided for the disinfection of hatcheries, among other control measures. In addition, it has prompted the veterinary check of farmed salmon, making the ordinance the starting point for salmon infectious disease control in Chile.

Summary of the Development Process of the Salmon Industry

Figure 3.4 roughly illustrates the development of the salmon industry in Chile. It shows the evolution of salmon industry companies from the 1970s, together with the research and development activities of Chilean National Fishery Services (SERNAPESCA) and Fishery Promotion Institute (IFOP) carried out with Japanese cooperation. After Nichiro Chile launched salmon sea farming in 1979, the Chile Foundation, a newly created, semi-governmental foundation, made an investment large enough to support salmon production through sea farming on a major scale and successfully recouped this investment, demonstrating the commercial feasibility at a scale of one thousand tons per year in 1988.

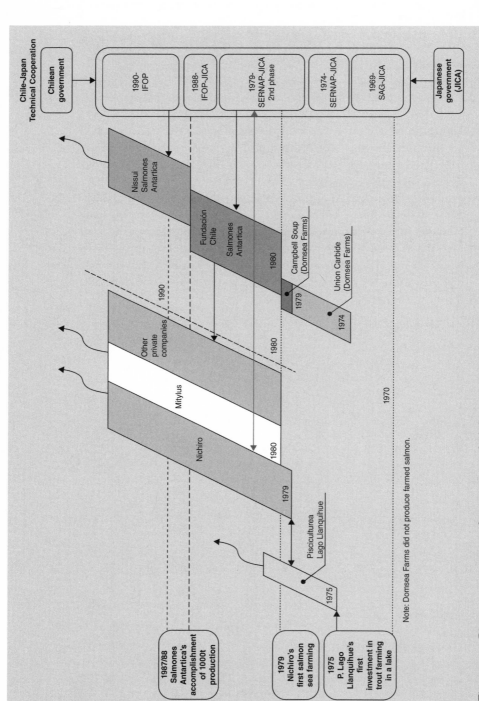

Figure 3.4 Pioneer companies and institutions of Chilean salmon industry

Source: Prepared by the author, based on Hosono (2010).

Case 5: Singapore

Singapore, a country without natural resources and with a large number of unemployed people at the time of its independence, is today one of the most competitive countries in the world. The experience of Singapore is particularly relevant as a small country that experienced highly successful industrial development and economic transformation. Its population was 2.6 million in 1985 and 4.8 million in 2008. A small country faces a different agenda than larger countries do and needs to adopt different strategies.

Singapore was one of the first Southeast Asian countries to promote export-led growth rather than import substitution-led growth. In the late 1970s, faced with rising competition from other exporters whose wage rates were lower, Singapore decided to transition from exports dependent on cheap labor into a knowledge economy based on skilled labor and higher value-added exports. During the last three decades, the country has continuously upgraded its industrial structure, overcoming the so-called middle income trap. As Yusuf and Nabeshima (2012) mention in their study on Singapore, Ireland, and Finland, by the 1980s it was becoming apparent that by betting on the technologically dynamic industrial subsectors—principally electronics, telecommunications, chemicals, and pharmaceuticals—small countries could improve their longer-term growth perspective. In this context, the rapid transformation demanded increasingly higher-level human resources and entrepreneurs. In many cases, in which foreign direct investment played an important role in transferring and disseminating cutting-edge technology, especially in the areas of electronics, the Internet, and biotech industries, transnational companies would not have been interested in investing in Singapore if the country did not have the human capital and knowledge base to absorb such technology.

The following section intends to get insights into how human resource development and accumulation of capabilities to address the global competition was achieved. Then the institutions that formulated the country's development strategy and facilitated the transformation will be discussed.

Human Resource Development and Accumulation of Knowledge and Capabilities

In the transformation process of Singapore, Yusuf and Nabeshima (2012, 34–36) emphasize the importance of general purpose technologies (GPTs). They further argue: "The revolution caused by advances in semiconductors, electronics, and telecommunication technologies is widely associated with new products and the ways products are manufactured. Undoubtedly, these advances have contributed significantly to economic changes, but product innovation was powerfully reinforced by numerous collaborative innovations in other areas—for example, in services, institutions, organizations, and habits and lifestyles. GPTs have proven to be an extraordinarily potent transformative force because the learning economy generated a cross-disciplinary matrix of supporting and intersecting innovations that enormously magnified the influence of core technologies."

Yusuf and Nabeshima (2012, 44) highlight that in embracing technology as a driver of long-term growth, Singapore, Finland, and Ireland successfully engaged in building capabilities. This success is the core of the three countries' models and resulted in the making of a networked learning and innovation system of the highest rank. The concept of such capabilities resembles the concept of "learning to learn" coined by Stiglitz and cited in the section of this chapter titled "An Analytical Perspective." He stresses that development strategies need to be focused on "learning to learn," especially in an era with fast-changing technologies in which specific knowledge learned at one moment risks rapid obsolescence.

So how did Singapore succeed in building such capabilities? A close look at Singapore's national initiative to increase productivity, strengthen quality, and later to support innovation will help us to understand Singapore's experience. According to Prime Minister Lee Kuan Yew, "The shift to a knowledge-intensive industrial structure with strong international competitiveness is only possible through the human-resource development of 2.6 million people, the only resource Singapore has" (Japan Productivity Organization 1990, 1).[17] Lee was concerned with how to organize and motivate Singapore's labor force in such a way as to make the most of plant modernization and skills development (JICA/IDCJ/IDJ 2010, 30). In April 1981, the Singaporean

Committee on Productivity was formed comprising representatives of enterprises, workers' organizations, government officials, and academia. The committee reviewed the experiences of productivity movements in Japan, another country without natural resources but with abundant labor. It then presented a report to the president of the National Productivity Board (NPB) of Singapore, which had been designated as the main body for promoting productivity development in Singapore. In June 1983, the Singapore Productivity Development Project (SPDP) was launched with the support of the Japanese government.

Some fifteen thousand Singaporean engineers, managers, and other professionals participated in the project. Two hundred engineers, managers, and other professionals from Singapore took part in training courses in Japan, and more than two hundred Japanese experts were dispatched to Singapore. In addition, more than one hundred textbooks and other training materials were prepared specifically for the project. During the period of SPDP and beyond, labor productivity in manufacturing industries improved by an annual average rate of 5.7 percent (1981–1986), 3.0 percent (1986–1991), and 4.8 percent (1991–1996).[18]

In 1990, when SPDP ended, 90 percent of workers in the country were involved in productivity development activities, compared with 54 percent in 1986. In 2001, 13 percent of the total labor force was participating in quality-control circles, in comparison with 0.4 percent in 1983, when SPDP started. Quality control circles are considered the most effective vehicle for improving quality and productivity with the active participation of workers. Through this participatory approach, workers' ideas are incorporated into the production process, leading to innovative solutions to address ever-changing challenges. Hence SPDP became one of the driving forces for productivity gains in Singapore.

NPB's activities gathered considerable momentum, progressing from the awareness stage (1982–1985), during which it created widespread awareness of productivity among companies and the workforce, to the action stage (1986–1988), when it translated awareness into specific programs to improve productivity in the workplace, and finally the follow-up stage (1988 to the present), in which it encouraged ownership of the productivity movement (see Ohno and Kitaw 2011; Ohno 2013). The NPB merged with the Singapore Institute of Standards and Industrial Research in 1996 to create the Productivity and Standards Board (PSB), bringing together the soft skills and the technical aspects of productivity. The PSB was later strengthened and reorganized into the Standards, Productivity, and Innovation Board (SPRING) in 2002.

NPB, PSB, and now SPRING became global centers of excellence in the field of productivity, quality, standards, and innovation. Other key factors that bolstered these institutions include the transition from a public sector–led entity to a private sector–led entity, active advocacy and publicity, human resource development inside and outside the institution, and the establishment of a skills development fund by the government. Singapore's productivity initiative was strongly encouraged by the country's senior leaders, especially Prime Minister Lee. He understood the need for institution building and the need to promote creativity and the capacity to innovate in order to sustain growth for Singaporeans.

Here it should be particularly emphasized that the previously mentioned process enhanced the capabilities of both individuals and organizations. Ohno (2013, 190) reiterates that a nationwide productivity drive requires a paradigm shift, a mindset change by which all people strive for and acquire the habit of improvement, and systems and practices that translate such an attitude into action. He further emphasizes that a new way of thinking, living, and working must be firmly built in the minds and actions of all leaders and actors and highlights the importance of strong political commitment from the top and strong organizational support.

Institutions that Enabled the Process of Transformation

Singapore's Economic Development Board (EDB) was a single agency with the task of delivering the key elements of a growth strategy (Yusuf and Nabeshima 2012, 105). It was established in 1961 with the original goals and organizational structure spelled out in its first annual report: "The primary function of the Board is to promote the establishment of new industries in Singapore and to accelerate the growth of existing ones" (cited by Schein 2001, 38). Schein, who described the culture of EDB as "strategic pragmatism" based on an extensive study of EDB, summarizes that Singapore displayed a remarkable adaptive and learning capability without sacrificing short-term problem solving (57–58).

Ohno (2013, 172–173) points out that EDB is a business-friendly, one-stop agency for domestic and foreign investors. EDB, in attracting

FDI in priority sectors, uses both broad-based approaches and targeted approaches. Holding first position among more than 180 countries in the World Bank Doing Business Reports for five consecutive years, EDB also engages in individual negotiations with foreign companies to offer company-specific support and incentives in what is called the "Queen Bee" approach.

Kuruvilla and Chua (2000, 40–41) consider the following, among others, to be the major reasons behind Singapore's remarkable success in upgrading workforce skills: a general link between economic development needs and skill formation/development facilitated by an institutional structure that places the EDB at the center of the efforts with responsibility for both areas; EDB's model of technological transfer linking FDI to skills development as well as of joint government-private sector operation for skill training; and educational reform for long-term skills development.

In the areas of productivity, quality, standards, and innovation, NPB, PSB, and now SPRING played a crucial role in mainstreaming cross-cutting general purpose technologies (GPTs) in Singapore's industrial development and economic transformation.

Furthermore, the provision of infrastructure for industrial development by Jurong Town Corporation (JTC) as the principal statutory board for industrial development cannot be overemphasized. JTC is seen as a strategic developer of cutting-edge industrial spaces bringing forth new paradigms in industrial planning and urban design (Kaushik 2012, 13). It now aims at strategic clustering and innovation providing new estates, cluster hubs, paradigms, land creation, and eco-sustainability.

Summary of the Process of Development of Institutions for Accumulation of Knowledge and Capabilities

Figure 3.5 roughly illustrates the development of institutions in Singapore responsible for economic development, productivity, standards and innovation, and infrastructure provision. It focuses on the evolution over fifty years of such institutions as the Productivity and Standards Board (PSB) and the Standard, Productivity, and Innovation Board (SPRING), both considered essential for productivity development, accreditation of products, standardization, and scientific research and development in Singapore.

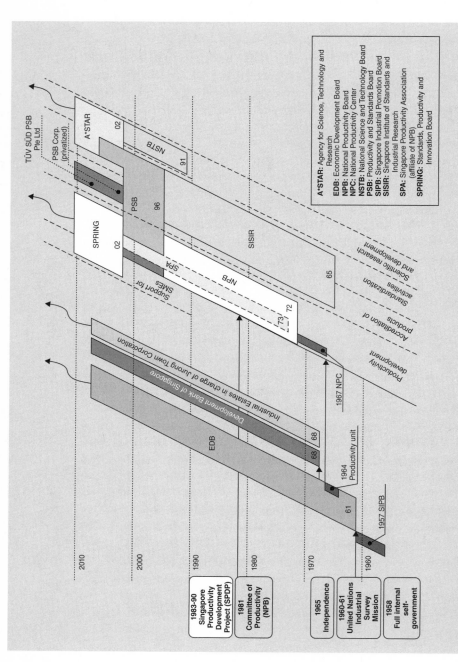

Figure 3.5 Major institutions of Singapore in areas of economic development, productivity, standards and innovation, and infrastructure provision

Source: Prepared by the author, based on JICA/IDCJ/IDJ (2010) and Ohno and Kitaw (2011).

CONCLUDING REMARKS: FINDINGS FROM
THE CASE STUDIES

The five cases presented here show how distinctive critical factors identified by several recent studies interact in practice. Learning and accumulation of knowledge and capabilities are essential, and occur in a gradual, incremental, and generally path-dependent process. However, the process is critical for changing the endowments to attain dynamic comparative advantage. Our case studies also bring out how the government or public institutions can facilitate the process. In Thailand, Bangladesh, and Singapore, the constant improvement of the capabilities of those involved in the new industries was crucial.

Change of endowments is also attained by infrastructure construction and technological innovation. They often trigger or accelerate industrial development and transformation. The Eastern Seaboard was crucial for the expansion of the automobile industry in Thailand, which eventually enabled the country to be labeled the "Detroit of Asia." In Bangladesh, construction of more efficient transport and logistics infrastructure facilitated and accelerated the process of transformation. In Brazil, technological breakthroughs changed the endowments and comparative advantage of the country and, together with institutional innovations, triggered the transformation of the Cerrado from barren land into one of the most productive agricultural regions in the world. In Chile, technological adaptation and development changed the endowments. But in all of these cases, industrial development and economic transformation could not have happened without constant development of capabilities and knowledge through learning. In Singapore, "learning to learn" was a key factor in the country's rapid and profound transformation.

Thus in all outstanding cases studied, economic transformation was achieved with changes in endowment and comparative advantage. The endowment changes were enabled both by the long-term process of accumulation of knowledge and capabilities and by investment in infrastructure and in technological innovation. In particular, the technology and knowledge necessary for new economic activities, especially in agriculture and aquaculture, are normally considered public goods. These public goods were provided by public institutions or via public-private collaboration.

In all five cases, effective institutions accomplished the role of facilitator or catalyzer of transformation. First of all, many of them had been created for specific purposes and had long-term visions and missions. Second, most such institutions regarded public-private interaction, consultation, or coordination to be of the highest priority, as was seen in the cases of Thai automobile industry policymakers, the Brazilian Agricultural Research Corporation, Bangladesh garment industry policymakers, the Chile Foundation, and Singapore's Economic Development Board and Standard, Productivity, and Innovation Board. Third, most of these institutions adapted flexibly to changes in the global market and phases of industrial development.

These findings generally confirm the conclusion of JICA/JBIC (2008) regarding drivers of economic growth found in the Asian experience, drawing from many other remarkable cases of changing endowments and transformation in the region. Particularly noteworthy are mid-to-long-term vision for development and associated strategies; flexibility in responding to a changing environment; the government's close ties with the private sector; and harnessing the private sector's capacity to the maximum.

NOTES

The author would like to express his gratitude to Yasuo Fujita, Go Shimada, and Ayako Otaguchi of JICA Research Institute for their valuable comments. Errors and omissions are the responsibility of the author.

1. Greenwald and Stiglitz (2012) use a similar definition: "Industrial policies are what we call those policies that help shape the sectoral composition of an economy. The term is used more broadly than just those policies that encourage the industrial sector. A policy which encourages agro-business, or even agriculture, is referred to as an industrial policy" (3).

2. This view is also similar to the recent argument on CD. The wider acceptance of systems thinking in the current CD discussion is based on the assumption that it can better capture and explain the complexities of multilayered transformative processes in a constantly changing external (that is, development) environment (Hosono et al. 2011, 181).

3. Kaizen is a Japanese concept that can be translated literally as "continuous improvement." It is not easy to define kaizen in a strict sense because it corresponds to evolving initiatives and activities in the areas of quality and productivity and can be very flexibly adapted to each factory floor's context. Despite flexibility in its application, kaizen has, among other things, common characteristics. It is: (1) not imposed by "top-down" orders or instructions, but is a "bottom-up process" implemented at the initiative of each worker, based on their observations, experiences, knowledge, wisdom, and so on; (2) not a one-shot activity, but is continuous and incremental; and (3) not strictly limited to production itself, but covers all aspects of production including

improvements in safety and morale, as well as improvement in quality, in operation efficiency, and in delivery (see Hosono 2009).

4. This typological approach is inspired by *World Development Report 2013* (World Bank 2012, 18–19).

5. It goes without saying that the automobile is a complex product consisting of a large number of parts and components that involve different production processes and factor proportions. Many of these parts and components are manufactured by independent suppliers in other industries such as textiles, glass, plastic, electronics, rubber products, and steel and other metals (Athukorala and Kohpaiboon 2011, 1).

6. Regarding this new policy, see Natsuda and Thoburn (2011, 13).

7. Starting in 1978, the LCR for passenger cars was increased from 25 percent to 35 percent in the first two years and was then raised by 5 percent every year until 1983, eventually reaching 50 percent, and for commercial vehicles from 20 percent to 45 percent. The new policy also required assemblers to localize the production of specific parts by introducing a "mandatory deletion" scheme targeting specific parts such as brake drums and exhaust systems. In 1994, the LCR was further raised to 60 percent for pickup trucks with gasoline engines and 72 percent for those with diesel engines. In 1996, the government announced the abolition of the LCR by 1998, prior to the WTO target date, although eventually the period was extended to 2000 (Natsuda and Thoburn 2011, 15).

8. Translation is by the author.

9. Cited in Techakanont (2008, 9).

10. This summary is based on JICA/JBIC (2008, 50).

11. Another study reached a similar conclusion: "It was the cumulative synergetic effect of a number of factors that had contributed to pushing the Eastern Seaboard Development Program forward. These included: Effective leadership to ensure the public's interest, competency of technocrats, powerful central economic agencies, special institutional settings, functioning coordination mechanisms, and external global factors" (Ohno and Shimamura 2007, 131).

12. This case study is based on Hosono, Magno Campos da Rocha, and Hongo, eds. (forthcoming).

13. The role of LGED in the rural development cannot be overemphasized. LGED is one of the largest public sector organizations in Bangladesh, with a staff exceeding ten thousand and a development budget accounting for 14 percent (fiscal year 2009–2010) of the total development budget of the government. For details of LGED, see Fujita (2011).

14. For details of this system, see Easterly (2002, 149).

15. This case study is based on Hosono (2010).

16. See the SalmonChile (The Salmon Industry Association of Chile) website (www.salmonchile.cl). This figure does not include people employed by upper-stream and downstream industries of salmon farming and processing value chain.

17. Remarks made by the prime minister when he visited Kohei Goshi, honorary president of Japan Productivity Center in June 1981.

18. The figures and those of the following paragraph are from JICA/IDCJ/IDJ (2010, 16 and 22).

REFERENCES

Alves, Eliseu Roberto de Andrade. 2012. "Embrapa: A Successful Case of Institutional Innovation." In *Brazilian Agriculture: Development and Changes*, ed. G. B. Martha Jr. and J. B. de Souza Ferreira Filho, 143–160. Brasilia: Embrapa.

AQUA. 2007. "Pioneros en Chile: Con la Acuicultura en las Venas." *AQUA* (December).

Athukorala, Prema-Chandra, and Archanun Kohpaiboon. 2011. "Thailand in Global Automobile Networks." Paper submitted to Study for the International Trade Center, Geneva.

Cimoli, Mario, Giovanni Dosi, and Joseph E. Stiglitz, eds. 2009. *Industrial Policy and Development: The Political Economy of Capabilities Accumulation*. Toronto: Oxford University Press.

Commission on Growth and Development. 2008. *The Growth Report: Strategies for Sustained Growth and Inclusive Development*. Washington, DC: World Bank.

Doner, Richard F. 1991. *Driving a Bargain: Automobile Industrialization and Japanese Firms in Southeast Asia*. Berkeley: University of California Press.

Easterly, William. 2002. *The Elusive Quest for Growth: Economists' Adventures and Misadventures in the Tropics*. Cambridge, Mass.: MIT Press.

Economist. 2010. "The Miracle of the Cerrado." *The Economist*, August 28.

Fujita, Yasuo. 2011. "What Makes the Bangladesh Local Government Engineering Department (LGED) So Effective?: Complementarity Between LGED Capacity and Donor Capacity Development Support." JICA Research Institute Working Paper No. 27 (January): 1–49.

Greenwald, Bruce, and Joseph E. Stiglitz. 2012. "Learning and Industrial Policy: Implications for Africa." Paper presented at New Thinking on Industrial Development: Implications for Africa for the International Economic Association.

Hosono, Akio. 2009. "*Kaizen*: Quality, Productivity and Beyond." In *Introducing KAIZEN in Africa*, ed. GRIPS Development Forum, 23–38. Tokyo: National Graduate Institute for Policy Studies (GRIPS).

——. 2010. *The Japanese Who Changed Chile into a Great Salmon-Exporting Country* (in Japanese). Tokyo: Diamond, Inc.

Hosono, Akio, Shunichiro Honda, Mine Sato, and Mai Ono. 2011. "Inside the Black Box of Capacity Development." In *Catalyzing Development: A New Vision for Aid*, ed. Homi Kharas, Koji Makino, and Woojin Jung, 179–201. Washington, DC: Brookings Institute.

Hosono, Akio, and Yutaka Hongo. 2012. "Cerrado: Brazil's Agricultural Revolution as a Model of Sustainable and Inclusive Development." Tokyo: JICA.

Hossain, Mahabub, Binayak Sen, and Yasuyuki Sawada. 2012. "Jobs, Growth and Development: Making of the 'Other' Bangladesh." In *World Development Report 2013 Companion Volume*, 1–53. Washington DC: World Bank.

Inter-American Development Bank (IDB). 2010. *The Age of Productivity: Transforming Economies from the Bottom Up*. Washington, DC: IDB.

International Labour Organisation (ILO). 2013. *Bangladesh: Seeking Better Employment Conditions for Better Socioeconomic Outcomes*. Geneva: ILO.

Japan International Cooperation Agency (JICA), International Development Center of Japan (IDCJ), and The International Development Journal (IDJ). 2010. *Data*

Collection Survey on Strategy Formulation on Human Resources Development in Southeast Asia. Final Report. Tokyo: JICA.

Japan International Cooperation Agency (JICA) and Japan Bank for International Cooperation (JBIC). 2008. *Report of the Stocktaking Work on Economic Development in Africa and the Asian Growth Experience.* Tokyo: JICA.

Japan Journal. 2014. "ODA, Japan's Way." *The Japan Journal* (October): 6–13.

Japan Productivity Organization. 1990. *Singapore Productivity Improvement Project.* Tokyo: Japan Productivity Organization.

Johnson, Simon, Jonathan D. Ostry, and Arvind Subramanian. 2007. "The Prospects for Sustained Growth in Africa: Benchmarking the Constraints." NBER Working Paper No. 13120.

Kaushik, Diwakar. 2012. "Evolution of Industrial Landscape in Singapore." Case study presented on the International Society of City and Regional Planning (ISOCARP) Congress. http://www.isocarp.net/projects/case_studies/cases/cs_info.asp?ID=2108.

Kuruvilla, Sarosh, and Rodney Chua. 2000. "How Do Nations Develop Skills?: Lessons from the Skill Development Experiences of Singapore." New York: Cornell University ILR School. http://digitalcommons.ilr.cornell.edu/cbpubs/8/.

Lecler, Yveline. 2002. "The Cluster Role in the Development of the Thai Car Industry." *International Journal of Urban and Regional Research* 26 (4): 799–814.

Lin, Justin Yifu. 2012. *New Structural Economics: A Framework for Rethinking Development and Policy.* Washington, DC: World Bank.

Maruha-Nichiro Salmon Museum. http://www.maruha-nichiro.co.jp/salmon/fishery/09.html.

Ministry of Foreign Affairs. 2005. *Japan's Official Development Assistance (ODA) White Paper 2005.* Tokyo: Ministry of Foreign Affairs.

Mostafa, Romel, and Steven Klepper. 2010. "Industrial Development through Tacit Knowledge Seeding: Evidence from the Bangladesh Garment Industry." Working paper, Washington University, St. Louis, Mo.

Mottaleb, Khondoker Abdul, and Tetsushi Sonobe. 2011. "An Inquiry into the Rapid Growth of the Garment Industry in Bangladesh." Discussion paper, National Graduate Institute for Policy Studies (GRIPS).

Natsuda, Kaoru, and John Thoburn. 2011. "Industrial Policy and the Development of the Automotive Industry in Thailand." Working Paper No. 11(5), Ritsumeikan Center for Asia Pacific Studies (RCAPS).

Noman, Akbar, and Joseph E. Stiglitz. 2012. "Strategies for African Development." In *Good Growth and Governance in Africa: Rethinking Development Strategies*, ed. Akbar Noman et al., 3–47. Oxford: Oxford University Press.

Ohno, Kenichi. 2013. *Learning to Industrialize: From Given Growth to Policy-aided Value Creation.* New York: Routledge.

Ohno, Izumi, and Daniel Kitaw. 2011. "Productivity Movement in Singapore." In *Kaizen National Movement: A Study of Quality and Productivity Improvement in Asia and Africa.* Japan International Cooperation Agency (JICA) and National Graduate Institute for Policy Studies (GRIPS) Development Forum. http://www.grips.ac.jp/forum-e/Kaizen_e.htm.

Ohno, Izumi, and Masumi Shimamura. 2007. *Managing the Development Process and Aid: East Asian Experiences in Building Central Economic Agencies*. Tokyo: National Graduate Institute for Policy Studies (GRIPS) Development Forum.

Organization for Economic Co-operation and Development (OECD). 2008. *Natural Resources and Pro-Poor Growth: The Economics and Politics*. Paris: OECD.

Rhee, Yung Whee. 1990. "The Catalyst Model of Development: Lessons from Bangladesh's Success with Garment Exports." *World Development* 18 (2): 333–346.

Rodrik, Dani. 2007. *One Economics Many Recipes: Globalization, Institutions, and Economic Growth*. Princeton: Princeton University Press.

Schein, Edgar H. 2001. *Strategic Pragmatism: The Culture of Singapore's Economic Development Board*. Cambridge, Mass.: MIT Press.

Shimomura, Yasutami, and Fumiharu Mieno. 2008. "Thailand Case Study." *Aid Effectiveness to Infrastructure: A Comparative Study of East Asia and Sub-Saharan Africa* JBICI Research Paper 36–2 (July): 1–51.

Stiglitz, Joseph E. 1987. "Learning to Learn, Localized Learning and Technological Progress." In *Economic Policy and Technological Performance*, ed. Partha Dasgupta and Paul Stoneman, 125–153. Cambridge: Cambridge University Press.

Techakanont, Kriengkrai. 2008. "The Evolution of Automotive Clusters and Global Production Network in Thailand." Discussion paper No. 0006, Faculty of Economics, Thammasat University.

T.J. 2013. "Thailand's Booming Car Industry: Detroit of the East." *The Economist*, April 4.

United Nations Conference on Trade and Development (UNCTAD). 2012. "Bangladesh Sector-specific Investment Strategy and Action Plan: G20 Indicators for Measuring and Maximizing Economic Value Added and Job Creation from Private Investment in Specific Value Chain." Pilot Study Results. http://unctad.org /Sections/diae_dir/docs/diae_G20_Bangladesh_en.pdf.

World Bank. 2012. *World Development Report 2013: Jobs*. Washington, DC: World Bank.

Yamashita, Shoichi. 2004. "Development of Automobile Parts Industry and Formation of Export Platform in Thailand" (in Japanese). International East Asia Research Center, ASEAN-Auto Project No. 04(1).

Yunus, Mohammad, and Tatsufumi Yamagata. 2012. "The Garment Industry in Bangladesh." In *Dynamics of the Garment Industry in Low-Income Countries: Experience of Asia and Africa*, ed. Takahiro Fukunishi, 1–28. IDE-JETRO Interim Report. http://www.ide.go.jp/Japanese/Publish/Download/Report/2011/2011_410.html.

Yusuf, Shahid, and Kaoru Nabeshima. 2012. *Some Small Countries Do It Better: Rapid Growth and Its Causes in Singapore, Finland, and Ireland*. Washington, DC: World Bank.

FURTHER READING

Bangladesh Garments Manufacturers and Exporters Association (BGMEA). 2013. "Trade Information." http://www.bgmea.com.bd/home/pages/TradeInformation.

Hosono, Akio, Carlos Magno Campos da Rocha, and Yutaka Hongo, eds. Forthcoming. *Development for Sustainable Agriculture: The Brazilian Cerrado*. London Palgrave Macmillan.

International Labour Organisation (ILO) and Asian Regional Team for Employment Promotion World Employment Programme. 1993. *Social Dimensions of Economic Reforms in Bangladesh*. Geneva: ILO.

International Trade Center. 2011. "Thailand in Global Automobile Networks." http://www.intracen.org/uploadedFiles/intracenorg/Content/Trade_Support_Institutions/Business_voice_in_policy_making/WTO_accession_implication_for_business/Thailand_in_global_automobile_networks.pdf.

Islam, Md. Zohurul, and Uzma Mukhtar. 2011. "EPZ History in Bangladesh and its Administration and Legislation for Economic Enclave." *Business and Management Review* 1 (7): 86–102.

Iwasaki, Ikuo. 2006. "Singapore no Kaihatsu to Good Governance" [The Development of Singapore and Good Governance]. In *Ajia no Governance [Governance in Asia]* (in Japanese), ed. Yasutami Shimomura, 159–187. Tokyo: Yuhikaku.

Japan International Cooperation Agency (JICA). 1985. "Meghna and Meghna-Gumti Bridge Construction Project Report." Tokyo: JICA.

Japan International Cooperation Agency (JICA) and Overseas Economic Cooperation Fund (OECF). 2000. *IV JICA/OECF Joint Evaluation: Eastern Seaboard Development Program*. Tokyo: JICA.

Kharas, Homi, Koji Makino, and Woojin Jung, eds. 2011. *Catalyzing Development: A New Vision for Aid*. Washington, DC: Brookings Institute.

Kuchiki, Akifumi. 2007. *Ajia Sangyou Cluster Ron: Flow Chart Approach no Kano-sei [Industrial Clusters in Asia: Possibility of Flow Chart Approach]* (in Japanese). Tokyo: Shoseki Kobo Hayakawa.

Lin, Justin Yifu. 2012b. *The Quest for Prosperity: How Developing Economies Can Take Off*. Princeton: Princeton University Press.

Noman, Akbar, Kwesi Botchwey, Howard Stein, and Joseph E. Stiglitz, eds. 2012. *Good Growth and Governance in Africa: Rethinking Development Strategies*. Oxford: Oxford University Press.

Schein, Edgar H. 1999. *The Corporate Culture Survival Guide*. San Francisco: Jossey-Bass.

Shimamura, Masumi. 2007. *Building Central Economic Agencies*. National Graduate Institute for Policy Studies (GRIPS) Development Forum. http://www.grips.ac.jp/teacher/oono/hp/course/index.htm.

Techakanont, Kriengkrai. 2011. "Thailand Automotive Parts Industry." In *Goods Trade in East Asia: Economic Deepening Through FTAs/EPAs*, ed. Kagami Mitsuhiro, 192–229. Research Report No. 5, Institute of Developing Economies Bangkok Research Center (IDE-BRC).

Teoh, Zsin Woon, Santitarn Sathirathai, David Lam, Chung Han Lai, and Kriengsak Chareonwongsak. 2007. "Thailand Automotive Cluster." Final paper, Macroeconomics of Competitiveness. http://www.isc.hbs.edu/pdf/Student_Projects/Thailand_AutomotiveCluster_2007.pdf.

World Bank. 2009. *World Development Report 2009: Reshaping Economic Geography*. Washington, DC: World Bank.

CHAPTER 4

The Economic Implications of a Comprehensive Approach to Learning on Industrial Policy

THE CASE OF ETHIOPIA

Go Shimada

Notwithstanding the much-improved economic performance of Africa in the past decade or so, industrial development continues to languish. The percentage of the GDP emanating from the manufacturing sector has been declining since the 1980s. Recent economic growth is dominated by the mining sector. Foreign direct investment (FDI) goes toward natural resources and not the manufacturing sector. As the population grows, youth unemployment will become a serious issue for sustainable growth and political stability in the region. Therefore industrial development that contributes to increases in employment and income can be crucial.

There has been heated debate over industrial policy elsewhere and a renewal of interest recently; it remains one of the most controversial topics (Noman et al. 2012; Lin and Chang 2009; Hausmann, Rodrik, and Velasco 2005).[1] This debate can be said to go back to nineteenth-century economists Ricardo and List, and there is still little consensus. A number of issues from the Washington Consensus that work against industrial policy—such as rent seeking, political capture, policy mistakes, and the misguided pursuit of picking the winners—have been raised (Krueger 2011). On the other hand, advocates of industrial policy have emphasized that markets do not function perfectly to achieve general Pareto optimality under the assumption of perfect information and perfect competition, among other things (Greenwald and Stiglitz 2012; Stiglitz, Lin, and Patel 2013).

This chapter will focus on the "learning" (or "learning how to learn") aspect of industrial policy. Knowledge gaps (not just resource gaps) have long been identified as issues requiring attention for development, but they have been neglected (Stiglitz 1998; Greenwald and Stiglitz 2012;

Noman and Stiglitz 2012). Further, there is a dearth in empirical analysis on learning in Africa. Due to the recent growing interest in this field, the number of empirical studies has been growing gradually (Dinh et al. 2012).

Regarding learning, it is important to disaggregate "what to learn." Technology and skill are not the only areas of importance for Africa. Industrial development does not occur by simply adopting new technology. There are other types of knowledge necessary for industrial development, such as policy planning and managerial skills, as we will elaborate later. Almost all the past literature on Africa, however, has focused mainly on the technology/skill aspects. There is only limited literature surveying the policy and managerial aspects of learning in Africa, and still further empirical studies on other aspects of learning are required to see how effective learning is for economic growth (Sonobe, Suzuki, and Otsuka 2011). This chapter intends to shed light on a comprehensive approach to learning. For this purpose, this chapter will look at the ongoing project by Japan International Cooperation Agency (JICA) in Ethiopia. Readers wishing to get to the case study that is the original aspect of this chapter may go directly to the section titled "Policy and Management Capital Learning in Ethiopia."

LITERATURE REVIEW

INDUSTRIAL POLICY

In the 1990s, development policy was based on a mantra of liberalization, privatization, and price stability that regarded industrial policy as a source of inefficient market distortion. In 1993, the Overseas Economic Cooperation Fund (OECF, now JICA) published Occasional Paper No. 1 titled "Issues Related to the World Bank's Approach to Structural Adjustment: Proposals from a Major Partner" (OECF 1993a), arguing in favor of infant industry protection and of credit subsidies for selected industries believed to have export potential, which was in opposition to the Bank's approach. In the same year, the World Bank published "The East Asian Miracle," which gave very guarded and qualified support to industrial policy, and that too only for export promotion, not on import protection and credit market intervention. The OECF (1993b) disagreed with its view (Mosley, Harrigan, and Toye 1995). Although the World Bank published the report, industrial policy was by and large sidelined in the Bank.

In the wake of the rise of emerging economies such as China, India, Brazil, and South Korea, a growing number of people have started to regard industrial policy as an important policy tool for economic and private sector development (Cimoli, Dosi, and Stiglitz 2009; Rodrik 2007). This trend is partly due to the response of developed economies after the financial crisis; Rodrik (2010) called this movement the "return of industrial policy." At least if and how donors should promote industrial policy has become a hotly debated subject in recent years.

Justin Lin (2012), the former chief economist of the World Bank, proposed what he calls new structural economics (NSE). The concept of NSE is controversial because it differs from the traditional World Bank approach. In his classification, the NSE is the third wave of developmental thinking. The first wave in the emerging and developing economies (old structural economics) emphasized market failure and proposed import substitution for structural changes. The results were disappointing. The second wave of thinking highlighted government failures and emphasized a "getting the prices right" policy. The third wave, which Lin proposed, intends to bring structural change back to the core of the discussion. He proposes to industrialize according to the comparative advantages under the given endowment structure, which old structural economics neglected or even contradicted. Regarding the last point, Ha-Joon Chang is against overreliance on comparative advantage, and he argues that developing countries need to adopt more proactive industrial policy beyond that called for by pursuit of static comparative advantage, as exemplified by the experiences of Japan and South Korea (Lin and Chang 2009).

Krueger (2011) commented on Lin's proposal, saying that his view is industrial and urban biased (distortion) and that there are many questions regarding the role of the state. Some of these questions are, for instance, whether support should be given to all industries or to a specific industry, and what incentives (for example, firm-specific treatment, subsidies, or tariffs) should be included. She also emphasized the risks of attempts at picking winners and government failure more generally.

On the other hand, Stiglitz (2011) expressed some sympathy for the NSE proposal and stressed, as Solow (1957) did, that advances in technology have been the source of increases in per capita income over the last two centuries. In his view, disparity in knowledge matters for developing countries, so Stiglitz proposes aiming to create "a learning society" that absorbs, adopts, and adapts knowledge, and eventually moves on to producing new knowledge. With regard to "learning," he also stressed the importance of "learning to learn" (or the ability to learn) (Greenwald and Stiglitz 2012; Stiglitz 1987).

LEARNING

Imperfect information and the nature of knowledge, with characteristics of public goods associated with externalities (spillovers), lead to under-investment in learning. With market imperfections the losses incurred by firms during a "learning phase" can act as a barrier to entry, implying a tendency toward monopoly (Stiglitz 2010 and 2012). Unlike the aggregate growth model of a closed economy with competitiveness assumed by Arrow (1962) and Kaldor and Mirrlees (1962), Dasgupta and Stiglitz (1988) found that market equilibrium is not efficient in the light of learning costs of firms. There is a potential for the state to play a rewarding role as a catalyst for learning.

Greenwald and Stiglitz (2012) posit the particular importance of the industrial sector at early stages of development because its growth is likely to be more learning intensive, with spillovers to the rural/agricultural sector. Learning linkages among the natural resource extraction sector and other sectors were typically much weaker than those among the manufacturing sector and the rest of the economy (Greenwald and Stiglitz 2012).

MANAGERIAL CAPITAL

When Lall (1987) surveyed Indian firms, he stressed the importance of technological capability (TC). He disaggregates the TC into five elements: (1) project execution; (2) product engineering; (3) process engineering; (4) industrial engineering and planning; and (5) technological transfer. This classification is useful to deepen our understanding of elements of technology/skill and what learning entails.

There is, however, bias in his definition of the technical aspects of the firm. In addition to these technological capabilities, private firms need to have other abilities: "management capabilities" that include marketing, finance, and external relations, among others (Wad 1991).

Although management capability is important, it has been neglected in development and growth literature. For Solow (1957), management capability is subsumed in the residual of a production function (the error term). In the early days, Lucas (1978) and Rosen (1982) proposed "talent for management" as an important factor of production. Few empirical studies, however, have been conducted on managerial capital. Bruhn, Karlan, and Schoar (2010) emphasized that a crucial dimension of capital missing in developing countries is "managerial capital." In their view, managerial capital can affect the production function through two channels. One is improving the marginal productivity of inputs (for example, labor and physical capital). The other is improving resource constraints (for example, access to capital or labor with better resource forecast). Recently, the greater attention to this issue is reflected in the increase in the number of empirical studies (Klinger and Schündeln 2007; Karlan and Valdivia 2011; Field, Jayachandran, and Pande 2010; and Bruhn, Karlan, and Schoar 2010).

Through an empirical study in Africa, Sonobe, Suzuki, and Otsuka (2011) also confirmed the importance of management capital, in that relevant technical assistance enables informal firms to expand operations and generate employment. As we will see in detail in the case of Ethiopia, a productivity and quality improvement method called *kaizen* provides inexpensive basic management skills and can improve management practices. Their study focuses mainly on business administration, basic business skill, and manufacturing floor management. They found that in Tanzania the training effects on record keeping and kaizen practices are highly significant. According to their study, a majority of entrepreneurs do not keep records of costs and revenues, and it hampers their objective judgment on their operation.

POLICY LEARNING

In addition to the managerial capital, there is another important element of learning: policy learning. When Lall (1987) surveyed Indian firms, he rightly pointed out problems of the methods by which individual firms acquired technological capability (TC). These firms considered policy environment an external factor and they got TC without any support from the government. As we have already seen, because of market imperfection, knowledge does not spill over automatically. It is important for governments in developing countries to promote knowledge spillover and to encourage learning.

There have been successful policies and failures in the past. Looking at the development cases of Asia, their recipes and timing vary from country to country. In other words, country context mattered greatly when planning industrial policy. Because country context matters, a government should not just blindly copy the successful policy of another country; they need to learn how to analyze country context and adapt to it. In other words, they need to "learn how to learn" selectively from the cases of various countries. For instance, the role of the public sector in developing small and medium enterprises (SMEs) changes according to the country context and to the stages of industrial development.

Regarding learning on a policy level, there are several attempts from donor countries. One example is the knowledge sharing program (KSP) of the Korean Development Institute (KDI). The case we will see in this chapter is JICA's program in Ethiopia. One feature distinguishing this program is a comprehensive approach, which we will discuss in the next section.

POLICY AND MANAGEMENT CAPITAL LEARNING IN ETHIOPIA

A Comprehensive Approach to Learning

As we have seen so far, two levels of learning are necessary: (1) policy level (policy learning) and (2) private firm level (technology/skill and management capital learning). The two of them are inseparable. Business environment affects private firms' strategy in the market. There are various elements in the business environment that private firms need to take into consideration. Among them the following elements are especially important: outlook on inflation and exchange rate, changes in the system of taxation, and industrial policy.

Here industrial policy is broadly defined to include an assortment of policy measures, including infrastructure development, education and vocational training, financial sector (especially loans to SMEs), FDI promotion, trade, intellectual property rights, and industrial standards. These types of policies will affect a private firm's long-term strategy, especially for its investments. If the future is uncertain, it will result in low investment by the private sector. The term "investment" includes investment in productivity and quality improvement, as well as physical investment.

A government policy will affect private firms' decisions in many ways. For instance, productivity and quality improvement will be discouraged under high inflation and exchange rate volatility. This is

CONTINUED

because it is difficult for private firms to recognize and measure the results of the improvements under uncertain situations. On the other hand, government support such as infrastructure development, education, vocational training, and SME development policy will encourage private firms to improve productivity. Thus policy and private firms' operations are closely connected to each other.

Each level can be disaggregated (figure 4.1). Regarding the policy level, these are (1–1) policy planning and (1–2) policy implementation. The capacity of policy planning is important, as the previous section discussed. The capacity for policy implementation is different from that of policy planning. How effectively a government can implement a policy largely depends on its organizational capacity. Industrial development is a multi-sector (or a multi-ministerial) task. Several sectors can be involved in exporting even a single agro-industrial product abroad (for example, the agriculture, manufacturing, and transport sectors). In addition, factors such as quarantine, tax and customs procedures, and exchange rate also affect export performance. In other words, promoting exports can require total governmental effort with intergovernmental coordination, as well as public-private consultation. Coordination with all stakeholders requires very high capacity and is a difficult task.

In some countries, excellent policy plans are drafted without taking feasibility and the capacity of government organizations into account. These two factors are correlated, but the issues that need to be learned

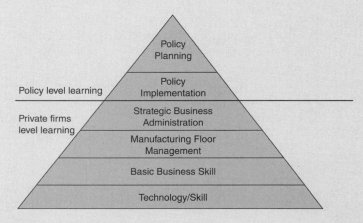

Figure 4.1   Structure of learning

are different. As Cimoli, Dosi, and Stiglitz (2009) discussed, "organization building" is one of the most difficult tasks, and policies and institution building have shaped the accumulation of both technological and organizational capabilities. These capabilities decide the national capabilities to catch up with crucial knowledge.

Turning now to the private firm level, there are four sublevels of entrepreneurial skills: (2–1) strategic business administration (including labor management and computerization); (2–2) manufacturing floor management (including inventory control); (2–3) basic business skill; and (2–4) technology/skill. The first three items are elements of managerial capacity. The capacity of strategic business administration (2–1) is required for employers and the business administration department. Manufacturing floor management (2–2) is required for factory workers as well as factory managers. Basic business skill (2–3) in many micro and small enterprises in Africa was found lacking by Sonobe, Suzuki, and Otsuka (2011). This includes skills such as record keeping, which is essential for effective and efficient day-to-day operation of a company. This chapter will look at the case of Ethiopia based on these considerations.

Background of the Program in Ethiopia

This chapter examines a program in Ethiopia supported by JICA in collaboration with National Graduate Institute for Policy Studies of Japan (GRIPS) that used a comprehensive approach to learning. This program was initiated in response to the request from late prime minister Meles and has two components: support to formulate industrial policy in the new five-year development plan (industrial policy dialogue) and support to develop private firms (a project for quality and productivity improvement). These two components are implemented side by side, taking the linkage between the policy and operation of private firms into consideration. This program started in 2009 and completed its first phase in 2011. The program was started with strong leadership by high-ranking government officials (top-down) and was implemented by equally strong ownership by government technocrats and private firms (bottom-up).

The late prime minister was critical of the Solow model because the model treats technological change as something external to the economic process: an exogenous factor (Zenawi 2012). In his view, technology is a public good, and there are market failures in providing it. Therefore he believed that developing countries should not leave technological development (innovation) to the market, and the

CONTINUED

key to this is learning from abroad. So he argued that technological capability accumulation is the central challenge for developing countries to achieve continued growth. It will enable developing countries to move up the technological ladder. He compared two types of national innovation systems and discussed the need for the system to reflect the structure of the economy. Those systems are the mission-oriented systems of the United States, United Kingdom, and France, and the diffusion-oriented systems of Germany, Sweden, and Switzerland. A mission-oriented system is a system to explore new technology by, for example first-rank universities. A diffusion-oriented system aims to exploit existing technologies through social mechanisms, such as standardization of products or an apprentice system of training craftsmen. For developing countries, he argued, it would be easier to adopt and adapt existing technology in developed countries rather than to pursue innovation.

With this view, he tried to learn from cases in foreign countries such as South Korea and Taiwan. He even sent government officials to these countries. In addition, he requested specific assistance in adopting and adapting existing technology from development partners such as Germany, Italy, and the United Nations Industrial Development Organization (UNIDO) (Ohno 2013). In response, Germany implemented the Engineering Capacity Building Program (ECBP). ECBP includes a technical and vocational education and training (TVET) system and engineering and private sector development, among other things. From Japan, he requested the specific support mentioned earlier.

Outline of the Program

Industrial Policy Dialogue: Mutual Learning

The industrial policy dialogue was started in June 2009 and ended the first phase in May 2011. The dialogue was started together with the pilot project for productivity and quality improvement (kaizen), which we will see in the next section. The aim of the dialogue was to exchange views on: (1) the new five-year development plan;[2] (2) issues needed to be tackled for policy planning and implementation (for example, intergovernmental coordination); and (3) progress and issues on the pilot project. These three elements complement each other and cover policy strategy to private sector operation on the ground.[3]

The dialogue was held quarterly eight times at three levels: (1) prime minister, (2) ministers and state ministers, and (3) heads of directorates and institutes. These three levels have different organizational responsibilities and authorities on policy planning and policy implementation. Therefore, naturally, even if the topic is the same, the contents of the discussion and the issues to be challenged are different. From the Japanese side, the core members of the JICA-GRIPS team were Professor Kenichi and Izumi Ohno.

The Pilot Project for Productivity and Quality Improvement (Kaizen)

In parallel with the policy dialogue, a pilot project for productivity and quality improvement started in October 2009 and ended in May 2011 (phase one). Phase two of the project has been underway since November 2011. The productivity and quality improvement is called *kaizen*. It is a method to continuously improve productivity and quality in a participatory process and a bottom-up approach. Under the structure of learning we discussed earlier, kaizen mainly focuses on (2–1) strategic business administration and (2–2) manufacturing floor management. It does not require additional cost from the employer or restructuring such as cutting employment, unlike business process reengineering (BPR).

Japan itself introduced productivity and quality improvement in 1955 at the start of Japan's era of rapid economic growth, learning from American business management tools.[4] There were dual aims. One was to enhance competitiveness to expand the market, utilizing resources effectively and scientifically, at the same time reducing production costs. The other was to boost employment and to enhance real wages and the standard of living.

Impacts and Their Causes

What kind of impact did the program have? Before examining overall impacts, we will start by looking at the impacts of the pilot project. There is a certain degree of limitation in this analysis due to lack of data (such as benchmarking data) because the program was not designed to

CONTINUED

be analyzed by econometric analysis like the randomized control trial (RCT). Therefore the analysis here is only a qualitative analysis. It is a future task after phase two to run a more rigorous impact analysis.

Regarding the pilot project, a team of JICA and Ethiopian experts together visited twenty-eight pilot private manufacturing firms ten times each and gave them questions, rather than answers, on what the companies needed to think about to improve their operations. The twenty-eight pilot private firms were from the (1) agro-processing, (2) chemical, (3) metal, (4) leather, and (5) textile industries. After the ten consultations over six months, as table 4.1 shows, the highest benefit

Table 4.1 Results observed from the pilot project companies (examples)

Quantitative Results (Monetary Impacts)

(1) Average quantitative benefit of ETB 500,000 (USD 30,030) per pilot company. Given that the average number of employees is 402 per company, the average benefit per head is ETB 1,240 (USD 74.50), which is comparable to the prevailing gross monthly wage (USD 75).

(2) Company A reduced costs by (a) ETB 10,000 (USD 600) per month and (b) ETB 78,000 (USD 4,685) per year.

(3) Company B generated additional income of ETB 1.2 million (USD 78,072) per year.

(4) Company C decreased downtime to ETB 204,000 (USD 12,252) per day.

(5) Company D rectified raw material defect used for manufacturing to ETB 2.4 million (USD 144,144).

(6) Company E identified repaired and reused usable machines and equipment worth USD 3.25 million.

Quantitative Results (Non-Monetary Impacts)

(1) Company F increased labor productivity by reducing time loss for searching for tools by on average 50 percent.

(2) Company G reduced floor space by around 50 percent.

(3) Company H improved the defect ratio in the range of 50 to 70 percent.

(4) Company I improved lead time in the range of 16 to 90 percent.

Qualitative Results

(1) Clean working environments created.

(2) Teamwork and motivation of workers developed.

(3) Health and occupational safety of workers improved.

(4) Increased employee participation.

(5) Knowledge obtained on how to meet quick delivery and to reduce costs.

Source: Based on Shimada, Homma, and Murakami (2013) and JICA (2011b).
Note: 1 ETB = USD 16.65

to a company was 3.25 million Ethiopian Birr (ETB), equivalent to around USD 195,195. The twenty-eight firms had obtained an average benefit of ETB 500,000 (equivalent to around USD 30,030). Given that the average number of employees was 402 per company, the pilot project generated a benefit of ETB 1,240 (USD 74.50) per head, which almost equaled the prevailing gross monthly wage (USD 75).

These improvements, having such significant impacts, were made without additional investment cost. The firms simply improved their method of operations through kaizen by conducting 5S activities (Sort, Straighten, Shine, Standardize, Sustain) and reducing seven types of waste (overproduction, inventory, repairs/rejection, motion, processing, waiting, and transport).

Table 4.2 shows qualitatively measured results by the Ethiopia-JICA team. Companies classified as grade 5 have a high possibility of being a model company, with the other grades as follows: grade 4 (good possibility); grade 3 (some possibility); grade 2 (low possibility); and grade 1 (no possibility). In short, this table shows that ten out of twenty-eight companies (more than one-third) are graded 5 and 4 as candidates for being excellent companies in the near future. These results indicate that even if the input is small, learning about (2–1) strategic business administration and (2–2) manufacturing floor management have certain positive impacts. In other words, according to the twenty-eight pilot companies experiment, there are huge possibilities for Ethiopian (or African) enterprises to improve productivity and quality greatly with small changes in (2–1) strategic business administration and (2–2) manufacturing floor management.

Table 4.2 Qualitatively measured results from the pilot companies

Subsector	Grade					Total No. of Companies
	5	4	3	2	1	
Metal	1	2	2	2	1	8
Textile	1	1	1	1	1	5
Agro-Processing	1	1	1	2	1	6
Chemical	3		2	1	3	9
Leather			2			2
Total Occurrences	6	4	8	6	6	30

Source: JICA (2011a).

CONTINUED

Factors of Different Pace of Progress: Clear Policy Message from the Government and Managers' Strong Commitment and Ownership

Is learning about (2–1) strategic business administration and (2–2) manufacturing floor management enough to improve private sector operation without any learning on the policy level? What are the decisive factors for success and failures among pilot companies? The pace of progress is different among companies participating in the kaizen project.

One of the important factors of success was the managers' strong commitment and ownership to introduce the new method. Managers of successful companies understood that the key to improving productivity and quality was a bottom-up approach at the manufacturing floor. They tried to build good management-employee relationships, appreciating communication with employees and employee training. This commitment of managers is difficult to measure. Before the project, kaizen was new to Ethiopia, and managers did not have knowledge about the method. Considering the situation, it was extraordinary that Ethiopian entrepreneurs showed strong commitment to the new method. What was the reason behind it?

It was the clear policy message from the government that the government will support the introduction of the new method. The late prime minister and other high-ranking government officials had mentioned the initiative to introduce kaizen on TV and in public speeches. This clear message reduced the entry barrier for private companies to learn the method and improve productivity and quality. Unlike under the condition of asymmetry of information, managers took the learning benefit into account, so the learning phase was not considered a loss for them. Because of this clear policy message, an introduction seminar in Addis Ababa on kaizen, held before the project started, attracted huge attention. Even though kaizen was very new to Ethiopian entrepreneurs, more than 320 entrepreneurs from 170 private companies attended the seminar. The policy message generated commitment and ownership of Ethiopian entrepreneurs.

Learning Policy Planning: Focus on Quality and Productivity

In spite of the clear message from high-ranking officials, the same policy message was not clear in the policy documents such as the five-year development policy and sectorial development policy. In the process of the preparation of the GTP, the policy message was discussed in the policy dialogue. The issue was how to synchronize the GTP, a guiding framework of national development plans, and activities on the ground. For that purpose, micro-small enterprises (MSE) policy was discussed in detail.

The Ethiopian government examined Asian cases by themselves, with JICA-GRIPS providing some comparative case studies from East Asia such as Japan's SME development policy and Singapore's nationwide movement of productivity and quality improvement. This self-learning increased policy space, and as a result, in the framework of the GTP, a new MSE development strategy was adopted, referring the introduction of kaizen to industrial development. This policy shows the policy direction and catalyzes learning in the private sector.

Learning Policy Implementation: Coordination and Capacity Development

Another important point pertains to policy implementation by government bureaucrats and technocrats. One of the issues raised and discussed in the policy dialogue was a policy coordination mechanism across ministries and agencies. For industrial development, as we saw, different ministries and agencies are involved. For any government, it is a challenge to build consensus on key policy directions and the way they are implemented among stakeholders inside and outside government. East Asian countries have certain mechanisms to coordinate this. JICA-GRIPS provided the Ethiopian government with various case studies of such mechanisms.

There are several ministries and agencies in Ethiopia in charge of MSE development, and the government setup is very complex. These include the Ministry of Industry (MoI), Ministry of Urban Development and Construction (MoUDC), Ministry of Education (MoE), TVET, and the EKI (Ethiopian Kaizen Institution). Learning the coordination mechanisms of East Asia, the Ethiopian government also developed several coordination mechanisms. For example, a national council was established to coordinate MSE development, co-chaired by MoUDC and MoI. This coordination mechanism reduces unnecessary fragmentation.

Further, regarding learning kaizen at the private firm level, the government agency plays an important role in catalyzing the learning. The important thing is that the impacts of the project were brought from the Ethiopian government experts who learned the method based mainly on on-the-job training (spillover effects based on the knowledge acquired by doing).

The experts belonged to the Kaizen Unit in the then Ministry of Trade and Industry (now the Ministry of Industry). The late prime minister established this new unit just before the start of the pilot project, as a part of his initiative. The members of the Kaizen Unit consisted of nine young Ethiopian professionals without any knowledge about the method. There was very clear policy guidance for them from the high-ranking government officials and the new MSE development policy. They also received higher demand from private firms other than the pilot companies (bottom-up needs), as they knew that the government supported the introduction of kaizen. These demands from the top and from the ground were the driving forces behind their self-learning.

Policy Learning and Expanding Policy Scope

The business environment for pilot companies was an important factor. The successful companies had no disruptive management condition. Companies with disruptive management conditions failed to progress. The condition was mainly being unable to procure essential materials for their operations due to the shortage of foreign currency. Ethiopia had difficulty with importing some of these essential materials.

The issue of shortage of foreign currency had been discussed at the policy dialogue, and the pros and cons of import substitution policy were discussed in the process to prepare the GTP. With careful examination, the government of Ethiopia expanded the scope of the policy from an export promotion policy focusing on a few selected sectors (such as leather and leather products, textile and garment, and agro-products) to an import substitution policy. The import substitution policy focuses on industries such as chemical, metal, and engineering. Dani Rodrik of Harvard University also advised the Ethiopian government regarding the expansion of policy scope in 2008 (Rodrik 2008; Ohno 2013).

Although this management skill was new to the Ethiopian experts before the project, after the project six out of nine experts were assessed as being level 3 experts (competent enough to be a consultant and provide a consultancy service), and three experts were assessed as assistant consultants (level 2). Please see table 4.3 for details of this level of expert.

As we have seen with the Ethiopian case, learning managerial knowledge improved the performance of private firms. The quality and productivity project focuses on strategic business administration and manufacturing floor management. Policy learning also contributed to the improvement, expanding the ability of the government to help private sector development. Selective policy learning from the successes and failures of East Asian countries enables the Ethiopian government to expand its policy options and learn lessons about implementation. The clear policy direction catalyzed learning on the ground. The coordination mechanism among ministries and government agencies made the approach to MSE development comprehensive rather than fragmented. The concerned government agency acquired practical knowledge on kaizen through learning by doing, and disseminated its knowledge to the private sectors to improve their productivity and quality.

Table 4.3 Assessment of capacity development of Ethiopian experts on kaizen

Level	Competence	Level of Knowledge and Skill	Assignment
5	Competent to provide consultancy services on kaizen	- Eight years of experience and more - Experience of consultancy services for at least thirty companies by him/herself in six years of service	Lead Consultant
4	Competent to provide consultancy services on kaizen	- Six years of experience - Experience of consultancy services for at least fifteen companies by him/herself in four years of service	Senior Consultant
3	Competent to provide consultancy services on kaizen	- Four years of experience - Acquired relevant knowledge and skills for kaizen in addition to TQM/QCC/5S/QC 7 tools - Acquired other knowledge and skill on industrial business engineering (financial management, human resource management, etc.) - Competent to prepare case materials for training exercise - Experience of consultancy services for at least five companies by him/herself in two years of service	Consultant
2	Competent to guide kaizen activities	- 2 years of experience - Acquired advanced and applied knowledge and skills on TQM/QCC/5S/QC 7 tools - Competent to present at least five case studies of kaizen for training purpose	Assistant Consultant
1	Competent to conduct kaizen activities for yourself	- Acquired person with no experience - Acquired basic knowledge and skill on TQM/QCC/5S/QC 7 tools - Competent to make at least two case analyses	Junior Consultant
0	No experience		

Source: JICA (2011a).
Note: TQM = Total Quality Management; QCC = Quality Control Circle; 5S = Sort, Set in Order, Shine, Standardize, and Sustain; QC = Quality Control.

CONCLUSIONS

This chapter examined the learning aspect of industrial policy, disaggregating the elements of learning, which mainly consists of policy-level and private company-level learning. Earlier literature focused mainly on introducing skills and technology into private companies. Recently, there has been a growing interest in managerial capability learning. This chapter explored the possibilities of a comprehensive approach because policy learning and managerial capability learning are inseparable, using a case in Ethiopia to study the impacts.

The results of the Ethiopian case imply that learning on various levels will strengthen Africa's private sector for industrial development, allowing it to become competitive. This comprehensive approach to learning is still new to the development partners. The approach will enable African countries to sustain their economic growth, diversifying their economies and generating jobs.

The ongoing empirical work on phase two of the Ethiopian case should provide the basis for a more thorough analysis.

NOTES

1. Following past literature such as Rodrik (2007) and Noman and Stiglitz (2012), this chapter also considers that industrial policy covers not only the manufacturing sector but also broad sectors such as the agricultural and service sectors.

2. The five-year plan (2005–2009) is the Plan for Accelerated and Sustained Development to End Poverty (PASDEP). The debate was also held for the new five-year plan, namely the Growth and Transformation Plan (GTP 2010–2015).

3. This dialogue was an approach to "mutual learning" between the Ethiopian side and the Japanese side. As discussed, context matters greatly for policy planning; the Japan side has rich knowledge on East Asian cases, but little knowledge on the Ethiopian economy. The Ethiopian side understands its own economy, but has little knowledge regarding East Asian cases. If policy prescription were one-size-fits-all, things would be much simpler. The dialogue approach provided mutual learning opportunities to find solutions.

4. The three guiding principles of productivity improvement were set out in 1955 in Japan, which were: (1) expansion of employment; (2) cooperation between labor and management; and (3) fair distribution of the fruits of productivity.

REFERENCES

Arrow, K. J. 1962. "The Economic Implications of Learning by Doing." *Review of Economic Studies* 29: 155–173.

Bruhn, M., D. Karlan, and A. Schoar. 2010. "What Capital Is Missing in Developing Countries?" *American Economic Review* (May): 629–633.

Cimoli, M. G. Dosi, and J. Stiglitz. eds. 2009. *Industrial Policy and Development: The Political Economy of Capabilities Accumulation.* New York: Oxford University Press.

Dasgupta, P., and J. Stiglitz. 1988. "Learning-by-Doing, Market Structure and Industrial and Trade Policies." *Oxford Economic Papers* New Series 40 (2): 246–268.

Dinh, H. T., V. Palmade, V. Chandra, and F. Cossar. 2012. *Light Manufacturing in Africa.* Washington, DC: World Bank.

Field, E., S. Jayachandran, and R. Pande. 2010. *Do Traditional Institutions Constrain Female Entrepreneurship? A Field Experiment on Business Training in India.* IFMR Working Paper Series No. 36, January. Chennai: Institute for Financial Management and Research.

Greenwald, B., and J. Stiglitz. 2006. "Helping Infant Economies Grow: Foundations of Trade Policies for Developing Countries." *American Economic Review* 96 (2): 141–146.

———. 2012. "Learning and Industrial Policy: Implications for Africa." New Thinking on Industrial Policy: Implications for Africa. Roundtable conference presented by the International Economic Association, cosponsored by the World Bank, United Nations Industrial Development Organization (UNIDO), and the South African Economic Development Department, Pretoria, South Africa.

Hausmann, R., D. Rodrik, and A. Velasco. 2005. *Growth Diagnosis.* Cambridge, Mass.: Kennedy School of Government, Harvard University.

Japan International Cooperation Agency (JICA). 2011a. *The Study on Quality and Productivity Improvement (Kaizen) in the Federal Democratic Republic of Ethiopia.* Tokyo: JICA.

———. 2011b. *Study on Industrial Policy Dialogue in the Federal Democratic Republic of Ethiopia.* Tokyo: JICA.

Kaldor, N., and J. Mirrlees. 1962. "A New Model of Economic Growth." *Review of Economic Studies* 29: 174–192.

Karlan, D., and M. Valdivia. 2011. "Teaching Entrepreneurship: Impact of Business Training on Microfinance Clients and Institutions." *Review of Economics and Statistics* 93 (2): 510–527.

Klinger, B., and M. Schündeln. 2007. "Can Entrepreneurial Activity Be Taught?: Quasi-Experimental Evidence from Central America." *World Development* 39 (9): 1592–1610.

Krueger, A. 2011. "Comments on 'New Structural Economics' by Justin Yifu Lin." *World Bank Research Observer* 26 (2): 222–226.

Lall, S. 1987. *Learning to Industrialize: The Acquisition of Technological Capability by India.* London: Macmillan.

Lin, J. 2012. *New Structural Economics: A Framework for Rethinking Development and Policy.* Washington, DC: World Bank.

Lin, J., and H-J Chang. 2009. "Should Industrial Policy in Developing Countries Conform to Comparative Advantage or Defy It? A Debate Between Justin Lin and Ha-Joon Chang." *Development Policy Review* 27 (5): 483–502.

Lucas, R. E., Jr. 1978. "On the Size Distribution of Business Firms." *Bell Journal of Economics* 9 (2): 508–523.

Mosley, P., J. Harrigan, and J. Toye. 1995. *Aid and Power: The World Bank and Policy-Based Lending.* Vol. 1, *Analysis and Policy Proposals.* New York: Routledge.

Noman, A., K. Botchwey, H. Stein, and J. Stiglitz. eds. 2012. *Good Growth and Governance in Africa: Rethinking Development Strategies.* New York: Oxford University Press.

Noman, A., and J. E. Stiglitz. 2012. "Strategies for African Development." In *Good Growth and Governance in Africa: Rethinking Development Strategies,* ed. Akbar Noman, Kwesi Botchwey, Howard Stein, and Joseph Stiglitz. 3–47. New York: Oxford University Press.

Ohno, K. 2013. *Learning to Industrialize: From Given Growth to Policy-Aided Value Creation.* Abingdon: Routledge.

Overseas Economic Cooperation Fund (OECF; now JICA). 1993a. "Issues Related to the World Bank's Approach to Structural Adjustment: Proposals from a Major Partner (Occasional Paper No. 1)." Tokyo: OECF.

——. 1993b. "The Intellectual Awakening of a Sleeping Partner: An OECF View of Structural Adjustment (OECF Research Quarterly No. 1)." Tokyo: OECF.

Rodrik, D. 2007. *Normalizing Industrial Policy.* Cambridge, Mass.: Harvard University.

——. 2008. "Notes on the Ethiopian Economic Situation." Unpublished manuscript, Cambridge, Mass.: Kennedy School of Government, Harvard University.

——. 2010. "The Return of Industrial Policy." *Project Syndicate,* April 12. www.project-syndicate.org/commentary/the-return-of-industrial-policy.

Rosen, S. 1982. "Authority, Control and the Distribution of Earnings." *Bell Journal of Economics* 13 (2): 311–323.

Shimada, G., T. Homma, and H. Murakami. 2013. "Industrial Development of Africa." In *Inclusive and Dynamic Development of Africa,* ed. JICA, 173–194. Tokyo: JICA Research Institute.

Solow, R. M. 1957. "Technical Change and the Aggregate Production Function." *Review of Economics and Statistics* 39 (3): 273–294.

Sonobe, T., A. Suzuki, and K. Otsuka. 2011. "*Kaizen* for Managerial Skills Improvement in Small and Medium Enterprises: An Impact Evaluation Study [Background Paper]." In Dinh et al. (2012).

Stiglitz, J. 1987. "Learning to Learn, Localized Learning, and Technological Progress." In *Economic Policy and Technological Performance,* ed. P. Dasgupta and P. Stoneman, 125–153. Cambridge: Cambridge University Press.

——. 1998. "Knowledge for Development: Economic Science, Economic Policy, and Economic Advice." In *Annual World Bank Conference on Development Economics* 20, ed. B. Pleskovic and J. Stiglitz, 9–58. Washington, DC: World Bank.

——. 2010. *Learning, Growth, and Development: A Lecture in Honor of Sir Partha Dasgupta.* Presented at the World Bank's Annual Bank Conference of Development Economics, Stockholm.

——. 2011. "Rethinking Development Economics." *World Bank Research Observer* 26 (2): 230–236.

——. 2012. "Creating a Learning Society." Lecture given at the London School of Economics and Political Science, London, July 4.

Stiglitz, J., J. Y. Lin, and E. Patel. 2013. *The Industrial Policy Revolution II—Africa in the Twenty-first Century.* New York: Palgrave Macmillan.

Wad, A. 1991. "Review of *Learning to Industrialize* by Sanjaya Lall." *Research Policy* 20 (1): 77–85.

Zenawi, M. 2012. "States and Markets: Neoliberal Limitations and the Case for Developmental State." In *Good Growth and Governance in Africa: Rethinking Development Strategies*, ed. Akbar Noman, Kwesi Botchwey, Howard Stein, and Joseph Stiglitz, 140–174. New York: Oxford University Press.

CHAPTER 5

Review of Industrial Policies in Ethiopia

A PERSPECTIVE FROM THE LEATHER
AND CUT FLOWER INDUSTRIES

Girum Abebe and Florian Schaefer

As early as the 1950s the Nobel Laureate economist Arthur Lewis (1955, quoted in Lin and Chang 2009) exclaimed, "No country has made economic progress without positive stimulus from intelligent government." The appropriate role for government in the economy has been a source of heated debate among academics and policymakers ever since. While the private sector is widely viewed as a driver of growth, there appears to have been little consensus on the role and ability of government to push the private sector toward promoting growth and development, let alone on whether such interventions are necessary for industrial takeoff. Proponents of free market policies claim government interventions in the economy distort relative prices and therefore diminish the allocative efficiency of the economy overall. Consequently, they argue for a minimalist state that confines itself to setting the legal boundaries necessary for market interaction.

Yet historical evidence suggests that, with the right policies, governments in poor countries can systematically improve the material welfare of their societies through technological catch up and industrial upgrading. In fact, given the ubiquity of market failures in these economies, ranging from information externalities to high levels of transaction costs and coordination problems, many argue that government intervention in the allocation of productive resources is unavoidable (for example, Lin and Chang 2009). Without decisive government intervention, it is likely that such market failures would hinder industries from being established in the first place, or else prevent them from taking off even when established.

A close reading of the well-known East Asian experience demonstrates the exceptional roles the states played in bringing about the transformation of these economies (Wade 1990). The Ethiopian government has been very keen to discover how such industrial upgrading and structural transformation was possible in the span of only a few years. One insight that is gleaned from the East Asian experience is the importance of industrial policies to stimulate the formation and growth of profitable industries that, in the absence of appropriate intervention, might not have happened.

Since the inception of the first industry strategy paper in 2002, the Ethiopian government has been actively promoting strategic sectors under the theme of an agricultural-led industrialization development policy (better known as Agricultural Development-Led Industrialization, or ADLI). The overarching focus of the strategy paper is to promote export-oriented and labor-intensive industries in line with the country's perceived comparative advantage. Textiles and garments, food processing, floriculture, and leather products all rely on relatively simple technology and require large amounts of labor, including low-skilled labor, making them well-suited to the labor abundant/capital scarce nature of the Ethiopian economy. The two recent five-year national plans, Plan for Accelerated and Sustained Development to End Poverty (PASDEP) and Growth and Transformation Plan (GTP), both included ambitious goals for cut flower and leather sectors as well as other sectors, and policies have been put in place to attract and nurture investments in these areas. Industrial policy was given focus in Ethiopia with the launching of the industry strategy paper in 2002. The strategy paper outlined policy measures in support of labor-intensive industries with particular emphasis on attracting investment toward the manufacturing sector and enhancing the competiveness of the export sector.

Within a few years of launching explicit industrial policymaking, striking success was recorded in the floriculture and leather goods industries in Ethiopia. For example, while leather goods exports were a paltry USD 59 million in 1997, they increased significantly to USD 120 million in 2012 and are poised for a dramatic takeoff with a large investment by a major international shoe producer. A remarkable growth pattern is also observed in the floriculture industry, in which exports were a little more than USD 150,000 in 1997, a figure that grew to more than USD 210 million in 2012. This chapter seeks to highlight Ethiopia's experience in experimenting with industrial policies, and more specifically to trace and evaluate the role industrial policy played in the growth of these two industries. We trace the evolution of industrial policies in both sectors and give a detailed account of the institutions created to deliver these policies. We place particular emphasis on the various setbacks and problems that both government institutions and private firms had to overcome, and we extract lessons for future policymaking.

The experiments with industrial policy in both the leather and floriculture sectors are especially useful for drawing practical lessons because Ethiopia enjoyed a clear and a priori comparative advantage only in one of them. The leather sector has vast potential resources for the commercialization of the leather products to draw on from Ethiopia's huge livestock sector. The large gap between the livestock resource base of the country and leather goods production is evidence of the potential for future growth, and the natural quality of Ethiopian leather is sought after in international markets for the production of high-quality footwear, bags, cases, gloves, and other leather articles. Of course favorable climatic conditions, proximity to the market, and low labor costs have by now made the floriculture industry viable in Ethiopia, but this was far from obvious at the outset. Floriculture is a knowledge-driven industry, and Ethiopian firms started at an immense disadvantage compared to their direct competitors in Kenya. Consequently, the Ethiopian government adopted quite different approaches in designing industrial policies to promote these two industries.

In the leather and leather products industry, mutually reinforcing problems at several stages of the leather value chain have kept production volume and quality low (Altenburg 2010). The government has thus devised policies to improve the supply and quality of raw materials and has sought to stabilize their prices. Efforts have also been made to upgrade the production facilities and technology of leather processing units while attempting to improve the international marketability of leather products. In short, government interventions in the industry range from the point of skin and hides collection to the leather production and marketing stages. These were problems that the market, left to its own devices, could not overcome. The government proactively identified bottlenecks along the value chain and compelled private sector companies to engage in a continuous program of upgrading and quality improvement.

In the floriculture industry, on the other hand, the government policies have generally been in response to specific problems raised by private actors. The industry is relatively new to the country and requires tacit and firm-specific knowledge at input procurement, production, and marketing stages. While the entry of large specialized private firms demonstrated the potential viability of the sector in Ethiopia, it was the rapid response of the government to eliminate constraints such as access to credit, land, and air freight services at affordable rates that led to the remarkable flourishing of the sector. The takeoff period of the floriculture industry overlapped with the launch of sector-specific support by the government in the early and mid-2000s. Although industrial policy measures in the cut flower sector have been more reactive compared to policies in the leather industries, they are much more interventionist than industrial policies in other flower-producing countries in Africa, including Kenya and Uganda.

We find that industrial policies in both sectors have been successful in driving their growth. The differentiated challenges in each sector were met with flexible policy regimes, tailored to the unique challenges in each sector. However, policy must continuously evolve as sectors mature and face new problems and opportunities. Impressive results to date notwithstanding, important improvements still need to be made in terms of policy responsiveness and in ensuring growth is broad based across relevant value chains.

The rest of the chapter is structured as follows: the section titled "The Leather Sector" provides an overview of the leather sector and reviews policy implementation. The next section in turn looks at the cut flower sector. The section titled "Conclusion and Recommendations" concludes by drawing out the main lessons to be learned for policymaking in the future.

THE LEATHER SECTOR

Ethiopia is generously endowed with livestock resources. Its cattle population of more than 53 million, along with sheep and goat populations of 25.5 and 24.1 million, respectively, put the country first in Africa (CSA 2013). With an annual off-take rate of nearly 10 percent for cattle, 33 percent for sheep, and 38 percent for goats, the country has enormous potential for cheap supplies of skins and hides. Policymakers in Ethiopia have long recognized the potential of the sector, as indicated by the Growth and Transformation Plan (GTP)[1] and several other national plans that preceded it. In the GTP the leather and leather products industry is one of six priority industries expected to contribute to export diversification and foreign exchange earnings. Unlocking this potential requires sustained productivity improvements to make the industry internationally competitive and allow for greater value addition prior to export (FDRE 2010).

Crucially, for a country that is still largely agrarian in its employment structure, the leather and leather products industry has multiple linkages to the rural economy. It is also highly labor intensive in the raw material sourcing, transportation, processing, and marketing phases, which are distributed across rural and urban areas. The industry thus possesses enormous potential to create much-needed nonagricultural employment, and looks set to play an important role in poverty reduction. Yet this potential has remained underexploited. Given the far-reaching structural problems unique to the leather sector, ranging from ad hoc hide and skin collection systems to poor marketing infrastructure, it is not immediately clear whether the sector could take off without coordinated policy support.

OVERVIEW OF THE LEATHER INDUSTRY

The leather sector is composed of leather tanneries, which source their supply mostly from the local market, and footwear producers, who use both local and international markets for raw material supply. The most important source of raw material for leather tanneries is hides and skins procured from skin collectors and traders. Larger tanneries that are fitted with machines and equipment to produce leather products higher up the leather value chain buy semi-processed leather products from tanneries with more simple production technology. More often than not, the footwear sector relies on imports for accessories, such as soles and laces. Owing to the problems with both quality and consistency of leather supplies by tanneries, footwear producers have had to supplement local purchases with imported leather to maintain output levels and meet contractual obligations. The largest component of raw material by both value and volume is, however, processed leather that is obtained from local tanneries. Figure 5.1 describes products and participants at various stages of the leather value chain.

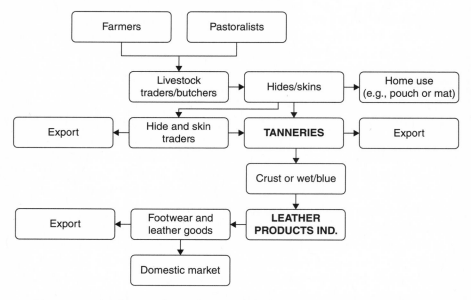

Figure 5.1   Products and participants in the leather value chain

Ethiopia has a long history of handcrafting and blacksmithing. As far back as the late 1920s and the 1930s, there were several leather processing and shoe manufacturing enterprises in the country. Despite the huge resource potential, commercialization was extremely slow and uneven, and consequently both production and export of leather products have remained disappointingly low for several decades.

In the 1950s and 1960s, for example, leather and leather goods production were small in volume and largely targeted the local market (Van der Loop 2003). In the 1980s, the socialist Derg regime banned the export of raw hides and skin in an attempt to encourage the domestic production of semi-processed leather articles. This ban radically altered the marketing structure of hides and skins by restricting exports to at least the wet-blue level. While the ban forced hide and skin traders to sell directly to tanneries for processing, it also encouraged illegal cross-border trade in both live animals and hides and skins. The ban had a limited impact in terms of improving the local leather tanning and leather goods manufacturing capacity. For example, there were only about six thousand jobs in large-scale tanning and manufacturing of leather products such as footwear, luggage, and handbags when the Derg regime was overthrown in 1991 (CSA 1994).

After the 1991 revolution, the new government began moving toward a market economy, although the state retained a prominent role in the economy. By 2008, there were twenty-one tanneries in Ethiopia with a combined tanning capacity of four thousand pieces of hide and thirty thousand pieces of skin per day. There are now twenty-six tanneries and more than fifteen large export-oriented footwear producers, as well as an untold number of micro- and small-scale shoemakers in Ethiopia. The tanneries have a combined tanning capacity of more than 170,000 pieces of skin and hide per day, and footwear producers can produce more than 20,000 pairs of shoes per day. However, industry representatives estimate the current annual capacity utilization of these tanneries at only about seventeen million pieces of skin and hide, that is, less than 50 percent of full capacity.

This lack of capacity utilization explains not just the inability of local leather goods producers to penetrate the export market, but also their failure to withstand competition from imports once the economy was liberalized after 1991. Not surprisingly, following the liberalization policy of the current regime in the late 1990s, the leather footwear sector was inundated with cheap imports. This drove many footwear producers out of business, "plunging the sector into slump" in the early 2000s (Sonobe, Akoten, and Otsuka 2009). Helped by improved local capability and effective industrial policies, the sector has since then registered impressive growth that has enabled it to reclaim some of the domestic market and even successfully venture into the export market. In the process, several enterprises improved the quality, design, and durability of their products by learning from their foreign-based trading partners. While credit must of course be given to the perseverance and resourcefulness of private entrepreneurs, the role government policies played in restructuring leather and leather goods production and marketing cannot be overestimated. The next subsection presents the features of industrial policies that were initiated to promote the sector.

INDUSTRIAL POLICY IN THE LEATHER
AND LEATHER PRODUCTS INDUSTRY

As part of a wide-ranging program of economic liberalization, the Ethiopian government has introduced several business-friendly policies since the early 1990s. The policy packages aim to mobilize domestic resources for investment and to attract investment funds from abroad, both from foreign nationals and from the Ethiopian diaspora. For example, investors are granted customs duty exemption, making imported capital goods and construction materials completely exempted from import duty. Customs duty drawbacks are also available for those who import raw materials and packaging supplies for processing exportable goods. To promote exports in the manufacturing sectors, a voucher scheme and bonded manufacturing warehouse facilities were introduced in 2001.[2] There is also a provision for income tax exemptions for between two and eight years, depending on the area of investment, export volume, and investment location. Investors are also allowed to forward losses incurred during the tax break period for half of the income exemption period.

All these are nondiscriminatory general incentives that are available to all investors irrespective of the investment sector and the nationality of the investor, although the exact levels of incentives on offer are tailored to the needs of different sectors. In addition to these general incentives, there have been several other policy measures and direct government interventions aimed specifically at promoting industrial upgrading and value addition in the leather and leather products industry.

These can be traced back to the Industrial Development Strategy (IDS) paper drafted in 2002. While specific policy menus were not articulated in the strategy paper, it broadly emphasized the need to work on problems associated with hide and skin production, collection, and processing.

The disappointing performance of the sector is mostly due to an inefficient supply chain, which is not capable of reliably delivering sufficient amounts of high-quality skins and hides at acceptable prices. There are several interrelated problems that plague the supply system. First, parasitic skin diseases in live animals affect the quality of skins and hides used in leather manufacturing. Second, commonly used traditional livestock husbandry practices, including flaying, branding, and curing, greatly deteriorate the quality of skin and hides. Lastly, rudimentary post-mortem management of skins and hides, including backyard slaughtering, poor and unorganized skin and hide collection, and substandard storage and transportation systems, results in both lower quality and an overall shortage of the raw materials required for leather processing. For example, 90 percent of sheep and goats and 70 percent of cattle slaughtering are carried out in the backyards of residential and farming units using traditional methods (UNIDO 2012). As a result, nearly 30 percent of hides and skins delivered to tanneries are rejected owing to poor quality (Bekele and Ayele 2008). These problems are further compounded by the unorganized supply of skin and hides. Downstream in the processing stage, challenges include rudimentary technology, insufficient capital, lack of skilled manpower, and marketing, among others.

Given that the production technology is standardized and markets are well established (if inefficient), the leather industry could expand by solving these problems at various stages of the leather value chain. This in turn requires the coordination of several activities to upgrade skin and hide collection systems upstream and processing downstream. As quality problems "travel" down the supply chain, and there are complex issues around price incentives for quality assurance and consistency, all stages of the supply chain must be tackled at the same time. In other words, this is a textbook coordination failure. No private entity, however, has the capacity (or size) to simultaneously overcome these problems that appear at multiple stages of the leather value chain, at least not in the context of Ethiopia (Altenburg 2010). Without the active involvement of the state, it is also not clear that there are adequate private incentives to improve the leather supply chain, which would involve properly reorganizing the livestock sector and the leather manufacturing sector, as well as several intermediary stages between the two. Recognizing the need for better coordination of the skins-to-leather value chain to exploit the potential provided by the leather resource base, the government of Ethiopia has initiated several interventions. It has been trying to remove barriers to expansion of the leather industry in particular.

To help overcome the problems associated with supply issues, the industry strategy paper stressed the importance of collective slaughtering and skin gathering. In the processing stage, the government was to be actively involved in establishing modern slaughterhouses, improving the capacity utilization of tanneries and the skills of workers involved at various stages of leather processing.

In fact, in 1994, eight years before the strategy paper was made public, the government helped organize six state-owned companies to form the Ethiopian Tanners' Association, which was later renamed Ethiopian Leather Industries Association (ELIA) in 2007. The establishment of this association was a first step to properly organize the market for raw hides and skins. Members of the association produce wet-blue, crust, and finished leather products from sheep and goat skins. Today ELIA brings together privately owned tanneries, footwear, and leather garment and goods producers with the objective of initiating and coordinating capacity-building activities through training programs, industry discussion forums, and pilot project developments. ELIA, in partnership with the Ministry of Industry (MoI), also coordinates the presence of Ethiopian firms at international trade fairs and organizes the All African Leather Fair (AALF), which has been hosted in Ethiopia every year since 2008. ELIA also provides marketing information to its customers and lobbies the government on behalf of its members. The association now encompasses the largest forty-seven leather goods producers as members.

Another milestone in the government's effort to promote the leather sector was setting up the Leather and Leather Products Technology Institute (LLPTI) in 1998. After a slow start owing to limited funds and a lack of skilled staff, it was languishing in near obscurity until the mandate of LLPTI was significantly expanded in 2010. It was renamed the Leather Industry Development Institute (LIDI) and was given direct responsibility for the development of the leather industry by the MoI. The rationale for setting up LIDI was threefold. First, the institute is to act as a conduit for the absorption, improvement, and diffusion of technologies in the leather and leather products industry, that is, it is to facilitate sector-wide learning, including learning from abroad. By working closely with tanneries and footwear manufacturers, the institute is tasked with conducting practical technology training that will help spread improved practices across the sector. Second, LIDI is expected to enhance the competitiveness of the leather industry by undertaking benchmarking studies and by introducing global excellence standards to domestic producers. LIDI's Quality Testing and Approval Laboratory is used not only to assess the quality and comfort of shoes produced but also to detect any chemical contamination in the shoes. Third, LIDI is tasked with providing high-quality consultancy and training services in various technical and managerial skills relevant to the industry, "such as branding and marketing, effluent management and laboratory testing of quality parameters" (Altenburg 2010).

Perhaps the second most influential policy paper from the leather industry's point of view was a sector master plan prepared by UNIDO in collaboration with the then Ministry of Trade and Industry (MoTI, now MoI). The collaboration between UNIDO and the MoI from 2005 onward resulted in two documents, a master plan and a business plan for the leather and leather products sector (UNIDO 2012). The master plan emphasized the need for the tanning industry to continuously improve both value addition and the quality of inputs supplied to the leather goods industry, including the footwear sector. The master plan also introduced the technical benchmarking of the Ethiopian leather and leather product industry against four countries with more technically advanced leather industries, namely Italy, China, Vietnam, and India.

Drawing on the master plan, the MoI prepared a concrete action plan that mainly consisted of upgrading programs for tanneries and footwear producers. The MoI has, in partnership with UNIDO and international donors, carried out several projects to put into practice the capacity-building and competitiveness programs articulated in the action plan. Of these, the "Made in Ethiopia" project, which introduced "Taytu," the first luxury designer label to originate from Ethiopia, to the high-end European and American markets, has been a notable success.

Since the early 2000s, the government, in collaboration with donors, also invested heavily into education and training initiatives for staff at LIDI itself. For example, from 2005 to 2008, foreign experts were invited to improve the basic training programs offered by LIDI by adapting the training manuals to international standards and best practices. LIDI's leather quality testing laboratory has also received assistance from donors including UNIDO.

The government's intervention in the leather sector was, however, not confined to large tanneries and footwear producers. There are more than two thousand micro- and small-scale shoemakers clustered in Ethiopia's largest market in Addis Ababa, called Mercato, where a plethora of shoe producers, parts suppliers, accessories retailers, machining and equipment service providers, and product outlets are concentrated. Most of these enterprises lack proper business premises and are forced to operate out of small rented cribs in the back alleys of businesses and residential houses in the area. The government responded to this lack of both retail and production space by offering fully constructed production sites at highly subsidized rental rates. A prominent example is an integrated shoe cluster development in six blocks of four-story buildings close to the market. These premises now house the Ethio-International Footwear Cluster Cooperative Society (EIFCCOS), the most important association of micro-, small-, and medium-scale shoemakers in Ethiopia, which has over one thousand members. This was a joint initiative by the government and an entrepreneur, who now is the chairman of the society, to unify the intermediate stages of the shoemaking process in a modern cluster to better exploit agglomeration economies.

In 2009 the MoI, in collaboration with UNIDO, designed a project titled "Technical Assistance Project for the Upgrading of the Ethiopian

Leather and Leather Products Industry" to be implemented by UNIDO experts by 2012. This involved "a wide range of technical assistance from production layout to management and marketing" (UNIDO 2012). The government also adopted a benchmarking exercise to upgrade the leather and leather products industry. To this effect, LIDI entered into a twinning arrangement with the Central Leather Research Institute (CLRI) and the Footwear Design and Development Institute (FDDI) of India to execute the benchmarking exercises at factory level. The government selected seven tanneries and seven footwear producers to implement UNIDO's initial benchmarking study recommendations. At the time of drafting this chapter, this has been an ongoing program, which is yet to be evaluated.

INTERVENTIONS AND OUTCOMES IN THE LEATHER AND LEATHER PRODUCTS INDUSTRY

The government's objective in all interventions in the leather sector is achieving the highest possible value addition at each stage of leather processing, that is, transforming leather production from unprocessed hide and skin to wet-blue and then to crust in the short run, and finally to finished leather products for the export market in the medium to long run. To begin with, the government had long banned the export of raw hides and skins to force firms to add value domestically and enhance supply to the local industry. More recently, the government considered banning the export of crusted leather in December 2011. Instead, the government decided to levy a 150 percent tax on the export of such leather in April 2012. A year before that, to protect input prices for tanneries, the Ministry of Industry had put a cap on market prices of hides and skins (at 47 Ethiopian Birr and 80 Ethiopian Birr, respectively) after prices rose steeply following the traditional mass slaughter of animals in celebration of the Ethiopian Easter festival. An important feature contributing to the success of such direct forms of intervention is that they were fully anticipated. These interventions did not take the private sector by surprise, as the government had announced its intentions long before such policies came into effect, allowing the private sector actors time to adapt their business practices and models. For example, the government's desire to tax the export of crusted leather "to discourage those who do not upgrade" was apparent as early as 2005 (Zenawi 2006). The taxes therefore led only to a relatively small and temporary drop in export revenues, as firms scrambled to upgrade their production capabilities.

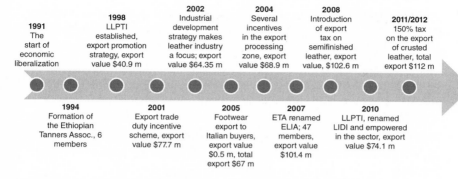

Figure 5.2 Timeline of important events in the leather industry

Source: Ethiopian Customs and Revenue Authority (ERCA), various years.

Growth of leather and leather product exports in Ethiopia has been rapid, albeit from a very low level to begin with. Regular exports of leather footwear, for instance, began with a small volume of sales to Italian buyers in 2004/2005. That year, total revenue from the export of leather footwear was worth less than USD 0.5 million. Three years later, export earnings had increased nearly twentyfold to USD 8.1 million. By 2012 export earnings from footwear had reached more than USD 11 million.

Export earnings from the wider leather and leather products industry have increased steadily from USD 67 million in 2004/2005 to USD 104 million in 2010/2011 (see figure 5.3). Correspondingly, formal

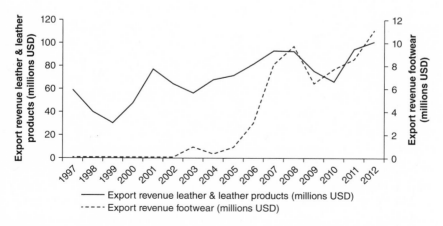

Figure 5.3 Trend in export earnings in the leather and leather products industry

Source: Ethiopian Customs and Revenue Authority (ERCA), various years.

employment has grown from 7,900 jobs in 2004 and 2005 to more than 14,100 jobs in 2010/2011 (CSA 2007 and 2012). Recent data also show that in 2012/2013, export earnings from processed leather and footwear were USD 123.4 million.

Figure 5.4 shows that real value added in the tanning and footwear industries has recently shown a significant upward trend. A remarkable shift in value addition is observed in both industries since the 2008/2009 fiscal year. The most likely cause is the heavy taxes levied on exports of the wet-blue and pickle stages of unfinished leather in order to promote production and export of finished leather. Indeed the export value of wet-blue and pickle leather has dropped drastically from a high point of more than USD 50 million in 2007/2008. As mentioned earlier, these taxes also partly explain the decline in export revenue from 2008 through 2010 seen in figure 5.3. In 2009/2010 there was a significant spike in formal employment in large- and medium-scale enterprises engaged in the leather processing business. Informal employment and employment in micro and small enterprises engaged in the leather industry is estimated to be much higher than these numbers suggest. EDRI's micro and small shoemakers' surveys conducted in 2008 and 2009 suggest that there could be more

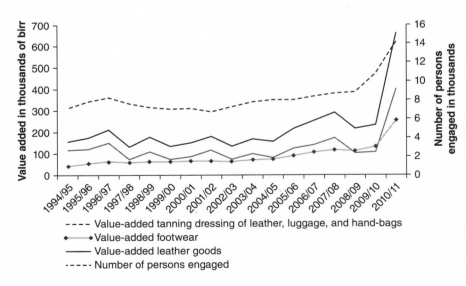

---- Value-added tanning dressing of leather, luggage, and hand-bags
◆——◆ Value-added footwear
—— Value-added leather goods
----- Number of persons engaged

Figure 5.4   Value addition and employment in the leather and leather products industry

Source: Authors' compilation using CSA's various large and medium enterprise reports.

than twelve thousand individuals working in the shoemaking business in the Mercato area alone.

Fiscal policies, combined with other interventions, have had the effect of pushing producers up the leather value chain. For example, McMillan (2012) reports that these interventions induced four large foreign-owned companies, who previously had exported only unfinished leather from Ethiopia, to procure machinery and equipment for the production and export of finished leather products. Local tanneries were initially forced to cut their exports due to limited capacity to produce finished leather products. Recently, however, there is evidence suggesting that they have upgraded their machinery and, as a result, are increasingly moving from selling semi-processed leather to other tanneries to involvement in the more lucrative export market. Indeed in both 2009 and 2011 the number of new leather product exporters far exceeded the number of incumbent exporters (World Bank 2014). What this episode clearly demonstrates is that information alone does not readily translate into capabilities. The tanneries knew of the coming export taxes on unfinished leather products in advance. However, they lacked the credit lines and technical expertise to upgrade in time. While information is vital, successful learning also requires making additional resources available at firm level.

In earlier periods, the local tanning industry was protected from competition, as foreign-based companies were not permitted to buy hides and skins, nor were they allowed to tan leather. Due to a lack of local capability, however, the ban on new foreign investment in these areas was removed for many years, before being restored in 2011. During this time, there were a number of new foreign investments in the leather sector. McMillan (2012) interviewed six new foreign investors who established tanneries in Ethiopia. The most striking feature to emerge from the interviews was that all of these companies were longtime buyers of Ethiopian leather, and that they decided to invest in production in Ethiopia because they wanted to "secure their leather supply."

Tanneries have received a wide-ranging support package to improve the quality of their products. LIDI offers training on production and managerial skills for workers and managers of tanneries free of charge. The government has also co-financed the employment of foreign experts and consultants who helped improve the production facilities of tanneries. Regarding land and finance, the government has offered land at reasonably low lease rates and provided export credit guarantees and loan facilities at highly subsidized rates.

The story is similar in the leather manufacturing sector. In the foot-wear sector, for example, while the importance of improving conditions for existing investors and attracting new investors has been high on the agenda, the government has largely shunned direct protectionist policies.[3] Instead, the government decided that the long-term sustainability of the industry hinged on upgrading the capability of local producers through skills formation and technology adoption. Enterprises that survived the intense competition from imports were those most able to improve their supply chain management, product quality, and delivery times of their product, and more generally upgrade their machinery and equipment, as well as labor and inventory management. In many cases, interna-tional buyers played a key role in these upgrading processes. In partic-ular, equipment and input manufacturers have every incentive to help Ethiopian producers employ increasingly sophisticated technology, as this of course necessitates purchasing the products of those very same provid-ers. Equipment providers dispatch engineers who not only help their cli-ents set up machines but also train local production engineers. Likewise, companies that provide the various chemicals needed at various parts of the production process are interested in broadening the product palette producers can offer, as this means buying more and different chemicals, and so they provide Ethiopian producers with seminars on market trends and fashions.

That said, the Ethiopian government has not simply let the industry fend for itself. A range of incentives instituted, was including, but not limited to, the provision of land in export processing zones, the provi-sion of cheap credit, subsidized and free training for workers and man-agers at LIDI, and co-financing the employment of foreign experts to temporarily work in the local shoe factories. The government freely pro-vided semi-constructed factories located in an industrial zone to firms that sought the production and export of footwear and other leather products in 2004 (Redi 2009), accompanied by tax breaks for import-ing machines for use in these plants. More recently, the government has granted three shoe producers, one Ethiopian, one Turkish, and the other Indian, tracts of land (approximately 2,800m^2 each) on which to build factories.

The government has also recognized the importance of attracting large-scale investment from global leaders in the footwear industry. A high-profile case is the Huajian group from China. The Huajian group is a global footwear manufacturer that uses its massive production site in Dongguan, Gaungdong Province, to churn out more than twenty million pairs of shoes annually, mostly for the Western markets. The former prime minister "head-hunted" the group, as he had taken a personal interest in seeing the formation of large-scale industrial clusters. After the group's representative met the former prime minister in August 2011, Huajian decided to invest in Ethiopia. This company now employs around 1,600 workers and produces nearly 2,000 pairs of shoes per day for well-known brands. The company intends to expand its production to generate export earnings equivalent to USD 4 billion per year within a decade. As part of the expansion scheme, it has recently acquired 300 hectares of land on the outskirts of Addis Ababa, and it plans to erect a complex of factories for the production of footwear, handbags, and accessories.

What sets this company apart from other foreign direct investment (FDI) in the footwear sector is its commitment to training local staff. It has selected and sent more than 130 young Ethiopian university graduates to China for training, with another batch of nearly 300 trainees soon to follow.[4] Such forms of training are vital in building local technological and managerial capabilities. For example, many studies attribute the rapid growth of the export-oriented garment industry in Bangladesh to young trainees who received intense training in production techniques, factory management, international procurement, and marketing in South Korea (for example, Mottaleb and Sonobe 2011). It remains to be seen whether such positive externalities will arise in the leather goods industry in Ethiopia.

INTERIM SUMMARY

Ethiopia is endowed with the resource base required for the commercial production of leather and leather products. The resources, however, still remained largely untapped due to a host of reasons ranging from poor hide and skin collection to limited technological sophistication at the leather-processing phase. The problems in the leather sector are multifaceted, and without a critical market size it is not clear that large private enterprises would emerge to improve the skin-to-leather value chain (Altenburg 2010). This would require coordinated action in which only states with long-term visions are willing (and able) to engage. The Ethiopian government has reacted by employing several forms of industrial policies. In addition to nondiscriminatory general incentives available to all investors, there have been several interventions aimed more explicitly at upgrading the leather and leather products industry. These interventions can be usefully subdivided into four forms of industrial policies.

First, the government is aggressively engaged in building the local production and marketing capacity through technology imports and learning from abroad. LIDI is used as an instrument to facilitate technology diffusion and upgrade the skills of workers and managers in the industry. To this end LIDI has organized training programs in collaboration with development partners, often involving foreign consultants. The government has also encouraged enterprises to use foreign experts by subsidizing the costs of their employment. Benchmarking exercises have been carried out in the hope of emulating more successful countries in the industry. Capacity building also means improving the institutional capacity of LIDI itself. As a result, LIDI has received direct support from both the government and international donors.

Second, due to its priority sector status, the leather and leather goods industry has had better access to finance from the Development Bank of Ethiopia (DBE). The familiar 70/30 credit modality accorded to industries in the priority sectors implies that the DBE would avail loans amounting to 70 percent of the total project cost once the investor raises equity equivalent to 30 percent of the investment cost.

Third, the government has provided land and semi-constructed factories to large- and medium-sized tanneries and footwear producers at highly discounted lease rates. The government has also erected several buildings that are given out to micro and small shoemakers at nominal rental fees. Both local and international investors are also offered huge tracts of land along with basic infrastructural facilities in the industrial zones strategically located in different parts of Ethiopia.

Fourth, the government has extensively used its tax and regulatory policies to encourage upgrading along the leather value chain. The export of raw hides and skins, for example, is banned to push local processing of leather. Similarly, the export of semi-finished leather products was subjected to a 150 percent export tax in 2008. In 2009, the same level of tax was imposed on the export of crust leather products. While limited local capacity might have attenuated the benefits of these interventions, studies suggest that they have encouraged the production of high-value leather goods. Such types of preannounced interventions are enormous disincentives to producers who are reluctant to move up the leather value chain, and they help push more innovative and efficient producers up the value chain.

All of these interventions have had the combined effects of improving value addition, export, and employment in the leather and leather products industry. Further, the provision of land at highly discounted lease rates, duty-free import of raw material and capital goods, as well as access to subsidized credit have attracted both foreign and domestic investors by reducing entry costs. These achievements are not, however, very large, particularly seen against the sector's potential, though as noted earlier the government's proactive attraction of investment by a large foreign producer of shoes is likely to make a dramatic impact. There remains much room for policy to improve several facets of livestock management and hide and skin collection. This would greatly improve raw material supply and quality for the leather processing enterprises.

THE CUT FLOWER SECTOR

The cut flower sector has the potential to make inroads into the twin problems of unemployment and the gap in technology between developed and developing countries. Unlike the traditional agricultural sector, the cut flower industry requires modern technologies during the production phase and more intense labor use per unit of land at the processing and post-harvest phases. It also provides a broader base for export through diversification, which improves export earnings while reducing their volatility. This is essential for low-income countries like Ethiopia that are dependent on traditional agriculture, which is highly sensitive to the vagaries of weather and provides only limited opportunity for additional technology and labor absorption.

Ethiopia is endowed with favorable climatic conditions for the production of different varieties of flowers, which presents it with a strategic advantage over other flower-growing countries. The possibility of high-altitude growing locations and suitable soil types constitute ideal conditions for producing higher-quality flower varieties. In addition to favorable climatic conditions, a reputable airliner and airport facilities and the physical proximity to the European market help reduce the cost of freight and enable the delivery of fresh, high-quality blossoms on time. Ethiopia's rural and urban poverty mean that wages are very low, which balances out the lower labor productivity and contributes to the low costs of production. The flower industry has thus developed mainly in the highlands, where climatic conditions are favorable, and is concentrated in areas that have relatively easy access to the airport.

OVERVIEW OF THE CUT FLOWER INDUSTRY

The earliest attempt to set up a flower farm for export to the European market dates back to the 1980s. In this period, it was state-owned farms that began exporting flowers to Europe. However, these projects failed. Following the economic liberalization in the early 1990s, two Ethiopian entrepreneurs established privately owned cut flower farms. Although these entrepreneurs have greatly contributed to the industry by way of information externalities regarding the feasibility of the industry, a major breakthrough came only in 1999 when an Indian owned (U.K.-based) company started rose production using steel structure greenhouses—a technology that hitherto had been adopted by neither the SOEs nor the two Ethiopian farms (Gebreeyesus and Iizuka 2010).

In the early 2000s, the industry started expanding with the entry of both domestic and foreign entrepreneurs. Yet the flower industry faced several challenges in the farm-to-market value chain (see figure 5.5 for a simplified presentation of the cut flower value chain). First, there was a problem associated with access to suitable land for floriculture development, that is, land that is located close to the airport. Investors acquired land through a time-consuming process of leasing from individual small-holder farmers, a process that then required the "consolidation of small contiguous holdings" (Gebreeyesus and Iizuka 2010). The second problem growers faced in the 1990s and early 2000s was the absence of regular and dependable air freight at rates competitive to the European market. Because cut flowers are a delicate product, post-harvest life and foliage are highly dependent on the availability of reliable and efficient air transport logistics. Along the farm-to-market value chain, air freight costs to market destinations often make up a substantial fraction of the total cost (GDS 2011). This cost factor is even more important in Ethiopia where, as noted earlier, wages are very low. Thus without ensuring cost-efficient structures at shipping and marketing phases, efficient flower production cannot be translated into profitability. The third commonly observed problem in the industry was the limited ability of firms to raise capital, as investment in cut flower farms required substantial amounts of upfront expenditure for fixed capital acquisition, such as greenhouses, pack houses, and cold storage facilities.

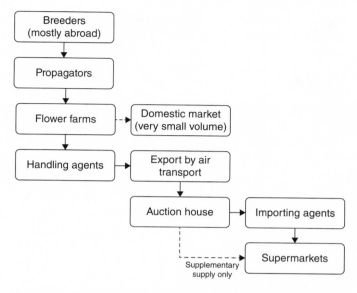

Figure 5.5 Participants and products in the cut flower value chain

All of these problems came to the government's attention in 2002, a period that also saw the establishment of the Ethiopian Horticulture Producers and Exporters Association (EHPEA). This business association was originally established by five investors and has since expanded considerably to incorporate more than eighty-five members. The EHPEA quickly proved itself a competent and effective lobbying agency, generously endowed with donor funds. Through consultation with the EHPEA, the government recognized the potential of the flower industry for export earnings and as a means to provide stable wage income to the landless and near-landless farming households.

Concerted measures were then taken to stimulate the sector. As a result, export earnings from the cut flower sector jumped from a paltry USD 150,000 in 2001 to USD 212.56 million in 2011/2012 (EHDA 2012). Similarly, land under flower cultivation drastically increased from less than 40 hectares in the early 2000s to 1,440 hectares in 2011/2012 (EHDA 2012). The question that then arises is: What role did policymakers play in boosting the sector? A recurrent finding in the studies of the industry is that takeoff only came about when the government started providing industry-specific supports in 2003 (Altenburg 2010; Taylor 2010;

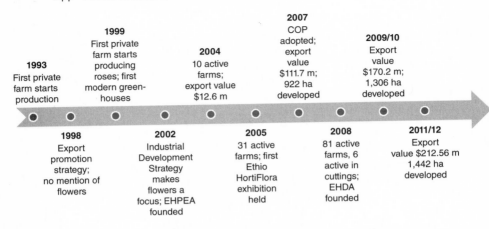

Figure 5.6   Timeline of important events in the cut flower industry

Gebreeyesus and Iizuka 2010). Figure 5.6 illustrates the evolution of the cut flower industry since the early 1990s.

INDUSTRIAL POLICY IN THE CUT FLOWER INDUSTRY

The government's early and continuous commitment to promoting the cut flower industry is one of the most important factors that enabled the industry to reach a critical mass for takeoff (Taylor 2010). In late 2002, the prime minister's office requested that the Ministry of Trade and Industry (MoTI) prepare a five-year action plan for the industry detailing potentials, problems, and possible solutions (Gebreeyesus and Iizuka 2010). Based on this plan, a five-year target was prepared and three concrete areas of intervention were identified. The latter involved the provision of land, long-term credit, and facilitation of air cargo logistics.

The government's initial support schemes primarily targeted the alleviation of the three major problems mentioned earlier. Suitable land located at reasonable distance from the airport was made available to investors at very low lease rates with extended lease periods. With regard to the air transport and logistics problem, the government "initiated discussion and cooperation between the flower exporters and the Ethiopian Airlines (EAL)" (Gebreeyesus and Iizuka 2010). The government then subsidized the air freight rates, and exporters were also granted the privilege to ship on EAL on a credit basis. The government also attempted to redress the financing problem by instituting a soft loan scheme at the

Development Bank of Ethiopia (DBE) with generous terms (Gebreeyesus and Iizuka 2010). The bank extends long-term credit based on a 70/30 debt-equity ratio modality, asking for no additional collateral except the investment project and the fixed capital employed therein.

To overcome the credit constraints faced by prospective investors, the government deployed the DBE as a prime lender in the sector. The DBE, as a result, has played a crucial role in the development of the cut flower industry. This role has evolved as the nature of the problems facing the industry changed and the sector matured. The next subsection presents a detailed account of the DBE's engagements in the cut flower industry.

FINANCE AND THE ROLE OF THE DEVELOPMENT BANK OF ETHIOPIA

Capital markets are either completely nonexistent or highly deficient in many developing countries. Particularly private sector financing of investments with long gestation periods and uncertain returns is challenging. Such forms of investments might be heavily discounted particularly when they result in substantial spillover effects in the form of knowledge that can spur complementary investments as the investors and the financier cannot appropriate the full benefits of their investments. Investors are also likely to be myopic and lack the knowledge to correctly appraise the risk involved in financing new projects. New industries are inherently more risky than established ones. As a result, investments with high social returns may not be able to attract sufficient capital if capital allocation is left purely to the market. In other words, markets by themselves will tend to maximize short-term returns, and will tend to underinvest in areas that carry high social returns, especially if these are only realized in the long run. Governments, especially in low-income countries, need to find alternative ways of financing medium- and long-term projects. Development banks are often established to finance projects in strategic sectors, as well as to provide technical support for investors with limited project management capacity (DBE 2010).

The Development Bank of Ethiopia was established in 1970 to streamline the limited financial resources of the country toward priority areas. According to a key respondent at the DBE, the bank is there "to take risks that commercial banks would not." To align the bank's role with the government's development plans, such as the PASDEP and GTP, the bank produces five-year strategic plans, which are then used to develop detailed annual plans. To increase its effectiveness, the government has limited the bank's role to supporting priority sectors.[5] Consequently, the bank provides medium- to long-term credit to investment projects in priority sectors and is willing to take short-term risks and shoulder costs in order to enhance the economic development of the country in the medium and long term.

Not surprisingly, at the early stage of the cut flower industry, commercial banks in Ethiopia were averse to lending to entrepreneurs who wanted to invest in the industry (Taylor 2010).[6] The government has thus used the DBE to meet the financial needs of prospective investors in the industry since the early 2000s.

Although the financing modalities available at the DBE from the outset were attractive compared to neighboring countries, credit take-up was initially low. Once the profitability of the sector became apparent, however, both foreign and local investors started borrowing from the DBE using the 70/30 modality, whereby the investor is required to pay down 30 percent of the project costs and the bank then lends the other 70 percent. Initially, interest rates on the loans were as low as 7.5 percent. Rates have since increased by one percentage point, but they remain lower than rates available either in commercial banks in Ethiopia or in other flower-producing countries in the region, such as Kenya and Uganda.

The DBE's initial lending experience in the flower industry was not all rosy. Because the cut flower industry was new to the country and had intricate production and marketing systems, local knowledge required for proper feasibility evaluation of investments in the industry was very limited. In the beginning, the bank lacked relevant knowledge and capacity to properly appraise business plans. For example, as the bank lacked experience in floriculture, it was not able to assess the veracity or accuracy of claims made by loan seekers about project costs (including, but not limited to, greenhouses, international staff, chemical inputs, and fertilizers). The bank had limited information on what the correct industry standard rates were, which led to significant overinvoicing in some projects. In particular, this affected the collateral the bank took for its 70 percent portion of the project costs. As most investors were unable to provide any collateral other than the fixed investments made in the projects themselves, and because this constituted part of the incentive package, the bank was forced to accept these overvalued assets as collateral. Floriculture by its nature has lower fixed capital content than other industries; this combined with the faulty project valuation implies that the collaterals collected by the bank were insufficient to cover even the 30 percent pay down required for loans disbursed by the bank. In other words, a larger proportion of the project risk was shouldered by the DBE. These highly favorable terms were in some cases exploited by unscrupulous investors who greatly overstated their costs to criminally extract funds from the bank (Taylor 2010).

Recognizing its initial weakness and under pressure from the highest echelons of the political system, the bank embarked on a drive to both engage more directly with the sector and to build up its own expertise. This resulted in a number of initiatives. First, the bank tailored its credit policy to better serve the idiosyncratic needs of the cut flower industry. Second, the bank started working with overseas development banks and local stakeholders to build its capacity and strengthen its own research department. Bank employees assigned to work on the cut flower industry received regular training in collaboration with the Ethiopian Horticulture Producers and Exporters Association (EHPEA). Partnerships were established with development banks in other countries, notably the Netherlands, Turkey, Korea, and India, the latter being the destination of large numbers of DBE staff sent for training. Third, since the establishment of the EHDA, the agency and the bank have been working closely together, holding monthly meetings and sharing relevant information. This has helped the bank to expand its learning scope and keep track of the status of each project through active follow up.

After undergoing a steep and painful learning curve, the DBE has now managed to learn the ins and outs of the industry. The bank has developed a credit policy specifically tailored to the cut flower industry, and its customer assistance framework has evolved. For example, each farm is now assigned a contact officer who is uniquely responsible for that farm, backed up by a team ready to lend assistance to the farm. This includes many forms of technical assistance, not just in purely financial terms but also in export and marketing knowledge, among other things. Regular inspection trips are undertaken to each farm, and the DBE staff is supposed to be aware of all relevant developments, irrespective of whether or not they are directly related to repayment capacity. In this way, whenever problems arise, the bank is able to quickly recognize the problem and can propose an appropriate solution.

THE FINANCIAL CRISIS AND STATE INTERVENTION

A defining moment in the interaction between the bank and its cut flower clients came in 2008 and 2009, when the cut flower industry was on the verge of collapse following the global financial crisis. With key export markets in economic turmoil, demand for flowers plummeted.

In 2008, the National Export Promotion Committee directed the EHDA to evaluate the health of the industry. At the time, forty-three flower farms had collectively borrowed more than one billion Ethiopian Birr from the Development Bank of Ethiopia (EHDA 2009). When flower prices spiraled downward during the global financial crisis, many of these borrowers were suddenly unable to service their debt. Faced with the possibility of large parts of the sector imploding, the government and the DBE engaged in a desperate attempt to stem the coming wave of farm bankruptcies.

A team comprising staff from the DBE, the National Bank of Ethiopia (NBE), the Ministry of Agriculture and Rural Development (MoARD), and the EHDA, as well as owners of the farms and sector representatives, was formed and tasked with evaluating each farm individually, with the aim of preventing foreclosures. Based on these evaluations, the team made recommendations for each farm. After reviewing the recommendations, the bank then implemented measures including rescheduling of loan repayments, additional credit for troubled farms, and even direct management intervention in some of the worst cases. To handle this process, the bank set up a special section, which has since been tasked primarily with following up on the status of borrowers in the cut flower industry.

The combination of these measures meant that foreclosures were avoided in all but two or three cases. All other afflicted farms are apparently still operational. The DBE summarized the bank's stance during the bailout process as follows: "If it is a genuine problem, we want to be part of the solution. We will reschedule the loans, we won't foreclose, and we will transfer sick loans to others who can manage the farm." The sentiment appears to be shared with investors in the cut flower industry. For example, an investor interviewed by Taylor (2010) reflects that "the government asked us what more mechanism should we put? Not many governments do this."

While the DBE's assistance in the form of loan rescheduling and cash injections was available for both foreign- and locally owned flower farms, Ethiopian-owned farms were more likely to be in financial distress and hence have benefited more from the intervention. This suggests that the financial crisis alone might not have precipitated the problems, but rather acted to exasperate and expose already existing structural weaknesses in the product portfolio, management capacity, and marketing knowhow of some Ethiopian-owned firms. Addressing these weaknesses required going beyond sector-specific interventions to targeted policy interventions aimed at improving the capacity of Ethiopian-owned farms. This motive partly lies behind the establishment of the EHDA.

A SECTORAL SERVICE AGENCY: THE ROLE OF THE ETHIOPIAN HORTICULTURAL DEVELOPMENT AGENCY

Since its establishment in July 2007, the EHDA has been the principal government institution designed to support flower growers in Ethiopia. The agency was set up to act as a one-stop shop for services required by investors. Prior to 2007, the sector was characterized by administrative dispersion, with investors having to deal with a number of different branches of government simultaneously to acquire the necessary licenses and other documents. The rationale behind the agency is to bundle these services in a single institution. It should be noted, however, that the agency is a service institution for investors and not a sector regulator. Regulatory functions for the sector remain in the hands of a variety of institutions, each of which is responsible for its field of authority.

The support the agency provides to investors can be subdivided into three broad pillars: capacity building, investment support, and market promotion. Capacity-building efforts are geared toward local investors who often (at least initially) have limited knowledge regarding production technologies, input procurement systems, and flower marketing chains. Some of these investors had no prior experience either in the cut flower industry or in sectors similar to flower farming. This is especially true for Ethiopian-owned farms, most of which had had no previous involvement in the sector. Foreign-owned farms, in contrast, are often run by specialized floriculture companies or are established by investors with many years of experience in the industry. To address these shortcomings, the agency launched the Integrated Capacity Building Program that, among other interventions, involved employing foreign consultants to assist Ethiopian-run farms with all aspects of the business, including production, product handling, farm management, and financial management. The Integrated Capacity Building Program also comprises short-term training programs for flower workers and managers on issues as diverse as benchmarking, farm management, harvesting, and marketing. These programs were implemented with assistance from Dutch training and research institutions (Boer and Pfisterer 2009).

The Ethiopian government quickly realized that strengthening the agricultural research and extension system would play a pivotal role in the long-term sustainability of the cut flower industry. Ethiopian farms, both foreign and domestic owned, for example, incur substantial costs in the form of royalty payments to international flower breeders, who tend to sit in the Netherlands and other advanced flower-producing countries. These breeders occupy a unique position in the floriculture value chain. They produce new varieties of flowers for which they then hold the intellectual property rights. Farms may plant these varieties in exchange for payment of royalty fees to breeders. Varieties rapidly go in and out of fashion, and the correct choice of varieties is often a life or death decision for flower farms. Farms owned by international companies, who often have their own breeding operations or have longstanding business relationships with renowned international breeders, are at a distinct advantage here vis-à-vis many Ethiopian-owned farms, who lack such connections and the intimate market knowledge they bring with them.

The country could retain some of the breeders' royalties by encouraging flower variety research and development locally in both the public and private research institutions. The EHDA is involved in some attempts to upgrade the existing local knowledge stock. One of the public universities has, for example, recently launched a regular education program for students in the field of horticulture at BSc and MSc levels (Gebreeyesus and Iizuka 2010). Similarly, to address the knowledge issue, a Horticultural Practical Training Centre has been established for graduates, investors, government staff, and stakeholders in the industry.

Under the second pillar of investment support, land provision constitutes the most important support the EHDA provides to investors. The EHDA has been working closely with the federal and regional governments to facilitate the acquisition of land suitable for growing flowers by investors. Initially, land located close to Addis Ababa was given to investors at low lease rates. The sector has, however, moved into a period in which most of the growth is driven by the expansion of existing projects rather than the establishment of entirely new farms. Expansion of existing projects, however, is hampered by the availability of suitable land. Suitable land for cut flower farming needs to be conveniently located, have leases that are not too expensive, and have the necessary infrastructure in place. Ideally, plots for expansion should be adjacent to existing projects.

Recently, there has been some migration of growers to areas outside of Addis. But most of the existing flower farms are located in close proximity to Addis Ababa, and they have already taken up nearly all the available government land situated in areas surrounding Addis Ababa. The remaining land is owned[7] by local farmers who mainly produce cash crops for the Addis Ababa market. They would, therefore, require substantial compensation to cede the land to flower farms. Two solutions are offered by the EHDA to resolve the land problem. First, the incentive package with respect to land is tailored so that farms located in less suitable locations, or far away from Addis Ababa, get bigger financial incentives to compensate for the drawbacks of the location. Second, the agency has recently started earmarking land in five "development corridors" across five regional states for horticulture development. Land located in these areas is registered in a "land bank" and will be fitted with the necessary infrastructure, including power, cold storage facilities, and transport linkages to and from either regional airports or Bole International airport in Addis Ababa for export and Djibouti port for imports. The corridors have the advantage of being geographically concentrated, which makes service provision easier. Infrastructure such as water reservoirs and pack houses can also be shared among farms. Uptake appears to have been limited.

As part of the investment support scheme, the agency also plays an arbitration role between investors and workers employed in the industry. The agency seeks to maintain good labor and community relations by avoiding industrial action and smoothing out conflicts that may arise between management and labor. Far from being a neutral arbitration body, the agency sees its role as maintaining production by preventing work stoppages or other forms of disruptive collective action on part of workers.

The third support pillar involves market promotion. By working closely with Ethiopian diplomatic missions abroad, the agency tries to promote both the products and the overall image of Ethiopian floriculture abroad. It aims to grow the Ethiopian flower industry's global market share and reach by distributing samples, finding new importers, and attending trade shows. To facilitate exports, the agency also works with public logistics providers such as EAL and Ethiopian Shipping Lines (ESL), as well as private logistics companies, to open up new routes and increase capacity on existing ones.

PERFORMANCE OF THE CUT FLOWER INDUSTRY

Figure 5.7 summarizes the growth of the cut flower industry in the past several years. Production and export of flowers were virtually zero during the 1990s. In the early and mid-2000s, two important developments helped unleash the growth of the industry. The Ethiopian Horticulture Producers and Exporters Association (EHPEA) was established by producers engaged in the cut flower industry in September 2002. The association started lobbying the government, stressing the potentials of the sector. As a result, the government initiated several incentive schemes that granted a number of privileges to the industry. Consequently, cut flower production and export increased substantially between 2002/2003 and 2005/2006. In three years' time, the number of flower stems exported rose by more than 1,000 percent, from 16 million to 186 million. Correspondingly, export revenue and the share of the flower industry in total export revenues grew from $1.8 million to $37.5 million and from 0.01 percent to 1.4 percent, respectively.

More aggressive support for the industry came with the five-year national development plan, the Plan for Accelerated and Sustained Development to End Poverty (PASDEP), covering 2006 to 2010. The

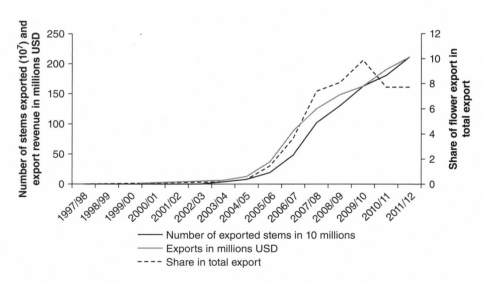

Figure 5.7   Volume and value of export in the cut flower industry

Source: ERCA and Ethiopian Horticulture Sector Statistical Bulletin (2012).

plan explicitly named the industry as one of the priority sectors that would receive direct state support, mostly in the form of investment incentives. The 1998 export promotion strategy had not even mentioned the cut flower industry (Gebreeyesus and Iizuka 2010). Once the industry's potential became apparent, it prompted support at the highest levels of government. The former prime minister, for example, got personally involved in the development of the sector, holding regular meetings with investors in the cut flower industry to get up-to-date information and seek immediate solutions to the business constraints faced by the industry in consultation with investors. Investors consistently stress how important this direct line of communication and the "open ears" at the top of the political leadership had been to their initial success.

The combined effects of these measures made the cut flower industry one of the major export earning sectors in the country. In 2009/2010, the cut flower industry generated 10 percent of total export earnings, an impressive expansion by about eight percentage points within just three years (see figure 5.8). The number of stems exported reached two billion in 2011/2012, generating revenue amounting to USD 212.6 million.

Labor intensity, and hence employment opportunity, is another beneficial feature of the cut flower industry. As shown in figure 5.8, employment has substantially increased in the sector in the period considered. Land development for flower production appears to follow a strikingly

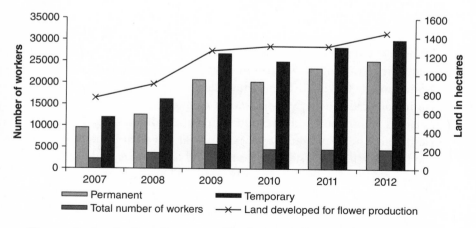

Figure 5.8   Levels of employment and land use in the cut flower industry (recent trends)

Source: EHDA (2012) statistical bulletin (for land coverage) and EDRI's panel surveys (for employment)

similar trend with employment levels. Unlike other industries in which expansion is often associated with the adoption of labor-saving technologies, figure 5.8 perhaps suggests that expansion in the flower industry remains highly labor intensive. This trend is good news given the severe unemployment problem in Ethiopia.

The employment figures might actually understate the actual number of jobs created in the sector. These figures were gathered from seventy farms in 2012, while EHDA data show that there were more than eighty flower farms in the same period. As a result, the EHDA official forecast puts employment in the cut flower industry at much higher levels. Accordingly, in 2011/2012, the number of workers engaged in the industry was 50,500.

Questions remain regarding pay and working conditions. Ethiopia has a single, state-affiliated labor union that, unsurprisingly, is thoroughly corporatist in outlook and does not engage in collective bargaining on behalf of workers. While the cut flower sector as a whole has been very keen to comply with international production standards, wages remain low and the use of pesticides and herbicides can pose serious health hazards.[8] While voluntary standards and government oversight are better than no regulation at all, independent labor organizations and mandatory collective bargaining could better balance the interests of investors and those of their—mostly young and female—workers.

INTERIM SUMMARY

The development of the cut flower industry in Ethiopia spans three decades since the 1980s, when state-owned farms attempted to export summer flowers for the first time. In the late 1990s, a large foreign-owned farm introduced innovative production techniques, and its success was emulated by both local and foreign investors, in addition to attracting the government's attention to the sector's potential and what it might be able to do to realize it. As a result, the number and relative size of flower farms had noticeably increased by the early 2000s. These early entrants, however, faced several problems. Access to suitable land, cheap and dependable air freight services, and start-up capital were some of the earliest constraints on the growth of the sector.

With the introduction of sector-specific support in 2003, the government of Ethiopia demonstrated its intentions to promote the cut flower industry. The establishment of the EHPEA and its strong ties with the government helped identify and quickly tackle problems in the sector. Policy measures that provided prospective investors with land at low lease rates, subsidized and reliable air freight services, and low-interest credit were introduced. Regarding the latter, for example, the DBE started generously tailoring its credit policy to better serve the industry. There is little doubt that such measures led to a radical shift in the industry, with the export revenue topping more than USD 100 million in 2006/2007. Similarly, the active involvement of the DBE is credited for stabilizing the industry when flower demand plummeted following the global financial crisis in 2008 and 2009. This is a clear demonstration of the value of development banks, which are of sufficient size to not only provide much-needed seed funding and start-up finance but also to act as backstops to protect investments in the face of external shocks.

Because the nature of farms in the cut flower industry is heterogeneous, not every farm will be affected by policy measures or external shocks in the same way. There are sophisticated foreign conglomerates that possess state of the art production technologies and that established robust market structures. On the other hand, there are Ethiopian investors who migrated from trading businesses in the hopes of exploiting the favorable agro-climatic conditions for growing flowers, while having limited technological and marketing knowledge in the cut flower sector. In order to improve local capacity, provide investment support for all types of investors, and search for new marketing frontiers for Ethiopian flowers, the EHDA was established in 2007 on the behest of the government. The EHDA was created as a one-stop shop to facilitate the development of the industry in close consultation with private sector representatives, most notably the EHPEA. Such forms of public-private partnerships can be used as instruments for continuous information exchange on constraints on and opportunities for growth. From interviews with relevant sector actors, we know that there is greater scope to utilize such arrangements to better inform and coordinate interventions in the sector, particularly when new rules and directives are to be enacted and promulgated.

CONCLUSION AND RECOMMENDATIONS

The government of Ethiopia has used industrial policy to both exploit and create (dynamic) comparative advantages in the priority sectors defined in its industrial strategy. This chapter has focused in particular on the policies employed to foster and support the leather and floriculture sectors. It has found that the mixture of general incentives and targeted interventions used in both sectors has been highly effective in nurturing entrepreneurship and investment and has resulted in remarkable growth in both sectors. Moreover, it is clear that takeoff in either sector would not have been possible without direct government intervention and support.

It is tempting to argue ex post that Ethiopia followed its comparative advantage in setting up a successful and internationally competitive floriculture sector and in providing for strong growth and a pathway to competitiveness through further investment in leather. After all, Ethiopia has cheap labor, and these are labor-intensive activities. Both require the application of modern technology with limited complexity and skill requirements, thereby suiting Ethiopia's "factor endowments." But this argument disregards the slow and complex process of discovery, testing, failure, and adaption that led to growing sectors in both cases. Especially in floriculture, by far the more successful of the cases—at least until recently—examined here, Ethiopia's supposed comparative advantage was hardly obvious at the outset. Instead, the competitiveness now achieved was consciously crafted by skilled entrepreneurs, hardworking laborers on low wages, and a government that did not shy away from repeated and direct involvement, right down to day-to-day management decisions in ailing farms. It is probably better to say that there was a *potential* for creating a competitive industry.

We agree with Altenburg (2010) that the challenges faced by both sectors were quite different and called for different policy responses. In the leather sector, the challenge was a classical coordination failure, whereby problems all along the value chain had to be tackled simultaneously to achieve the necessary quality of inputs and outputs for global competitiveness. In the absence of large, fully vertically integrated private companies, such coordination and concomitant investment could only be undertaken by government. By contrast, the floriculture sector did not lack private sector coordination capacity, but instead required interventions to create an enabling environment, in particular to overcome weaknesses in logistics and initial capital formation. By adopting a flexible and differentiated policy regime, the government is able to meet the requirements of both sectors.

Because both sectors are, in their modern forms, new to the Ethiopian economy, these successes were the result of sometimes painful learning processes and were not achieved without cost. It is therefore necessary to draw lessons from the experiences gained.

BUILDING IMPLEMENTING CAPACITY EARLY

Industrial policy necessarily implies a process of testing and experimentation with new industries. To be able to effectively support infant industries, the relevant government bodies must strive to equip themselves with appropriate technical knowledge before support to these sectors is commenced. As the experience of early support to floriculture demonstrates, a lack of sector-specific knowledge can result in costly misallocation of scarce capital resources and funds. Sector-specific knowledge also allows government bodies to build the kinds of close collaborative partnerships that are now in evidence in both the leather and floriculture sectors. International assistance can be sought to pull in relevant knowledge at relatively little budgetary cost.

RESPONSIVE REGULATION

Regulation is a vitally important aspect of industrial policy. Regulatory regimes must be transparent, predictable, and easy to comply with, while at the same time holding companies to the high standards expected of them. By its very nature the regulation of complex agricultural, agro-industrial, and industrial sectors is often spread across a variety of different government institutions, including line ministries and authorities. The role of government here is twofold. First, the government has to assure effective communication across responsible institutions, allowing them to build a coherent and consistent regulatory regime. Second, the government has to make sure that regulations are technically feasible and will not place unnecessary burdens on companies. To ensure this, draft regulations should be communicated to sector actors in advance, and opportunities for feedback should be provided. Regular sector roundtables involving all stakeholders could be used to achieve this. That being said, regulators must also be able to hold individual companies and their owners accountable. In sectors that require larger initial capital outlays, there may then well be a trade-off between minimum efficient scales and companies that are effectively too big to regulate.

DIFFERENTIATE COMPANIES

There can be huge differences between companies *within* a single sector in terms of both initial endowments and the speeds with which they are able to move up respective learning curves. A salient difference in the context of the Ethiopian economy is that between foreign- and domestic-owned companies. These will frequently face different challenges and require different types of support to succeed. Foreign companies often have greater access to capital resources and tend to have greater knowledge of relevant production systems and demand structures in final markets. Ethiopian-owned companies are often initially behind in these respects, but they tend to be much more familiar with the Ethiopian regulatory and legal framework within which they operate. To reach the greatest efficiency and effectiveness of support possible, some types of interventions should be tailored to these differentiated requirements. Difficult decisions also have to be made in considering how long to support ailing companies. Every company must be given a chance to move up the sector learning curve, and this will generally entail some false starts. But not every company will succeed, and some must be allowed to fail so that their capital can be put to more productive uses.

CONTINUOUS DIALOGUE

It is important to note that the lessons discussed here were drawn from the successes in fostering newly grown industries. As these industries achieve takeoff, mature, and face new and different challenges, industrial policy will have to change with them. In maturing industries, problems shift from capital formation and market making to upgrading and sustainability. For this to occur, industrial policy must move toward sustainable knowledge creation and training, as well as the implementation of labor and environmental standards to ensure the long-term viability of industries. Labor income acts as an important transmission mechanism for benefits to society, and government should consider policy levers such as minimum wage requirements to guarantee that expanding economic opportunities are translated into improving livelihoods. Labor standards are important to help ensure that success is not achieved on the backs of workers. To know when and how support must shift, it is important that regular channels of communication, but also of close monitoring and evaluation, are kept open between government and sector actors.

DEVELOPMENT FINANCE

Both sectors benefited from finance made available by the Development Bank of Ethiopia. DBE loans are slightly cheaper than commercial loans, but this is not why they are important. In many low-income countries, the private banking sector has neither the size nor the administrative capacity to lend to risky projects with long gestation periods, as characterized by the establishment of entirely new sectors or the comprehensive overhaul of existing ones. A state-owned development bank of sufficient size can shoulder such risks and, as we have seen, can even act as implicit insurance against external shocks. Crucially, though, such banks have to be able to work in close consultation with the sector to offer not just financial advice but also direct technical and commercial expertise. They will have to hire a broad selection of technical staff with sector-relevant knowledge, going far beyond financial specialists. Their staff should be embedded directly in larger clients and at the very least make regular visits to smaller borrowers. Working closely with private sector firms also gives development banks an important oversight role. They must be willing and able to enforce disciplinary measures against companies when necessary, and they should be sufficiently independent to terminate loans when companies are either unable or unwilling to perform.

NOTES

1. The GTP is the latest development plan initiated by the Ethiopian government and developed in consultation with the private sector and the public at large. The plan's main objective is to sustain the high and broad-based economic growth trajectory the country enjoyed from 2003 to 2010, with the aim of reducing poverty and ensuring a high standard of living.

2. The Export Trade Incentive Scheme Establishing Proclamation enacted in July 2001 introduced these two schemes, along with a range of other incentives. Investors engaged in the manufacturing sector with export licenses are eligible for the voucher scheme, and those who are wholly engaged in exporting their products but are not eligible for the voucher scheme can apply for the bonded warehouse facilities. The voucher scheme allows the investors to deposit the voucher with customs authorities and customs formalities to be carried out after raw materials (imported for producing exportable commodities) are kept in the private warehouse of the investor in the production site. This, while saving time on customs clearance procedures, enables duty-free importation and use of raw materials. Similarly, the bonded warehouse facility provides duty-free privileges for raw materials used for manufacturing exportable commodities and allows customs clearance activities to be carried out at the warehouse of the investor. This requires the physical presence of a customs officer whenever raw materials are removed from the warehouse for production.

3. The onslaught from foreign competition in the early 2000s was certainly the result of the liberalization policy that opened the Ethiopian market to cheap imports from more productive foreign producers. As ever in such cases, the longer-term costs to local productive capacities, with effects on employment, have to be weighed carefully against the benefit to consumers from cheaper commodities. In particular, the

questions should be whether the poorest benefit more from increased consumption through employment expansion or through cheaper goods. The answer may well depend on the timescale of the analysis.

4. It is not clear whether this is a condition imposed by the Ethiopian government, but it seems likely that this is the case.

5. The horticulture sector is one of the priority sectors identified in the five-year national plans, including the GTP. In addition, in the GTP there are eight priority industries for medium/large enterprises: textile and apparel, leather and leather products, sugar and sugar-related products, cement, metal and engineering, chemical, pharmaceutical, and agro-processing industries (FDRE 2010).

6. This has hardly changed since the early days of the emergence of the cut flower industry. While commercial banks have financed a few projects in the cut flower industry, these investments have faced difficulties due to the limited expertise and capability regarding the industry on the part of the financier. This has led the DBE to buy out some of the loans from the privately held commercial banks.

7. In Ethiopia, all land is ultimately owned by the government, but individuals hold land in forms of private quasi-ownership.

8. The EHPEA has recently taken the initiative to develop its own industrial code of practices with the aim of achieving global standards.

REFERENCES

Altenburg, T. 2010. "Industrial Policy in Ethiopia." Discussion paper, Deutsches Institut für Entwicklungspolitik 2: 0–34. http://dspace.cigilibrary.org/jspui /handle/123456789/28303.

Bekele, Mekonnen, and Gezahegn Ayele. 2008. "The Leather Sector: Growth Strategies through Integrated Value Chain." *EDRI: Research Report* 11 (June): 1–51.

Boer, Diederik de, and Stella Pfisterer. 2009. "Review of the WSSD Public-Private Partnership Program in Ethiopia: Final Report." *Expert Centre for Sustainable Business & Development Cooperation* (March): 1–58.

Central Statistical Agency (CSA). 2007. "Report on Large and Medium Scale Manufacturing and Electricity Industries Survey 2005–2006." *Statistical Bulletin* 403 (October): 1–209.

———. 2012. "Report on Large and Medium Scale Manufacturing and Electricity Industries Survey." *Statistical Bulletin* 531 (August): 1–229.

———. 2013. "Agricultural Sample Survey 2012/13 [2005 E.C.]: Report on Livestock and Livestock Characteristics (Private Peasant Holdings)." *Statistical Bulletin* 570 (2): 1–188.

Development Bank of Ethiopia (DBE). 2010. *Corporate Balanced Scorecard (2010–2015)*. Addis Ababa, Ethiopia: DBE.

Ethiopian Horticulture Development Agency (EHDA). 2009. "Performance Evaluation of the Ethiopian Floriculture Industry (Three DBE Client Farms Targeted as a Case Study)." (March): 1–35.

———. 2012. "Ethiopian Horticulture Sector Statistical Bulletin." Issue 01. Addis Ababa, Ethiopia: EHDA.

Federal Democratic Republic of Ethiopia (FDRE). 2010. *Growth and Transformation Plan (GTP)—Vol I: Main Text.* Government of Ethiopia, Addis Ababa, Ethiopia.

Gebreeyesus, Mulu, and Michiko Iizuka. 2010. "Discovery of the Flower Industry in Ethiopia: Experimentation and Coordination." *UNU-MERIT Working Paper Series,* 2010-025: 1–42.

Global Development Solutions (GDS). 2011. "Towards a Globally Competitive Ethiopian Economy: The Role of Services and Urbanization Case Studies—Rose and Polo Shirt Value Chains." (February 18): 1–78.

Lin, Justin, and Ha-Joon Chang. 2009. "Should Industrial Policy in Developing Countries Conform to Comparative Advantage or Defy it? A Debate Between Justin Lin and Ha-Joon Chang." *Development Policy Review* 27 (5): 483–502.

McMillan, Margaret. 2012. "The Role of Foreign Investment in Ethiopia's Leather Value Chain Lessons for Ghana." *Ghana Strategy Support Program* 22 (November): 1–5.

Mottaleb, Khondoker Abdul, and Tetsushi Sonobe. 2011. "An Inquiry into the Rapid Growth of the Garment Industry in Bangladesh." *Economic Development and Cultural Change* 60 (1): 67–89. http://www.jstor.org/stable/10.1086/661218.

Redi, Omer. 2009. "From Ashes, an Industry Reborn." *Addis Fortune* (March 22): 464.

Sonobe, Tetsushi, John E. Akoten, and Keijiro Otsuka. 2009. "An Exploration into the Successful Development of the Leather-Shoe Industry in Ethiopia." *Review of Development Economics* 13 (4): 719–736.

Taylor, B. 2010. "Labour Patterns in Export Floriculture: The Case of the Ethiopian Flower Industry." Conference paper prepared for the Working for Export Markets: Labour and Livelihoods in Global Production Networks Conference, University of Sussex, U.K., July 1–2.

United Nations Industrial Development Organization (UNIDO). 2012. "Technical Assistance Project for the Upgrading of the Ethiopian Leather and Leather Products Industry: Independent Evaluation Report." UNIDO project number TE/ETH/08/008.

Van der Loop, Theo. 2003. "The Importance of the Leather Footwear Sector for Development in Ethiopia." *RLDS Policy Brief* 1. Addis Ababa University, Ethiopia.

Wade, Robert. 1990. *Governing the Market: Economic Theory and the Role of Government in East Asian Industrialization.* Princeton: Princeton University Press.

World Bank. 2014. "3rd Ethiopia Economic Update: Strengthening Export Performance through Improved Competitiveness." June.

Zenawi, Meles. 2006. "African Development: A Policy Maker's Perspective." Speech to the Initiative for Policy Dialogue—Brooks World Poverty Institute Africa Task Force, Manchester University, U.K., August.

CHAPTER 6

The Return of Industrial Policy

(WHAT) CAN AFRICA LEARN FROM LATIN AMERICA?

Annalisa Primi

Africa is growing. The development debate in Africa has shifted from how to overcome poverty in a low-growth continent to how to profit from the high-growth momentum. The rise of China and its demand for raw materials have contributed, to a large extent, to the boost in growth and to the rise of dynamism in African markets. Poverty has been decreasing, access to information technologies has increased in most of the countries of the region, and new partners have emerged in trade and investment. Media, on their side, are playing their part portraying Africa as the next "booming" continent, with a growing and young population that could be a big reservoir for growth and development in the medium term. However, all that glitters is not gold, and Africa still suffers from deep structural problems (AfDB, OECD, UNDP, ECA 2012, 2013; ECA/AU 2013; ECA 2013, 2014). Youth employment is high and growing; middle classes are emerging with new demands and aspirations that need to be addressed. The African production structure is still weak, with few domestic companies operating at the technological frontier and with the majority of firms lagging behind in terms of productivity and innovative capabilities. Diversification and upgrading are, in fact, often confined to "islands of excellence" within the countries of the region.

While optimism regarding growth and development opportunities abounds, there is growing recognition that the new context is not a guarantee of structural transformation and job creation for Africa unless targeted policies are implemented (Chang 2012; Greenwald and Stiglitz 2012; Noman 2012; Noman et al. 2012; ECA 2013, 2014). In addition, the new global economic context is changing the debate on development policy and is reopening the debate on industrial policies. The Washington Consensus had wiped them away from the policy mix, but the new global economic context and the growing discontent with conventional economic approaches are contributing to bringing industrial policies back to the development agenda. Few would believe today that open and free global markets would allow each country to specialize in the "best" possible sector/activity. However, what to do and how to do it are questions with no easy answers (Lin and Chang, 2009). In Africa, in particular, most of the good practices and policy advice look even more difficult to implement: corruption, weak states, lack of public resources, low entrepreneurial culture, elites, and poor infrastructure and skills are often quoted as barriers to designing and implementing effective industrial policies in the countries of the region. This, matched with the recognition that "most of the policy tools applied by Southeast Asian economies during their catching up are not available anymore," turns industrial policy into an option with low feasibility and low political acceptability in many countries of the region. Yet things are changing (ECA 2014).

Industrial policy in the new global economic landscape is much more than the policies applied by Southeast Asian countries in the past. During the last decade there has been a resurgence of interest in industrial policy at the global level, in the Organization for Economic Co-operation and Development (OECD), and in developing countries (Cimoli, Dosi, and Stiglitz 2009; Naudé 2010; Lin 2012; OECD 2012a, 2013a). Latin America has often been regarded as a "failure" in contrast with the "success" of Southeast Asian economies.[1] However, the region has accumulated experience in the challenges of designing and then trying to implement industrial policies, and has advanced, particularly in the last decade, through a process of trial and error (Peres 2009; Peres and Primi 2009; Ocampo and Ros 2011; Devlin and Moguillansky 2012; Coutinho et al. 2012). Latin America is far from having solved its development problems, and it is still struggling to tackle inequalities and achieve economic transformation. But the region has been witnessing high growth, the emergence of new middle classes with new aspirations and demands, and a renewed commitment of many governments to promote science, technology, and innovation as pillars of new development strategies more in line with the new global economic landscape. Like Africa, Latin America is also varied, with countries that differ in endowments, geography, and institutions, as well as in size.

Can the recent experience of Latin America in industrial policies offer lessons for Africa? Policies are always time and context specific, but they are also shaped by regularities and general principles that make the sharing of practices and challenges in design and implementation a valuable exercise. The point is not to find shortcuts or easy answers but to enrich the policy framework through the experience of others, to identify lessons that can make the process of industrial policy planning and implementation more effective.

This chapter aims to contribute to the renewed debate on industrial policy in Africa. It focuses on the changing global economic landscape, as the setting in which Africa is developing, and it looks at the experience of Latin America to identify some principles that could be of help in the policymaking process in Africa. The chapter is structured in three sections. The first describes the changes in the global economic landscape, focusing on the new geography of growth, production, trade, and innovation. The second discusses the implications of the new global context on development policy and the resurgence of interest about industrial policies. The third section focuses on what lessons for Africa can be derived from the recent Latin American experience.

A CHANGING GLOBAL ECONOMIC LANDSCAPE

We are living in a fast-changing world, and our economies and societies are experiencing major transformations. Among the multiple (and interrelated) issues that are contributing to the redefinition of development opportunities today, I will recall two aspects that are, in my opinion, crucial to understand and contextualize the return of industrial policies on the development agenda and that are determining some of the major policy challenges that developing economies are facing today:

1. A new geography of growth, production, and trade is emerging due to the rise of China and its growing integration into world trade.
2. A new geography of innovation is emerging, too, but at a much slower pace. The increased diffusion of information technologies and the growing priority given to science and technology in emerging countries are defining new micro-dynamics of learning, knowledge circulation, and innovation and are contributing to the creation of new innovation hubs in the world. However, Africa, even in the renewed context, still lags behind other developing regions, including Latin America.

AN EVOLVING GEOGRAPHY OF GROWTH,
PRODUCTION, AND TRADE

Developing countries have been growing more than advanced economies since the late 1990s. Despite recent concerns about global economic slowdown, this trend is likely to continue, even though many
emerging economies will be advancing at a slower pace than their
previous two-digit growth pattern (OECD 2010, 2013a). This shift
of the center of gravity of the world economy toward the East (and
partially the South) has also contributed to make Africa the fastest
growing continent in the world (figure 6.1). The experience of many
countries has shown that growth is not enough for development, but
that it opens up opportunities for development and it challenges the
political economy's dynamics for industrialization in developing countries. Policy priorities (and consequent agreements and disagreements),
in fact, tend to change when investment options are discussed in low-
growth or high-growth contexts.

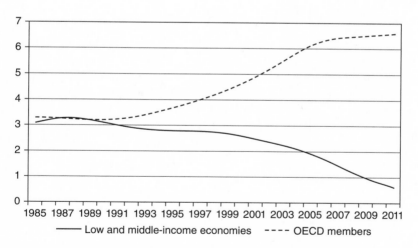

**Figure 6.1   Annual GDP growth rates by income group, 1985–2011;
smoothed rates**

Note: Chile, Mexico, and Turkey are included both in low- and middle-income economies
and in the OECD.

Source: OECD (2013a), based on World Development Indicators (2012) and OECD National
Accounts data files.

We are witnessing a new geography of growth. Growth poles are grow-ing in number and are increasingly localized in the East and the South. These changes are coming together with new forms of organization of production at a global scale and with new trade and investment pat-terns. Today China is the world's largest manufacturer. Its share of total world manufacturing value added (18.9 percent) outperformed that of the United States (18.2 percent) in 2010 (figure 6.2). Over two decades its share in world manufacturing output has increased sixfold. The rise of this giant is reshaping the global landscape, and countries are aware that they need to take this into account when designing their strategies for the future (Barros de Castro 2009; Castro and Castro 2012).

Manufacturing is not only shifting to China but is growing in many developing economies. In parallel, OECD countries are putting in place

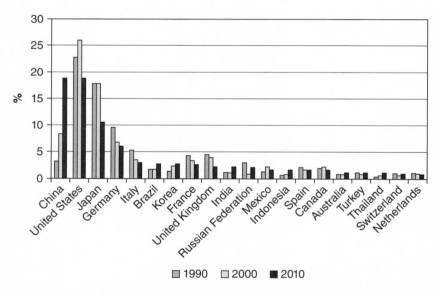

Figure 6.2   World top-twenty manufacturers, 2010; country share in total world manufacturing value added

Note: Manufacturing refers to industries belonging to International Standard Industrial Classification (ISIC) divisions 15–37. Value added is the net output of a sector after adding up all outputs and subtracting intermediate inputs. It is calculated without making deductions for depreciation of fabricated assets or depletion and degradation of natural resources. The origin of value added is determined by the ISIC, revision 3.

Source: OECD (2013a), based on United Nations Statistical Division, National Accounts Main Aggregates Database, March 2012.

new strategies for manufacturing to address the economic slowdown and preserve their leadership in technological development; for example, the Advanced Manufacturing Supply Chain Initiative in the United Kingdom and the U.S. Advanced Manufacturing Partnership. The share of non-OECD economies, without China, in total world manufacturing value added rose from 14 percent in 1990 to 20 percent in 2010 (UN, National Accounts Main Aggregates Database 2012). Even though Africa is suffering from deindustrialization, more recent trends indicate a renewed dynamism in the countries of the region. For example, Egypt, Morocco, and South Africa have much lower shares of manufacturing in their GDP than the OECD average, but their manufacturing output has been growing more rapidly than in OECD countries between 2005 and 2010 (figure 6.3).

These changes in growth and production are accompanied by growing trade among developing economies. China, India, and Brazil are emerging trade partners for Africa. India and Brazil increased their share of total African trade from 2.3 percent and 1.7 percent, respectively, in 2000 to 7 percent and 3 percent in 2011 (OECD 2013a). China accounted,

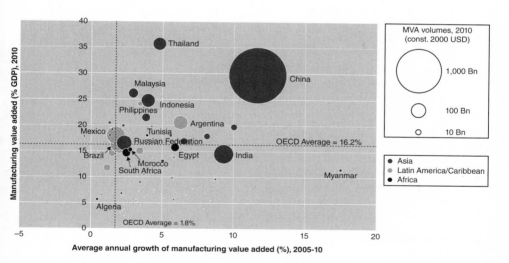

Figure 6.3   Manufacturing, intensity, and dynamism in developing economies, 2005–2010

Note: OECD average: Manufacturing value added (% GDP) = 2009 data or latest.

Source: OECD (2013a), based on UN National Accounts Main Aggregates Database, World Bank, World Development Indicators, and OECD STAN Database, for OECD average, July 2012.

in 2011, for 19 percent of total African exports, while in 2000 this share
was only 5 percent. African imports from China also grew from 5 percent
of total imports in 2000 to 17 percent in 2011 (OECD 2013a). China
has also started to generate foreign direct investment (FDI) outflows in
a growing number of African countries (figure 6.4). These new trade
partnerships could contribute to opening new technology transfer and
learning opportunities.

In addition, the emerging middle classes in developing economies
are expressing new and diversified demands, opening new consumer
markets to be captured. These new consumers represent an enormous potential, and companies will struggle to gain their confidence
and sell to them. This is happening not only in Asia but also in Latin
America and Africa. This rising demand can represent a strong incentive for domestic companies to develop new products and services and

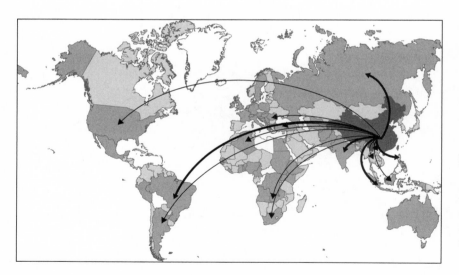

**Figure 6.4   Top fifteen destinations of Chinese foreign direct investment,
2003–2012**

Note: The size of the arrows indicates the number of jobs created by Chinese FDI from January
2003 to December 2012 in the top fifteen recipient countries. The graphic only includes data
from greenfield and expansion-related investments; merger and acquisition transactions are
not captured. This map is for illustrative purposes and is without prejudice to the status of or
sovereignty over any territory covered by this map.

Source: OECD (2013a), based on FDI Markets. A service from the Financial Times Ltd., 2012.

to customize existing solutions to domestic market needs. But the competition to gain those markets will be harsh. So far, established multinational companies have not been particularly active in targeting the emerging middle classes, but everything points to the fact that they will increasingly do so (McKinsey 2012). It is probable that multinational corporations (MNCs) will partner with local firms and institutions in order to penetrate the new market segments, thus opening potential learning opportunities in hosting economies.

A NEW GEOGRAPHY OF LEARNING AND INNOVATION IS EMERGING, TOO, BUT AT A MUCH SLOWER PACE

In addition to the new growth, production, and trade patterns, a new geography of innovation is emerging, but at a much slower pace. The diffusion of information technologies has contributed to increasing the possibilities for knowledge transfer. Learning is increasingly happening not only through market channels. The new forms of knowledge flows go beyond capital imports or FDI, happening through networks and growing mobility of skilled personnel as well. A growing number of cities and regions, hosting specific competences, are investing in "branding" themselves to reach out to new partners. In some cases these local efforts are coordinated with the country strategies; in others they are carried out in an autonomous way. The French city of Lyon, for example, hosts a cluster of companies with high-tech and logistical competences in urban lighting; the city is involved in a knowledge transfer partnership with some cities in Vietnam willing to implement new forms of urban lighting. This is not an isolated trend; in the new global context, new forms of partnership are developing by which highly localized competences and businesses can establish global partnerships to open new business and learning opportunities. But often only the localities with empowered governments and with at least basic capabilities are taking advantage of these new opportunities.

A growing number of developing economies are becoming attractive locations for research and innovation. For example, a rising number of research and development (R&D) centers have been opened in emerging and developing countries thanks to a mix of public policies and new business strategies of MNCs that increasingly perceive developing economies as future markets. These actions have opened opportunities for learning and accumulating capacities in developing economies that were not

available during the first generation of FDI, which only included delo-
calization of the lowest levels of production phases. However, the debate
on re-shoring in some leading manufacturing economies could change
the setting in this realm, calling for new and quicker policy responses in
emerging economies.

Developing countries are also increasing their investment in skills,
science, and technology. Nonetheless, the gap with OECD countries
persists (figure 6.5). China is emerging as an innovator. Its image as a
low-cost competitor is still present, but it is not predominant anymore.
Chinese factories have accumulated capabilities and learning and are
now moving up in the value chains. China more than doubled R&D
expenditures over the last decade and in 2009 invested 1.5 percent of its
GDP in R&D (the OECD average for the same year was 2.3 percent),
and it is increasing its training of technical workers and scientific and
engineering personnel. In Latin America, innovation is, at least in terms
of declarations, a key priority for most countries (Primi 2014). However,
the countries of the region are far from the OECD average in R&D

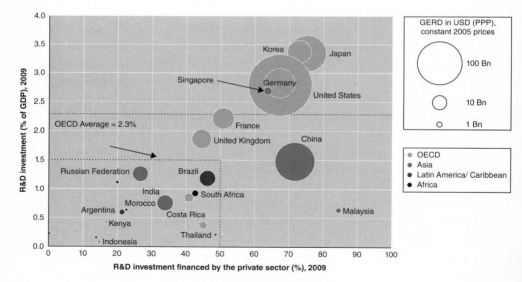

**Figure 6.5 R&D intensity and private sector commitment in selected countries,
2009**

Note: 2009 or latest available year.

Sources: OECD (2013a), based on OECD MSTI Database for OECD countries, RICYT for Latin
America and the Caribbean, RICYT and UNESCO for other countries.

expenditures, patents, and trademarks. Brazil, for example, is the leading country in the region, and its investment in R&D was 1.2 percent of GDP in 2010. Africa lags behind; investment in R&D, patents, and trademarks is minimal when compared to other regions. The majority of African countries invest little in R&D, and the private sector hardly engages in innovation activities. No African country devotes more than 1 percent of GDP to R&D, and most of the financing comes from the public sector.

CHANGES IN DEVELOPMENT POLICY AND THE "RETURN" OF INDUSTRIAL POLICY

THE QUEST FOR NEW FORMS OF ECONOMIC THINKING

The new geography of growth, trade, and innovation is not only changing development opportunities, it is also contributing to the redefinition of development policy and the development agenda. On the one hand, there are emerging global development challenges like health and environment that are calling for new forms of global governance. On the other hand, there is wide consensus that growth, albeit necessary, cannot be an end in itself. Growth needs to be inclusive and sustainable, not only for reasons of external pressures but also for growing internal demands. The new "middle classes" and the growing young populations in emerging and developing countries are increasingly expressing new aspirations and demands, putting pressures on national policy choices, and calling for new responses to increase their opportunities and achieve better lives. These new demands represent a growing source of pressure for governments in emerging and developing economies to shift toward new development models that match global aspirations with local needs. Examples of these trends range from the growing demand for better and fairer education in Chile, a high-growth country in Latin America that performs well in exports, to the call for social and economic fairness expressed by society during the Arab Spring.

On the finance side, countries are discussing how to close the financial gap and mobilize new sources of finance for development. The project of the BRICS bank could represent a major novelty in development finance (and hence in priorities for investment); however, the agreement between these emerging countries will require some time, as many fear the potential predominance of China in this sphere. In addition, the 2008 financial and economic crisis has contributed to shaking the fundamentalism in beliefs in free markets and has reopened a debate on the role of the state in contemporary capitalist economies (Skidelsky 2009; Griffith-Jones, Ocampo, and Stiglitz 2010). A growing quest for new forms of economic thinking and policy models is arising in OECD and non-OECD countries due to the growing recognition that markets alone do not always perform optimally for the society.

As the promises of the Washington Consensus were not fulfilled, from the 2000s onward developing countries have started to look at new development models. The rise of political leadership concerned with the welfare impact of traditional market-led growth policies together with the growing discontent with conventional growth recipes and the more ambitious demands and aspirations of the societies in developing countries are concurring to define a new landscape in which the trust in self-correcting markets is being questioned, or at least not automatically assumed as the reference for policy action. On the one hand, this has implied the return to classical ideas of economic development, including the recognition that production activities differ in their capacity to generate linkages and raise aggregate productivity, and a growing attention toward the role of demand, especially the domestic role of demand. But it has also required searching for new policy models capable of taking into account the specificities of the new landscape, characterized by the increasing relevance of (local, regional, and international) networks for production and innovation, higher speed of diffusion of information (when not of knowledge), and higher mobility of capital and talents.

How the changing economic landscape will affect development policy is still to be clarified on many fronts (including the future of aid, development finance, and development cooperation priorities). However, a major difference with respect to the previous decades has already emerged: production structure (that is, what countries produce and trade and how they organize these processes) is back on the development agenda. Production structure is, once again, seen as an essential determinant of growth, productivity, and income distribution. Even the discussion on the post–2015 development agenda has revealed that neglecting the "production and structural side" in the first generation of MDGs was a weakness that needed to be addressed in the next generation of development goals because often poverty and inequality outcomes are shaped by structural issues. However, there is also a growing recognition that the development debate and the challenges differ today from the ones of the 1950s and 1960s, when the structural issues were at the core of the development agenda. Today the level of integration of global economies (especially on the financial side) is much higher, thus requiring different types of policy approaches. On the other hand, the diffusion of information technologies has deeply changed the speed of information flows, thus creating new pressures for the accountability of policy actions.

THE RESURGENCE OF INTEREST
IN INDUSTRIAL POLICIES

Together with the renewed interest in the "structural" dimension of development comes the resurgence of interest in industrial policy. After its golden age—which spanned from the 1940s to the 1970s—industrial policy was banned from development strategies in the name of structural adjustment programs. From the late 1940s onward, the majority of developing economies had put in place strategies, with mixed results, to foster the creation of endogenous technological and production capabilities to shift from agricultural to industrialized societies (Amsden 1989; Wade 1990; Reinert 2007). With the upsurge of the debt crisis, the development agenda shifted from policies to foster structural change and productivity catch-up to narrowing poverty gaps. Poverty was considered as an area that needed targeted strategies and active policy support, while the development of industrial capabilities was assumed to be an automatic process guaranteed by open capital and good markets that, once freed from the ties of state intervention and regulation, would have conduced countries to specialize in exporting what they were best at. This was not the case in practice. While structural adjustment programs and globalization contributed to macroeconomic stability and fostered modernization of production activities, they also brought about job losses and the dismantling of production and institutional capabilities in key manufacturing and technology areas, contributing to the truncation of the state-led industrialization efforts started in many developing economies in the previous decades (Fajnzylber 1983).

The resurgence of interest in industrial policy does not mean that the controversy surrounding it is over. But it seems that after decades of "good" and "bad" examples of industrial policies and in the presence of a new, more challenging economic landscape, the discussion is shifting to a more pragmatic level in which economists and policymakers discuss not the need (or lack thereof) of industrial policy but what to do and how to do it (Chang 2011). Somehow there has been a convergence toward recognizing that state intervention is needed in order to engender processes of structural change and to favor the transition of the economy toward superior stages of development in which rents are extracted more from knowledge than from capital accumulation or raw materials (Reinert 2007; Cimoli, Ferraz, and Primi 2009; Chang 2012; Lin 2012).

A major novelty in the current debate about industrial policies is the growing recognition that they are more diffused and varied in implementation than what was assumed by the conventional approach. Industrial policies today are, in fact, much more than a "Southeast Asian phenomenon." The interest for industrial policies today is coming from different countries in different ways (Rodrik 2004; Chang 2011; Cimoli, Dosi, and Stiglitz 2009; Noman 2012; ECLAC 2012; Lin 2012; OECD 2012a and 2013a). China is a peculiar case: it has been implementing industrial policy for a long time, mixing open economy approaches with strategic management of accumulation of capabilities and technology transfer for domestic learning. Most Southeast Asian economies are implementing production transformation strategies, each with a peculiar focus: Malaysia is fostering FDI spillovers and SMEs development, Singapore is promoting technological upgrading and global integration, and Korea is focusing on promoting national champions and the development of new key technologies.

A growing number of OECD countries are reopening the debate on industrial policies due to the long-lasting effects of the 2008 economic and financial crisis (OECD 2012a). Austria, France, and the United Kingdom are implementing new industrial policies to boost the competitiveness of their domestic industries and to create better jobs. The United States is crafting new strategies to face the increasingly competitive global scenario by implementing new manufacturing and innovation initiatives to strengthen the national production and technology clusters, as well as by promoting the creation of new U.S.-based firms. In Latin America, the return of industrial policy predated the 2008 financial and economic crises. Brazil has relaunched its industrial policy in 2003 and since then has been refining the institutional and financial arrangement for its production transformation strategy based on technological upgrading, diversification, and specialization. Industrial policy is also rebounding in Africa (ECA 2014). South Africa has a multi-annual Industrial Policy Action Plan (Zalk 2012), and Morocco is implementing a new industrial policy to better leverage, growing FDI in key strategic sectors like the car industry. Ethiopia is pursuing industrial policies with particular success, as some of the other contributions to this volume point out. Senegal is planning to re-create a national development bank to channel resources to production development, just to name few examples.

Several issues are contributing to the resurgence of interest in industrial policy in developing economies:

1. Inclusive and sustained growth is not a low-hanging fruit for most countries. Globalization and the development of China open new opportunities and threats for developing economies, and it is requiring new strategic approaches to grasp the benefits of the new scenario (Dahlman 2011). The China effect varies according to each country. In natural resource–rich economies, it is contributing to sustained growth, fostering new investment flows, and contributing to the new dynamisms in African markets, but it is also reinforcing specialization in raw materials and challenging the survival of low-cost assembly and manufacturing in most developing economies, calling for new development strategies. The rise of China is pushing countries to look at trade, manufacturing, and defense at new angles due to the changes in the global geopolitical order. Creating and retaining manufacturing, technological, and scientific capabilities is becoming more difficult, and it is rising up in countries' priorities.

2. Growth in emerging and developing economies has also opened spaces for proactive policies that were not available in the 1980s and 1990s. In Brazil, it allowed boosting investment for production development and social inclusion, contributing to the creation of incentives both on the supply side and the demand side since the early 2000s. In Colombia, the increase of revenues from natural resources has recently contributed to the reopening of the debate on the competitiveness strategy and on how to channel funds from natural resource extraction to support innovation and regional development. The coming into power of political leaderships in favor of a proactive role of the state in fostering structural change also contributed to the creation of pressures to design and implement industrial policies in countries like Brazil and South Africa.

3. The costs of low industrial and innovation capabilities became more visible. No country has developed without the creation of a sound and productive scientific and manufacturing base (Amsden 1989; Wade

1990; Chang 1994, 2002; Reinert 2007; Cimoli, Dosi, and Stiglitz 2009; Lin 2012). This is even truer in global economies. The existence of knowledge-based capabilities is the precondition for grasping the benefits of global markets. The issue is not merely to be a part of value chains but to be in a position that allows the capture of most of their value. Manufacturing has been changing in nature and cannot be the only locus for absorbing the rising mass of workers, neither in OECD nor in emerging markets (IDA 2012). But it is a key area for creating better jobs, promoting productivity growth, and engendering linkages with other sectors. History shows that manufacturing is the key to contributing to and sustaining growth and productivity and that it fosters the accumulation and diffusion of technical change. Advanced economies are also increasingly worried about their loss of manufacturing competences, especially in the aftermath of the 2008 financial and economic crisis (OECD 2012a; IDA 2012).

When governments envisage a more proactive role of the state in the economy, the risks of capture and rent mismanagement are of course high. Policymakers and the public administration are aware of the major bottlenecks in the policy processes and of the difficulties in implementing industrial policies. But many developing countries are focusing on how institutions and performance-based management schemes can help to maximize the effectiveness of government intervention to reduce lock in and capture, instead of preaching for a minimalist policy approach to avoid mistakes and failures.

In the last decade many developing countries have designed and implemented new industrial policies in a variety of ways. In general, industrial policies involve a set of actions directed toward changing the prevailing specialization pattern of a country over the medium and long term by increasing the rents derived from knowledge and innovation with respect to the ones deriving from the extensive use of raw material and labor. Industrial policies include government actions designed to support the creation of endogenous production and technological capabilities in areas that are considered strategic for national development. The identification of these activities is country and time specific, but it is also based on the emulation of successful cases (Chang 1994; Reinert 2007; Cimoli, Dosi, and Stiglitz 2009).

By observing the conception and practice of industrial policies in different countries, we see that the production development initiatives

Table 6.1 Main features of contemporary industrial policies

Policy Model Governance	**Plan-based:** Formalized in national development plans/strategies. *Ex. Brazil, India, Korea, South Africa*	**Top-down:** Low responsibilities for regional/local governments. *Ex. South Africa*
		Mixed: Coexistence of national and regional/local initiatives. *Ex. China, Brazil, Italy*
	Initiative-based: Based on multiple government-led initiatives. *Ex. United States*	**Bottom-up:** High responsibilities for regional/local governments. *Ex. Germany, Spain, India*
Priorities/Scope	**Traditional**	**Growth; Job creation; International competitiveness**
	Emerging	**Territorial inclusion and competitiveness; Social inclusion; Sustainable/green economy**
Objectives	**Diversification** (entry in new sectors/types of activities)	
	Specialization and upgrading (scaling up in local and/or global value chains)	
	Increasing the density of the production system (fostering entrepreneurship, linkages, networks)	
Policy Mix	**Industrial policy tools *strictu-sensu*** (direct and indirect incentives to firms; business regulation)	**Infrastructure building and upgrading** **Financing** (development banks)
	Trade policy and FDI	**Macroeconomic policy** (i.e., exchange and interest rate management
	Support to science and technology	**Competition policy**
	Skills development	

FDI: foreign direct investment

differ or resemble across countries because of governance, priorities, objectives, and policy mix (table 6.1). Some countries have a centralized/plan-based industrial policy model. Targets are set and objectives and lines of action are formalized in national plans. This is the case in many East Asian economies, as well as in Brazil, Morocco, and South Africa. The countries without a formalized "industrial policy plan" or strategy implement de facto industrial policies through several initiatives, financing research and technology transfer, setting up regulations that favor certain types of agents over others, and promoting trade in specific industries. This is, for example, the case of the United States, where industrial policy follows a "decentralized/initiative-based" approach in which a variety of federal- and state-led programs and initiatives contribute to the establishment of a preference for the U.S. industry, including the intellectual property regimes and some of its provisions, such as the Bayh-Dole Act (Cimoli, Coriat, and Primi 2009; Block and Keller 2011).

Industrial policy often has a strong regional and/or local component. In some countries, a bottom-up approach prevails in which most competences at the level of industrial and technological capabilities are managed at the subnational level: Germany and India are cases in point. Other countries follow a more top-down approach with reduced margin of maneuver for regional and/or local authorities, as happens in South Africa. In other cases, a more mixed approach prevails in which national initiatives coexist in a more or less coordinated way with regional actions. This is the case in China, Brazil, and Italy, for example.

In addition, industrial policy needs to deal with the issue of the greening of the economy. The green economy represents a potential new paradigm for which industries need to be prepared (Mathews 2012). Not all will be leaders in green production and technologies, but there are windows of opportunities for first comers in this area that should not be disregarded by developing countries. In fact, developing economies include territorial and social inclusion (for example, Brazil and India) and green (for example, China and South Africa) as priorities in their industrial policies.

Developing countries often face multiple challenges when designing their industrial policies. Some industrial policy actions aim at diversifying the production structure, contributing to the creation of capacities in new economic sectors (for example, electronics, pharmaceuticals, biotechnology, etc.), or in new types of activities (for example, design, research and development, value-added services, etc.). Other actions aim at fostering the specialization and upgrading of existing activities and sectors. This means favoring modernization of production, increased efficiency, and improved performance of existing companies and clusters of entire sectors. But industrial policy also aims at strengthening the density of a production system by fostering entrepreneurship, networks, and collaborations on the basis of the recognition that more dense systems are more resilient, innovative, and productive. This also implies including specific policies to address the drawback of persistent informality in developing countries (Srinivas 2012). Each of the objectives poses specific challenges to the policymakers: How should the beneficiaries and stakeholders be identified? Which incentives are needed to get them interested in the policy, and which forms of dialogue are better suited to foster the necessary public-private partnership required for going from design to implementation?

Industrial policy is often nested in a strategic vision about the country's development path. The ultimate goal is not to strengthen specific economic actors (whether large or small firms or clusters) or sectors; the objective should be to activate learning, to achieve higher growth, and to create better jobs. This strategic dimension of industrial policy requires actions in multiple fields. For an industrial policy to be effective, targeted actions in finance, skills, infrastructure, and trade are needed, as well as alignment with macroeconomic and competition policy. This systemic dimension is often difficult to achieve, but it is what ultimately determines the effectiveness of industrial policy in the medium and long term.

(WHAT) CAN AFRICA LEARN FROM THE RECENT LATIN AMERICAN EXPERIENCE IN INDUSTRIAL POLICY?

There are no blueprints for designing and implementing a "good" industrial policy. Each country will need to identify its own approach, taking into account its vision for development and its endowments and challenges. However, countries can learn from the experience of others. We are often told by experts on Africa that "Africa has another history, challenges and heritage" and thus that most policy recommendations valid in other parts of the world do not apply. Africa is highly heterogeneous; it includes small and large economies, natural resource–rich and -poor countries, landlocked countries and islands, and countries at war and countries that are consolidating their democratic systems. Even though every country is unique and faces challenges that require a context-specific approach, lessons can be learned from the experiences of others.

Countries learn how to implement policy by trial and error and by accumulating knowhow and expertise. The past and the current successful cases show that industrial policy works better when it has clear priorities, is capable of getting a constructive dialogue between the public and the private sectors, and mobilizes investments in bundles in critical areas, including infrastructure, skills, and finance. Because some Southeast Asian countries have been successful in implementing industrial policies and achieving structural transformation, it is common to look at their experience and try to identify lessons for other developing countries. Often the "success" of the East Asian experience is confronted with the perceived "failure" of Latin America. However, Latin America has also accumulated relevant learning in the political economy of industrial policies, not only in the past, but also in the last decade. The region has witnessed a (slow) return of industrial policies (Peres 2009). The fact that industrial policies are back in the region to a different extent and under different forms is not proof of their effectiveness and good management; structural transformations tend to occur over decades, and often industrial policies deliver results in the medium and long run. But lessons can be learned from the recent experience of Latin American countries in designing industrial policies in the new and changing economic landscape.

The learning in industrial policies in Latin America can contribute to Africa's debate for several reasons. Both regions have been growing since the late 1990s and are facing the challenge of sustaining this growth and reducing inequalities in the long run. They are both influenced by the new trends in their traditional OECD trade partners and in their emerging partners, which are redefining their development opportunities. In addition, they are both profiting from a good global momentum in which windows of opportunity for newcomers seem to be more accessible due to (1) increased diffusion of information and communications technology (ICT), (2) emerging global challenges such as the search for new and renewable energy sources and greener production and consumption modes, and (3) changes in the organization of production at a global level, with growing specialization opportunities. In addition, countries in Latin America and in Africa are increasingly involved in developing new visions for their development in the context of new societal demands and growing concern about equity. Most countries in the two regions have in fact suffered from a process of institutional weakening in the realm of science, technology, and production in the aftermath of the structural reforms, and are now facing the challenge of designing and implementing industrial policies with old or weak institutions.

Since the 2000s, Latin America has witnessed a resurgence of interest in industrial policies. Brazil has been the pioneer, with the Integrated Industrial, Technology, and Trade Policy introduced in 2003 that evolved into the Production Development Policy in 2008 and in the *Plano Brasil Maior* in 2012. Other countries in the region have had a more shy approach toward explicitly using the term *industrial policy*, but in practice sectoral technology initiatives and government incentives to promote domestic scientific, technological, and industrial development have been strengthened in most countries of the region. Argentina, for example, created its Ministry for Science, Technology, and Productive Innovation in 2007, signaling the willingness of the country to increasingly shift toward a more knowledge-based growth pattern. Chile has focused on promoting industrial clusters and has made new government funds available to promote innovation by utilizing rents from mining.

The return of industrial policy comes in a new and rapidly evolving global context that calls for new policy approaches. The reshaping of the global development landscape and the rise of China are neither a blessing nor a curse for developing countries. In the medium and long term, much of the global impact on other emerging and developing economies will depend on the strategies and policies they will implement in the short and medium term. If the ultimate goal of industrial policy is still sustaining growth, productivity, and employment, countries today need to do it by operating in global knowledge economies and by fostering social and territorial inclusion, as well as the greening of production and consumption modes. The broadening scope of industrial policy and the increased interdependency of economic agents pose new challenges to the creation and retention of production and knowledge capabilities. How better to tap into the resources and competences available elsewhere? How better to create the incentives to go beyond easy short-term gains and engage in the costly and painstaking effort of building domestic capabilities?

Latin American countries are recognizing the importance of strengthening their production and innovation capacities. Despite the still prevailing suspiciousness about the risks of failure of industrial policy, the wind is changing. The new context and the increased availability of information about countries' strategies are showing that a great deal of state intervention is needed to back up private sector dynamics and to boost development. In the last decade, several emerging and developing economies reengaged in active industrial policies in Africa, Asia, and Latin America. Many lessons could be drawn from the "dos" and "don'ts" in Latin America. Taking into account the current debate in Africa, the following eight points on the political economy of industrial policy seem the most relevant.

REHABILITATING THE PLANNING FUNCTION IN GOVERNMENTS

Industrial policy is back in Latin America, but with different strengths and nuances in the different countries. Brazil is the country that more openly speaks about its industrial policy; however, most Latin American countries have reinforced government actions to strengthen domestic entrepreneurial activities and/or to promote a better inclusion in global value chains by promoting new forms of FDI and by increasing support to science and innovation in the last decade. Achieving structural transformation in Latin American countries means overcoming several barriers such as low skills, poor infrastructure, low demand, and scant financing, for example. Critics often argue that getting all these conditions right is a luxury that most developing countries cannot afford. But clarifying the objectives of structural transformation helps reveal the barriers and create a demand for articulating the necessary actions.

Regardless of the specific country approach, the countries of the region are facing a major governance challenge in rehabilitating the planning functions in countries where these capabilities were reduced due to the extensive application of the structural reforms packages of the 1990s. In the last decade, Argentina, Brazil, Chile, and smaller countries like Costa Rica have restrengthened their planning functions by creating interministerial bodies for policy coordination. The institution of these councils is not a guarantee of their capacity to operate, but when matched by presidential commitment they help create spaces for aligning the actions of different ministries to the objective of structural transformation and production upgrading. In certain cases they can help in building trust and alignment with the Ministries of Finance, which often are the most averse to endorsing production transformation strategies.

RECOGNIZING THAT IT IS POSSIBLE (AND LEGITIMATE) TO GO BEYOND CURRENT COMPARATIVE ADVANTAGES

The heritage of the structural reforms has contributed to the induction of a generalized perception that production activities and sectors are all alike and that deliberate efforts to "build" competences in given technological and production fields were doomed to failure. However, one of the most welcomed changes in the policy discussion in Latin America in the post–Washington Consensus period has been the return of the sectoral dimension in innovation and competitiveness strategies; that is, sectors differ in their impact on aggregate productivity, in intersectoral technological spillovers, and in the ways in which they create, absorb, and diffuse knowledge. Hence policies need to openly take into account the sectoral dimension.

However, many countries in Latin America struggle when it comes to deciding how to prioritize actions. Often policymakers feel more comfortable (or face less opposition) when dealing with horizontal measures. The discussion on how ambitious the policy should be and how far from existing assets and competences a country should go are controversial issues. A large economy like Brazil, with a quite articulated industrial matrix and a young and growing population, is putting in place a strategy (Plano Brasil Maior) with multiple targets: some incentives target the creation of frontier knowledge and technology, others aim at boosting the competitiveness of existing sectors, and others target priority sectors like energy and health. For smaller economies, the issue is more challenging. Costa Rica has opted for a competitiveness model that focuses of the attraction of FDI as a lever to transform the economy, while Chile has followed a softer approach by promoting cluster development in areas in which the country already had some advantages and capabilities (copper and mining, wine, and ICT, among others). Despite the efforts, structural heterogeneity persists. In many cases, some firms operate at the frontier and are well integrated in global production networks. Yet most of the domestic firms are small and characterized by low productivity and reduced international competitiveness when they do not operate in conditions of informality. The experience of Latin American countries shows that horizontal measures have limited impact in contexts characterized by high structural heterogeneity.

The return of industrial policy is contributing to the redefinition of the development debate and to the relegitimization of the interventions to create new capabilities. This can be done in several ways: by promoting the upgrading and diversification of existing companies, fostering the creation of new companies, and strategically dealing with foreign ones. While there is disagreement on how to choose the direction of technical change and who should do it, there is consensus on the fact that the new context opens opportunities for going beyond the current specialization pattern. Countries can mobilize different levers for strengthening capabilities, including financing of science and technology development, public procurement, FDI, and entrepreneurship promotion. Those instruments are not novel but can be designed in new ways to be in line with the new scenario and thus be more effective.

Science, technology, and innovation do not receive the same attention in all Latin American countries. Some countries are trying to exploit the synergies between industrial development and promotion of science, technology, and innovation. Brazil is a case in point in which the partnership among the Ministry of Science and Technology, Ministry of Development, Industry, and Foreign Trade, and the Brazilian Development Bank (BNDES) is an advance in institutional design. Fostering science, technology, and innovation requires new spaces for vertical and horizontal coordination. Innovation is increasingly a cross-cutting issue in the agendas of different sectoral ministries (such as health, energy, environment, and education) beyond its traditional role of development in agriculture and manufacturing. There is an increasing need for more coordination among different sectoral agendas (of the various ministries) to increase the effectiveness of public action. Brazil has responded to these challenges by creating coordination mechanisms between innovation policy and productive development policy. At the same time, in line with the recent national strategy for growth with social inclusion, the Ministry of Science and Technology has supported the strengthening of institutions in Brazil's federal states in order to promote production structure diversification and to increase the country's scientific, technological, and productive strength.

Among some of the recent tools that Latin American countries are introducing to foster the strengthening of domestic innovation capabilities and sustain learning processes are the following:

- The strategic management of FDI. While in the past FDI was considered a potential threat for the creation of endogenous technological and production capabilities, many countries in Latin America are now trying to profit from the new generation of FDI. Companies have, in fact, started to delocalize not only assembly functions but also more knowledge-intensive activities, including design, testing, and R&D. Some countries in the region have started to put in place incentives to attract these types of FDI and to promote the generation of backward and forward linkages with the local economy. Costa Rica is probably the best-known example in the region (OECD 2012b), but some states in Brazil and Chile have also been active in this field, accumulating institutional capacities to negotiate with investors.

- Public procurement that until few years ago was a taboo is now starting to be included among the tools to strengthen the domestic industry and to attain social goals (for example, in the health care sector). Often it is used in areas like health, defense, infrastructure, and energy in which there are high social and economic issues at stake, and in which in general the state is involved with the research, use, service delivery, and/or production. However, the effective management of public procurement requires strong government capabilities and appropriate legal frameworks. Often there are controversies, especially from foreign companies that clamor for the application of the WTO principle of equal treatment. Developing countries would benefit from building institutional capabilities at the national, regional, and local levels to allow policy learning in the management of public procurement (Kattel and Lember 2010).

- A recent and fashionable trend in Latin America is the setting up of programs to promote the creation of start-ups. These have low operation costs and are contributing to the creation of an image of Latin America as a new place for innovation (OECD 2013b). Initiatives of this type are flourishing in many countries in the region, including Brazil, Chile, Colombia, and Peru. Some are more oriented toward the attraction of foreigners with entrepreneurial skills and experience, like the Chilean program. Others, like the Brazilian program, target mostly national entrepreneurs, even though 25 percent of total beneficiaries can be from outside the country.

A major puzzle for Latin America, as well as for Africa, is how to promote the transformation and the upgrading of the agricultural sector while promoting diversification and industrialization. Brazil offers an interesting example. In the 1970s, Brazil had instituted a National Corporation for Agricultural Research (EMBRAPA), a public company in charge of carrying out frontier research to increase the productivity of the national agro-industrial production, while at the same time preserving the environment. The organization is financed by the general government budget, but it is also allowed to receive additional contributions from external partners, including multilateral financing agencies, private companies, and foundations. EMBRAPA is managed with high research standards, but it is strongly oriented toward technology transfer and productive application. It works both with small rural producers and in partnership with large domestic and foreign companies. The work with local producers relied on the existence of rural extension services that have been closed or impoverished by the structural reforms, inducing EMBRAPA to develop ways to share solutions with agricultural producers. Some of its offices had to develop new "mobile units" that travel to the regions and help the small producers introduce the innovations in their processes.

FINDING APPROPRIATE SOURCES OF FINANCE AND TAILORING FINANCING SCHEMES TO THE NEEDS OF BENEFICIARIES

The recent experience of Latin America shows that long-term financing schemes are necessary. Industrial policy needs to get the private sector on board, and for this long-term and stable financing are required.

Development banks can be powerful allies in channeling financial resources to production development and innovation. But these institutions need to introduce innovations in their management and operational routines to be able to foster innovation and operate in a fast-changing environment. For example, in Brazil the National Development Bank (BNDES) is a key actor in the design and implementation of the national industrial and innovation policies. The bank has introduced new procedures to evaluate intangibles in order to be more capable of screening projects with higher innovation potential, and it has introduced new tools for targeting the different demands. For example, a key challenge for Brazil is increasing SME financing. Not only is scanning and evaluating credit requests for SMEs challenging and time consuming, it also requires multiple operations that could result in delays that actually inhibit the operation of the firms and their investment in innovative projects. The BNDES has introduced a credit card for SMEs (*cartão* BNDES) that allows them to easily access the government's credit lines in a quicker and safer way, through credit cards operated by other first-tier banks.

Latin American countries have also developed new forms of partnership with the private sector to match funds and finance innovation and production development. On the one hand, some countries have introduced sectoral technology funds to finance mission-oriented research programs and innovation projects in fields of strategic importance (for example, oil, energy, and water management in Brazil, and software and biotechnology in Argentina). Sectors matter for industrial policy because production, technology, and innovations have specific organizational, technical, skills, and infrastructure requirements that are highly sector specific. These financing systems that channel private and public resources to innovation projects are operative in Argentina, Brazil, and Mexico, among other countries in the region. Brazil has a system of sectoral technology funds that has financed R&D and innovation in specific sectors by matching public and private resources since 1999 (Cimoli, Ferraz, and Primi 2005, 2009; Primi 2014). The existence of these funds is contributing to the building of partnerships and trust between universities and the private sector. The operation of these funds is complex because they require coordination between industry and academy. The experience of Brazil has shown that time is needed to develop trust, and that these funds work better when they mobilize a sufficient critical mass of financial resources; if they are too little, transaction costs are too high.

Natural resource–abundant countries have also introduced new forms of financing for innovation. The rising prices of raw materials created opportunities for extracting rents from these activities and channeling them to development. In 2005, Chile issued a law to channel royalties from mining exploration to a public fund for innovation (Primi 2014). Colombia and Peru have introduced similar mechanisms. The use of this source of finance for production development and diversification requires addressing the territorial dimension because consensus is needed both on the sectoral allocation of those resources and on their territorial destination. The communities hosting the natural resource–related activities claim rights on the use of those resources, and consensus-building efforts are needed. While the creation of funds based on natural resource rents is a step in the right direction, it is not a panacea. The design and management of those financing schemes is complex and requires strong learning processes both at the central and at the regional levels. Strong political leadership and long-term support are required to allow the mechanisms to function and be effective.

CLARIFYING WHO THE STAKEHOLDERS ARE AND BUILDING TRUST

In Latin America, a major challenge is to identify the stakeholders and the beneficiaries of the industrial policy initiatives, as well as to get a consensus for these policies in context with big social and poverty challenges. The conformation of the "elite" challenges the capacity of industrial policy to get the private sector on board and to establish a pact for national development. Often the "elite" is well connected with foreign stakeholders but shows a low level of trust in domestic financing and production agents. Today the option of picking a few national companies as major beneficiaries and stakeholders of the policy would not be feasible. Not only is the context characterized by a variety of agents that the policy is called to act upon, but it would not be socially sustainable to make industrial policy a "policy for the few." Even accepting that a degree of concentration of efforts and resources is needed because scattered interventions are inefficient, the new industrial policy needs to be inclusive. Countries need to decide how to deal with a variety of stakeholders, including SMEs, start-ups, and foreign companies operating in the country with the nationals installed abroad. A key challenge for Africa and for Latin America is how to create the incentives for the creation and strengthening of a national entrepreneurial class. It is not only about having companies operating in the country; it is about creating a system in which nationals can grow as Schumpeterian entrepreneurs.

MOBILIZING REGIONS AND TERRITORIES AS AGENTS OF CHANGE

The return of industrial policy in Latin America is characterized by a growing attention to the "territory." In the past, industrial policies have often been territory blind. Today this option is not sustainable and not desirable. In some countries in Latin America, including Chile, Colombia, and Peru, the willingness to channel resources from the mining sector toward innovation is helping to create a demand for strengthening institutions at the regional level. In Argentina and Brazil, the governments are increasingly concerned about promoting a more balanced development pattern and finding new sources of growth in provinces and states.

Regions and cities can be powerful additional sources of growth and innovation, while industrialization needs to take into account its impact on urbanization and territorial management. Many countries in Latin America (as well as in Africa) are consolidating their democratic systems, and their industrial policies need to be nested in these political schemes. It cannot be a closed-door bureaucratic exercise that then has to permeate the whole country. The development of production capabilities in Latin America is not happening in a harmonious way within countries. Often, rising growth and accumulation of production and innovation capabilities is happening in specific locations within the country, while the majority of the territory lags behind. If this agglomeration trend is not counterbalanced with active policies for territorial development, it might undermine potential growth in the future by underestimating new sources of growth and engendering growing social tensions.

PLANNING INCENTIVES FOR THE NEXT PARADIGM: INVESTING IN GREEN SOLUTIONS

Despite the disagreement at the multilateral level, many developing economies are recognizing the opportunities and challenges of the new green economy paradigm. On the one hand, they need to foster learning and increase participation in global production networks, which in many cases are still based on "back" technological paradigms, but on the other hand, they will all need to invest and prepare themselves for the future. This means being involved in research, as well as profiting from importing greener technologies that are increasingly cheaper in the markets thanks to the Chinese action (Mathews 2012). Brazil, for example, is investing in green technologies, building off of government-led efforts started in the 1970s. Environmental sustainability is a priority also for small economies like Costa Rica and Panama, but it is still not high up in the priorities of most other countries in the region. In addition, most of the green transformation programs focus on the technological dimension, like in Brazil, while the green paradigm would require addressing, in addition to the technological dimension, the consumption side and the change in behaviors, service delivery, and urban planning. These are all areas in which developing countries could take big steps.

INVESTING IN STRENGTHENING STATE CAPABILITIES

The role of institutions is vital in development. These are created through time in a cumulative process. The countries in which the government administration has been delegitimized (minimized) due to the implementation of the structural reforms are in a difficult position when they are called upon to implement more and better policies. While the conventional argument calls for "getting the institutions right" and then "getting the policies right," often in reality things work the other way round. Institutions coevolve with the challenges they are called to face and with the policies that they are administrating and implementing. Poor institutional capabilities are no excuse for calling for low state intervention. Investing in institutional strengthening is part of a proactive policy package. Latin American countries have started to strengthen their institutions for innovation in the last decade. Argentina created a Ministry of Science, Technology, and Productive Innovation in 2007 to signal the willingness of the country to promote knowledge-based growth. Brazil has introduced innovation among the priorities of its national development bank (BNDES), and it is promoting the creation of a new corporation to promote mission-oriented research. Chile has created a Ministerial Council for Innovation. Smaller economies have made progress too: Costa Rica has created a ministerial council to promote the coordination between FDI policy and innovation, and Uruguay has created a National Agency for Innovation.

DO NOT LEAVE EVALUATION AS AN ADDITIONAL ITEM ON THE "TO-DO" LIST

Latin American countries have been investing more in policy planning than in implementation and have been traditionally sloppy in policy evaluation. Most countries lack systems for policy monitoring and evaluation. In the last decades, the diffusion of the use of ICTs in government has helped to increase information quality, quantity, and accessibility favouring monitoring. But impact evaluation still has not been developed in an adequate manner. In addition, even in countries in which there is a favorable climate for industrial policy today, like Brazil and South Africa, proponents are required to be "accountable" for the executed actions and to prove the effectiveness of the implemented measures. The slowdown of the global economy in the aftermath of the 2008 crisis (and the entry into a non-expansionary phase of the economic cycle) led to advocate for fiscal consolidation in order to stabilize the economy.

The experience of Latin American countries shows that targeted efforts to create a culture of evaluation are needed. They will not develop spontaneously in most countries. Evaluation is more useful when it is conceived as an integral part of the policy cycle and not as an "external" function of control of checks and balances. In small countries, external support is often essential to carry out policy evaluation; however, even in those cases, direct participation of local constituencies is essential to ensure meaningful evaluation exercises. Some Latin American countries have introduced industrial and innovation surveys to monitor trends and assess policy impact (Cimoli, Primi, and Rovira 2011). Improving the capacity to use surveys is a mid- to long-term process requiring a permanent dialogue among experts, statisticians, and policymakers.

While impact assessment is rare in Latin America, most countries have advanced in creating and facilitating access to information about policy programs and their implementation. In some countries, agile agencies like "observatories" are contributing to information generation and analysis. For example, in Argentina, the Observatory on Employment monitors job creation and production trends and favors policy fine tuning by cooperating with the Ministry of Labor. In Colombia, the Observatory for Science and Technology (OCyT), created in 1999 as a public-private partnership initiative, is responsible for the elaboration of qualitative and quantitative indicators to monitor trends and support the process of strategic decision making.[2]

CONCLUSIONS

The new economic landscape is opening up opportunities for Africa, but market forces alone will not be enough. Creating more and better jobs, improving the participation of Africa in production networks, and increasing scientific and technological capabilities in the countries of the region are still goals to be reached by African countries. History shows that development is a process that goes hand in hand with the building of domestic institutions, strengthening of domestic demand and supply, and the creation of backward and forward linkages within the economy and with foreign partners. These processes entail accumulation of scientific, technological, and production capabilities, as well as intensive institutional learning. Creating the conditions for promoting learning and structural change in Africa could help the countries of the continent to fully grasp the opportunities of the new global economic scenario and reduce the deep gap that still separates opportunities and living standards in Africa from most of the rest of the world.

The relegitimization of the "production structure" as an area for policy intervention and the resurgence of interest in industrial policies can be allies in engaging African countries in implementing new transformation strategies, improving the participation of its countries in the global economy, and achieving progress on the domestic fronts. For example, South Africa is engaged in Multi-Annual Industrial Transformation Plans, and Morocco has a new industrial policy aimed at strengthening domestic production leveraging on FDI in priority sectors, including the automotive sector. Ethiopia has been vigorously implementing and refining its industrial policies. However, designing and implementing industrial policies is easier said than done, especially in the new economic landscape characterized by high mobility of capital and labor, growing relevance of international knowledge, and production networks. In addition, in many countries there is still resistance to accepting the legitimacy of embracing ambitious transformational strategies.

Southeast Asian countries are the common examples for deriving lessons about industrial policies. This chapter has tried to highlight some lessons that could be learned from Latin America, especially in the realm of the political economy of industrial policy. It seems that both in Latin America and in Africa it is difficult to accept "ambitious" policies. Countries should not underestimate the importance of claiming the right to deliberately intervene to alter the production structure and favor specialization in more knowledge- and technology-intensive sectors. There is no automatism in development processes, and market incentives alone are not generally enough to promote a transition toward superior stages of development. Science, technology, and innovation, as well as learning processes, are paramount in development. Investing in building learning and absorptive capacities is crucial in order to be able to tap into existing knowledge and to open opportunities for leap frogging. Latin America has started to advance in this area by increasing the importance of the innovation agenda in the countries' development strategies. Africa has much to do in this respect. Creating a culture for innovation and stimulating domestic entrepreneurship are important components of development strategies. But these are costly and long-term efforts.

Industrial and innovation policies are effective when they manage to get the private sector on board. This is an open challenge for countries in Latin America, as well as for countries in Africa. It is not uncommon that business and political elites are responsible for the low impact of government industrial development strategies because they tend to have low trust in domestic production. Creating a national entrepreneurial class is a key component of the development process. Africa has a big asset to help break this vicious cycle and grasp the opportunities of the new global economic and political context: the potential of its young and growing population. Africa's youth are increasingly skilled and have new aspirations. These issues are at the heart of the "animal spirits" that are behind the dynamism of our economies. Industrial policies should be able to mobilize them, whether they are in the continent or abroad, to make Africa the next rising giant.

NOTES

The views expressed in this chapter are those of the author and do not necessarily reflect those of the organization. This chapter is part of the background research carried out by the author in the framework of the elaboration of the OECD (2013) *Perspectives on Global Development 2013—Shifting Up a Gear: Industrial Policies in a Changing Economic Landscape* (Paris: OECD).

1. What constitutes a "failure" in the Latin American experience is also part of the debate. Some argue that the import substitution policies of the 1950s and 1960s have been a failure. Others see the Washington Consensus recipes and their diligent application by the countries of the region as the main reason for the "failure" of the Latin American catch-up. Others have a more balanced view, taking into account the concurrence of external and internal factors, as well as the behaviors of the Latin American elites (Ocampo and Ros 2011). What is important to clarify is that the approach of dismissing the Latin American experience of the 1950s and 1960s as a total failure cannot be accepted because these decades have set the basis for the industrial, technological, and institutional capabilities of today.

2. In South Africa, for example, the Department of Trade and Industry (DTI) has to report to the Parliament the implementation results of the Industrial Policy Action Plan anually. It is also required to present a mid-term implementation review, including quantitative and qualitative achievements of strategic and sectoral targets, the number of beneficiary firms, the number of jobs created, the allocation of government support, and any changes in legal framework. The evaluation process includes a review of mid-term challenges and opportunities and a reassessment of strategic priorities, taking into account what has been achieved through policy implementation and the eventual rise of new challenges. In South Africa the industrial policy implementation mid-term review also clarifies the coordination requirements with other policies, including trade, competition, technology, innovation, and green economy.

REFERENCES

African Development Bank, Organization for Economic Co-operation and Development, United Nations Development Programme, Economic Commission for Africa (AfDB, OECD, UNDP, ECA). 2012. *African Economic Outlook 2012: Promoting Youth Employment*. AfDB, OECD, UNDP, ECA Publishing

——. 2013. *African Economic Outlook: Structural Transformation and Natural Resources*. AfDB, OECD, UNDP, ECA Publishing.

Amsden, A. 1989. *Asia's Next Giant: South Korea and Late Industrialization*. New York: Oxford University Press.

Barros de Castro, A. 2009. "The Impact of Public Policies in Brazil along the Path from Semi-Stagnation to Growth in a Sino-Centric Market." In *Industrial Policy and Development: The Political Economy of Capabilities Accumulation*, ed. M. Cimoli, G. Dosi, and J. E. Stiglitz. New York: Oxford University Press.

Block, F., and M. R. Keller. 2011. *State of Innovation: The U.S. Government's Role in Technology Development*. Boulder, Colo.: Paradigm Publishers.

Castro, A. C., and L. Castro. 2012. *Do Desenvolvimento Renegado ao Desafio Sinocêntrico: Reflexões de Antonio Barros de Castro sobre o Brasil*. Rio de Janeiro: Elsevier Editora, Ltda.

Chang, H-J. 1994. *The Political Economy of Industrial Policy*. London: McMillan.

——. 2002. *Kicking Away the Ladder—Development Strategy in Historical Perspective*. London: Anthem.

——. 2011. *Industrial Policy: Can We Go Beyond an Unproductive Confrontation?* Annual World Bank Conference on Development Economics 2010, World Bank, Washington DC.

——. 2012. *Industrial Policy: Can Africa Do It?* Paper presented at the International Economic Association Roundtable Conference on New Thinking on Industrial Policy: Implications for Africa, Pretoria, South Africa, July 3–4.

Cimoli, M., B. Coriat, and A. Primi. 2009. "Intellectual Property and Industrial Policy: A Critical Assessment." In *Industrial Policy and Development: The Political Economy of Capabilities Accumulation*, ed. M. Cimoli, G. Dosi, and J. E. Stiglitz, 506–538. New York: Oxford University Press.

Cimoli, M., G. Dosi, and J. E. Stiglitz. 2009. *Industrial Policy and Development: The Political Economy of Capabilities Accumulation*. New York: Oxford University Press.

Cimoli, M., J. C. Ferraz, and A. Primi. 2005. "Science and Technology Policy in Open Economies: The Case of Latin America and the Caribbean." Production Development Series, no. 165, Economic Commission for Latin America and the Caribbean (ECLAC), United Nations, Santiago.

——. 2009. "Science, Technology and Innovation Policies in Global Open Economies: Reflections from Latin America and the Caribbean." *Globalization, Competitiveness and Governability Journal* 3 (1): 32–60.

Cimoli, M., A. Primi, and S. Rovira. 2011. *National Innovation Surveys in Latin America: Empirical Evidence and Policy Implications*. Santiago, Chile: Economic Commission for Latin America and the Caribbean (ECLAC)-IDRC, United Nations.

Coutinho, L., J. C. Ferraz, A. Nassif, and R. Oliva. 2012. "Industrial Policy and Economic Transformation." In *The Oxford Handbook of Latin American Political Economy*, ed. J. Santiso and J. Dayton-Johnson, 100–133, Oxford: Oxford University Press.

Dahlman, C. 2011. *The World under Pressure: How China and India Are Influencing the Global Economy and the Environment.* Stanford: Stanford University Press.

Devlin, R., and G. Moguillansky. 2012. *What's New in the New Industrial Policy in Latin America?* Paper prepared for the International Economic Association (IEA)-World Bank Round Table, Washington, DC, May 22–23.

Economic Commission for Africa of the United Nations (ECA). 2013. *Economic Report on Africa 2013: Making the Most of Africa's Commodities: Industrialising for Growth, Jobs and Economic Transformation.* Addis Ababa, Ethiopia: UN-ECA.

———. 2014. *Economic Report on Africa 2014: Dynamic Industrial Policy in Africa: Innovative Institutions, Effective Processes and Flexible Mechanisms.* Addis Ababa, Ethiopia: UN-ECA.

Economic Commission for Africa of the United Nations (ECA) and African Union Commission (AU). 2013. "Industrialisation for an Emerging Africa." Issue paper, Sixth Joint Annual Meetings of the ECA Conference of African Ministers of Finance, Planning and Economic Development and AU Conference of Ministers of Economy and Finance, Abidjan, Côte d'Ivoire, March.

Economic Commission for Latin America and the Caribbean (ECLAC). 2012. "Structural Change for Equality: An Integrated Approach to Development" Document for the Period of Session, 2012, Santiago, Chile, United Nations.

Fajnzylber, F. 1983. *La industrialización trunca de América Latina.* Mexico City: Editorial Nueva Imagen.

Greenwald, B., and J. E. Stiglitz. 2012. *Learning and Industrial Policy: Implications for Africa.* Paper presented at the International Economic Association Roundtable Conference on New Thinking on Industrial Policy: Implications for Africa, Pretoria, South Africa, July 3–4.

Griffith-Jones, S., J. A. Ocampo, and J. E. Stiglitz. 2010. *Time for a Visible Hand: Lessons from the 2008 World Financial Crisis.* New York: Oxford University Press.

Institute for Defense Analysis (IDA). 2012. "Emerging Global Trends in Advanced Manufacturing." IDA Paper P-4603.

Kattel, R., and V. Lember. 2010. "Public Procurement as an Industrial Policy Tool: An Option for Developing Countries?" Working Papers in Technology Governance and Economic Dynamics 31.

Lin, J. 2012. *New Structural Economics: A Framework for Rethinking Development and Policy.* Washington, DC: World Bank.

Lin, J., and H-J Chang. 2009. "Should Industrial Policy in Developing Countries Conform to Comparative Advantage or Defy it? A Debate Between Justin Lin and Ha-Joon Chang." *Development Policy Review* 27 (5): 483–502.

Mathews, J. A. 2012. "Why Should Developing Countries Be Concerned about Green Growth?" Background paper prepared for the OECD Development Centre's Perspectives on Global Development 2013, OECD, Paris.

McKinsey. 2012. *Winning the $30 Trillion Decathlon: Going for Gold in Emerging Markets.* McKinsey Quarterly, August, 2012. McKinsey & Company.

Naudé, W. A. 2010. "Industrial Policy: Old and New." UNU-WIDER Working Paper 106.

Noman, A. 2012. "Infant Capitalists, Infant Industries and Infant Economies: Trade and Industrial Policies for Early Stages of Development in Africa and Elsewhere." IPD working paper, Columbia University.

Noman, A., K. Bothchwey, H. Stein, and J. E. Stiglitz, eds. 2012. *Good Growth and Governance in Africa: Rethinking Development Strategies*. New York: Oxford University Press.

Ocampo, J. A., and J. Ros. 2011. *The Oxford Handbook of Latin American Economics*. New York: Oxford University Press.

Organization for Economic Co-operation and Development (OECD). 2010. *Perspectives on Global Development 2010: Shifting Wealth*. Paris: OECD Development Centre.

——. 2012a. "Beyond Industrial Policy—Emerging Issues and New Trends." Draft STI working paper on Industrial Policy DSTI/IND (2012) 19.

——. 2012b. "Attracting Knowledge-Intensive FDI to Costa Rica: Challenges and Policy Options." *Making Development Happen Series*, No. 1. Paris: OECD.

——. 2013a. *Perspectives on Global Development 2013—Shifting Up a Gear: Industrial Policies in a Changing Economic Landscape*. Paris: OECD.

——. 2013b. *Start-up Latin America: Promoting Innovation in the Region*. OECD Development Centre Study. Paris: OECD.

Peres, W. 2009. "The (Slow) Return of Industrial Policies in Latin America." In *Industrial Policy and Development*, ed. M. Cimoli, G. Dosi, and J. E. Stiglitz, 175–202. New York: Oxford University Press.

Peres, W., and A. Primi. 2009. "Theory and Practice of Industrial Policy: Evidence from the Latin American Experience." *Serie Desarollo Productivo* 187, CEPAL/ECLAC.

Primi, A. 2014. "Promoting Innovation in Latin America: What Countries Have Learned and (What They Have Not) in Designing and implementing Innovation Policies and Intellectual Property Policies." PhD diss., Maastricht University.

Reinert, E. 2007. *How Rich Countries Got Rich and Why Poor Countries Stay Poor*. London: Constable and Robinson.

Rodrik, D. 2004. "Industrial Policy for the 21st Century." Centre for Economic Policy Research discussion paper 4767.

Skidelsky, R. 2009. *Keynes: The Return of the Master*. New York: Public Affairs.

Srinivas, S. 2012. "Development Strategies and Industrial Policy: What Can Be Learned from the Indian Experience?" Background paper prepared for the OECD Development Centre's Perspectives on Global Development 2013, OECD, Paris.

Wade, R. 1990. *Governing the Market: Economic Theory and the Role of Government in East Asian Industrialization*. Princeton: Princeton University Press.

Zalk, N. 2012. "South African Post-Apartheid Policies Towards Industrialisation: Tentative Implications for Other African Countries." In *Good Growth and Governance in Africa: Rethinking Development Strategies*, ed. A. Noman, K. Bothchwey, H. Stein, and J. E. Stiglitz 345–370. New York: Oxford University Press.

CHAPTER 7

Can the Financial Sector Deliver Both Growth and Financial Stability in Sub-Saharan Africa?

Stephany Griffith-Jones with Ewa Karwowski

Finance provides a particularly challenging area for policy design and research, especially if placed in the context of those countries' needs for development. The policy challenges and research needs are very large, due in part to a major rethinking of the role, scale, and structure of a desirable financial sector, as well as its regulation, in light of the North Atlantic financial crisis that started in 2007/2008. This major crisis also challenged the view that developed countries' financial and regulatory systems should be emulated by developing countries, given that developed countries' financial systems have been so problematic and so poorly regulated. Furthermore, it is important to understand the implications of the major international policy and analytical rethinking for Sub-Saharan Africa (SSA) and adjust it to the features and needs of their economies.

The financial sectors of African low-income countries (LICs) are still at an early stage of development, so lessons from the crisis could inform their financial sector development strategies. Moreover, their financial sectors, while generally still shallow, are experiencing fairly rapid growth. Combined with African countries' existing vulnerabilities, such as limited regulatory capacity, this might pose risks to financial system stability. Despite the infrequent appearance of systemic banking crises on the African continent over the past decade, fast credit growth in many economies—even if at comparatively low levels—calls for caution, signaling the need for strong and countercyclical regulation of African financial systems. For policymakers and researchers, this poses the challenge of applying the lessons from the crisis in developed and previously emerging countries to African LICs, while paying careful attention to the specific features of African financial systems.

There are also more traditional policy challenges and research gaps on financial sectors in LICs and their links to inclusive growth. To support growth, there are a range of functions that the financial sector must meet in African LICs, such as helping to mobilize sufficient savings; intermediating savings at low cost and long- and short-term maturities to investors and consumers; ensuring that savings are channeled to the most efficient investment opportunities; and helping companies and individuals manage risk. There are also large deficiencies in these areas originating from specific market failures and/or gaps. For example, there is a lack of sustainable lending at relatively low spreads, including with long maturities to small and medium enterprises (SMEs), which is particularly constraining for growth in LICs.

This chapter presents two key areas for a policy, as well as a corresponding research agenda on finance and growth in Sub-Saharan Africa building partly on lessons from the global financial crisis: (1) the desirable size and structure of the financial sector and (2) new challenges for financial regulation. Discussions in these two areas are important to advance understanding on the links between the financial sector and inclusive as well as sustainable growth.

FINANCIAL SECTOR DEVELOPMENT AND GROWTH

Central bankers and financial regulators in African LICs have always faced major conceptual and institutional challenges in striking the right balance in their policy design to achieve the triple aims of financial stability, growth, and equity.

These challenges acquired a new dimension in the light of numerous financial crises, initially in the developing world, but recently in developed countries. The latter led to a major reevaluation of the role of the financial sector, its interactions with the real economy, and the need for major reform of its regulation, especially in developed and emerging economies (see, for example, Griffith-Jones, Ocampo, and Stiglitz [2010]; IMF [2011]; and Haldane and Madouros [2012] on the need to simplify regulation); the latter resonates very well with LICs. Before examining the implications of this analysis for SSA countries, we will first look at how the global financial crisis affected SSA countries.

Interestingly, although the global financial crisis originated in and strongly hit developed economies, its cost to developing SSA countries (in contrast to all LICs on average) in terms of foregone growth and investment, as well as falling tax revenue with increasing budget deficits, is quite substantial. Developing SSA suffered a GDP growth slowdown to 4 percent in the aftermath of the crisis (2008–2010) in comparison to average growth rates of 4.7 percent between 2000 and 2007, according to World Bank data. This is equal to a loss in GDP growth of 0.7 percentage points. SSA growth was much more affected by the recent slowdown in economic activity around the world—mainly driven by recession and stagnation in developed economies—than that of all LICs on average, countries that have managed to grow by 0.4 percent more in the same period, according to World Bank data (2008–2010, compared to 2000–2007). Similarly, the crisis impact on tax revenue is potentially larger in SSA than in low-income economies on average. While LICs did not see a reduction in tax revenue in the aftermath of the crisis, taxes collected in SSA fell by 1.7 percent of GDP in comparison to pre-crisis levels. Concurrently, budget positions in SSA countries worsened by 1 percent of GDP on average.

Furthermore, the question can be raised as to whether SSA growth in investment rates would have been faster in the absence of the global financial crisis. Figure 7.1 illustrates this point. Gross capital formation (investment), as share of GDP, peaked at 22 percent in 2008, falling by almost 1.5 percentage points in the following year. The 2008 level has not been recovered as of 2011, the latest year for which data are available.

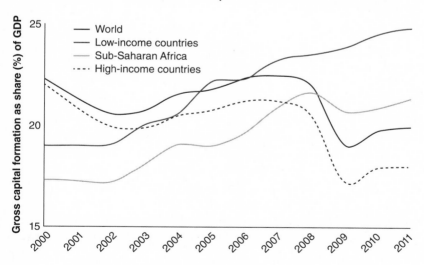

Figure 7.1   **Impact of the global financial crisis on gross capital formation, 2000–2011**

Source: World Bank (2013b).

It is interesting that the number of banking crises on the African continent has overall been remarkably low over the past decade (2000–2009), potentially indicating increased resilience of African financial systems, particularly in comparison to the 1990s (see figure 7.2).

This argument is in line with the observation that the dissemination of the financial crisis from strongly affected advanced economies to African low-income countries has mainly happened through the trade channel, falling commodity prices, shrinking remittances, and official development assistance budgets.

In this context, the Nigerian banking crisis—discussed shortly—is seen by some as a "sporadic outlier" (Beck et al. 2011, 3). There is nevertheless the danger that lack of recent crises can lead to policymaker and regulator complacency (as well as that by the financial actors), which could increase the risk of future crises. This phenomenon, known in the literature as "disaster myopia," has contributed to increased risk of crises in other regions in the past.

There has been relatively little research and policy analysis on the implications of the global financial crisis for African countries and LICs more generally, with some valuable exceptions (see, for example, Kasekende, Bagyenda, and Brownbridge [2011] and Murinde [2012] for

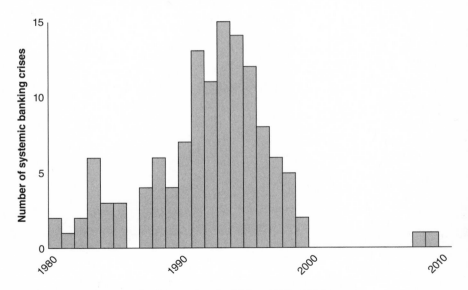

Figure 7.2   Systemic banking crises in Africa, 1980–2010

Source: Laeven and Valencia (2008 and 2012).

good analyses of regulatory issues in LICs). Because African financial sectors are growing quite quickly, they may be more vulnerable to threats to their financial stability. The value added of policy analysis and research on finance and development that explores the right lessons to learn from the global crisis—and previous ones in emerging economies—for African LICs is thus likely to be high. This research might help answer the question of how the need to ensure financial stability interacts with the need for a financial system in LICs that assures enough access to sustainable finance for the different sectors of the economy, including long-term finance to fund structural change, as well as different segments such as small- and medium-sized enterprises (SMEs) and infrastructure.

AREAS OF ANALYSIS

There are two areas of inquiry for understanding the links between the financial sector and inclusive, as well as sustainable, growth: (1) What is the desirable size and structure of the financial sector in LICs? (2) What are the regulatory challenges to maximize the likelihood of achieving financial stability while safeguarding inclusive and more sustainable growth? Political economy might be a fruitful lens through which to perform such analysis because it sheds light on the political determinants of financial policy.

SIZE AND STRUCTURE OF THE FINANCIAL SECTOR

At a broad level, what is the desirable size and structure of the financial sector in African countries in order to maximize its ability to support the real economy? What are the desirable paths of development of the financial sector in Africa in order to help it maximize its contribution to growth, considering features of African countries and lessons from recent crises?

The traditional positive link between the deeper and larger financial sector and long-term growth—that started in the literature with Bagehot and Schumpeter, but then was reflected in quite a large part of the empirical literature, such as Levine (2005)—is being increasingly challenged. Authors like Easterly, Islam, and Stiglitz (2000) had already suggested that financial depth (measured by private credit to GDP ratio) reduces volatility of output up to a point, but beyond that actually increases output volatility. More recently, a number of papers have shown an inverse relation between the size of the financial sector and growth, especially beyond a certain level of financial development, which is estimated at around 80 to 100 percent of private credit to GDP. Thus Bank for International Settlements (BIS) economists (Cecchetti and Kharroubi 2012, 1) reach the following conclusions based on empirical work, which challenges much of earlier writing: "First, with finance you can have too much of a good thing. That is, at low levels, a larger financial system goes hand in hand with higher productivity growth. But there comes a point, where more banking and more credit lower growth. Secondly, looking at the impact of growth in the financial system—measured in employment or value added—on real growth, they find clear evidence that faster growth in finance is bad for aggregate real growth. This implies financial booms are bad for trend growth. Hence, macro prudential or counter-cyclical regulation . . . is important."

Finally, in their examination of industry-level data, they find that industries competing for resources with finance are particularly damaged by financial booms. Specifically, manufacturing sectors that are R&D-intensive suffer disproportionate reductions in productivity growth when finance increases.

Similarly, an IMF discussion paper (IMF 2012a) suggests empirical explanations for the fact that large financial sectors may have negative effects on economic growth. It gives two possible reasons. The first has to do with the increased probability of large economic crashes (Minsky 1974; Kindleberger 1978; Rajan 2005), and the second relates to potential misallocation of resources, even in good times (Tobin 1984). De la Torre and Ize (2011) point out that "too much finance" may be consistent with positive but decreasing returns of financial depth that, at some point, become smaller than the cost of instability. It is interesting that the IMF discussion paper (IMF 2012a) results are robust to restricting the analysis to tranquil periods. This suggests that volatility and banking crises are only part of the story. The explanation for the "too much finance" result is not only due to financial crises and volatility but also due to misallocation of resources.

It is also plausible that the relationship between financial depth and economic growth depends, at least in part, on whether lending is used to finance investment in productive assets or to feed speculative bubbles. The effect of financial depth on economic growth seems limited not only where credit serves to feed speculative bubbles—where excessive increases can actually be negative for growth—but also where it is used for consumption purposes as opposed to productive investment. Using data for forty-five countries for the period from 1994 to 2005, Beck et al. (2012) and Beck et al. (2011) show that enterprise credit is positively associated with economic growth but that there is no correlation between growth and household credit. Given that the share of bank lending to households increases with economic and financial development, and household credit is often used for consumption purposes whereas enterprise credit is used for productive investment, the allocation of resources goes some way toward explaining the nonlinear finance-growth relationship. In African countries, only a small share of bank lending goes to households. However, as financial sectors and economies grow, this will change, as has been the case in South Africa.

Rapidly growing credit to households—even though desirable and potentially welfare enhancing when strengthening reasonable levels of domestic demand and financial inclusion in a sustainable way—might, however, cause financial instability if not regulated prudently. This is especially the case if lending is excessively channeled into the construction sector, creating a housing bubble. The two most advanced African economies, South Africa and Mauritius—both upper-middle-income countries—have recently experienced or are currently experiencing a construction boom. Both economies possess relatively deep financial markets with strong private domestic lending, including significant consumption credit extension. Figure 7.3 shows that private credit in high-income economies was around 100 percent of GDP on average in 2010, while it accounted for 70 to 80 percent of GDP in Mauritius and South Africa.

In international comparison, South Africa was the country in Africa that experienced the strongest real estate price gains between 2004 and 2007, by far exceeding even the price growth in the booming residential property markets of the United States and the United Kingdom. In South Africa, the ratio of household to business credit is approximately 1:1. The large majority of household borrowing takes on the form of mortgage finance. During the early 2000s, this led to an unprecedented housing boom in South Africa fed by growth in housing loans of over 150 percent in real terms between 2000 and 2010 (see figure 7.4). This was largely absorbed by upper-income South African households accounting for three-quarters of total household credit created (DTI 2010). In an attempt to reduce inflation, asset price increases, and potential macroeconomic overheating, the South African Reserve Bank gradually initiated

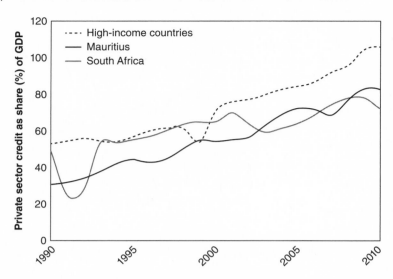

**Figure 7.3   Private credit extension in African middle-income
countries compared to high-income countries, 1990–2010**

Source: World Bank (2013b).

monetary tightening in June 2006, accelerating the rise in interest rates
the following year.

The subsequent economic slowdown in South Africa was to a large
extent based on domestically accumulating economic and financial
imbalances, while the global financial crisis merely intensified the recession of 2008/2009. The fact that credit- and consumption-led growth
was unsustainable in South Africa was illustrated in almost one million
jobs shed in 2008/2009, largely in low-skilled consumption-driven sectors. A positive aspect was that there was no financial crisis, perhaps
because of the positive policy response from the economic authorities;
however, as mortgage credit picks up, and especially if it does so at a very
fast pace, care has to be taken to regulate this. The South African experience reiterates that private sector credit expansion at very high levels
might lead to output volatility and adverse growth effects (see Easterly,
Islam, and Stiglitz [2000] and Cecchetti and Kharroubi [2012]). In order
to prevent future crises and to foster economic development, a reorienta-
tion toward more business credit, particularly for productive investment,
might be needed.

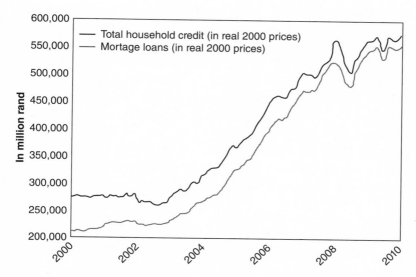

Figure 7.4 **South African private sector credit extension by purpose, 2000–2010**

Source: SARB (2013).

In Mauritius almost one-third of private sector credit flows to households, equaling 20 percent of GDP by late 2012. The majority of household borrowing is mortgage finance (60 percent of total household credit), with the rest used to fund consumption (40 percent). Given sustained demand for residential property, housing credit had been growing close to 20 percent annually on average until 2012 (Bank of Mauritius 2013). Simultaneously, foreign direct investment (FDI) that flowed into the country concentrated on real estate activities, with the bulk in tourist-related building. The construction industry accounted for approximately half of FDI inflows in recent years (2008–2012). Mauritius's construction boom should be monitored with caution, which has also been pointed out by the IMF Article IV Mission Consultation. Financial vulnerabilities appear to be accumulating in the industry with potential adverse impact on balance sheets of domestic commercial banks. Even though nonperforming loans as share of total credit are at reasonably low levels, they have increased. Furthermore, nonperforming loans in the construction industry (excluding housing loans) as share of sectorial credit are more than twice as high, rising from around 5 percent in 2010 to 8 percent

2012. This development is worrying and calls for countercyclical regulation, especially because year-on-year growth in construction credit has shot up sharply recently.

Limited data availability makes it difficult to measure to what extent consumption credit is on the rise in most African economies. This would seem to make the case for more disaggregated credit data, as well as monitoring by regulators and policymakers, more urgent.

One of the few low-income SSA countries providing disaggregated domestic lending data is Mozambique (Banco de Moçambique 2013). Private sector credit has increased significantly between 2000 and 2010 in the southern African country, from 15 percent to 23 percent of GDP (see table 7.1). During this period, consumer borrowing almost tripled as share of total credit while it grew almost eightfold between 2001 and 2012 in real terms (see figure 7.5). Mozambique has had a strong growth performance, implying a robust medium-term economic outlook (IMF 2013).

Nevertheless, falling consumer price inflation has been accompanied by potential price pressures present in urban housing markets, which are difficult to assess due to lack of house price data for Mozambique. Central

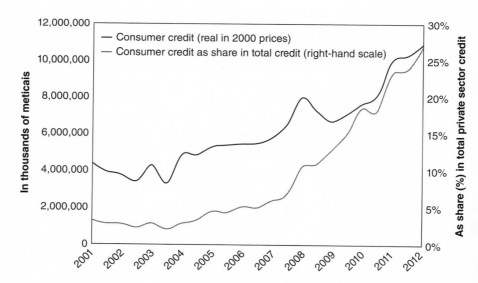

Figure 7.5   Mozambican consumer credit in real terms and as share of total private sector credit, 2001–2012

Source: Banco de Moçambique (2013).

areas in Mozambican towns and cities have been observed to experience property price growth of 100 percent annually (CAHF 2012).

More broadly of relevance for growth, as we began to discuss earlier, is the link between the structure of the financial sector and growth. The IMF in its Global Financial Stability Report (IMF 2012b) has interesting further empirical analysis of the relationship between the structure of the financial sector and economic growth, as well as the volatility of this growth and financial stress. This is a fairly understudied area, and one that has hardly been applied to LICs. The preliminary empirical results of the IMF report suggest that cross-border connections through foreign banks may be associated with instability during crises, though their role may be more beneficial in normal times.

Crucial in the context of policymaking and research on finance in Africa is the extent to which the findings on the relationship between the structure and size of the financial sector and growth in more developed economies are relevant for and apply to African LICs because their financial systems are markedly different. In particular, these countries' banking systems are small in absolute and relative size, many of them reaching the size of mid-sized banks in high-income countries. For instance, Beck et al. (2011) report that if measured in relative size, based on the claims on the private domestic nonfinancial sector to GDP (private credit), the median for African countries as a whole (that is, including North African countries) was 19 percent in 2009, while it was 49 percent for non-African developing countries. African financial sectors also show levels of financial intermediation, and access to financial services has remained limited for large segments like SMEs, the agricultural sector, or poor households. Many of those use informal financial services.

Given the importance of SMEs in creating employment, the lack of financial infrastructure supporting their activity in African financial systems is a major drawback for development. International financial indicators show that African businesses in general are disadvantaged through less access to finance than competitors in other regions. Concurrently, SMEs enjoy particularly poor access to sources of finance, leaving them with internal cash flow as their main source for investment finance. As a consequence, enabling African SMEs to better access financing sources has the potential to strengthen and accelerate growth if done on sustainable grounds, at reasonable cost, and under adequate regulation.

The obstacles African SMEs experience in their domestic financial systems are mainly concentrated on the insufficient support by banking institutions, as well as the lack of alternative sources of finance. Therefore

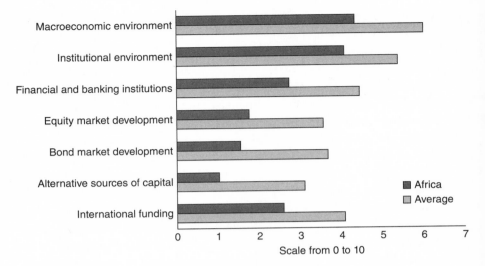

Figure 7.6   CAI components for Africa compared to the average, 2009

Source: Barth et al. (2010).

recent developments of deepening African financial markets might help SME growth if successfully and sustainably channeled into this segment. International indicators such as domestic analysis via enterprise surveys, by company size, support the view that African SMEs have limited access to finance, as argued shortly. Figures 7.6 and 7.7 illustrate the difficulties

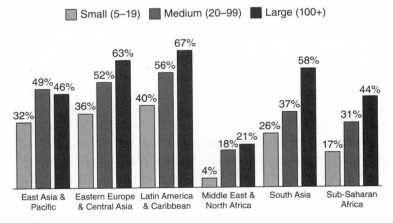

Figure 7.7   Regional percent of firms by firm size with a bank loan/line of credit

Source: World Bank (2013a).

that African businesses and entrepreneurs have in accessing finance, in comparison to the average for all countries.

Assessing the ability of firms to access finance more deeply, the percentage of small, medium, and large firms that have a bank loan or a credit line can serve as a measure. Sub-Saharan African small- and medium-sized firms have poor access to finance when compared to other developing regions (only 17 percent, as opposed to 40 percent in Latin America and 32 percent in East Asia), performing only better than the Middle East and North Africa region (see figure 7.7). This analysis of access to credit by firm size is taken further in figure 7.8 by looking at some Sub-Saharan African countries' firms of different sizes and the implications on the ability of the firm to have a bank loan or a credit line.

In general, between 60 and 70 percent of SMEs in Sub-Saharan Africa need loans, however, only 17 percent of small- and 31 percent of medium-sized firms actually have access to finance. As a consequence, firms in Sub-Saharan Africa have to finance a high proportion of investment through internally generated cash flows (82 percent among small Sub-Saharan African firms, 78 percent among medium firms, and 72 percent among large firms, according to World Bank data). This reflects the Capital Access Index (CAI) finding that African countries lack developed

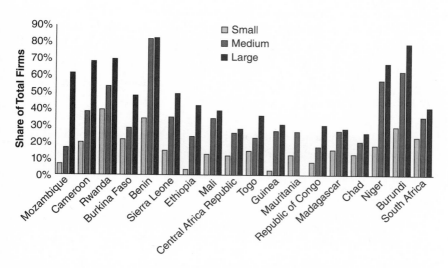

Figure 7.8   Access to bank loans and/or lines of credit by some SSA countries' firms

Source: World Bank (2013a).

equity and bond markets and alternative sources of capital, and that there are low levels of lending by banking institutions (with the latter two probably the most appropriate forms of funding SMEs).

Not surprisingly, according to the World Bank, 48 percent of small enterprises and 42 percent of medium enterprises in Sub-Saharan Africa have identified access to finance as a major obstacle to their business activities. This is an extremely high proportion, though some caution should be expressed, in that only creditworthy—and not all—SMEs should be granted credit.

In an effort to increase the level of participation of financial institutions to finance small and medium enterprises, public banks, such as the African Development Bank (AfDB), are driving a number of initiatives designed to encourage the participation of financial institutions. One notable initiative is the African Guarantee Fund (AGF), which is a for-profit social investment fund. The AGF is owned by AfDB, Agencia Española de Cooperación Internacional para el Desarrollo (AECID), and Danish International Development Agency (DANIDA) ,with contributions of USD 10 million, USD 20 million, and USD 20 million, respectively (AfDB 2012). Over the next three to five years, this share capital is expected to increase to USD 500 million, giving the institution capacity to guarantee up to USD 2 billion-worth of SME loans. The additional capital will be coming from bilateral donors, private investors, and development finance institutions (DFIs) (AfDB 2012). The AGF will select certain financial institutions to be partner institutions by assessing their commitment to grow their SME portfolio and by improving financial product offerings to SMEs. For these partner institutions, AGF will have two lines of activity:

1. Partial credit guarantees: the provision of partial guarantees for financial institutions on the African continent to incentivize them to increase debt and equity investments into SMEs. These guarantees, with different fee structures, will support: (a) loans made by client financial institutions to SMEs through a hybrid approach (portfolio and individual loan basis); (b) funds mobilization (that is, issuance of bonds) by financial institutions in support of their SME financing activities; and (c) equity capital financing for SMEs.
2. Capacity development: supporting AGF's partner institutions enhancement of their SME financing capabilities through assisting to improve the capacity to appraise and manage SME portfolios (AfDB 2013).

Operationally, the AGF will work on a risk-sharing basis with financial institutions, and the maximum risk coverage ratio will be 50 percent. The balance of risk will be borne by the financial institutions (AfDB 2013). AGF is designed to achieve a triple-A rating in order to attract a zero percent risk weight on SME loans provided by partner institutions. This will allow these institutions to lend money with limited need to set aside regulatory capital because of the guarantee from the highly rated AGF. The tenor of the guarantee will be for 80 percent of the life of the underlying transaction.

It is worth noting for the purposes of future research that, over and above the general consensus that SMEs lack long-term finance at reasonable lending rates, working capital facilities are also starting to be emphasized. The AfDB notes that "SMEs . . . complain . . . how banks are hesitant to provide long-term lending and working capital facilities, both of which they need for growth" (AfDB 2012, 3). Currently, 15 percent of small enterprises in Sub-Saharan Africa use banks to finance working capital; however, only a small proportion (6 percent) of their working capital needs are covered by this type of finance (see figure 7.9).

The need for working capital finance from financial institutions is echoed by Standard Bank, which found that there is a need for working

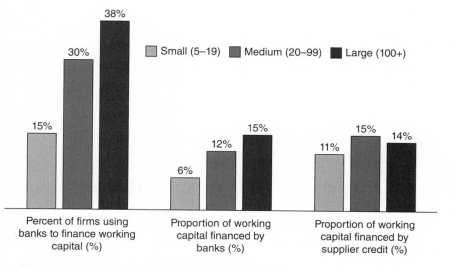

Figure 7.9   Financing of working capital by SSA firms

Source: World Bank (2013a).

capital facilities for SMEs in Sub-Saharan Africa (Botha 2011). To this end, Standard Bank has launched a product called Quick Loans, which provides unsecured loans of between USD 300 and USD 30,000 for three to twelve months, as well as other forms of finance to traders (Standard Bank 2013). Standard Bank (2013) has established SME banking in thirteen African countries (excluding South Africa), and during 2011 it provided financial services to more than 150,000 SMEs across these countries.

In general, data on the asset composition of banks across different regions show that, unlike banks in other regions of the world, African banks hold a much smaller share of their assets in private sector loans and a much larger share in government securities, foreign assets, and liquid assets (Beck et al. 2011). Household credit constitutes only a small share in bank credit, except in countries where financial sectors are more developed, like South Africa.

Banking sectors in most African countries are highly concentrated. In many countries, banks are predominantly foreign owned, many of them regional banks from other African countries. Banks also operate very profitably, with subsidiaries of foreign banks in Sub-Saharan Africa having higher returns on assets than subsidiaries of the same banks in other regions (Honohan and Beck 2007).

It is not clear the extent to which the findings on the reverse link between financial depth and growth found in the context of developed and emerging economies is relevant for low-income countries (which have a much lower level of financial development and large parts of the population and companies lacking any access to financial services, as compared to countries with far deeper financial sectors). However, these findings will certainly be relevant for designing policies that will influence their future evolution. Furthermore, it may well be that in the near term, the issue relates more to avoiding excessive speed of growth of finance, that we started to illustrate earlier, which may be more of a threat to financial stability in the case of Sub-Saharan Africa. Indeed, as shown in figure 7.10, financial deepening in SSA has accelerated in recent years. The amount of private credit as share of GDP almost doubled from an average of 10 percent during the 1990s to 18 percent by 2010. Bank deposits as share of GDP grew from 13 percent (in 1990–1999) to more than 20 percent (in 2010), while liquid liabilities (also known as broad money or M3)[1] to GDP rose by more than 10 percentage points over the same period, from 20 percent to more than 30 percent.

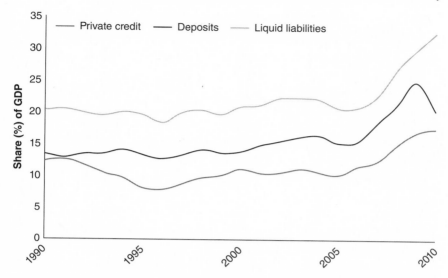

Figure 7.10 **Financial deepening in Sub-Saharan Africa, 1990–2010**

Source: World Bank (2013b).

The aggregate figures do not do justice to the fast pace of credit expansion in certain SSA economies. Table 7.1 provides country data on credit extension as share of GDP for all SSA economies individually. It highlights countries that have experienced a doubling of private credit to GDP within the past decade (2000–2010) in light gray. Economies in which

Table 7.1 Credit extension in Sub-Saharan Africa by country, 1990, 2000, and 2010

Country	1990 (%)	2000 (%)	2010 (%)	Credit growth 2000–2010(%)
Sub-Saharan Africa (developing)	9.2	11.0	17.5	59.1
Angola	n/a	1.1	18.1	1545.5
Benin	n/a	11.1	22.1	99.1
Botswana	7.8	13.9	22.3	60.4
Burkina Faso	16.2	10.8	16.5	52.8
Burundi	7.4	17.3	20.0	15.6
Cameroon	27.1	7.7	11.1	44.2
Cape Verde	4.0	37.5	59.2	57.9
Central African Republic	7.4	4.4	7.4	68.2
Chad*	6.5	3.4	5.0	47.1

(continued)

Table 7.1 (*Continued*)

Country	1990 (%)	2000 (%)	2010 (%)	Credit growth 2000–2010(%)
Comoros*	n/a	8.3	12.2	47.0
Congo, Dem. Rep.	n/a	n/a	n/a	n/a
Congo, Rep.	n/a	5.7	4.1	−28.1
Côte d'Ivoire	36.4	15.2	17.3	13.8
Eritrea	n/a	n/a	n/a	n/a
Ethiopia*	1.6	18.2	17.2	−5.5
Gabon	n/a	8.3	8.1	−2.4
Gambia, The	10.0	11.6	17.7	52.6
Ghana	5.0	11.7	13.7	17.1
Guinea	n/a	n/a	n/a	n/a
Guinea-Bissau*	13.0	7.6	5.8	−23.7
Kenya	17.7	25.6	30.6	19.5
Lesotho	13.8	14.0	12.6	−10.0
Liberia*	n/a	n/a	13.8	n/a
Madagascar	14.5	8.0	11.1	38.8
Malawi	9.2	4.5	14.2	215.6
Mali	9.2	4.5	17.4	286.7
Mauritania	31.1	n/a	n/a	n/a
Mauritius	30.1	54.2	82.3	51.8
Mozambique	n/a	15.4	23.2	50.6
Namibia	n/a	39.1	43.7	11.8
Niger	12.8	4.3	11.8	174.4
Nigeria	8.8	11.1	30.3	173.0
Rwanda	7.4	9.5	n/a	n/a
Sao Tome and Principe*	n/a	4.1	33.2	709.8
Senegal	27.5	16.5	24.5	48.5
Seychelles	7.0	15.2	22.9	50.7
Sierra Leone	3.3	1.9	9.2	384.2
Somalia	n/a	n/a	n/a	n/a
South Africa	49.1	65.0	71.7	10.3
South Sudan	n/a	n/a	n/a	n/a
Sudan	4.3	1.8	10.9	505.6
Swaziland	14.2	12.6	23.1	83.3
Tanzania	12.4	3.9	14.6	274.4
Togo	22.7	15.7	20.7	31.8
Uganda	2.5	5.3	13.4	152.8
Zambia	6.8	6.7	10.7	59.7
Zimbabwe	0.0	0.8	n/a	n/a

Source: World Bank (2013b).

* Where 1990 or 2010 data were unavailable, 1991 or 2009 data were used if possible.

Countries where private credit extension has (almost) doubled between 2000 and 2010 are highlighted in light gray.

Countries where private credit extension has increased threefold or more (but less than tenfold) are highlighted in medium gray with black font.

Countries where private credit extension has increased tenfold or more are highlighted in dark gray with white font.

private credit tripled or increased up to tenfold over the same period are highlighted in medium gray with black font. SSA states that saw a rise in lending to the private sector of ten times or more are highlighted in dark gray with white font.

This analysis shows that in the recent decade there have been a considerable number of SSA countries with very rapid credit growth, namely:

- Benin and Swaziland, where credit to GDP (almost) doubled;
- Malawi, Mali, Niger, Nigeria, São Tomé and Príncipe, Sierra Leone, Sudan, Tanzania, and Uganda, where credit to GDP increased threefold and more (but less than tenfold);
- Angola, with private credit growing by a factor of more than fifteenfold, or 1,500 percent.

Though this is a rough indicator, countries in the last two categories would seem more vulnerable to potential crises, so they may need to examine whether they need to introduce tighter regulations in general, or in particular sectors.

Financial systems in many African countries share features that seem to increase their vulnerability to shocks in the economic and financial system, including limited financial regulatory capacity, macroeconomic volatility linked to the economic structure of the countries (for example, natural resource dependence, which implies volatility of their terms of trade), and political pressure for financial deepening with a view to develop the real economy.

Fast credit growth might exacerbate vulnerabilities and enhance the risk of financial crises, as it has done in all other regions of the world. In the African context, the case of Nigeria provides a recent illustration that banking crises might cause a negative link between financial deepening and growth, even at relatively low levels of financial development. In 2004/2005, the Central Bank of Nigeria (CBN) mandated a steep increase of minimum bank capitalization with a view to create large internationally competitive banks and increase financial depth (Soludo 2004). Banks achieved this capitalization, which was high even by international standards, by means of equity investment, mergers, and acquisitions, resulting in the consolidation of the banking sector from eighty-nine to twenty-five banks. The consolidation in the domestic banking sector, along with abundant capital in the wake of rising oil prices, increased the speed of credit creation with significant flows to sectors with little growth impact. Between 2006 and 2009, private credit tripled from 12 percent to

36 percent of GDP. In real terms (2002 prices), this meant that domestic borrowing by the private sector grew almost fivefold.

This growth of credit included loans used to finance share purchases, clearly an undesirable practice, setting the stage for a financial asset bubble, particularly in bank stocks (Sanusi 2010). The financial sector boom ended in a bust, with a systemic banking crisis in 2009 due to excessive financial sector growth, partly because it had not been accompanied by the corresponding regulatory and supervisory upgrade. Consequently, nonperforming loans as percentage of gross loans rose sharply from 9.5 percent in 2007 to almost 30 percent in 2009. Finally, nine financial institutions that were close to collapse had to be rescued at the cost of USD 4 billion. The cost of cleaning up the balance sheets and recapitalizing the banks concerned is estimated at about 2.4 trillion naira, equivalent to almost 8 percent of GDP (IMF 2011). The Nigerian crisis shows there is no reason for complacency about the need for rigorous financial regulation in African economies, especially in the face of rapid credit expansion.

With respect to the effect of foreign bank presence on financial stability and growth in Africa, the existing evidence is somewhat ambiguous and requires further research (for an interesting book, see Beck et al. [2014]). There are indications that foreign banks can bring in experience from other regional economies and can help exploit scale economies in small host countries. Yet the benefits for financial access remain ambiguous, partly because of the greater reliance of foreign banks on "hard" information about borrowers as opposed to soft information that often implies a focus on prime borrowers (Detragiache, Tressel, and Gupta 2008; Sengupta 2007). Furthermore, it seems that foreign banks are fundamentally different from domestic banks. As argued by Rashid (2011), foreign banks seem less inclined to lending, and their loans are likely to be more volatile than those offered by domestic banks. Despite strong foreign bank presence, the effects of the global financial crisis on African banks have been limited. This is due in part to the relatively limited presence of banks from developed economies in Africa (with a high proportion of foreign banks currently being regional ones, which is different from previous decades in which foreign banks were predominantly developed country ones; see Kasekende, Bagyenda, and Brownbridge [2011]) and the fact that existing subsidiaries mostly fund themselves locally and not via their parents; this, however, limits the contribution these foreign banks make to national savings (Fuchs et al. 2012). In addition, reportedly large capital buffers—often above levels required by Basel III—have served to increase the resilience of African banks during the global financial crisis, although this may have involved some costs for intermediation (Fuchs, Losse-Mueller, and Witte 2012).

The fact that financial sectors in LICs tend to be relatively smaller and simpler provides an advantage in that governments have more policy space to influence the future nature and scale of their financial system. Furthermore, the fact the financial sector is smaller may imply it is less powerful politically; thus this potentially gives more autonomy to regulators—and more broadly to governments—to shape the financial sector.

LICs thus have the advantage of being latecomers to financial development and can benefit from positive and negative lessons from experiences and research on other countries. On the other hand, the incompleteness of LIC financial systems means that important challenges remain on extending access (to all types of financial services) to those excluded, such as a high proportion of poor households, microenterprises, and SMEs. More generally, it is difficult to fund working capital and investment in sectors such as agriculture and industry, especially for SMEs (and particularly at low spreads and longer maturities) crucial for growth and employment generation. The financing of infrastructure is a well-known problem in LICs, and the mobilization of sufficient long-term finance, as well as the most effective way to channel it to investment in that sector, is a key area of policy, where research, including clear understanding of market gaps—as well as effectiveness of policy interventions—could be very valuable.

Policy and research challenges on the desirable structure of the financial sector include the following research themes and questions:

1. What functions are particularly important to meet in African LICs? What are the deficiencies and needs in these areas in LICs? For example, how can sustainable lending at relatively low spreads and sufficient maturities to SME best be encouraged? What are the main challenges for delivering that type of finance in LICs? What are the specific needs of particular sectors?

2. What combination of public/private institutions/mechanisms may be desirable to best achieve the three objectives of growth, financial stability, and equity? This would look—in general and in country settings—at the existence of market gaps and market failures in specific areas (for example, long-term finance) in LICs, as well as potential government failures. Careful review of theoretical and empirical work needs to be combined with analysis of experiences to offer a balanced menu

of policy options for the most effective institutional arrangements in particular country contexts. What mechanisms (public guarantees, first losses assumed) are desirable to encourage private financing? How can they best be structured to avoid excessive contingent public liabilities in order for them to be effective? What experiences exist that have worked well? How can they best be applied to LICs?

3. Since the 2007/2008 crisis, increased interest has emerged in expanding the role of national and regional development banks to provide countercyclical lending when private credit falls. Also, public banks can be valuable for incorporating environmental externalities to give LICs the opportunity to "leap frog" by adopting low-carbon technologies. More broadly, public development banks can be a valuable mechanism for financing particular strategies of development. What are the incentives and institutional arrangements that are required to make such development banks effective and efficient in LICs? What lessons can be learned from successful banks in developed countries (for example, the European Investment Bank, German KfW) and emerging economies (for example, the Brazil Development Bank [BNDES] in Brazil, as well as Asian development banks)? Most research on the experiences with development banks in Africa dates from the 1980s and 1990s, and evaluations report fairly negative experiences (see Brownbridge, Harvey, and Gockel 1998). However, many development banks have been reformed over the past decade so that reevaluations of their effectiveness are necessary. What are the criteria for defining what is a "good development bank," and how can this be achieved best in an African context? Returning to the theoretical issues, what are the specific market gaps and failures that need to be addressed in specific LIC contexts, and how best can government failures be minimized? A hypothesis to be explored is that the effectiveness of development banks depends substantially on governance arrangements and political economy factors. What are the preconditions, including political economy ones, for such banks to be effective in LICs in ways similar to how they have been in emerging and developed economies?

4. In the case of private banks, should a particular model (for example, with respect to size) be encouraged? Many African countries' banking systems have an oligopolistic structure in which a small number of banks dominate the market and competition is limited. Is there a case that smaller, more decentralized banks are better for reducing asymmetries of information? Are there more benefits from increased

competition? Or are economies of scale an important factor for determining bank efficiency? Are potential costs of increased systemic risk of large banks so high that smaller, narrower banks may be preferable (Demirgüç-Kunt and Huizinga 2010)? What are the lessons, if any, for African LICs from the debate in developed countries on the structure of banking? What should be the preferred model for international banks in African LICs? Should LIC regulators encourage/require international banks to act as subsidiaries, rather than branches, as the UN Stiglitz Report proposes, to facilitate the task of national regulation? In India and some other developing countries, branching regulations are in place. What have been the experiences with such regulations? Should international banks (and possibly all large banks) be required to have branches not just in large cities but also in smaller cities?

5. To what extent is it best to concentrate on the development of banking in LICs, or should nonbanking institutions (like stock markets and insurance markets) also play an increasingly important role? Both financial and human resources for developing and regulating nonbank institutions tend to be limited in African countries, so that efforts to develop such markets that are resource demanding should be based on evidence-based policy advice. Should specialized lending institutions, like leasing or factoring companies, as well as low-end financial institutions such as cooperatives, credit unions, and microfinance, be promoted, as suggested in Beck, Demirgüç-Kunt, and Singer (2011)? If the insights of imperfect and asymmetric information are central, such information tends to be local and specialized (Stiglitz 2012); this may provide an important theoretical and practical justification for greater use of more low-end and more decentralized institutions. Would the latter, for example, be particularly effective for the financing of SMEs, and more broadly for the so-called missing middle? For many African households, such low-end financial institutions constitute the only form of financial access. In Uganda, for instance, only 21 percent of adults above the age of fifteen have an account at a formal financial institution (Demirgüç-Kunt and Klapper 2012). Governments have hence promoted cooperatives, credit unions, and microfinance. How can a more desirable mix be encouraged? What is the empirical evidence on which to base such decisions?

6. How can development of primary public debt markets be encouraged to establish risk-free benchmark curves? Based on deepening of the public bond market, how can the local corporate bond market best be

developed, including for long-term institutional investors to buy? What are relevant lessons from the analysis of experiences in other parts of the world and of recent empirical work on growth impact of structures of different financial sectors?

7. What kind of institutional developments and financial innovations are valuable for promoting inclusive and more sustainable growth without increasing systemic risk excessively? More specifically, what systems can improve access by the poor and by SMEs to sustained credit, which do not create systemic risk for the financial system? Mobile banking, which should be regulated proportionate to its risk, is an example for such an innovation. How can the poor not only have access to sufficient and sustainable credit but also be protected in times of crisis so that the poor are "not too small to be counted" during crises, while banks are rescued because they are considered too big to fail (BIS paper 2012)? What are the complementarities among financial and other policies, for example, for increasing productivity of SMEs?

THE CHALLENGES OF FINANCIAL REGULATION

A key lesson from recent crises has been the need for regulation to be both countercyclical and comprehensive to avoid the build-up of systemic risk (Griffith-Jones, Ocampo, and Stiglitz 2009; Saurina and Repullo 2011). Though there is agreement on these principles, there is far less consensus on how these should be implemented. A great deal of research and policy analysis is being carried out in the BIS, the IMF, and the Financial Stability Board on these issues.

One of the key problems is that LICs are not represented at all or are heavily underrepresented in these bodies. Therefore there is insufficient focus in their work on how relevant these issues are for LICs and how they should be implemented in them.

It may be useful to carry out research that would synthesize ongoing discussions on these issues of countercyclicality and comprehensiveness, as well as other key issues that LIC regulators and policymakers define as a priority for them. Over the past decade, there has been rapid credit growth in a number of African countries, including Angola, Democratic Republic of Congo, Equatorial Guinea, Ghana, Guinea-Bissau, Liberia, Malawi, Nigeria, São Tomé and Príncipe, Sierra Leone, Swaziland, Tanzania, and Zambia (Iossifov and Khamis 2009). Whether a manifestation of a credit boom or driven by fundamentals, rapid credit growth can give rise to systemic financial and macroeconomic risks, making the design and implementation of appropriate macroprudential regulation and supervision a policy priority in Africa. For example, the final report of *Making Finance Work for Africa*, in collaboration with the Association of African Central Banks (AACB) and the Bank of Uganda (2011), defined as most relevant and urgent for African LICs—within Basel III—the incorporation of macroprudential supervision.

In the case of macroprudential regulation, an important research issue is how can it be complementary to monetary policy in LICs? Macroeconomic volatility, for instance, remains a problem, partly because many African countries' exports are concentrated in a few commodities, which makes their economies vulnerable to the large price shocks characteristic of commodities.

Furthermore, practical issues on how best to implement macroprudential policy would require research. These could include the following:

1. What, in the LIC context, is the best choice of regulatory instrument through which countercyclical regulation can best be implemented both for solvency and liquidity? What are the best indicators to determine when capital requirements or provisions need to be increased in boom times in LICs, or allowed to be drawn down in bad times? How should the variables and methodologies suggested internationally for countercyclical regulation be adapted to realities in LICs as regards data limitations, as well as broader context of the smaller financial sector and existing financial regulation (Bank of Uganda 2012)?

2. Should countercyclical regulation of banks be done in LICs mainly at an aggregate level and/or in specific sectors, for example, where lending is increasing fastest? Should such measures be implemented through ex-ante rules or have some flexibility?

3. Focusing on the issue of comprehensiveness: How relevant are the international analyses of comprehensive regulation for African LICs and how should any international conclusions be modified for the LIC context? This requires taking into account the different nature of the financial system in LICs, where, for example, many financial transactions go through informal channels or financial services are provided by non-banking institutions like retail shops or mobile service providers. The mobile payment service M-Pesa, developed in Kenya, is a case in point. M-Pesa was launched to target mobile subscribers who were unbanked

and now has over seven million customers, both banked and unbanked. Light regulation in the testing phase of the financial product, on the principle of proportionate supervision, contributed to M-Pesa's rapid growth. However, at a later stage of product development and at a higher level of outreach, regulation may need to become significantly more stringent for M-Pesa's success to be sustainable. Yet comprehensive regulation of M-Pesa and other financial innovations may call for closer coordination between regulators of such institutions (for example, tele-communications regulators in mobile banking) and banking regulators. Therefore the challenge of comprehensive regulation has a very different institutional character in LICs.

4. Also in relation to aims of financial regulation, in LICs these include more explicitly the purpose of inclusive growth. Can regulations go beyond stability and be designed more explicitly for growth? How can lending best support industrial policies and regional mandates to ensure poor regions have more access to credit? What is the experience on establishing minimums and maximums of lending in certain categories, for example, SMEs? Are experiences like the U.S. Community Reinvestment Act or the Small Business Administration successful and relevant to LICs? Are there similar successful experiences in LICs?

Also of high priority are regional/cross-border issues. This refers not only to regulation of traditional international banks but also to the rapidly emerging pan-African banks. As Fuchs, Losse-Mueller, and Witte (2012) point out, recent reforms of the international supervisory architecture concentrated on creating colleges of supervisors for all internationally operating banks. Representation of African supervisors (especially LICs) is very limited; this is a source of concern because an international bank may have a small part of its portfolio in an African country while implying a very large share of their market for a particular LIC country. The role of the LIC supervisor in these colleges becomes too small, if there is any at all, with potentially serious consequences for financial stability and growth impact in the LIC country. Key are the political economy of how to practically enhance the "voice" of LIC supervisors in cross-border supervisory processes that have strong impacts on their economy, and to overcome asymmetries of power that can lead to economically inefficient outcomes for LICs.

A key source of macroeconomic volatility, as well as of financial systemic risk, is generated by certain types of capital flows. As a result, there has been growing recognition, in IMF and BIS, as well as in the academic literature (for example, Stiglitz and Ocampo 2008; Korinek 2011; Gallagher, Griffith-Jones, and Ocampo 2012), on the need for management of the capital account. One of the newest research and policy challenges is how to most effectively combine regulation of capital flows and national countercyclical regulation. Again discussion in LICs has been more limited. Are capital account management measures also needed in LICs, and under what circumstances? In best practice, when are capital account regulations more effective, and when are domestic prudential regulations, which focus on currency mismatches? How best can they complement each other? The large volume of bond issues by Sub-Saharan African sovereigns recently implies access to new sources of capital, but poses new risks, as international experience tells us.

The types of issues to be examined on capital account management for LICs would relate to issues of: (a) Timing, relating to how soon after a surge of capital flows starts occurring should measures to discourage more short-term flows be used; (b) Should they be temporary or part of a permanent system that can be suspended? (c) If and when should these regulations be price or quantity based? and (d) How can avoidance be prevented?

Our analysis has focused more on discouraging excessive short-term capital flows when they threaten to cause macroeconomic overheating, overvalued exchange rates, and increased financial sector systemic risk. However, there is also the important issue of attracting long-term capital flows, especially where it can provide technology transfer and access to new markets. This is a topic that now has new dimensions, such as the increased role of Chinese and other southern investors. Such new sources and modalities have both potential positive impact and risks to the financial sector.

CONCLUSION

While the 2007/2008 crisis originated in, and strongly hit, developed economies, African economies and financial systems were relatively unscathed. However, there is no reason for complacency in regulating African financial sectors. Fairly rapid credit growth in the late 2000s, in the context of limited regulatory and supervisory capacity (especially in some countries), suggests that the time is ripe to draw appropriate lessons for African countries from the North Atlantic crisis. There is also no reason to believe that if major private financial crises have hit all other continents, Africa would be an exception, unless it proceeds very cautiously with financial liberalization and financial development, as well as accompanying it with strong and effective regulation.

Regulation of the financial sector should be countercyclical, to prevent boom-bust cycles that can lead to developmentally costly crises, and comprehensive, to include all institutions that provide credit. Capital flows should also be prudently managed and, where appropriate, capital account regulations should complement domestic financial regulation, as is increasingly recognized by institutions such as the IMF and the BIS. Furthermore, the rapidly growing borrowing on the international bond markets by SSA sovereigns could lead to future problems, so it needs careful monitoring.

The fact that African LICs' financial systems are still relatively small in relation to the size of their economies allows more space for African policymakers and regulators to try to shape their financial systems so they serve the needs of the real economy well by helping support inclusive and sustainable growth (for example, by supporting much-needed lending to SMEs), as well as desirable structural change.

Furthermore, the fact that the financial sector is smaller in SSA countries, as a proportion of GDP, may imply it is less powerful politically; thus this potentially gives more autonomy to regulators—and more broadly to governments—to shape the financial sector to serve the real economy.

A key issue is not just the size but also the structure of the financial sector. Because financial sectors are riddled with market imperfections and market gaps, it is important to have government interventions to correct these market imperfections (for example, the pro-cyclical nature of private lending) and institutional arrangements to fill market gaps (for example, sufficient long-term finance for helping finance private sector investment). Furthermore, to implement a particular vision and strategy of development, it is valuable for governments to have institutions and mechanisms to help finance development of particular sectors. In this context, it is important to design instruments and institutions that can perform such functions. Public development banks have worked well and often played a very important role in the development of many successful countries, such as Germany, Japan, South Korea, Brazil, and others. It is therefore an important research and policy challenge to help define the conditions for "good" (that is, well functioning, in terms of their objectives) development banks to be created and to operate in low-income countries in Sub-Saharan Africa.

There is also growing consensus that smaller, more decentralized banks may be more appropriate in low-income countries, especially to lend to small and medium enterprises, partly because they can know their customers better, reducing asymmetries of information. Overall, a more diversified banking system, with large and small banks, as well as private and public development banks, seems to offer benefits of diversification (and thus less systemic risk), complementarities in serving different sectors and functions, as well as providing competition for providing cheap and appropriate financial services to the real economy.

NOTES

We are very grateful to Joseph Stiglitz for valuable comments on an earlier draft of this chapter. We are also very grateful for very good comments received at the IPD Africa Task force meetings in New York and Yokohama, especially those from Akbar Noman. Charles Harvey also gave detailed comments. We thank ESRC/DFID for their support for the research leading to this chapter. We are also grateful to Florence Dafe for her valuable input and Nshalati Hlungwane for excellent research assistance.

1. They are the sum of currency and deposits in the central bank (M0), plus transferable deposits and electronic currency (M1), plus time and savings deposits, foreign currency transferable deposits, certificates of deposit, and securities repurchase agreements (M2), plus travelers checks, foreign currency time deposits, commercial paper, and shares of mutual funds or market funds held by residents. This definition of broad money is used by the IMF and the World Bank.

REFERENCES

African Development Bank (AfDB). 2012. *African Guarantee Fund for Small and Medium-Sized Enterprises Information Memorandum.* Tunis: AfDB.
———. 2013. *Our Operations: African Guarantee Fund.* Tunis: AfDB. http://www.africanguaranteefund.com.
Association of African Central Banks (AACB) and the Bank of Uganda Financial Action Task Force. 2011. *Final Report of the Making Finance Work for Africa Conference.*
Banco de Moçambique. 2013. *Statistics, Overall Credit Statistics by Purpose.* Maputo: Banco de Moçambique. http://www.bancomoc.mz/Default_en.aspx.
Bank of Mauritius. 2013. *Financial Stability Report.* Port Louis: Bank of Mauritius.
Bank of Uganda. 2012. *Financial Stability Report (June).* Kampala: Bank of Uganda.
Barth, J., T. Li, W. Lu, and G. Yago. 2010. *Capital Access Index 2009.* Santa Monica: Milken Institute.

Beck, T., B. Buyukkarabacak, F. Rioja, and N. Valev. 2012. "Who Gets the Credit? And Does it Matter? Household vs. Firm Lending across Countries." *BE Journal of Macroeconomics* 12 (1): 3–44.

Beck, T., A. Demirgüç-Kunt, and D. Singer. 2011. "Is Small Beautiful? Financial Structure, Size and Access to Finance." World Bank Policy Research Working Paper No. 5806 (September): 1–32.

Beck, T., M. Fuchs, D. Singer, and M. Witte. 2014. *Making Cross-Border Banking Work for Africa.* Bonn: GIZ and World Bank.

Beck, T., S. Munzele Maimbo, I. Faye, and T. Triki. 2011. *Financing Africa. Through the Crisis and Beyond.* Washington, DC: World Bank.

Botha, A. 2011. "Interview Titled: Finance Strategies for SME Development." *CNBC Africa,* May 5.

Brownbridge, M., C. Harvey, and F. Gockel. 1998. *Banking in Africa: The Impact of Financial Sector Reform Since Independence.* Oxford: James Currey and Africa World Press.

Cecchetti, S. G., and E. Kharroubi. 2012. "Reassessing the Impact of Finance and Growth." BIS Working Papers 381 (July): 1–17. http://www.bis.org/publ/work381.pdf.

Centre for Affordable Housing Finance in Africa (CAHF). 2012. *Housing Finance in Africa, 2012 Year Book.* Johannesburg: CAHF.

De la Torre, A., and A. Ize. 2011. "Containing Systemic Risk: Paradigm-based Perspectives on Regulatory Reform." World Bank Policy Research Working Paper No. 5523 (January): 1–26. http://elibrary.worldbank.org/doi/pdf/10.1596/1813–9450–5523.

Demirgüç-Kunt, A., and H. Huizinga. 2010. "Are Banks Too Big to Fail or Too Big to Save? International Evidence from Equity Prices and CDS Spreads." World Bank Policy Research Working Paper No. 5360 (May): 1–50.

Demirgüç-Kunt, A., and L. Klapper. 2012. "Measuring Financial Inclusion: The Global Findex Database." World Bank Policy Research Paper No. 6025 (April): 1–58. http://elibrary.worldbank.org/doi/pdf/10.1596/1813–9450–6025.

Department of Trade and Industry (DTI). 2010. *The New Growth Path.* Pretoria: DTI.

Detragiache, E., T. Tressel, and P. Gupta. 2008. "Foreign Banks in Poor Countries: Theory and Evidence." *Journal of Finance* 63: 2123–2160.

Easterly, W., R. Islam, and J. Stiglitz. 2000. "Shaken and Stirred, Explaining Growth Volatility." Annual Bank Conference on Development Economics, World Bank, Washington, DC.

Fuchs, M., T. Losse-Mueller, F. Strobbe, and M. Witte. 2012. *African Financial Sectors and the European Debt Crisis: Will Trouble Blow across the Sahara?* Washington, DC: World Bank.

Fuchs, M., T. Losse-Mueller, and M. Witte. 2012. "The Reform Agenda for Financial Regulation and Supervision in Africa." In *Financial Sector Development in Africa: Opportunities and Challenges,* ed. T. Beck and S. M. Maimbo. Washington, DC: World Bank.

Gallagher, K. P., S. Griffith-Jones, and J. A. Ocampo. 2012. "Capital Account Regulations for Stability and Development: A New Approach." *Issues in Brief* 22: 1–8.

Griffith-Jones, S., J. A. Ocampo, and A. Ortis. 2009. "Building on the Counter-Cyclical Consensus: A Policy Agenda." Paper prepared for the High-level Roundtable, Towards Basel 3? Regulating the Banking Sector after the Crisis, Brussels, October 12.

Griffith-Jones, S., J. A. Ocampo, and J. Stiglitz. 2010. *Time for a Visible Hand: Lessons from the 2008 World Financial Crisis*. New York: Oxford University Press.

Haldane, A. G., and V. Madouros. 2012. "The Dog and the Frisbee." Bank of England speech given at the Federal Reserve Bank of Kansas City's 36th Economic Policy Symposium, The Changing Policy Landscape, Jackson Hole, Wyoming, August 31.

Honohan, P., and T. Beck. 2007. *Making Finance Work for Africa*. Washington, DC: World Bank.

International Monetary Fund (IMF). 2011. "Nigeria: Staff Report for the 2010 Article IV Consultation." *IMF Country Report*. Washington, DC: IMF.

———. 2012a. "Walking Hand in Hand: Fiscal Policy and Growth in Advanced Economies." Discussion paper, IMF, Washington, DC.

———. 2012b. *Global Financial Stability Report: Restoring Confidence and Progressing on Reforms*. Washington, DC: IMF.

———. 2013. *Republic of Mozambique. Staff Report for the Article IV Consultation*. Washington, DC: IMF.

Iossifov, P., and M. Khamis. 2009. "Credit Growth in Sub-Saharan Africa—Sources, Risks, and Policy Responses." IMF Working Paper No. 180: 1–30.

Kasekende, L. A., J. Bagyenda, and M. Brownbridge. 2011. *Basel III and the Global Reform of Financial Regulation: How Should Africa Respond? A Bank Regulator's Perspective*. Washington, DC: New Rules for Global Finance. http://www.new-rules.org/storage/documents/g20-fsb-imf/kasakende.docx.

Kindleberger, C. P. 1978. *Manias, Panics, and Crashes: A History of Financial Crises*. New York: Basic Books.

Korinek, A. 2011. "Systemic Risk-taking: Amplification Effects, Externalities, and Regulatory Responses." Working Paper Series 1345 (June): 1–41. http://www.ecb.europa.eu/pub/pdf/scpwps/ecbwp1345.pdf.

Laeven, L., and F. Valencia. 2008. "Systemic Banking Crises: A New Database." IMF Working Paper No. 224: 1–78. https://www.imf.org/external/pubs/ft/wp/2008/wp08224.pdf.

———. 2012. "Systemic Banking Crises: An Update." IMF Working Paper No. 163 (June): 1–32. http://www.imf.org/external/pubs/ft/wp/2012/wp12163.pdf.

Levine, R. 2005. "Finance and Growth: Theory and Evidence." In *Handbook of Economic Growth*, ed. P. Aghion and S. Durlauf, 1: 865–834. Amsterdam: Elsevier.

Minsky, H. P. 1974. "The Modeling of Financial Instability: An Introduction." In *Modeling and Simulation*, vol. 5, Proceedings of the Fifth Annual Pittsburgh Conference, Instruments Society of America, 267–272.

Murinde, V. 2012. *Development-Orientated Financial Regulation*. Washington, DC: New Rules for Global Finance. http://www.new-rules.org/storage/documents/g20-fsb-imf/murinde-kups.pdf.

Rajan, R. G. 2005. "Has Financial Development Made the World Riskier?" Proceedings of the Jackson Hole Conference organized by the Kansas City Fed, Jackson Hole, Wyoming.

Rashid, H. 2011. "Credit to Private Sector, Interest Rate Spread and Volatility in Credit Flows: Do Bank Ownership and Deposits Matter?" UN DESA Working Paper No. 105 (May). http://www.un.org/esa/desa/papers/2011/wp105_2011.pdf.

Sanusi, L. S. 2010. "The Nigerian Banking Industry: What Went Wrong and the Way Forward." Convocation lecture delivered at the Convocation Square, Bayero University, Kano, February 26.

Saurina, J. S., and R. Repullo. 2011. "The Countercyclical Capital Buffer of Basel III: A Critical Assessment." Centre for Economic Policy Research Discussion Paper No. DP 8304. http://www.cemfi.es/ftp/wp/1102.pdf.

Sengupta, R. 2007. "Foreign Entry and Bank Competition." *Journal of Financial Economics* 84: 502–528.

Soludo, C. 2004. "Consolidating the Nigerian Banking Industry to Meet the Development Challenges of the 21st Century." Address delivered to the Special Meeting of the Bankers' Committee, Abuja, Central Bank of Nigeria, July 6.

South African Reserve Bank (SARB). 2013. *Annual Report*. Pretoria: SARB.

Standard Bank. 2013. *Supporting SMEs*. http://sustainability.standardbank.com /socioeconomic-development/enterprise-development/supporting-smes/.

Stiglitz, J. 2012. "Monetary Policy in a Multipolar World." Paper presented in IEA Conference, Turkey, November.

Stiglitz, J., and J. A. Ocampo. 2008. *Capital Market Liberalization and Development*. New York: Oxford University Press.

Tobin, J. 1984. "On the Efficiency of the Financial System." *Lloyds Bank Review* 153: 1–15.

World Bank. 2013a. *Enterprise Surveys, What Businesses Experience*. Washington, DC: World Bank. http://www.enterprisesurveys.org.

——. 2013b. *World DataBank*. Washington, DC: World Bank.

FURTHER READING

Basel Committee on Banking Supervision. 2010. *Microfinance Activities and the Core Principles for Effective Banking Supervision*. Basel: Bank for International Settlements.

Beck, T., A. Demirgüç-Kunt, and R. Levine. 2010. "Financial Institutions and Markets: Across Countries and Over Time." *World Bank Economic Review* 24 (1): 77–92.

Central Bank of Nigeria. 2013. *Data and Statistics*. http://www.cenbank.org/Rates.

Economics Intelligence Unit (EIU). 2011. *Private Consumption*. London: EIU.

Emerging Markets Consultants. 2012. *Blog Mozambique (Maputo)*. http://www .emergemarkets.com/blog.

Financial Action Task Force. 2013. *Anti-Money Laundering and Terrorist Financing Measures and Financial Inclusion*. Paris: FATF.

Financial Services Authority. 2009. *The Turner Review: A Regulatory Response to the Global Banking Crisis*. London: Financial Services Authority.

Global Partnership for Financial Inclusion. 2011. *Global Standard-Setting Bodies and Financial Inclusion for the Poor Toward Proportionate Standards and Guidance, A White Paper*. Prepared by CGAP on behalf of the G-20.

HM Treasury. 2012. *Vickers Report*. Independent Commission on Banking, Draft Banking Reform Bill.

International Monetary Fund (IMF). 2009. *Impact of the Global Financial Crisis on Sub-Saharan Africa*. Washington, DC: IMF, Africa Department.

——. 2012c. "Fourth Review Under the Policy Support Instrument and Request for Modification of Assessment Criteria." *IMF Country Report*. Washington, DC: IMF.

Reddy, Y. V. 2012. "Society, Economic Policies and the Financial Sector." Presented at the Jacobsson Lecture, the Bank for International Settlements, Basel, June 24.

Ren, H. 2011. "Countercyclical Financial Regulation." World Bank Policy Research Working Paper No. 5823. http://elibrary.worldbank.org/doi/pdf/10.1596/1813-9450-5823.

Sriram, M. S., V. Chaturvedi, and A. Neti. 2012. "Too Big to Fail Versus too Small to be Counted." *BIS Papers* 62. http://www.bis.org/publ/bppdf/bispap62j.pdf.

CHAPTER 8

Growth Strategies for Africa in a Changing Global Environment

POLICY OBSERVATIONS FOR SUSTAINABLE AND SHARED GROWTH

Danny Leipziger and Shahid Yusuf

Following decolonization in the 1950s and the 1960s, growth accelerated in several of the leading African economies with the flowering of long-delayed industrial activity, the modernization of physical infrastructure, and the quickening of urbanization. However, by the mid-1970s this initial phase of catching up had run out of steam as countries fell prey to political turbulence, internal and cross-border conflicts, and economic distortions introduced by policy mismanagement and import substituting industrialization. Problems internal to the continent were exacerbated by the weakening performance of Africa's main trading partners in the West. African countries entered a long economic twilight that extended through the mid-1990s;[1] since then and for over a decade, Africa has benefited from a widely shared revival of economic activity. Reasons for this revival include the spurt in growth worldwide that can be traced to globalization; the upsurge in innovations triggered by the advent of the Internet and advances in semiconductor/digital technologies, by expansionary monetary policies, and by the extraordinary economic prowess of China and other Asian countries that raised the tempo of industrialization; the demand for mineral resources; and the volume of trade, particularly South-South trade. Other causes for this resurgence are internal to Africa. On balance, there is greater stability and a democratization of politics, macroeconomic policy is better managed, African economies are more open, and human development indicators have improved. Also, higher primary product prices have enhanced export earnings and increased the volume of foreign direct investment (FDI) in resource-based sectors and linked infrastructures.[2]

With growth averaging over 5 percent per year during 2000 and 2011, both African policymakers and external observers are confident that the continent has turned the corner and its long-term prospects are brighter than at any time in the recent past. But this newfound momentum cannot be taken for granted, and sustaining or even improving on this performance will depend on how effectively African countries, both individually and collectively, respond to a number of challenges—old and new. In particular, the financial crisis of 2008/2009 has seriously weakened some of Africa's principal Western trading partners and suspended questions over the future contribution of industrialization, trade, and the flow of aid to Africa's growth. Aid fatigue, and doubts as to its efficacy,[3] is being compounded by the budgetary woes of Western countries that are unlikely to be resolved during this decade.[4] Moreover, the sources (and the future[5]) of growth are less easy to discern than was the case just five years ago. Even the East Asian economies are casting around for additional drivers of growth with services including nontradable ones becoming the focus of policy attention.[6] The fragmentation of production and its offshoring from Western countries might by now be well past its high water mark, and in fact there is some evidence of a reflux of certain kinds of manufacturing activities back to the industrialized nations. Whether the transfer of some industrial activities from East Asia (China in particular) to Africa will offset a slowing of offshoring from the West remains to be seen. A sharp and sustained increase in capital investment, rapid technological advance, and innovation complemented by human capital deepening and a strengthening of governance institutions are plausible options, but all demand a commitment to long-term development strategies backed by the sort of sustained political resolve that has been in short supply in Africa.

So much is at stake that inaction is not a viable option. African countries will need to adopt a proactive approach and capitalize on both the newly gained confidence in the continent's future and the mineral and energy discoveries that have brightened the growth prospects of countries such as Mozambique,[7] Ghana, Tanzania, and Uganda, among others. Several attempts have been made to craft a strategic framework for African countries,[8] but the uncertainties injected by the lingering aftermath of the financial crisis have complicated the situation and made it harder to chart a course forward. While recent research offers a plethora of findings, these too add to the confusion because not infrequently their relevance for Africa and the practical policy implications are left unstated.

The purpose of this chapter is to sketch a strategy for African late starters that identifies the key objectives and the mix of policy initiatives appropriate for a post–financial crisis environment in which South-South trade and capital flows are taking on a greater salience. In sketching this framework, the chapter will draw on the empirical work that is helping spell out the constants in growth economics and what our new knowledge suggests are the changes that need to be factored into policies.[9] The chapter is divided into three parts. The first part briefly reviews the performance of African economies over the past decade; it highlights the factors that enabled the continent to escape from a prolonged spell of stagnation. The second part notes the challenges for African countries and how these have been sharpened by the crisis and by other developments, such as the greatly enlarged role of China in both the global economy and in Africa. The third part defines a diversified strategy[10] that could help African countries remain on their current growth paths while addressing challenges they cannot afford to sidestep.

AFRICAN ECONOMIC PERFORMANCE, 1990–2011

The first half of the 1990s was a low point for growth in Sub-Saharan Africa—0.8 percent per year. In the latter half of the decade, growth rose to an average of 3.9 percent per year, well in excess of the 2.4 percent average of the 1980s,[11] and it continued accelerating into the first decade of the twenty-first century.[12] Growth between 2000 and 2010 averaged 5 percent per year and, in spite of spreading gloom in the European Union, was 5.1 percent in 2011. Growth slowed to 3.7 percent in 2012 but then rose to 4.7 percent in 2013–2014.[13] This performance was supported by a rise in investment rates from an average of 18 percent in 1990 to 21 percent in 2012[14]—not comparable to East Asian levels, but respectable nonetheless—and by an increase in total factor productivity from –0.5 percent per year between 1980 and 1994 to 1.3 percent per year since 1995.[15] Exports grew from just over 26 percent of GDP in 1990 to almost 32 percent in 2012.[16] Several countries also improved their social and Doing Business indicators,[17] and foreign investment in Africa rose from USD 9 billion in 2000 to USD 57 billion in 2013,[18] with African countries attracting 3.9 percent of global inflows. Remittances also climbed to USD

41.6 billion in 2011.[19] And African countries reduced their external debt in 2012 to 22 percent of GDP from 63 percent in 2000 (Severino and Debled 2012).

The stronger growth performance is reflected in some progress toward several Millennium Development Goals (MDGs). The region has achieved 35 percent of its poverty target of halving the population living on less than USD 1.25 (in 2005 prices)—from 57 percent in 1990 to 48 percent in 2010 (World Bank 2014b), although according to Sala-i-Martin and Pinkovsky (2010), Africa is en route to halving its poverty rate by 2017. Moreover, growth was pro-poor with inequality diminishing since 1995.[20] In a recent paper, Alwyn Young (2012) goes further to claim that income statistics might be seriously underestimating the actual gains. By using the Demographic and Health Surveys, which collect data on household ownership of durables, he concludes that household consumption has in fact been increasing by between 3.4 and 3.7 percent per year, which is three to four times the rate reported by international data sources. Declining rates of poverty have had positive spillover effects, with the percentage of underweight and malnourished children declining by 25 percent. Furthermore, primary school completion rates rose to 79 percent in 2009, with countries such as Burundi, Madagascar, and Rwanda achieving near-universal primary enrollment; child mortality dropped from 181 to 130 percent over the same period; and there was a significant slowing in the growth of new HIV infections by up to 74 percent in some of the worst affected countries (United Nations 2012; *Economist* 2013, 3).

Other indicators convey a less positive picture. Gross savings fell from an average of 24.6 percent in 2006 to 20 percent in 2012.[21] Although gross capital formation was increasing, private fixed investment was unchanged at 13.4 percent of GDP from 2006 to 2009, and the infrastructure deficit scarcely narrowed.[22] In a disturbing trend, the share of manufacturing in GDP for Africa as a whole declined from 13 percent in 2000 to 10 percent in 2012.[23] It was 9.7 percent in East Africa, 5 percent in West Africa, and 18.2 percent in Southern Africa.[24] Moreover, most manufactures are resource based with low domestic value added, and they register limited productivity gains and spawn few linkages with the rest of the economy (UNCTAD 2011). Diversification of manufactured exports was correspondingly limited. The share of manufactured exports in total merchandise exports, which was 27 percent in 2000, fell to 26 percent in 2012,[25] and Africa was responsible for just 1.3 percent of global manufactured exports in 2008 (and 1.1 percent of global manufacturing value added in 2009), against 1 percent in 2000 (and 1.2 percent of global manufacturing value added). The principal exports of even the more industrialized African countries were resource based. For example, South Africa's top two exports were platinum and gold; Kenya's were tea and cut flowers; Ethiopia's were coffee and sesame seeds (the lackluster performance of manufacturing is noted in *Economist* [2013]);[26] Tanzania's were coffee and tobacco; and Ghana's were cocoa beans and manganese ores (World Bank 2011b).

CONTRIBUTING TO GLOBAL PUBLIC GOODS AND RAISING GROWTH POTENTIAL

The accumulated experience of more than half a century has substantially enhanced the developmental potential of the African continent. Technological advances and globalization have improved the growth prospects of late starters and opened up avenues for leap frogging in areas such as telecommunications, banking, and power generation. The scope for internalizing decades of lessons makes it possible for African countries to pursue smart urban development and avoid the many missteps of countries at a more advanced stage of urbanization. Increased South-South trade and capital flows and Africa's diminishing reliance on its traditional trading partners reduces the continent's vulnerability to a prolonged stagnation of Western economies. In comparison to the 1970s, Africa is in a better position to sustain its regained growth momentum. But success continent-wide will rest on two factors. First, Africa must increase the supply of global public goods that have helped foster recent prosperity but are currently inadequate to sustain future growth. Second, African countries must take a strategic and methodical approach to transforming economic assets into innovative drivers of economic performance.

Africa faces a host of challenges and an exhaustive listing serves no useful purpose. However, a small subset of global public goods is likely to exert a profound influence on Africa's prospects. These include continued integration with the global trading environment in a manner that contributes to the diffusion of capital and ideas; continent-wide political stability; and a wide-ranging, multisectoral response to global climate change that minimizes economic costs while containing the increase in greenhouse gas emissions.

INCREASING THE PROVISION OF PUBLIC GOODS

PRESERVING GLOBALIZATION

The past decade has witnessed a sea of changes in international relations alongside a rebalancing of the global GDP. It appears that we are entering a multipolar world in which a number of regional hegemons are vying to displace a single superpower. This could have political and economic consequences. On the political front, the risk of regional tensions leading to arms races and flaring into sharp and costly conflicts is greater. On the economic front, the stalemated Doha Round and climate change–related negotiations (UNFCCC)[27] provide a foretaste of what a multipolar world may be like. There is a nontrivial risk of a slide back to a more protectionist environment if countries are unable to correct trade imbalances, and industrial hollowing and associated unemployment could induce politicians to buy short-term relief by raising barriers to trade. The term "murky protectionism" has been coined to describe the creeping revival of trade impediments, which if not reversed, could begin to eat into the gains from trade and the opportunities for export-led growth (Baldwin and Evenett 2009, Evenett 2013[28]). Following the financial crisis, worries have again resurfaced over untrammeled flows of international capital and the possibility of "sudden stops" to some countries when investors panic, the appreciation of exchange rates in others faced with a surge in inflows, and the inflating of asset bubbles as a consequence of quantitative easing by central banks in some of the leading economies. Similarly, the backlash against financial innovations (including securitization and exotic derivatives), and the havoc some have caused, is leading to a tightening of regulations. These could not only curb the excesses of financial globalization but also limit the benefits to developing countries in the form of productivity gains from financial development (Bekaert, Harvey, and Lundblad 2011), equity capital for industrialization, and sophisticated banking technologies that improve access of local businesses to capital and resource allocation.[29]

Although its promoters[30] can exaggerate the advantages of globalization and a tempering of certain trends may well be desirable,[31] a reversal would not be in the interests of the community of nations. The world has lived through one such reversal in the early decades of the twentieth century, and a recurrence is best avoided. But unless the widening cleavages between the interests of the advanced countries and the interests of developing countries can be bridged, a partial retreat from globalization and a weakening of the institutions that contribute to the benefits from closer integration are unwelcome possibilities.

Africa cannot afford to remain a largely passive bystander, and the challenge for African countries is how to collectively work with and influence other nations to secure and improve the institutional underpinnings of globalization. This institutional infrastructure, painfully pieced together over the past several decades, is an enormous asset. It has its deficiencies; however, the priority should be to fix the problems so that the gains from economic globalization are more widely shared and there are effective procedures and fora for settling political differences. In an increasingly fractious world, the importance of the latter and its bearing on the former cannot be minimized. Africa will need to use "voice," diplomacy, and its growing economic clout to help safeguard the future of "good" globalization.

Sustaining globalization and contributing to the public goods that will maximize its advantages need to be complemented by continent-wide efforts at trade integration that could serve as an additional engine of growth. In particular, Africa's many small, landlocked countries stand to benefit from increased intra-African trade. This has risen more rapidly since 2000 than exports to the rest of the world, but it still amounts to less than 10 percent of Africa's total trade, with the large countries accounting for the lion's share.[32] Intraregional trade confers an additional advantage on the smaller countries because it favors the exports of processed goods to partner countries in Africa instead of the export of unprocessed goods overseas.[33] Regional institutions supporting trade liberalization, and backed by domestic policies promoting export-oriented development, will contribute to greater integration, as will investment in infrastructure to close the wide remaining gaps and pruning other behind-the-border impediments to the flow of trade.[34]

POLITICAL STABILITY AND INSTITUTIONS

It is commonplace to note that political stability and conflict avoidance are critical for growth to be sustainable. Africa has had its share of local conflicts[35] and has experienced their destructiveness.[36] With the spread of democratic and more inclusive regimes, the continent is enjoying a period of relative respite. But the threat of renewed instability has not disappeared. Internal conflicts continue to smolder in Sudan, Uganda, Mali, Nigeria, and the Democratic Republic of Congo. Democratic rules of government appear to be widely applied throughout the region with all countries except Eritrea holding elections, but both the Mo Ibrahim Index and the Freedom House Index point to a decline in "full electoral democracy" and in political participation since 2007. Joshua Kurlantzick (2013) has reinforced this view in a recent book describing the retreat of democracy worldwide.[37] Only Mauritius can be classified as a "full democracy."[38] However, as the *Economist* (2012a) notes, there are grounds for optimism in the blurring of ideological fault lines, the increasing numbers of young voters, the information and media access made possible by information and communication technology, and more carefully supervised elections in some countries. Nevertheless, Africa's political institutions are at the embryonic stage, and the recent progress seems tentative and precarious. There is an unabated need for continuing national and Pan-African efforts to secure the gains achieved and create the political milieu that can underpin inclusive growth. How to minimize economic instability, political tensions, corruption, and violent conflict will be a continuing test for many African countries.[39]

CLIMATE CHANGE

The third most pressing challenge, which is entwined with preserving globalization, is climate change. Many African countries are at the epicenter of the changes to come that will result in higher temperatures, desiccation, worsening water scarcities,[40] extreme weather events, and coastal flooding.[41] Adaptation will undoubtedly provide partial relief, and as Africa becomes more prosperous, the continent will find it easier to absorb the additional costs. But early and concerted efforts to mitigate climate change would ease the burden on later generations. In this regard, the challenge for Africa is to play a proactive role in international negotiations—because it has so much at stake—and for Africa's leaders to make an early commitment to greening growth. With the advanced economies preoccupied with their fiscal and employment problems, by default the baton is passed to developing countries. They should engage in bold commitments followed by determined efforts at implementing difficult and initially unpopular policies. With so much urbanization, industrialization, and transport development ahead, Africa could embark on a path that efficiently manages the growth of energy, water, and resource utilization. Similarly, Africa could constrain increasing greenhouse gas emissions caused by deforestation by preserving carbon-sequestering forests. This step would help Africa avoid becoming locked into less resource-frugal technologies and forms of urbanization. It would also protect the continent's wealth of biodiversity (Steiner 2010). The (evidence-based) policy options and technologies to achieve these objectives are well known, if governments can muster the political will and the administrative capacities to put them into effect. In the long run, such green policies are likely to prove much more inclusive than current strategies, which will entail costly adjustments that could destabilize societies and be especially hard on the poor.[42]

In part, growing sustainably will depend on global developments, which Africa can influence—if it tries. Successful intervention would require a joint and unified approach predicated on an alignment of key objectives among African countries, using existing Pan-African institutions, making common cause with other developing nations, and articulating the approach forcefully in international bodies such as the G-20, which have the capacity to affect the direction of global change.

RAISING AFRICA'S GROWTH POTENTIAL

How Africa mobilizes its own resources and enlarges its economic potential will largely determine its future. The potential differs significantly among countries, which range in size from Nigeria, with a population of 175 million, to the Comoros and Cape Verde, with populations of just half a million, and will evolve at differing rates. Moreover, natural resource endowments vary widely among countries. Hence strategies and policy options will vary and need to be country specific. These country characteristics will affect how countries respond to trends and harness their factor endowments. Nevertheless, broadly speaking, growth potential is likely to be keyed to the following conditions.

NATURAL RESOURCES

Africa's decade-long growth spurt is closely tied to the export of mineral resources and to the higher prices these now command. Looking ahead, the abundance of natural resources will be a major determinant of future potential. Therefore it will be vital to accurately assess the magnitude of resources; adopt a rate of exploitation that maximizes long-term benefit streams, while taking account of absorptivity; and carefully choose options for investing the proceeds from the mineral wealth.[43] Furthermore, augmenting resources through discovery[44] and with the help of technological advances will further contribute to the potential. Arable land and water resources are no less important. Both are scarce in a number of countries, and their efficient utilization can be enhanced with the help of new technologies that minimize the wastage of water and the degradation of arable land through erosion. More fortunate countries, such as Zambia, by effectively husbanding their water resources,[45] can benefit from the food security and agricultural exports that could derive from an abundance of cultivable land.

POPULATION AND THE YOUTH DIVIDEND

Demographics will have a large hand in the fortunes of African countries, all of which have growing populations. Between 1950 and the end of the century, Africa's population ballooned from 230 million to 811 million and by 2010 had passed the 1 billion mark (Deen 2011). At current trend rates of growth of 2.2 percent per year, it will approach 2.4 billion by 2050.[46] There is scope for reaping a demographic dividend because more than one-half of Africa's population is under the age of twenty (Fine 2012) and Africa will add 122 million people to its workforce between 2010 and 2020. Whether the dividend, which offers a window of opportunity,[47] is realized will depend on the quality of education provided,[48] measures to secure the health of the population, and most important, investment that generates jobs by enabling existing firms to grow and induce start-up activity.[49]

EXPORT-ORIENTED INDUSTRIALIZATION

The development of productive activities, mainly by the private sector, and their composition will decisively affect growth potential and employment. How these evolve is a function of entrepreneurship (including from the large African diaspora), investment, and technological change. As noted earlier, investment in productive assets and in infrastructure has been low. Some observers of the East Asian experience are of the view that a WTO-compatible variant of industrial policy that (with suitable safeguards) nurtures new and potentially competitive activities may be appropriate for some countries.[50] Absent such policies, African economies will struggle to build manufacturing capabilities and/or export-oriented services—other than tourism comparable to those of Southeast Asian countries—and be unable to create the millions of new jobs that the continent urgently needs. Such policies suitably embedded within a competitive business environment could also assist with the growth of African firms: with the exception of South Africa, African countries host very small numbers of companies employing more than one hundred people,[51] the sort of companies likely to venture into overseas markets. Moreover, as evident from the Boston Consulting Group's report on Africa's new challengers, the vast majority of the larger firms are in services (such as banking, telecommunications, transport, and construction) (Ndulu et al. 2007). Strengthening and diversifying the base of tradable products, not only in urban areas but also in the agricultural sector, will ultimately determine if Africa can reap the advantages of globalization. It will also determine whether African firms can integrate with global value chains with the help of FDI,[52] especially those that will tighten Africa's links with markets in developing countries in which demand is likely to be growing faster.

RURAL ECONOMY

The demographic center of most African economies is in the rural sector. In Sub-Saharan Africa, 63 percent of the population was rural in 2013,[53] although on average agriculture generated just 16 percent of the GDP. Nevertheless, the unexploited agricultural potential is large (60 percent of the world's uncultivated cropland is in Africa[54]), and as global population grows and food security becomes an issue, some African countries could emerge as major exporters. In 2008, arable land per one hundred people amounted to over 24 hectares—well above the average for low- and middle-income countries. Moreover, because of the neglect of agricultural R&D, fertilizer inputs,[55] irrigation infrastructure, and better tillage practices, agricultural productivity is the lowest in the world—grain yields average 900 pounds per acre with one-fifth of those in China. Yield increases have contributed to 34 percent of the increase in production since 1960 compared to 80 percent in South Asia (Smith et al. 2010).[56] The opportunities for catching up are considerable, and with climate change the development of drought- and disease-resistant crop strains and lean irrigation techniques is rapidly becoming a priority.

TECHNOLOGY, INNOVATION, AND FDI

Africa has gained relatively little from the huge advances in industrial, agricultural, and services-based technologies, although mobile telephony has made substantial inroads (475 million people had mobile phone subscriptions by 2012 compared to 90 million people seven years ago[57]). There is a wealth of opportunity for late starters if they can mobilize skills and capital. For Africa, the shorter route to growth could be via human capital deepening and determined efforts at raising its quality so that it can harness the technologies now available. Once a pool of human capital initiates a virtuous spiral, the supply of capital can follow from local sources and overseas. Casual empiricism suggests that there is no shortage of capital globally that is searching for profitable opportunities. Over the medium term, FDI could substitute for domestic savings if the business climate is propitious and foreigners can perceive the market opportunities. In addition to capital, FDI can be a source of much-needed technologies and it can help stimulate local innovation. For Africa, the benefits of plugging into the global innovation system will increase commensurately as innovation becomes a bigger source of growth.

DEMAND AS A DRIVER

Africa's growth is unlikely to be constrained by a dearth in the demand for its mineral resources. However, that alone might not be enough for the continent as a whole to sustain the growth and to create the jobs that it needs to—and in fact, a number of mineral-rich African countries have suffered from the growth-retarding "resource curse" or are susceptible to it.[58] Future growth will rest on the pace and composition of agro-industrial development and a robust services economy producing tradables that the rest of the world demands, and they must, to varying degrees, figure in the strategies of all countries. However, as seen in the case of South Africa, rich in resources, stable in politics, and large in size, the development of new industries, especially manufacturing, has been limited (Yusuf 2011). Africa will need to derive a substantial boost from the growth of its own middle classes eager to raise their own consumption standards—especially the younger elements (Fine 2012). By 2020, this class is projected to number 130 million, which will generate a strong demand for consumer goods (Fine and Lund 2012). This potential source of future growth must be facilitated and factored into any calculation of longer-term growth prospects.

A FRAMEWORK FOR SUSTAINABLE GROWTH

A two-pronged strategy straddling the global and the local is central to the achievement of sustainable economic growth; African economies will have to conduct policy on both registers depending on their international salience and capabilities. Here we will focus on how countries might go about augmenting and realizing their growth potential, starting with the minimum objectives for sustainable and inclusive growth: the rate of increase of GDP; employment opportunities for the vast majority of the workforce; the avoidance of wide income disparities without eliminating "good inequality" that sharpens incentives; and containment of the eco-logical/resource footprint.

A growth rate averaging 7 percent per year would bring Africa to the level reached by the Republic of Korea at the end of the twentieth century.[59] Although higher than what most African countries have registered during the past decade, it is a desirable target for a number of reasons. Africa's current low per capita income and large technological gaps permit an acceleration of growth; they also present well-charted opportunities for catching up. The current overhang of unemployment, which exceeds 20 percent of the workforce in countries such as South Africa, and the anticipated increase in the labor force[60] cannot be accommodated except through growth in excess of current levels. Capital-intensive and unskilled, labor-displacing, technological change is also reducing the elasticity of labor demand in manufacturing and in services (and, at least in the advanced countries, resulting in jobless growth) (Kapsos 2005). Therefore absorbing Africa's growing pool of workers will call for faster growth than in the past, even if most of the jobs are in light industry and services. Ensuring an acceptable sharing of the fruits of growth will be a challenge, but one that could be manageable if more of the growth derives from (1) labor-intensive manufacturing (some of it shifting from East and Southeast Asia to Africa), (2) relatively labor-intensive tradables, and (3) labor-intensive services. Finally, green growth (which encapsulates some of the messages embedded in "sustainable") will be a function of price signals that encourage conservation and changing life styles. But it will equally be influenced by regulatory policies; government procurement; standards (for vehicles, equipment, and durables, among others) and their enforcement; technological change; and the pace of absorption of new ideas into equipment and in production practices.

Looking forward, we elaborate the five elements of a strategic framework for sustainable growth in Africa: (1) the political system; (2) state policymaking as well as regulatory and implementation capacities; (3) resource mobilization, investment, and total factor productivity (TFP); (4) learning and innovation systems; and (5) management of the urban system. Although many of these elements are not new, the global situation in which economic growth is proving more difficult for all economies makes this a necessary list of priorities in our view to propel Africa's future growth.

POLITICAL SYSTEM

There has never been much doubt that economic policies are almost always freighted with myriad political concerns. They leave an imprint on policy design, affect implementation, and influence both the outcomes and how the public perceives them. The varied and, in many instances, partial and halting responses to the financial crisis across the world have brought home once again the far-reaching role of politics and of political institutions in how countries respond to crises and how they struggle to arrive at a consensus on longer-term strategies.[61]

What kind of a political system delivers the better economic results has been endlessly debated, and accumulating experience has been subjected to rigorous testing. A prior belief in the efficacy of democracy and the enlightened resilience of democratic institutions has been challenged by the superior economic performance of a handful of countries all in East Asia; they achieved outstanding results under autocratic regimes and without the benefit of institutions that credibly protected individual rights to speech and to property against the grasping hand of the state.[62] With two exceptions, China and Vietnam, all of the East Asian star performers have embraced democracy, and the two African countries that vied with the East Asian ones with regard to economic performance—Botswana and Mauritius—managed to grow rapidly under democratic regimes. But the belief lingers that the wise and far-seeing autocrat who can create an effective bureaucratic machinery is more likely to deliver the prosperity that developing countries are seeking—and, as noted earlier, democracy has lost some of its appeal worldwide. The empirical research suggests, however, that the prior belief in democracy has considerable merit (Radelet 2010). At worst, democracy does not impede growth, and for developing countries that are taking the democratic road, the direct and indirect benefits of democracy can be large.[63] Pereira and Teles (2010) state that political institutions supporting a more pluralitarian electoral system are important determinants of growth in incipient democracies, but political institutions have a weaker bearing on growth in consolidated democracies that have already internalized their effects. Indirect benefits of democracy derive from increased stability; a higher degree of account-ability; lower rates of inflation; the greater protection afforded to property rights; and the responsiveness to popular demands for education, health care, and a safety net.[64]

In a globalized world, countries are more exposed to external shocks and will require collective action and sacrifices if a liberal multilateral trade regime is to be sustained and climate change curbed. Under such conditions, democracies are better placed to win the support of the majority and to more equitably distribute rewards or burdens. For African countries that have embraced democracy (and the majority have), the priority is to continue the process of building institutions and strength-ening those already in place. African democracies have been buoyed by good economic times, but the danger of slippage is by no means past. A precondition of future sustained and inclusive growth is surely the com-mitment of governments and of the public to making democracies work better. To this end, Africa's democracies should use the political leverage of representative government to craft long-term growth strategies.

STATE CAPACITY

Democratic institutions can serve as the foundation of growth, but absent state capacity to frame and implement policies derived from an overarch-ing strategy, progress is unlikely.[65] For example, East Asian economies notably have delivered good economic results under both autocratic and democratic regimes and have performed credibly on the international stage. To be successful, they have all relied on the capacity of the state's bureaucratic machinery to efficiently conduct wide-ranging development activities—including long-range planning policies to develop compara-tive advantage—and to steadily build the market and regulatory institu-tions that determine how well or poorly an economy functions. Weak state governing and policymaking capacities have been the bane of many African countries. These deficiencies should be remedied through public sector reforms that address problems with recruitment, culture, incen-tives, accountability, and the motivations to serve the public and to deliver results. A reformed public sector is the necessary complement to a development strategy aimed at prolonging the recent growth spurt and tackling the challenge of sustainability.

State capacity might be even more vital in the future because the financial crisis has stirred doubts and forced a rethinking of neoliberal policies.[66] The retreat of the state in developing economies (if such a retreat was ongoing or in the offing) is over, for the time being at least. As indicated earlier, a number of countries—including some advanced economies—are taking a second look at updated variants of industrial policies practiced by China[67] (and earlier by the Republic of Korea, Taiwan, China, and other Asian "tigers"). There is also a renewed push to fashion policies that do not undermine allocative efficiency and competitiveness and minimize the risk of public agency capture by industrial entities.[68] Structural (and youth) unemployment might also demand a more active role in creating jobs (as is currently the case in the Middle East and a number of African countries). However, for industrial, active labor market and redistributive policies to succeed, state policymaking and implementation capacity must be augmented. Thus far, only a tiny handful of African countries can claim to have reached the requisite level of public sector efficiency and transparency needed to accomplish the task.[69]

RESOURCE MOBILIZATION, INVESTMENT, AND TFP

Capital investment in infrastructure,[70] housing, and productive assets is critical in the earlier stages of industrialization. However, as countries develop, more of the growth is derived from total factor productivity (TFP), which reflects embodied and disembodied technological change, innovation, tacit knowledge, and gains in efficiency from a variety of sources. Income gaps and the slow speed of income convergence among countries are associated with slowness in assimilating technologies and persisting technology gaps.[71] When technology gaps are wide, as in most African countries at an early stage of industrialization, more of the TFP accrues from investment in fixed assets and linked processes embodying the latest technologies. Jorgenson and Vu (2007) estimate that between 1989 and 1995, capital accounted for 41 percent of growth and TFP accounted for 22 percent of growth in the 110 countries analyzed. By 2000–2004, the share of capital had declined to 34 percent, while that of TFP had risen to 37 percent. In developing Asia, the share of TFP was 39 percent, while that of capital was 35 percent. In other words, between 70 and 74 percent of growth is from these interlinked sources. For African countries, during 2000–2004, capital contributed 21 percent of growth and TFP contributed 23 percent. Much of the growth in Africa came from labor inputs, with quantity prevailing over quality gains. Ndulu et al. (2007) point to the low or negative contribution of physical capital and TFP to growth in Africa between 1990 and 2003. However, recovery in the late 1990s was substantially aided by improved TFP.

If African countries want to follow the path of other industrializing economies over the next couple of decades, particularly East Asian economies, then they may need to invest heavily to generate growth and make up for infrastructure deficits in the agricultural and urban sectors, and also widen and deepen the productive base. Further down the road, TFP could move into the lead once incomes are considerably higher. For this reason, measures to raise investment in specific areas with the highest growth potential deserve priority. These are likely to differ from ones that have been the principal sources of recent growth. One-third of Africa's growth in the past decade was from the exploitation of natural resources; the balance was from development of wholesale and retail activities (13 percent), transport and telecommunications (10 percent), real estate and construction (10 percent), financial intermediation (6 percent), and public administration (6 percent). The real sectors—manufacturing and agriculture—contributed 9 percent and 12 percent, respectively.[72] In contrast, over the same period these latter subsectors were the main sources of growth and employment in East Asia, and will arguably play a vital role in enabling Africa to grow at higher and sustainable rates.

The markedly small share of manufacturing in African economies is responsible for weaknesses in the export mix. Abdon and Felipe (2011), using the product space methodology[73] devised by Hidalgo and Hausmann (2009), show that the export structure of resource-rich African countries barely changed between 1962 and 2007. They remained exporters of a narrow range of products, almost all lying on the edges of the product space (although it should be noted that exports from Ghana, Kenya, and South Africa are dominated by manufactures). A few land-locked countries added exports to their portfolio that were closer to the networked interior of the product space, while coastal countries revealed a comparative advantage in more networked products, particularly garments. But the results for African coastal economies were dominated by South Africa, which has the most products in the core of the product space. Abdon and Felipe observe that Africa's poorly diversified productive structure and the high proportion of standardized ubiquitous (peripheral) products exported by many countries seriously compromise their export prospects. Especially for the smaller countries that need external markets to generate sufficient demand for rapid growth, export diversification and upgrading is a must.

Moreover, as Easterly and Reshef (2010) note, the desired growth outcomes will depend on achieving "big hits," that is, large exports of a few products to a single market or a limited number of markets.[74] They claim that a disproportionate share of export earnings derive from big hits that are difficult to anticipate; in addition, the composition of the big hit is itself subject to churning.[75] The winning recipe, discerned from the experience of leading export nations, consists of conditions facilitating the entry and maturing of companies that can opportunistically become exporters with global value chains of garments, footwear, metal products, consumer electronics, food products, and auto parts, providing points of entry for firms capable of meeting price, quality, volume, and delivery standards. Creating these export-friendly conditions requires a long-term strategy to stimulate domestic and foreign investment (supported by domestic saving) by improving the business climate, access to financing at reasonable cost,[76] and ease of importing intermediates, and through incentives for entrepreneurs. The strategy can be supported by investments in infrastructure that do away with troublesome logistics constraints for businesses, but infrastructure building by itself will not lead to a crowding in of industrial investment needed to deepen and diversify the industrial sector. For that, some form of state-led, industrial policy–based inducements might be required as well, and East Asia is replete with such examples.

LEARNING AND INNOVATION SYSTEM

If growth is sustained, domestic, public, and private savings could rise and help finance increased investment. However, it is unlikely that Africa will be able to realize East Asian levels of resource mobilization; if so, increased TFP will be an asset. The road to higher TFP winds through the learning and innovation system, which is a weak point for all African countries, even South Africa. But it is a weakness that can and must be addressed.

The research of Hanushek et al. (2011)[77] suggests that such a growth path will require improving and deepening human capital with the help of education and related health policy reforms. And recent research by Glewwe, Maiga, and Zheng (2014) indicates that because of poor school quality, Africa is deriving less benefit from growth than other regions.[78] If African economies can substantially raise the quality of their workers, and if this in turn makes it possible for businesses to step up the pace of technology absorption, research, and development and innovation, then it is possible to envisage a shift to a sustainable high-growth path less reliant on capital accumulation. In fact, the quality of the labor force affects economic performance through multiple channels. Human capital is key to the building of research infrastructure, the production of ideas, and their commercialization. And human capital, suitably motivated, will influence the vigor of entrepreneurship. The difficult part—a difficulty underscored by the Glewwe et al. (2011) review—is actually identifying and implementing the policies that will produce results within the space of five or ten years (for example, improved performance of teachers),[79] and then translating the gains in human capital quality into growth performance. No country has found a durable recipe, although small countries such as Finland and Singapore can claim a measure of success.[80]

For health policies, Africa's disease burden and epidemiological profile raise the challenge for policymakers by an order of magnitude.[81] The widespread prevalence of debilitating infectious diseases and helminthic infections erodes efforts at building human capital, but these have been joined by the spread of chronic diseases arising from changing lifestyles and eating habits associated with urbanization and rising incomes (Aikins et al. 2010). As with education, there is some low-hanging fruit to harvest with the help of policy changes, the harnessing of appropriate technologies, and foreign assistance. But the key to success again lies with implementation, monitoring of results followed by policy adjustment as needed, and persistence.[82]

Development thinking buttressed by the experience of East Asian countries devotes most attention to manufacturing and tradable services. However, for decades ahead, Africa's growth and export prospects will also hinge on the productivity and diversification of the agricultural economy. In almost every African country, agriculture is the largest employer, especially of women; and given Africa's reserves of unused arable land, agriculture is a potentially large source of exports.[83] Africa has lagged behind in agricultural research, and as a result labor and land productivity is well below levels elsewhere (Paarlberg 2008). African researchers are making limited progress in developing disease-resistant and drought-resistant strains of the crops most vital for farmers.[84] Compounding the problem is increasing water scarcity in a number of countries, particularly in the north and the east of the continent. This is likely to become more acute as populations expand, industrial and urban demand increases, and global warming leads to worsening desertification that is already apparent in Ethiopia and Kenya. Both rural and urban dwellers will need to come to terms with water scarcity in the coming decades,[85] and the risk is that difficulties in agreeing on fair sharing of water resources could lead to tensions between riparian nations. A combination of pricing, conservation, and many technological fixes will be part and parcel of development strategies, but recent history offers scant encouragement. Evidence of shrinking freshwater resources has been growing, but African countries have yet to take the needed initiatives to manage their water resources, which will be a key to sustainable growth.[86] Whether independently or in conjunction with agricultural development, water must figure prominently in the defining of a sustainable growth strategy. Water management will be an ongoing and expensive undertaking.[87] However, if neglected, poor water management will lead to rising food prices, trade imbalances, and water stress, and cities will suffer under the weight of unchecked migration from rural areas.

URBAN SYSTEMS

Industrial and innovation policies (which have a bearing on the business climate) are intermeshed with urbanization policies. Together these affect what sort of productive activities cluster and flourish, where they cluster and flourish, their competitiveness, how much employment they generate, their growth potential, and the revenue they produce for cities. Managing the process and the characteristics of urbanization in Africa to extract the productivity gains from efficient land use, services provision, and agglomeration economies will be a crucial test for policymakers. This challenge must be successfully tackled while containing per capita resource and energy costs, and also minimizing the negative externalities that undermine the quality of urban life and contribute to environmental degradation.[88] Policymakers will have to battle the inertial patterns of sprawling urban development prevalent in almost all countries because of widening private automobile use, the problems caused by past infrastructure and housing development, and resistance from all those who benefit from the existing land use and urbanization patterns. But neglect of urbanization strategy and enabling policies would seriously compromise an important strand of development and also cripple efforts to limit climate change and mitigate its consequences. Urbanization strategies can be highly complex, and most African municipal administrations will need to develop the technical capacity, the administrative skills, and the financing to craft and implement workable strategies that take full advantage of new technologies, hard as well as soft.[89]

CONCLUDING OBSERVATIONS

The current decade is likely to differ markedly from the preceding one, and this will have significant implications for national growth policy formulation in Africa and for the policies of others, principally donors and foreign investors (see Rodrik 2012a and 2012b). The evolving global economic environment is both a blessing and a curse. It is a blessing because the high-growth engine of the world economy, China, is generating substantial demand for raw materials that Africa has in abundance, and because China's financial status and its willingness to use its surpluses make Africa a privileged destination. Moreover, China's resource commitment to Africa in recent years exceeds that of the World Bank and the African Development Bank (AfDB) combined, if one looks at lending and foreign direct investment flows.[90] Hence Africa has everything to gain under current circumstances. Of course, the generalized global slowdown is not good news for the export of manufactures; however, it will take a while for Africa to reach the stage at which it can compete in many developed markets, and by then the outlook may well have improved. Moreover, while some of the advanced economies are struggling to extricate themselves from the financial crisis aftermath, Africa until now has been largely spared these dislocations, and its growth is close to recent trend rates.

This growth momentum benefits from the policy dividend arising from favorable macroeconomic developments. Independent examination by the IMF, the World Bank, and others show that macroeconomic management has been increasingly prudent in many African countries.[91] By any number of measures of macroeconomic probity—fiscal and current account balances, foreign exchange reserves, and access to capital markets or inflation—the situation is generally propitious, and governments are well positioned to take advantage of this. Moreover, the historically low interest rates that now prevail and are likely to continue in the medium term are another reason to attract capital for the myriad of needed investments previously mentioned. Hence there is ample reason to act vigorously.

So what constitutes a vigorous growth policy and how might governments act so as to achieve the elusive 7 percent per year growth rate that doubles GDP in a decade? From past experience, it is clear that few countries have managed growth acceleration without considerable policy effort (Commission on Growth and Development 2008). Rapidly growing countries have generally made conscious choices to defer some consumption in order to promote investment. While a country is living near subsistence, this may be a difficult tradeoff to manage; yet Africa as a region is no longer in this absolutely dire situation (although there are of course counterexamples and special cases). The policy elements that have worked have included high and effective investments in human capital; strong efforts on infrastructure; the channeling of savings into productive export-led growth spearheaded by manufacturing (executed by the private sector but supported by public sector policies); well-coordinated, yet malleable programs; and a long-term vision to propel the economy forward.

Some of the necessary, but not in and of themselves sufficient, conditions have already been mentioned, in particular capable bureaucracies, effective public spending, low levels of corruption, and a workable relationship between business and government. With respect to a key point on cooperation between business and government, it should be noted that local entrepreneurs with the ability to tap informal overseas financial markets can be effectively mobilized—provided they understand what is expected of them. African countries can augment local entrepreneurial resources by tapping the offshore diaspora (Ratha and Plaza 2011), and East Asian financing can be an asset if properly exploited.

While structural change that is transferring labor from agriculture to the urban sector has served to raise productivity in recent years,[92] future gains, as in East Asia, will depend on the dynamism of firms producing manufactures and tradable services. As noted earlier, the manufacturing sector's share in GDP is shrinking in part because African labor costs (productivity adjusted) are high and because of other constraints.[93] Enlarging the role of manufacturing and strengthening the productivity of tradeable services will be a central developmental objective of all African countries.[94]

East Asian experience shows that vigorous competition is a good thing. In some countries, such as the Republic of Korea, access to scarce finance was used as the lever to force firms to compete for export markets, with the successful ones being given the opportunity to grow and ultimately become national champions.[95] If firms are protected in the domestic market, they will have little incentive to improve productivity, pursue innovation, and shift their energies to exports.[96] Examples from Latin America abound, where either a lack of domestic competition has resulted in high-cost services (for example, Mexican telecommunications charges are the highest in the OECD) or comfortable domestic markets have limited the export drive in new products (for example, Chilean manufacturing). Where domestic markets are small, as in most African economies, the focus should be on regional markets supported by regional trading arrangements. These can be encouraged by cross-border policies on infrastructure, regulations, and standards (as has been happening in East Africa with some success).[97]

The interest on the part of China in both exploiting natural resources on the continent and also providing infusions of capital provides an opportunity that is not infinite in duration. The rules of the game, therefore, become quite crucial in determining how natural resource rents will be used, what kinds of enticements will be offered and in exchange for what, how infrastructure projects will be sequenced, how much job creation will occur, and how much technical knowhow will be transferred. Africa's policymakers can take advantage of favorable circumstances, provided that they have strong and viable development strategies prepared. This is a clear lesson of East Asia's success.[98]

Finally, the role of bilateral and multilateral donors in helping Africa to make maximum use of this "decade of opportunity" requires some elaboration. The stories of bilateral assistance programs that are too small to be effective, too narrowly focused on areas that seem to generate support in donor capitals, and too short term in duration to generate sustainable impact are well known. Also well established is the insufficient level of cross-border financing for projects, especially in infrastructure needed on the continent, but that cannot command sufficient international development assistance. To break free of their low-manufacturing, low-value-added export structure, African countries need a significantly altered flow of assistance. Priority needs to be given to those flows that can be leveraged with private sector investments in energy, transport, ports, and rails. The analytic work of the Stern Report on Infrastructure (Commission for Africa 2005) and the follow-up work by the World Bank (Foster and Briceno-Garmendia 2010) leave no doubt that there are myriad high-return projects waiting to be funded. Action on these, some of which the New Partnership for Africa's Development (NEPAD) has identified, is long overdue.[99]

Africa is the last region to be facing the huge development challenges of today. In the past, much time was spent lamenting what did not happen and explaining why, and much of the scholarly work was excellent in its diagnostics.[100] The game has to move on to the phase in which action is required to enable Africa to make the necessary strides forward. A great deal can be learned from the policies of other regions, particularly East Asia. After all, Vietnam twenty years ago had an average per capita income of around USD 100 and a poverty rate of 70 percent; by 2014, its average per capita income was USD 2,000 and poverty was below 20 percent. While still an agricultural exporter, Vietnam managed to attract FDI and expatriate capital and move into new and higher value-adding industries. Vietnam was better endowed with energy than other poor developing countries, had a population of close to seventy million and thus a large domestic market, and is not landlocked. Nevertheless, Vietnam's vital statistics as of 1990 were far worse than those of many African economies. Yet it has begun transforming into a more modern economy. Africa can and should do no less.

A final observation is that countries that radically transformed themselves and grew at high and sustainable rates decade upon decade did so not with the stroke of the pen or a single policy intervention but with the help of many coordinated policy interventions. The Growth Report (Commission on Growth and Development 2008) enumerates these interventions, and most have found their way into this diagnostic paper on Africa's future growth. The salient finding of that exhaustive exercise, however, was that countries needed to get many policies right, needed to have coherence among policies, needed effective leadership and political stability, and needed a long-term vision of where the economy was headed. Africa is at a moment in history, in our modest opinion, in which it must grasp the opportunities that exist and propel itself forward. The time is now!

NOTES

1. Only two countries, Botswana and Mauritius, bucked the trend and grew strongly during this period. The former grew because political stability, sound governance, and the effective management of the production and export of diamonds

yielded steady returns; the latter successfully used policy measures to attract FDI into the apparel industry and to capitalize on preferential access to European markets. See Noman et al. (2008).

2. See Miguel (2009).

3. Aid effectiveness is the subject of a meta-study by Doucouliagos and Paldam (2009) and a literature review by Roodman (2007). Both conclude that there is little evidence that aid raises investment and growth or reduces poverty. Likewise, Angus Deaton (2013) is also unable to find credible evidence that aid supports growth; in fact, he thinks that it might be a hindrance and may undermine state capacity building (see   http://www.project-syndicate.org/commentary/economic-development-requires -effective-governments-by-angus-deaton). Bill Easterly (2009) has poured cold water on the efforts of Western countries to transform Africa instead of supporting dispersed and incremental efforts at home-grown improvement that are seen to yield results. Nancy Qian (2014) notes that little of the aid goes to the poorest countries and the objectives pursued are all too frequently those of the donors. Greater initiative by African governments to promote their own brand of development is also favored by contributors to Noman et al. (2008). That aid can play a valuable role is articulately argued by, among others, Jeffrey Sachs (2005, 2014). http://www.foreignpolicy.com /articles/2014/01/21/the_case_for_aid.

4. Chinese aid to Africa provides a partial offset; however, through 2011, it probably did not amount to much more than USD 18 billion or about one-half of Chinese ODA to date.

5. See Rodrik (2011) and Rogoff (2012).

6. Turner (2014) views the slowing of the growth in world trade as inevitable. http://www.project-syndicate.org/commentary/adair-turner-explains-why -more-trade-may-no-longer-mean-more-growth.

7. See Smith (2012).

8. See, for example, the New Partnership for Africa's Development (NEPAD), which defines a strategic framework covering six thematic areas and the Programme for Infrastructure Development (www.nepad.org).

9. See Growth Dialogue (2012).

10. Minerals and petroleum accounted for well over half of Africa's exports and are key to the prosperity of countries such as Botswana and South Africa. They also sustain the economies of others such as Ghana, Nigeria, the United Republic of Tanzania, and Zambia. Diversifying the sources of growth is a priority for all mineral exporters, a point driven home yet again by the crisis.

11. See UNCTAD (2001).

12. See, for example, Radelet (2010).

13. See http://www.imf.org/external/pubs/ft/reo/2012/afr/eng/sreo1012.htm; http:// www.worldbank.org/en/publication/global-economic-prospects/regional-outlooks /ssa.

14. See http://wdi.worldbank.org/table/4.8. The investment rate was 22.9 percent excluding South Africa and Nigeria. It is increasing at a 0.5 percent per year rate according to the most recent calculations. World Bank (2014a); http://www.worldbank.org /content/dam/Worldbank/document/Africa/Report/Africas-Pulse-brochure_Vol7.pdf.

15. Martinez and Mlachila (2013). http://www.imf.org/external/pubs/ft/wp/2013 /wp1353.pdf.

16. Some researchers (Gruber and Koutroumpis 2011) claim that the penetration of mobiles has contributed to innovation—such as the justly famous M-Pesa mobile banking innovation in Kenya and Tanzania—and to growth, especially in the higher-income countries with greater mobile penetration. Annual growth in the higher-income countries has risen by 0.2 percent per year, whereas in the lower-income countries it is up by 0.11 percent. Seventy-four percent of Kenyans now use a mobile phone (the average for SSA in 2012 was 60 percent), and a quiet digital revolution appears to be stirring in the country (*Economist* 2012a). M-Pesa (and its five domestic competitors) has facilitated bank transfers and encouraged users to put their money in banks rather than in rural credit co-ops. See Mbiti and Weil (2011). It is estimated that the mobile money transfer system now serves to channel a third of Kenya's GDP. See http://www.economist.com/news/leaders/21572773-pride-africas-achievements -should-be-coupled-determination-make-even-faster.

17. Between 2000 and 2010, the time required to register property was almost halved to sixty-five days on average. Furthermore, time required to enforce contracts and to obtain construction permits were among the areas showing improvement.

18. UNCTAD (2014) http://unctad.org/en/pages/PressRelease.aspx?OriginalVersion ID=192.

19. See IMF (2011) and African Economic Outlook (http://www.africaneconomi -coutlook.org/ en/outlook/financial_flows/remittances/). The African diaspora totals some 30.6 million people, and their remittances account for a large part of the GDP of countries such as Lesotho (30 percent) and Cape Verde (10 percent).

20. Martinez and Mlachila (2013); http://www.imf.org/external/pubs/ft/wp/2013 /wp1353.pdf

21. See IMF (2012). Gross savings in East Asia reached 47 percent in 2009—a figure that is somewhat biased because of China's weight in the total and its very high savings. See http://wdi.worldbank.org/table/4.8.

22. According to some estimates, the incremental capital output ratio (ICOR) for Sub-Saharan Africa during the period from 1980 to 2010 averaged 5.23, which is high in comparison with East Asian countries during the period from 1970 to 2000. See Kumo (2011).

23. See http://wdi.worldbank.org/table/4.2.

24. Manufacturing accounted for 32 percent of GDP in East Asia in 2009.

25. See http://wdi.worldbank.org/table/4.4.

26. See http://www.economist.com/news/special-report/21572377-african-lives -have-already-greatly-improved-over-past-decade-says-oliver-august.

27. See http://www.davidsuzuki.org/issues/climate-change/science/international -climate-negotiations/history-of-climate-negotiations/.

28. See http://www.voxeu.org/article/five-more-years-g20-standstill-protectionism.

29. Beck et al. (2012) present evidence on the links between financial innovation and growth, and also the link between innovation and financial fragility.

30. See Bhagwati (2007) and Wolf (2004). See also review summaries of Wolf at http://www.complete-review.com/reviews/economic/wolfm.htm.

31. Sundaram, Schwank, and von Arnim (2011) claim that much of the FDI in Sub-Saharan Africa, courtesy of globalization, has gone into mineral extraction and that trade liberalization, by exposing infant African industries to competition, has stunted their development.

32. See Broadman (2007) for a detailed account of Africa's trade prospects with Asia and the trade facilitation issues that dog the growth of trade.

33. See Douillet and Pauw (2012). Severino and Debled (2012) cite a higher figure—15 percent.

34. The defragmenting of African markets would be a boon for Africa's exporters, especially smaller firms (see Brenton and Isik 2012). Also helpful would be progress at strengthening road and rail infrastructures and reduced delays at customs and border checkpoints (see Rippel 2011). African countries rank low on the World Bank's Logistics Performance Index (2012). See http://siteresources.worldbank.org/TRADE/Resources/239070–1336654966193/LPI_2012_rankings.pdf. African countries are also clustered in the lower half of the World Economic Forum's Enabling Trade Index (2012); see http://www3.weforum.org/docs/GETR/2012/GlobalEnablingTrade_Report.pdf. Infrastructure gaps in Sub-Saharan Africa are spelled out in World Bank (2011b) and according to some estimates cost Africa a 2 percent loss of GDP growth; see http://www3.weforum.org/docs/AF13/WEF_AF13_Report.pdf. Closing these by 2020 could require as much as USD 93 billion. Maintaining the infrastructure, another major issue in Africa, would demand adequate budgetary provisioning thereafter (see AfDB 2010).

35. Some of these conflicts were the result of interventions by the superpowers and were in effect proxy wars fought in Africa. See Hironaka (2005), Shah (2012), and Gettleman (2010).

36. According to Paul Collier (2003), the "conflict trap" is one of the causes of stalled development in many African countries. Some others are reliance on natural resources, being landlocked, and bad governance.

37. See http://yalepress.yale.edu/yupbooks/book.asp?isbn=9780300175387.

38. See the *Economist* (2012a).

39. Acemoglu and Robinson (2012, 1) refer to the failure of countries "not with a bang but with a whimper" because they are "ruled by extractive economic institutions, which destroy incentives, discourage innovation, and sap the talent of their citizens by creating a tilted playing field and robbing them of opportunities." http://foreignpolicy.com/2012/06/18/10-reasons-countries-fall-apart/.

40. World Bank (2013b) http://www.worldbank.org/en/news/feature/2013/06/19/what-climate-change-means-africa-asia-coastal-poor; on water stress in Africa, see Tatlock (2006).

41. Cities at risk in Africa include Abidjan, Accra, Dakar, Dar es-Salaam, Durban, Maputo, Mombasa, and Port Elizabeth. See the figure "African cities at risk due to sea-level rise" in UH-HABITAT (2008).

42. The desirability of greening urbanization and in the process making it more inclusive is discussed in ADB (2012) and McKinsey Global Institute (2010).

43. An assessment of Africa's mineral resource potential can be found in Custers and Matthysen (2009).

44. Gelb, Kaiser, and Viñuela (2012) show that new discoveries have substantially replenished mineral resources and contributed to national wealth.

45. World Bank (2009b).

46. See http://www.usatoday.com/story/news/world/2013/06/13/un-world-population-81-billion-2025/2420989/.

47. In the form of lower dependency rates, higher savings, a more elastic labor supply, and increased entrepreneurial energy.

48. About 42 percent of the twenty- to twenty-four-year-olds have some secondary education.

49. See AfDB et al. (2012). The official unemployment rate for the continent is 9 percent. However, only 28 percent of the workforce has stable and well-paid jobs and the safety net is nonexistent in most countries (McKinsey Global Institute 2012).

50. See Noman et al. (2008).

51. The UNCTAD (2011) report observes that small firms dominate African manufacturing. See also Mckenzie (2011).

52. See Farole and Winkler (2013). FDI from China in countries such as Ethiopia is a start at creating new linkages and South-oriented GVCs. See http://www.bloomberg.com/news/2014–07–22/ethiopia-becomes-china-s-china-in-search-for-cheap-labor.html.

53. See http://data.worldbank.org/topic/agriculture-and-rural-development#tp_wdi.

54. See Fine and Lund (2012).

55. African farmers apply on average only seven pounds of fertilizer per acre, and a factory in Nigeria is the sole producer of low-cost urea in all of Sub-Saharan Africa. See http://ngm.nationalgeographic.com/2013/05/fertilized-world/charles-text.

56. Collier and Dercon (2014) maintain that productivity gains call for an increase in the share of large commercialized farms and a decreasing focus on smallholder agriculture, which is the norm in Africa. Most farms tend to be small, well under five hectares each. See also Dercon and Gollin (2014).

57. See http://ngm.nationalgeographic.com/2013/05/fertilized-world/charles-text.

58. Van der Ploeg (2011). See https://www.aeaweb.org/articles.php?doi=10.1257/jel.49.2.366; see Frankel (2010); http://www.nber.org/papers/w15836.

59. The Growth Report (Commission on Growth and Development 2008) also recommended a growth target of 7 percent.

60. Africa's population is expected to grow by 2.4 percent per year during the period from 2009 to 2015, although the rate is likely to slow further down the road, reaching replacement-level fertility by 2050.

61. The political economy of Botswana's growth and stability is analyzed by Acemoglu, Johnson, and Robinson (2001). Acemoglu and Robinson (2010) claim in another paper that "the main reasons why African nations are poor today is that their citizens have very bad interlocking economic and political institutions" (22).

62. Easterly (2011) finds that, on balance, the occasional and temporarily benevolent autocrat does not promote long-term economic growth.

63. Whether there is a causal relationship running from democracy to growth is contested with some research suggesting that democracy is more likely to take root once countries have passed a certain income threshold.

64. See Doucouliagos and Ulubasoglu (2010); Feng (2003); Gerring et al. (2005); Knutsen (2009); Pereira and Teles (2010); and Rock (2009).

65. Pritchett, Woolcock and Andrews (2010) point to the existence of capability traps that constrain policy implementation by state agencies.

66. Among the expressions of doubt that have surfaced since the crisis, see Turner (2011).

67. See the championing of the Chinese approach by Justin Yifu Lin (in Chandra, Lin, and Wang 2012), who is of the view that as China vacates certain industries as its costs rise, African countries could move in.

68. See Aghion, Boulanger, and Cohen (2011); Leipziger (2012); Yusuf (2011).

69. See the World Bank's Public Expenditure and Financial Accountability Assessment Reports (PEFA) for African countries at http://web.worldbank.org/WBSITE /EXTERNAL/PEFA/0,,contentMDK:22687152~menuPK:7313203~pagePK:7313176~ piPK:7327442~theSitePK:7327438,00.html.

70. The recent adoption of the Programme for Infrastructure Development in Africa is a step toward a regionally coordinated approach that responds to the anticipated growth in demand.

71. See Parente and Prescott (2000) and Comin and Hobijn (2010). Francesco Caselli (2005) shows that an equalization of physical and human capital across all countries would explain only 37 percent of the differences in GDP per capita. The balance is due to productivity differences arising from technology of all kinds.

72. See McKinsey & Company (2010). See also UNCTAD (2011).

73. The product space refers to a network that brings out the interrelationships between products traded in the global marketplace. See http://www.chidalgo.com /productspace/.

74. See also Lederman and Maloney (2010).

75. The composition of the Republic of Korea's exports changed from one decade to the next. Garments, steel, and footwear in the 1980s were displaced by semiconductors, computers, and cars in the 2000s, and by semiconductors, vessels, and cars in the 2010s.

76. The cost of financing and limited access is frequently blamed for the slow entry growth and lagging export capacity of firms in Africa. See Venables (2010).

77. See http://hanushek.stanford.edu.

78. Increased enrollment that results in overcrowding of schools might be partly to blame.

79. On recipes and progress to date in Africa, see World Bank (2009a).

80. See Yusuf and Nabeshima (2012).

81. The outbreak of Ebola virus disease in Guinea and its spread to neighboring countries also points to the continuing danger from outbreaks of virulent infectious diseases. See http://www.cdc.gov/vhf/ebola/outbreaks/guinea/.

82. Glewwe and Kremer (2005) present the findings from research on initiatives in the area of education and deworming of school children in Africa.

83. See Klaus Deininger and Derek Byerlee (2011). They note that of the ten countries with large stocks of potentially cultivable land, five are in Africa. Globally there are 446 million hectares of such unutilized land that is unforested, uncultivated, and

with less than twenty-five people per square kilometer. Of this stock, 201 million are in Africa. Chad, the Democratic Republic of the Congo, Mozambique, the Sudan, and Zambia head the list.

84. The breakthrough will come from replacing annuals with equivalent perennials so as to reduce erosion and enable soils to hold on to nutrients.

85. See UNEP (2008), Chapter 2, "Freshwater Resources," section on "A Scarce and Competitive Resource," graphic on "The coming water scarcity in Africa." Available at www.unep.org/ dewa/vitalwater/article83.html.

86. This is changing as a result of Chinese funding for large dams in several African countries including the Sudan, Ethiopia, Zambia, Congo, and others. See http://www.internationalrivers.org/campaigns/chinese-dams-in-africa; http:// www.internationalrivers.org/resources/african-dams-briefing-map-4037. Whether these prove to be the solution or bring other problems in their wake remains to be seen. See http://www.internationalrivers.org/resources/big-dams-bringing -poverty-not-power-to-africa-2006.

87. See Schaefer (2008) and *Science* (2006).

88. The urbanization rate in Africa was 36 percent in 2011. See http://data.worldbank .org/topic/urban-development.

89. See Yusuf (2014) for a synthesis of recent research on the economics of urbanization.

90. Although data are often imprecise and confusing, Fitch reported that China's Exim Bank lending over the period from 2001 to 2010 totaled USD 67.2 billion compared with USD 54.7 billion for the World Bank, and that in 2011 lending from China was an estimated USD 11 billion without counting either Chinese grant aid or its considerable FDI in the continent, a stock figure reported to be USD 40 billion. See www.bloomberg.com (12–28–2011) and www.ChinaDaily.com as well as Ali and Jafrani (2012).

91. See IMF (2010). More generally on China's contribution to Africa's investment and growth, see, among others, Weisbrod and Whalley (2011), Kaplinsky and Morris (2009), and Renard (2011).

92. McMillan and Harttgen (2014).

93. Gelb, Meyer, and Ramachandran (2013).

94. Rodrik (2014) observes that Africa might not be able to mobilize the manufacturing growth engine, in which case it will need to rely more on the competitiveness of agro-processing activities and services.

95. See Amsden (1989) and Kim and Leipziger (1993).

96. In his recent book on the making of an antifragile system, Nassim Taleb (2012) makes the case for tough love.

97. On East African trade-related arrangements, see "EAC and China Discuss Partnerships for Trade and Investment" and "The Future of East African Integration," at www.eac.int.

98. See Leipziger (1997) and World Bank (1993).

99. The role of NEPAD and Africa's regional infrastructure needs are outlined in Estache (2011).

100. See Collier (2007).

REFERENCES

Abdon, Arnelyn, and Jesus Felipe. 2011. "The Product Space: What Does It Say about the Opportunities for Growth and Structural Transformation of Sub-Saharan Africa?" Levy Economics Institute Working Paper No. 670. papers.ssrn.com/sol3 /papers.cfm?abstract_id=1846734.

Acemoglu, Daron, and James A. Robinson. 2010. "Why Is Africa Poor?" *Economic History of Developing Regions* 25 (1): 21–50.

——. 2012. "10 Reasons Countries Fall Apart." *Foreign Policy* June 18. http://www .foreignpolicy.com/articles/2012/06/18/10_reasons_countries_fall_apart.

Acemoglu, Daron, Simon Johnson, and James A. Robinson. 2001. "An African Success Story: Botswana." MIT Department of Economics Working Paper No. 01–37. http://ssrn.com/abstract=290791.

African Development Bank (AfDB). 2010. "Infrastructure Deficit and Opportunities in Africa." *Economic Brief* 1 (September). Abidjan, Côte d'Ivoire: AfDB. http: //www.afdb.org/fileadmin/uploads/afdb/Documents/Publications/ECON%20 Brief_Infrastructure%20Deficit%20and%20Opportunities%20in%20Africa _Vol%201%20Issue%202.pdf.

African Development Bank (AfDB), Organization for Economic Co-operation and Development (OECD), United Nations Development Programme, and United Nations Economic Commission for Africa. 2012. *African Economic Outlook 2012.* Paris and Tunis OECD Publishing.

Aghion, Philippe, Julian Boulanger, and Elie Cohen. 2011. "Rethinking Industrial Policy." *Breugel Policy Brief* 2011/4. http://www.bruegel.org/publications /publication-detail/publication/566-rethinking-industrial-policy/.

Aikins, Ama de-Graft, Nigel Unwin, Charles Agyemang, Pascale Allotey, Catherine Campbell, and Daniel Arhin. 2010. "Tackling Africa's Chronic Disease Burden: From the Local to the Global." *Globalization and Health* 6: 5. www.globalizationandhealth .com/content/6/1/5.

Ali, S., and N. Jafrani. 2012. "China's Growing Role in Africa: Myths and Facts." *International Economic Bulletin* (February 9). Carnegie Endowment for Peace. http://carnegieendowment.org/ieb/2012/02/09/china-s-growing-role-in-africa -myths-and-facts/9j5q.

Amsden, A. 1989. *Asia's Next Giant: South Korea and Late Industrialization.* New York: Oxford University Press.

Asian Development Bank (ADB). 2012. *Key Indicators for Asia and the Pacific 2012.* Manila: ADB.

Baldwin, Richard, and Simon J. Evenett. 2009. "Don't Let Murky Protectionism Stall a Global Recovery: Things the G20 Should Do." *VoxEU.org*, March 5. www.voxeu .org/index.php?q=node/3206.

Beck, Thorsten, Tao Chen, Chen Lin, and Frank Song. 2012. "Financial Innovation: The Bright and the Dark Sides." *VoxEU.org.* http://www.voxeu.org/article /financial-innovation-good-and-bad.

Bekaert, Geert, Campbell R. Harvey, and Christian Lundblad. 2011. "Financial Openness and Productivity." *World Development* 39 (1): 1–19. http://www0.gsb.columbia .edu/faculty/gbekaert/papers/openness.pdf.

Bhagwati, Jagdish. 2007. *In Defense of Globalization*. New York: Oxford University Press.

Brenton, Paul, and Gözde Isik, eds. 2012. *De-Fragmenting Africa: Deepening Regional Trade Integration in Goods and Services*. Washington, DC: World Bank.

Broadman, Harry. 2007. *Africa's Silk Road*. Washington, DC: World Bank.

Caselli, Francesco. 2005. "Accounting for Cross-Country Income Differences." In *Handbook of Economic Growth*, ed. Phillipe Aghion and Steven Durlauf, 1:679–741. Amsterdam: North Holland.

Chandra, Vandana, Justin Yifu Lin, and Yan Wang. 2012. "Leading Dragons Phenomenon: New Opportunities for Catch-Up in Low-Income Countries." Policy Research Working Paper 6000, World Bank, Washington, DC. http://ideas.repec.org/p/wbk/wbrwps/6000.html.

Collier, Paul. 2003. *Breaking the Conflict Trap: Civil War and Development Policy*. Policy Research Reports. Washington, DC: World Bank.

———. 2007. *The Bottom Billion*. New York: Oxford University Press.

Collier, Paul, and Stefan Dercon. 2014. "African Agriculture in 50 Years: Smallholders in a Rapidly Changing World?" *World Development* 63: 92–101.

Comin, Diego, and Bart Hobijn. 2010. "Technology Diffusion and Postwar Growth." NBER Working Paper No. 16378.

Commission for Africa. 2005. "Going for Growth and Poverty Reduction." In *Our Common Interest: Report of the Commission for Africa*, 219–254. http://www.commissionforafrica.info/2005-report.

Commission on Growth and Development. 2008. *The Growth Report: Strategies for Sustained Growth and Inclusive Development*. Washington, DC: World Bank.

Custers, Raf, and Ken Matthysen. 2009. *Africa's Natural Resources in a Global Context*. Antwerp, Belgium: International Peace Information Service (IPIS). http://www.ipisresearch.be/att/20090812_Natural_ Resources.pdf.

Deaton, Angus. 2013. *The Great Escape: Health, Wealth and the Origins of Inequality*. Princeton: Princeton University Press.

Deen, Thalif. 2011. "Africa Faces Explosive Population Growth." *Inter Press Service (IPS)*, June 20. http://www.ipsnews.net/2011/06/africa-faces-explosive-population-growth/.

Deininger, Klaus, and Derek Byerlee. 2011. *Rising Global Interest in Farmland*. Washington, DC: World Bank.

Dercon, Stefan, and Douglas Gollin. 2014. "Agriculture in African Development: A Review of Theories and Strategies." CSAE Working Paper No. 2014–22, Center for the Study of African Economies, Oxford.

Doucouliagos, Hristos, and Martin Paldam. 2009. "The Aid Effectiveness Literature: The Sad Results of 40 Years of Research." *Journal of Economic Surveys* 23 (3): 433–461.

Doucouliagos, Hristos, and Mehmet Ali Ulubasoglu. 2010. "Democracy and Economic Growth: A Meta-Analysis." SSRN Working Paper. http://ssrn.com/abstract=1014333 or http://dx.doi.org/10.2139/ssrn.1014333.

Douillet, Mathilde, and Karl Pauw. 2012. "Trade Integration in Sub-Saharan Africa: Lessons from Malawian Trade Policy." Policy Note 10. International Food Policy Research Institute, Washington, DC.

Easterly, William. 2009. "Can the West Save Africa?" *Journal of Economic Literature* 47 (2): 373–447.

——. 2011. "Benevolent Autocrats." Draft paper. http://williameasterly.files.wordpress .com/2011/05/benevolent-autocrats-easterly-2nd-draft.pdf.

Easterly, William, and Ariell Reshef. 2010. "African Export Successes: Surprises, Stylized Facts, and Explanations." NBER Working Paper No. 16597. www.nber.org /papers/w16597.pdf.

Economist. 2012a. "A Glass Half-Full: Representative Government Is Still On the March in Africa, Despite Recent Hiccups." March 31. http://www.economist.com /node/21551494/.

——. 2012b. "Upwardly Mobile: Kenya's Technology Start-up Scene Is About to Take Off." August 25. http://www.economist.com/node/ 21560912.

——. 2013. "A Hopeful Continent." March 2. http://www.economist.com/news/special -report/21572377-african-lives-have-already-greatly-improved-over-past-decade -says-oliver-august.

Estache, A. 2011. "Africa's Regional Infrastructure Needs." The Growth Dialogue's Lisbon Policy Forum. http://www.growthdialogue.org/ events/regional-events/high -level-policy-forum-regional-infrastructure-constraints-africas-growth or http:// www.growthdialogue.org/ sites/default/files/event/document/ESTACHE_0.pdf.

Evenett, Simon. 2013. "Five More Years of the G20 Standstill on Protectionism?" VOX September 3. http://www.voxeu.org/article/five-more-years-g20-standstill -protectionism.

Farole, Thomas, and Deborah Winkler. 2013. "Making Foreign Direct Investment Work for Sub-Saharan Africa: Local Spillovers and Competitiveness in Global Value Chains." *Directions in Development.* Washington, DC: World Bank Group. http://documents.worldbank.org/curated/en/2013/12/18680570/making-foreign -direct-investment-work-sub-saharan-africa-local-spillovers-competitiveness -global-value-chains.

Feng, Yi. 2003. *Democracy, Governance and Economic Performance.* Cambridge, Mass.: MIT Press.

Fine, David. 2012. "Inside Africa's Consumer Revolution." *Project Syndicate.* November 7. http://www.project-syndicate.org/commentary/inside-africa-s -consumer-revolution-by-david-fine.

Fine, David, and Susan Lund. 2012. "Jobs: The Next Piece of Africa's Growth Jigsaw." *VoxEU.org*, December 4. http://www.voxeu.org/article/ jobs-next-piece -africa-s-growth-jigsaw.

Foster, V., and C. Briceno-Garmendia. 2010. *Africa's Infrastructure.* World Bank Report. Washington, DC: World Bank.

Frankel, Jeffrey, A. 2010. The Natural Resource Curse: A Survey. NBER Working Paper No. 15836. http://www.nber.org/papers/w15836.

Gelb, Alan, Kai Kaiser, and Lorena Viñuela. 2012. "How Much Does Natural Resource Extraction Really Diminish National Wealth? The Implications of Discovery." Working Paper No. 290, Center for Global Development, Washington, DC. http://www.cgdev.org/content/publications/ detail/1426040/.

Gelb, Alan, Christian Meyer, and Vijaya Ramachandran. 2013. "Does Poor Mean Cheap? Comparative Look at Africa's Industrial Labor Costs." Working Paper No. 325, Center for Global Development, Washington, DC.

Gerring, John, Philip Bond, William T. Barndt, and Carola Moreno. 2005. "Democracy and Economic Growth: A Historical Perspective." *World Politics* 57 (April): 323–364.

Gettleman, Jeffrey. 2010. "Africa's Forever Wars: Why the Continent's Conflicts Never End." *Foreign Policy* February 11. http://www.foreignpolicy.com /articles/2010/02/22/africas_forever_wars.

Glewwe, Paul W., Eric A. Hanushek, Sarah D. Humpage, and Renato Ravina. 2011. "School Resources and Educational Outcomes in Developing Countries: A Review of the Literature from 1990 to 2010." NBER Working Paper No. 17554. http:// www.nber.org/papers/ w17554.

Glewwe, Paul, and Michael Kremer. 2005. "Schools, Teachers, and Education Outcomes in Developing Countries." Second draft of chapter for *Handbook on the Economics of Education.* http://www.imap.givewell.org/files/DWDA%202009 /Interventions/EconEducationHandbook.pdf.

Glewwe, Paul, Eugenie Maiga, and Haochi Zheng. 2014. "The Contribution of Education to Economic Growth: A Review of the Evidence with Special Attention and Application to Sub-Saharan Africa." *World Development* 59: 379–393.

Growth Dialogue. 2012. *The Bellagio Symposium on New Growth Paradigms: A Growth Dialogue White Paper.* Washington, DC: The Growth Dialogue. http://www .growthdialogue.org/sites/default/files/event/document/Bellagio_paper_FINAL _proof_6–18–12-a.pdf.

Gruber, Harald, and Pantelis Koutroumpis. 2011. *Mobile Telecommunications and the Impact on Economic Development.* London: Centre for Economic Policy Research. http://www.cepr.org/meets/wkcn/9/979/papers/Gruber_Koutroumpis.pdf.

Hidalgo, César A., and Ricardo Hausmann. 2009. "The Building Blocks of Economic Complexity." Harvard University Center for International Development Working Paper No. 186. http://chidalgo.com/Papers/HidalgoHausmann_PNAS_2009 _PaperAndSM.pdf.

Hironaka, Ann. 2005. *Neverending Wars: The International Community, Weak States and the Perpetuation of War.* Cambridge, Mass.: Harvard University Press.

International Monetary Fund (IMF). 2010. "Regional Economic Outlook: Sub-Saharan Africa: Resilience and Risks." October 10. Washington, DC: IMF. http://www .imf.org/external/pubs/ft/reo/2010/afr/eng/pdf/ sreo1010.pdf.

———. 2011. "Harnessing Diasporas." *Finance & Development*, September. Washington, DC: IMF. http://www.imf.org/external/pubs/ft/fandd/ 2011/09/pdf/ratha.pdf.

———. 2012. *Regional Economic Outlook.* Washington, DC: IMF.

Jorgenson, Dale W., and Khuong Vu. 2007. "Information Technology and the World Growth Resurgence." *German Economic Review* 8 (2):125–145.

Kaplinsky, R., and M. Morris. 2009. "Chinese FDI in Sub-Saharan Africa: Engaging with Large Dragons." *European Journal of Development Research* 21 (4): 551–569.

Kapsos, Steven. 2005. "The Employment Intensity of Growth: Trends and Macroeconomic Determinants." Employment Strategy Paper, International Labour Organization, Geneva.

Kim, Kiwhan, and D. Leipziger. 1993. "Korea: A Case of Government-Led Development." Washington, DC: World Bank. http://books.google.com/books?id=G33jcR lzgQUC&printsec=frontcover&source=gbs_ge_summary_r&cad=0#v=onepage& q&f=false.

Knutsen, Carl Henrik. 2009. "Democracy and Economic Growth." Working paper, University of Oslo. http://folk.uio.no/carlhk/publications/DemocracyGrowth _Survey.pdf.

Kumo, Wolassa L. 2011. "Investment Efficiency, Savings and Economic Growth in Sub-Saharan Africa." *Afro Articles.* http://www. afroarticles.com/article-dashboard /article.php?id=222601.

Kurlantzick, Joshua. 2013. *Democracy in Retreat.* New Haven, Conn.: Yale University Press.

Lederman, Daniel, and William F. Maloney. 2010. "Does What You Export Matter? In Search of Empirical Guidance for Industrial Policies." Washington, DC: World Bank. http://siteresources.worldbank.org/EXTLACOFFICEOFCE/Resources /DoesWhatYouExportMatterSept2010.pdf.

Leipziger, Danny M. 1997. *Lessons of East Asia.* Ann Arbor: University of Michigan Press.

——. 2012. "The Competition between Western Capitalism and State Capitalism as Drivers of Economic Growth." Policy Brief #7, 2012. Washington, DC: Growth Dialogue.

Martinez, Marcelo, and Montfort Mlachila. 2013. "The Quality of the Recent High Growth Episode in Sub-Saharan Africa." IMF Working Paper No. WP/13/53, Washington, DC: IMF.

Mbiti, Isaac, and David N. Weil. 2011. "Mobile Banking: The Impact of M-PESA in Kenya." NBER Working Paper No. 17129.

Mckenzie, David. 2011. "How Can We Learn Whether Firm Policies Are Working in Africa?" Washington, DC: World Bank. http://elibrary. worldbank.org/content /workingpaper/10.1596/1813–9450–5632.

McKinsey & Company. 2010. *McKinsey on Africa.* McKinsey & Company. http:// mckinseyonsociety.com/mckinsey-on-africa/.

McKinsey Global Institute. 2010. *India's Urban Awakening: Building Inclusive Cities, Sustaining Economic Growth.* McKinsey & Company. http://www.mckinsey.com /insights/mgi/research/urbanization/urban_awakening_in_india.

——. 2012. *Africa at Work: Job Creation and Inclusive Growth.* 2012. McKinsey & Company. http://www.mckinsey.com/insights/mgi/research/africa_europe_middle _east/africa_at_work.

McMillan, Margaret M., and Kenneth Harttgen. 2014. "What Is Driving the African Growth Miracle?" NBER Working Paper No. 20077.

Miguel, Edward. 2009. *Africa's Turn.* Cambridge, Mass.: MIT Press.

Ndulu, Benno, L. Chakraborti, L. Lijane, V. Ramachandran, and J. Wolgin. 2007. *Challenges of African Growth: Opportunities, Constraints, and Strategic Directions.* Washington, DC: World Bank.

Noman, Akbar, K. Botchwey, H. Stein, and J. E. Stiglitz. 2008. *Good Growth and Governance in Africa: Rethinking Development Strategies.* New York: Oxford University Press.

Paarlberg, Robert. 2008. *Starved for Science: How Biotechnology Is Being Kept Out of Africa.* Cambridge, Mass.: Harvard University Press.

Parente, Stephen L., and Edward C. Prescott. 2000. *Barriers to Riches.* Cambridge, Mass.: MIT Press.

Pereira, Carlos, and Vladimir Teles. 2010. "Political Institutions, Economic Growth, and Democracy: The Substitute Effect." *Brookings Institution*, January 19. http://www.brookings.edu/research/opinions/ 2011/01/19-political-institutions-pereira.

Pritchett, Lant, Michael Woolcock, and Matt Andrews. 2010. "Capability Traps? The Mechanisms of Persistent Implementation Failure." Working Paper No. 234, Center for Global Development, Washington, DC.

Qian, Nancy. 2014. "Making Progress on Foreign Aid." NBER Working Paper No. 20412. http://www.nber.org/papers/w20412.

Radelet, Steven. 2010. *Emerging Africa: How 17 Countries Are Leading the Way*. Washington, DC: Center for Global Development.

Ratha, Dilip, and Sonia Plaza. 2011. "Harnessing Diasporas." *Finance & Development* (September): 48–51. http://www.imf.org/external/ pubs/ft/fandd/2011/09/pdf/ratha.pdf.

Renard, Mary-Francoise. 2011. "China's Trade and FDI in Africa." Working Paper No. 126, African Development Bank, Abidjan, Côte d'Ivoire.

Rippel, Barbara. 2011. "Why Trade Facilitation Is Important for Africa." Policy Note No. 27. Washington, DC: World Bank. http://go.worldbank.org/CYT7YFM2G0.

Rock, Michael T. 2009. "Has Democracy Slowed Growth in Asia?" *World Development* 37 (5): 941–952. http://EconPapers.repec.org/RePEc: eee:wdevel:v:37:y:2009 :i:5:p:941–952.

Rodrik, Dani. 2011. "The Future of Economic Growth." *Project Syndicate*, July 25. www.project-syndicate.org/commentary/rodrik58/English.

———. 2012a. "No More Growth Miracles." *Project Syndicate*, August 8. http://www .project-syndicate.org/commentary/no-more-growth-miracles-by-dani-rodrik.

———. 2012b. *The Globalization Paradox: Democracy and the Future of the World Economy*. New York: W. W. Norton.

———. 2014. "An African Growth Miracle?" NBER Working Paper No. 20188.

Rogoff, Kenneth. 2012. "Rethinking the Growth Imperative." *Project Syndicate*, January 2 www.project-syndicate.org/commentary/rogoff88/English.

Roodman, David. 2007. "The Anarchy of Numbers: Aid, Development, and Cross-Country Empirics." *World Bank Economic Review* 21 (2): 255–277.

Sachs, Jeffrey D. 2005. *The End of Poverty: Economic Possibilities for Our Time*. New York: Penguin Press.

———. 2014. "The Case for Aid." *Foreign Policy*. January 21. http://foreignpolicy .com/2014/01/21/the-case-for-aid/.

Sala-i-Martin, Xavier, and Maxim Pinkovsky. 2010. "African Poverty Is Falling . . . Much Faster Than You Think!" NBER Working Paper No. 15775. http://www.nber .org/papers/w15775.

Schaefer, M. 2008. "Water Technologies and the Environment: Ramping Up by Scaling Down." *Technology in Society* 30 (3–4): 415–422. http://www.sciencedirect.com /science/article/pii/S0160791X08000183.

Science. 2006. "Freshwater Resources." (Special issue on freshwater resources.) *Science* 313 (5790): 1005–1184. www.sciencemag.org/content/ 313/5790.toc.

Severino, Jean-Michel, and Emilie Debled. 2012. "Africa's Big Boom." *Project Syndicate*. http://www.project-syndicate.org/commentary/the-challenges-and-opportunities -of-african-economic-growth-by-jean-michel-severino-and-emilie-debled.

Shah, Anup. 2012. "Conflicts in Africa." *Global Issues*. http://www.globalissues.org
    /issue/83/conflicts-in-africa.
Smith, David. 2012. "Boom Time for Mozambique, Once the Basket Case of
    Africa." *The Guardian*, March 27. http://www.guardian.co.uk/ world/2012/mar/27
    /mozambique-africa-energy-resources-bonanza.
Smith, Pete, Peter J. Gregory, Detlef van Vuuren, Michael Obersteiner, Petr Havlík,
    Mark Rounsevell, Jeremy Woods, Elke Stehfest, and Jessica Bellarby. 2010. "Com-
    petition for Land." *Philosophical Transactions of the Royal Society* 365: 2941–2957.
Steiner, Achim. 2010. "Africa's Natural Resources Key to Powering Prosperity." *Envi-
    ronment & Poverty Times* No. 5. UNEP/GRID-Arendal. http://www.grida.no
    /publications/et/ep5/page.aspx.
Sundaram, Jomo Kwame, with Oliver Schwank and Rudiger von Arnim. 2011. "Glo-
    balization and Development in Sub-Saharan Africa." DESA Working Paper No.
    102, Department of Economic and Social Affairs (DESA), United Nations, New
    York. http://www.un.org/esa/desa/ papers/2011/wp102_2011.pdf.
Taleb, Nassim. 2012. *Antifragile: Things That Gain from Disorder*. New York: Random
    House.
Tatlock, Christopher W. 2006. "Water Stress in Sub-Saharan Africa." New York: Coun-
    cil on Foreign Relations. http://www.cfr.org/africa/ water-stress-sub-saharan-africa
    /p11240.
Turner, Adair. 2011. *Economics After the Crisis*. Cambridge, Mass.: MIT Press.
——. 2014. "The Trade Delusion." *Project Syndicate*. July 18. http://www.project
    -syndicate.org/commentary/adair-turner-explains-why-more-trade-may-no-longer
    -mean-more-growth.
United Nations. 2004. *World Population to 2300*. New York: United Nations. http:
    //www.un.org/esa/population/publications/longrange2/WorldPop2300final.pdf.
——. 2012. *The Millennium Developments Goals Report 2012*. New York: United
    Nations.
United Nations Conference on Trade and Development (UNCTAD). 2001. "Eco-
    nomic Development in Africa: Performance, Prospects and Policy Issues." New
    York: UNCTAD. http://unctad.org/ en/Docs/pogdsafricad1.en.pdf.
——. 2011. "UNIDO and UNCTAD Economic Development in Africa 2011: Special
    Report." New York: UNCTAD. http://unctad.org/en/docs/aldcafrica2011_en.pdf.
——. 2014. *World Investment Report 2014*. Geneva. http://unctad.org/en/pages
    /PressRelease.aspx?OriginalVersionID=189.
United Nations Environment Programme (UNEP). 2008. *Vital Water Graphics: An
    Overview of the State of the World's Fresh and Marine Waters*. 2nd ed. Nairobi,
    Kenya: UNEP.
United Nations Human Settlements Programme (UH-HABITAT). 2008. "Drowned
    and Dangerous: Cities and Climate Change." New York: UH-HABITAT. www
    .unhabitat.or/downloads/docs/ presskitsowc2008/Drowned n dangerous/pdf.
Van der Ploeg, Frederick. 2011. "Natural Resources: Curse or Blessing." *Journal of Eco-
    nomic Literature* 49(2):366–420.
Venables, Anthony J. 2010. "Economic Geography and African Development."
    Papers in Regional Science 89 (3): 469–483. http://ideas.repec. org/a/bla/presci
    /v89y2010i3p469–483.html.

Weisbrod, A., and J. Whalley. 2011. "The Contribution of China's FDI to Africa's Pre-Crisis Growth Surge." NBER Working Paper No. 17544.

Wolf, Martin. 2004. *Why Globalization Works.* New Haven: Yale University Press.

World Bank. 1993. *The East Asia Miracle.* Washington, DC: World Bank.

——. 2009a. *Accelerating Catch-Up: Tertiary Education for Growth in Sub-Saharan Africa.* Washington, DC: World Bank.

——. 2009b. *Zambia: Managing Water for Sustainable Growth and Poverty Reduction.* Washington, DC: World Bank.

——. 2011a. *Global Statistics: Key Indicators for Country Groups and Selected Economies.* Washington, DC: World Bank. http://data.worldbank.org/sites/default/files/gsapril2011.pdf.

——. 2011b. *Africa Development Indicators 2011.* Washington, DC: World Bank. http://data.worldbank.org/sites/default/files/adi_2011-web.pdf.

——. 2013. *Fact Sheet: Infrastructure in Sub-Saharan Africa.* Washington, DC: World Bank. http://web.worldbank.org/WBSITE/EXTERNAL/COUNTRIES/AFRICAEXT/0,,contentMDK:21951811~pagePK:146736~piPK:146830~theSitePK:258644,00.html.

——. 2013. *What Climate Change Means for Africa, Asia and the Coastal Poor.* World Bank. http://www.worldbank.org/en/news/feature/2013/06/19/what-climate-change-means-africa-asia-coastal-poor

——. 2014a. *Africa's Pulse.* Vol. 9. April. http://www.worldbank.org/content/dam/Worldbank/document/Africa/Report/Africas-Pulse-brochure_Vol9.pdf; http://www.worldbank.org/content/dam/Worldbank/document/Africa/Report/Africas-Pulse-brochure_Vol9.pdf.

——. 2014b. *Africa's Pulse.* Vol. 10 October. http://www-wds.worldbank.org/external/default/WDSContentServer/WDSP/IB/2014/10/23/000470435_20141023112521/Rendered/PDF/912070REVISED00oct2014ovol100v120web.pdf.

Young, Alwyn. 2012. "The African Growth Miracle." NBER Working Paper No. 18490. http://www.nber.org/papers/w18490.

Yusuf, Shahid. 2011. *East Asian Experience with Industrial Policy and the Lessons for South Africa.* Washington, DC: World Bank.

——. 2014. "Will Cities Continue Driving Economic Growth?" Working Paper No. 6, Washington, DC: The Growth Dialogue.

Yusuf, Shahid, and Kaoru Nabeshima. 2012. *Some Small Economies Do It Better: Rapid Growth and Its Causes in Singapore, Finland, and Ireland.* Washington, DC: World Bank.

CHAPTER 9

Measuring Policy Performance

CAN WE DO BETTER THAN THE WORLD BANK?

Julia Cagé

This article questions the relevance of the different measures of policy performance that are currently used by international organizations to allocate Official Development Assistance (ODA). It evaluates more especially the pertinence of the World Bank's Country Policy and Institutional Assessment (CPIA) and of the various alternatives that have been proposed in the literature. It suggests a new way of assessing aid effectiveness. Measuring policy performance is of particular importance: ODA represents a limited but needed resource for developing countries. Finding criteria to allocate it selectively is thus of great concern for donors.

Using a yearly panel dataset of over 146 developing and emerging countries between 1977 and 2008, I first show that the CPIA is correlated with current growth rates. This contemporaneous correlation can be explained in part by the fact that the assessments of the World Bank staff are colored by perceptions of countries' current performances. Next I show that the CPIA is not a good predictor for future economic growth. I also find a positive and statistically significant correlation between the correlation of developing countries' votes in the United Nations General Assembly (UNGA) and those of the United States and their CPIA scores (other things equal). This is obviously subject to a variety of interpretations about causality, but it can be seen as an indication of the influence of a pro-U.S. disposition in foreign policy on the CPIA.

I thus argue in favor of other measures of policy performance. I show that performance-based measures, as opposed to measures implying ex-ante conditionality, are more accurate instruments for aid allocation. In particular, I discuss the relevance of Kanbur's proposal (Kanbur 2005) of introducing some "outcome criteria" in the CPIA. I show that introducing straightforward outcome variables would be a significant improvement on the CPIA.

Finally, I make concrete proposals for the development of new performance indicators. The basic idea beyond these indicators would be to use "aid effectiveness" to allocate aid selectively. Such indicators are supposed to compute one "aid effectiveness" coefficient per country and year. I show how this can be done in a tractable manner, using the "local Gaussian-weighted ordinary least squares" econometric method.

RELATED LITERATURE

This chapter is first related to the literature that evaluates the relevance of the existing indicators measuring policy performance. The main focus of this literature is the World Bank.[1] Kurtz and Schrank (2007) evaluate the World Bank's coding of "good governance" by exploiting the time dimension of the data. Using Granger-style causality tests, they found weak support for the notion that "better governance" was connected with successive improvements in growth. Other studies focus more specifically on the CPIA. Because the CPIA data was not disclosed until recently, they mainly emanate from the World Bank. For example, Gelb, Ngo, and Ye (2004) show that CPIA ratings have been quite strongly associated with medium-run growth performance. On the contrary, in a review of the performance-based allocation system, the World Bank (World Bank 2001) underlines that, on average, CPIA ratings may be considerably affected by contemporaneous growth, with only modest predictive power with respect to future growth or poverty reduction. This is consistent with the empirical findings I obtain in this chapter. But while World Bank (2001) simply states this fact,[2] I establish it using a careful empirical analysis. Kraay and Nehru (2004) use CPIA ratings and find a significant inverse correlation between the quality of a country's policies and institutions on the one hand and its probability of debt distress on the other hand. Outside of the World Bank, however, other articles are much more critical toward the CPIA. For example, Herman (2004) calls for appreciating the weaknesses of this indicator, especially its low ability to discriminate among countries or over time. This chapter contributes to this debate by analyzing both conceptually and empirically the relevance of the CPIA. To the extent of my knowledge, this is the first systematic evaluation of the CPIA using data for 146 countries' votes over a thirty-year period (from 1977 to 2008).

This chapter is also related to the literature that proposes alternatives to the CPIA or other performance indicators. Kanbur (2005) argues in favor of introducing some outcome variables in the CPIA. His proposal is in the spirit of Collier et al.'s (1997) outcomes-based allocation. They indeed propose a basis for aid allocation in terms of retrospective assessment of a few major outcomes such as growth. Similarly, Barder and Birdsall (2006) defend the idea of *payments for progress*. I contribute to this literature by opening the way for a new indicator that improves upon the previous proposals that have been done.

Finally, this chapter is related to a growing literature on optimal aid allocation that emphasizes the necessity to take into account the level of policies as a selectivity criterion. This necessity was first highlighted by Burnside and Dollar (2000) and further examined in the World Bank report *Assessing Aid* (Dollar and Pritchett 1998). Using these findings, Collier and Dollar (2001) derive an effective allocation of aid in terms of poverty reduction and compare it to the current allocation. They find out that the current allocation is radically different from the allocation that would be effective on poverty reduction. They stress that an optimal allocation of aid not only depends on levels of poverty but also on the political environment. Moreover, they further develop this idea by applying their approach to the dynamic question of poverty reduction (Collier and Dollar 2001). Cogneau and Naudet (2007) propose an alternative allocation based on the principle of equality of opportunity: they take into account structural growth handicaps rather than the quality of past policies (see also Llavador and Roemer [2001]). In the same spirit, Wood (2007) presents a more general model of optimal allocation of aid in which donors take into account future poverty as well as current poverty. Finally, Amprou, Guillaumont, and Guillaumont-Jeanneney (2006) argue in favor of considering vulnerability to exogenous shocks and low levels of human capital as selectivity criteria. All this literature takes the level of policy or of performance in the effective use of development assistance as given. In this chapter, I determine the optimal performance indicator one can use in the selectivity formula for aid allocation.

The rest of the chapter is organized as follows. The next section presents descriptive evidence about the CPIA and assesses its relevance. The following section provides new ways of improving upon the CPIA. The final section concludes.

THE CPIA: A GOOD MEASURE OF POLICY PERFORMANCE?

One of the most influential tools for measuring policy performance as of today is the Country Policy and Institutional Assessment (CPIA), which is the World Bank's tool. In this section, I analyze the relevance of this tool as a measure of policy performance.

SOME HISTORY OF THE CPIA

Since 1977, the World Bank has carried out an annual performance assessment of its client countries' capacity to effectively absorb development assistance. This assessment, the CPIA, is one of the main criteria used to allocate International Development Assistance (IDA) resources among low-income developing countries. The CPIA is an assessment tool for the Bank used to gauge the likely return to development assistance in specific countries and to guide IDA allocations to countries below the income threshold. CPIA assessments do not directly reflect specific "outcome" criteria as set out in the Millennium Development Goals (MDGs)—for example, poverty reduction, school enrollment, maternal health, etc.—neither do they directly rest on proxy outcome variables such as GDP, export, or investment growth rates. The emphasis is on policy actions and institutional effectiveness. They rely on the judgments of technical analysts to assess how well a country's policy and institutional framework fosters poverty reduction, sustainable growth, and the effective use of development assistance (Gelb, Ngo, and Ye 2004).[3] Ratings are against specific criteria but are subjective. Indeed, the CPIAs are produced by the Bank's own staff, that is, its country teams.

In the past, CPIA results were not made available to the public. Only recently have governments themselves, whose policies are assessed in a particular CPIA, come to be informed of the numerical ratings on a confidential basis. Since 2000, there has been a public quintile-based disclosure. The exact numerical values of the CPIA have been disclosed starting with the results of the 2005 CPIA exercise. They now are fully available to the public.

The criteria used in the CPIA have evolved over the years in response to new analytical insights and lessons the Bank feels it has learned from experience. Originally called Country Performance Ratings (CPR), the assessment exercise acquired the name CPIA with the 1998 redesign to emphasize that it was the policy and institutional environment that was being assessed, not economic outcomes. The definition of the criteria, their relative importance, the rating, and disclosure procedures have undergone important changes over the years (Van Waeyenberge 2006).

During the 1980s, the emphasis moved from an initial concern with both policy inputs and economic performance indicators (growth and savings rates) to a predominant concern with policy inputs. By the early 1990s, an exclusive emphasis on policy inputs prevailed. In 1997, criteria covering governance-related issues were added. In 2001, several changes were introduced. As shown in the data appendix at the end of this chapter, the CPIA currently comprises sixteen criteria divided into four clusters. It is split into two groups, the CPIA Cluster A-C (Economic Management; Structural Policies; Policies for Social Inclusion/Equity), and the CPIA Cluster D (Governance Rating: Public Sector Management and Institutions). The CPIA Cluster A-C includes eleven items, and the CPIA Cluster D includes five items.

Using the guidelines, the Bank's country team gives a score to every country comprised between one and six for each of the sixteen criteria and gives each cluster the same weight in producing the overall country assessment.[4]

DESCRIPTIVE EVIDENCE

In this chapter, I use the annual series of the CPIA for 146 countries between 1977 and 2008. Table 9.1 presents summary statistics by decade. Despite fundamental changes in the CPIA design and a general understanding that developing country policies have improved on average since 1977, average CPIA results across countries have remained remarkably steady between 1977 and 2008.[5] Moreover, CPIA results have been concentrating increasingly around the median. This steadiness cannot come from the fact that some developing countries have improved substantially while others have declined, given that the standard deviation of the CPIA ratings has decreased since the 1990s. According to Gelb, Ngo, and Ye (2004), some inertia is to be expected in the ratings because they assess institutions and capacity to implement policies rather than just "stroke-of-the-pen" policy changes. This can cause CPIA scores to lag reform efforts, as better policies can require time to become properly reflected in the ratings. However, the concentration of the results around the same median for thirty years seems hardly explainable by such a lag.

Table 9.1 CPIA, summary statistics by decades, 1977–2008

	1970s	1980s	1990s	2000s
Average CPIA	3.00	2.93	3.06	3.43
Median CPIA	3.00	2.96	3.13	3.45
Standard Deviation of the CPIA	0.86	0.86	0.75	0.61
Observations	3	10	10	9

Source: CPIA data, World Bank.
Note: The table presents annual descriptive statistics of the CPIA between 1977 and 2008 (by decade).

Table 9.2 presents summary statistics by region. Some differences across regions appear. At the end of the 1970s, South Asia had the lowest score with an average score below three, followed by Sub-Saharan Africa. However, Asia improves its rating since the 1990s much more than Sub-Saharan Africa. Latin America and the Caribbean also improve

Table 9.2 CPIA, summary statistics by region, 1977–2008

	Average CPIA			
	1970s	1980s	1990s	2000s
Sub-Saharan Africa	2.72	2.73	2.77	3.17
Latin America and the Caribbean	3.17	2.89	3.25	3.69
Middle East and North Africa	3.30	3.31	3.17	3.39
Eastern Europe and Central Asia	3.50	3.37	3.11	3.77
South Asia	2.54	2.93	3.39	3.61
East Asia and the Pacific	3.59	3.33	3.29	3.37
Observations	3	10	10	9

Source: CPIA data, World Bank.
Note: This table presents annual descriptive statistics of the CPIA between 1977 and 2008 (by decade and region).

their rating during the 1990s. The regions that have the best average CPIA score today are Eastern Europe and Central Asia, which, despite a slight decrease during the 1990s, are back to their end of the 1970s average score. However, despite these small changes, the average CPIA score for each region has been incredibly stable during the period from 1977 to 2008.

THE RELEVANCE OF THE CPIA: REVIEW OF THE EXISTING EVALUATIONS

Ex-ante conditionality: The first caveat of the CPIA is that it relies on policies rather than on outcomes. From this point of view, it corresponds to a model of "ex-ante conditionality." The main problem of ex-ante conditionality is that until now it has never worked. As underlined by Stiglitz (1999), "good policies cannot be bought." Moreover, ex-ante conditionality goes against democratic accountability and economic sustainability that require that each country takes ownership of its development strategy.

Hidden conditionality: A second shortcoming of the CPIA comes from the fact that it may include hidden conditionality. According to van Waeyenberge (2006), there is an increasing contradiction between the rhetoric and the practice of the World Bank. He argues that with the recent changes made to the CPIA, the imperatives that have disappeared from the narrative guidelines of the CPIA may have somehow become "embedded" and now steer the CPIA exercise in less visible ways. He illustrates this point with the assessment of trade policy in the 2004 CPIA questionnaire (World Bank 2004). This questionnaire focuses exclusively on the policy framework regarding trade in goods, without reference to the rules and regulations affecting capital flows. However, closer scrutiny of the guideposts that accompany the narrative guidelines reveals how some specific policy imperatives have in fact been subsumed in the "diagnostic reports" that now serve as guideposts to staff's assessment: "these typically embody a bias in favor of foreign investment and trade, and are anchored in a framework of traditional welfare economics where government intervention is tolerated only in the context of static market failure."

According to these criticisms, the CPIA is not a good tool for allocating aid, at least conceptually. In the next section, I show empirically that it is not a good predictor for economic growth.

IS THE CPIA A GOOD PREDICTOR FOR
ECONOMIC GROWTH? AN EMPIRICAL ANALYSIS

In this section, I test empirically whether the CPIA is a good predictor for economic growth, using an annual panel dataset of over 146 countries between 1977 and 2008.

DATA DESCRIPTION AND DESCRIPTIVE STATISTICS

In order to determine whether the CPIA is a good predictor for economic growth, I run growth regressions with the CPIA score and the annual change in the CPIA as control variables in a panel of 146 developing countries over the period from 1977 to 2008.[6] As a dependent variable, I use the growth rate of per capita GDP. Usual controls in cross-country growth equations, used for example in Levine and Renelt (1992), Ramey and Ramey (1995), and Aizenman and Marion (1999), are the initial log level of real GDP per capita; the initial fraction of the relevant population in secondary schools; the initial growth rate of the population; and the average share of trade in GDP over the period. However, because all these controls are fixed at the country level, I directly introduce country-fixed effects in all the specifications for robustness reasons. I also control for M2 as a share of GDP lagged one period and aid flows. Panel data on aid flows are taken from the OECD Development Assistance Committee (DAC) annual series. Following Roodman (2006), I use the Net Aid Transfers (NAT) variable for measuring aid flows.[7] Table 9.3 provides summary statistics for a few key statistics.

EMPIRICAL SPECIFICATION

Equations are estimated using a panel of eight four-year periods from 1977 to 1980 through 2005 to 2008. Thus, an observation is a country's performance average over a four-year period. The averaging over a four-year period, which is usual in the literature, allows me to avoid the nonstationarity problem for the growth rate.

The baseline empirical specification is:

(1) $g_{it} = \alpha + \beta \, \text{CPIA Score}_{it} + \text{CPIA Change}_{it} + X'_{it}\lambda + \vartheta_{it} + \gamma_{it} + \varepsilon_{it}$

Where i index is the countries and t stands for the eight four-year periods (from 1977 to 1980 to 2005 to 2008); g is the growth rate of per

Table 9.3 Summary statistics

	(1)
	mean/sd
CPIA Score	3.16
	(0.77)
CPIA Change	2.10
	(8.13)
Per Capita Growth Rate	1.74
	(5.15)
Aid/GDP	7.95
	(10.93)
Observations	1095

Note: Numbers in parentheses are standard deviations and the others are averages. They have been computed using a panel of 146 developing countries over the period from 1977 to 2008. Variables are described in the data appendix.

capita GDP; "CPIA Score" is the average CPIA score over the period; and "CPIA Change" is the average of the annual change in CPIA rating over the period. X_{it} is a vector of control variables that vary with the specification considered. ϑ_i are country-fixed effects; γ_t is period-fixed effects; and ε_{it} is a country-period shock.

I estimate equation (1) using both Ordinary Least Squares (OLS) with robust standard errors and two-step Arellano-Bond GMM (table 9.4). The use of two-step Arellano-Bond GMM is driven by possible endogeneity concerns. Endogeneity may come from the fact that the CPIA is a subjective assessment. Subjective assessments are influenced by the perceptions of development outcomes—analysts use whatever information is available, including information from outcomes to set ratings—and ratings are therefore likely to be somewhat endogenous to outcomes.[8] The advantage of the system GMM method is that it helps to overcome endogeneity concerns in the absence of any strictly exogenous explanatory variables or instrument.[9] The results are robust to both methodologies.

RESULTS

Table 9.4 presents the results of the impact of performance as measured by the CPIA score and the annual changes in this score on the growth rate of per capita GDP (estimation of equation [1]). I find a positive and statistically significant coefficient for the CPIA score using both OLS (upper table) and two-step Arellano-Bond GMM (bottom table, columns 1 and 2). However, these estimates do not prove causality. As acknowledged by

Table 9.4 CPIA score and GDP growth rate

Panel A: OLS Estimations

	(1)	(2)	(3)	(4)	(5)	(6)
	OLS	OLS	OLS	OLS	OLS	OLS
	b/se	b/se	b/se	b/se	b/se	b/se
CPIA Score	1.819***	1.561***	1.954***	1.957***	1.889***	2.183***
	(0.352)	(0.408)	(0.406)	(0.410)	(0.425)	(0.326)
CPIA Change		0.060*	0.015	0.015	0.014	−0.020
		(0.032)	(0.036)	(0.035)	(0.035)	(0.029)
(One-Period) Lag of CPIA Score			−0.923**	−0.981**	−0.993**	−0.859**
			(0.423)	(0.435)	(0.436)	(0.337)
Period and Country FE	Yes	Yes	Yes	Yes	Yes	Yes
Aid	No	No	No	Yes	Yes	Yes
Aid Square	No	No	No	No	Yes	Yes
Outliers Included	Yes	Yes	Yes	Yes	Yes	No
R-sq	0.48	0.53	0.54	0.54	0.54	0.59
Observations	766	748	734	722	722	717

Panel B: GMM Estimations

	(1)	(2)	(3)	(4)	(5)	(6)
	GMM	GMM	GMM	GMM	GMM	GMM
	b/se	b/se	b/se	b/se	b/se	b/se
CPIA Score	2.343***	1.482***	1.814***	1.752***	1.763***	2.143***
	(0.462)	(0.546)	(0.452)	(0.554)	(0.547)	(0.464)
CPIA Change		0.085***	0.003	0.008	0.007	-0.008
		(0.032)	(0.040)	(0.037)	(0.037)	(0.034)
(One-Period) Lag of CPIA Score			−1.325***	−1.440***	−1.458***	−1.439***
			(0.349)	(0.335)	(0.350)	(0.333)
Period and Country FE	Yes	Yes	Yes	Yes	Yes	Yes
Aid	No	No	No	Yes	Yes	Yes
Aid Square	No	No	No	No	Yes	Yes
Outliers Included	Yes	Yes	Yes	Yes	Yes	No
Observations	741	723	710	698	698	693
Instruments	69	103	109	111	111	111
Hansen test	0.153	0.172	0.301	0.222	0.204	0.151
Arellano-Bond test for AR(1)	0.002	0.001	0.000	0.000	0.000	0.000
Arellano-Bond test for AR(2)	0.182	0.572	0.696	0.641	0.642	0.681

Note: $*p < 0.10$, $**p < 0.05$, $***p < 0.01$.

Panel A reports OLS estimates. Standard errors in parentheses are robust. Panel B reports two-step system GMM with Windmeijer's (2005) finite sample correction for standard errors for two-step GMM. I report the p-values for the Hansen test of overidentifying restrictions and the Arellano-Bond test for AR(1) and AR(2) in first differences. The unit of observation is a country/period. The dependent variable is the growth rate of per capita GDP. All the regressions include M2 as a share of GDP as a control. The variables are described in more detail in the text.

Gelb, Ngo, and Ye (2004), despite the use of clear benchmarks to derive CPIA ratings, it is possible that assessments are colored by perceptions of "how well the country is doing," which are influenced by recent growth trends. In this case, the positive coefficient I obtain for the CPIA score would simply reflect the fact that CPIA scores themselves respond to observed growth rates and so is not indicative of the fact that this score can be interpreted as a good predictor for growth rates.[10]

In order to test whether the CPIA score can be interpreted as a good growth predictor, I introduce as a control variable the CPIA score lagged one period. Obviously, this cannot be determined by the current growth rate. But a strong positive correlation between the CPIA score lagged one period and the following period growth rate would mean that the CPIA score is a good predictor of future growth.

When I estimate equation (1) with this new control, I find a negative and statistically significant coefficient for the CPIA score lagged one period, using both OLS and two-step Arellano-Bond GMM (column 3). Hence the CPIA score seems to be a bad predictor for future growth rate: countries with the lowest CPIA scores one period ago are those that do better in terms of growth during the following period.

Robustness checks: A possible issue may come from the fact that these estimates do not distinguish between the effects of performance as measured by the CPIA and other influences on growth that may themselves reflect the CPIA rating. For example, growth in high-performing countries may be partly driven by increased ODA flows in response to higher CPIA scores. In order to control for these other influences, I include aid flows normalized by GDP as a control variable (column 4) as well as the square of these flows to control for decreasing returns of development aid (column 5). The introduction of these controls, whether I use OLS or Arellano-Bond GMM estimations, does not change the results.

Moreover, the results are robust to dropping the outliers: I identify influential observations using the method of Hadi (1992), which classifies nine observations as outliers at the 5 percent level.[11] Removing these observations does not change the results (column 6).

Finally, I run a series of tests to address the potential pitfalls with GMM, namely instrument proliferation[12] and serial correlation in the error term (see Roodman 2009a and b). I report the *p*-values for the Hansen test of overidentifying restrictions and the Arellano-Bond (2001) test for first- and second-order serial correlation in the first difference in the error term. The AR(1) and AR(2) tests are satisfactory; they suggest

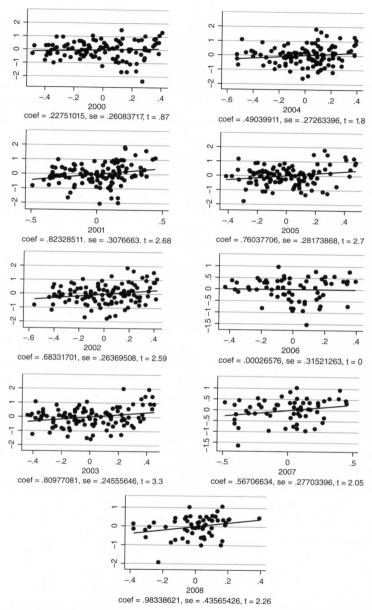

Figure 9.1 CPIA score and the correlation of the votes with those of the United States in the UNGA, 2000–2008

Note: The figures present, for each year between 2000 and 2008, the correlation between the CPIA scores of developing countries and the correlation of their votes with those of the United States in the UNGA.

that first-order serial correlation is present but second-order serial correlation is not, which is consistent with the identifying assumption of no serial correlation. Instrument proliferation can lead to implausibly high p-values of the Hansen statistic, so it is reassuring that the p-values are high enough to reject endogeneity but always below 0.4. Finally, I use the Windmeijer's (2005) finite sample correction for standard errors for two-step GMM.

The negative coefficient I obtain for the CPIA score lagged one period and therefore seems to be robust.

VOTES IN THE UNGA

I finally find a strong and statistically significant positive correlation between the CPIA scores of developing countries and the correlation of their votes with those of the United States in the UNGA. This appears clearly in figure 9.1. For each year between 2000 and 2008, I plot the relationship between the correlation of the votes with those of the United States in the UNGA and the CPIA score of the countries. This relationship is positive and statistically significant: the higher the correlation of the votes, the higher the CPIA score.

Obviously, correlation is not causality, but it seems hard to find an intuitive causal link going from the CPIA score to the correlation of the vote in the UNGA. On the contrary, one can argue that CPIA scores are biased in favor of countries having political links with the United States. The literature on aid allocation has shown that aid may be used to buy political support from the recipients (Alesina and Dollar 2000; Alesina and Weder 2002; Schraeder, Hook, and Taylor 1998; Kuziemko and Werker 2006). Another interpretation could therefore be that countries to which the World Bank is willing to give more aid obtain a higher CPIA score in order for these countries to effectively receive more aid through the Bank allocation formula. Whatever the precise sense in which that might or might not be the case, this questions the relevance of the CPIA.

HOW CAN WE IMPROVE UPON THE CPIA?

In this section I first consider the alternative proposals to the CPIA that have been formulated in the literature and in particular the one of Kanbur (2005). I then make concrete proposals for the development of new possible allocations based on the idea of using "aid effectiveness" as an allocation tool.

CRITERIA FOR AID ALLOCATION

One of the main uses of the CPIA is as a criterion in the development aid allocation formula. When a country is eligible for the International Development Association (IDA)—the development aid agency of the World Bank—the IDA formula to allocate aid is made of four different terms: (1) the CPIA; (2) the portfolio performance that is used to determine a rating for each country's implementation performance; (3) population; and (4) per capita income.[13] The combination of the CPIA and of the portfolio performance forms the Country Performance Rating (CPR):

$$CPR = 0.24 \times CPIA_{A-C} + 0.68 \times CPIA_D + 0.08 \times Portfolio$$

$CPIA_{A-C}$ stands for the clusters A through C of the CPIA; $CPIA_D$ for the cluster D; and Portfolio for the portfolio performance rating.

The IDA allocation formula is then computed as follows:

$$IDA\ Country\ Allocation = F\left[CPR^{0.5}, Population^{1.0}, \left(\frac{Gini}{Population} \right)^{-0.125} \right]$$

EXISTING ALTERNATIVE PROPOSALS TO THE CPIA

KANBUR'S PROPOSAL

Underlying that the CPIA implicitly relies too heavily on a uniform model of what works in development policy, Kanbur (2005) proposes to introduce outcome variables in the development aid allocation formula.

Indeed, as it clearly appears from the formula, the IDA essentially captures needs through the income criterion, and does not go directly to indicators such as infant mortality, maternal mortality, girls' education, and other components of the Millennium Development Goals. Moreover, the CPIA itself does not contain any final outcome variables like poverty, extreme poverty, girls' enrollment, etc. What it has instead is a series of intermediate variables like trade policy, regulatory policy, property rights, corruption, etc.

On the contrary, Kanbur argues in favor of an outcomes-based aid allocation, or at least in favor of introducing some outcome variables in the CPIA itself.[14] His main idea is to measure the needs side by the levels of the outcomes one is interested in, while measuring the performance side by the rate of improvement of these outcome variables over a given period of time up to the point of assessment, suitably normalized by the total aid flow over this period. He gives the following example: a country that has very low levels of girls' enrollment in primary schools should get more aid on grounds of need. But a country that is showing rapid improvements of girls' enrollment from this low level, relative to the aid it is receiving, should get even more. A country that is showing relatively slow rates of improvement should get relatively less on account of this measure of performance. The main advantage of this focus on outcomes is that it prevents the easy temptation of a one-size-fits-all approach to development.

As he acknowledges himself, this proposal is in the spirit of Collier's outcomes-based allocation (Collier et al. 1997). They propose a basis for aid allocation in terms of retrospective assessment of a few major outcomes such as growth. They show how outcome measures can control for influences on growth over which the government has no control and argue that donors should switch from attempting to "purchase" a pre-specified menu of policy changes to the allocation of aid on the basis of periodic overall assessments of government achievements.

Similarly, Barder and Birdsall (2006) defend the idea of "payments for progress," the main objective being to link additional aid to clear evidence on progress already achieved on the ground. In order to do so, payments would be determined as a function of the outcomes and not linked to the implementation of any particular policies or any other intermediate outputs, or tied to purchases from particular suppliers or companies.

ADVANTAGES OF KANBUR'S PROPOSAL

Kanbur's proposal relies on performance-based measures—on actual performance—and so does not imply ex-ante conditionality. Indeed, rating countries according to their rates of improvement of certain outcomes rather than according to their policies corresponds to an "ex-post" approach of conditionality: one has to reward countries that used past aid well (ex-post conditionality) without conditions (ex-ante conditionality). This is in the spirit of the Paris Declaration (2005) and of the following Accra Agenda for Action (AAA) (2008)[15]: "Developing countries and donors will work together at the international level to review, document and disseminate good practices on conditionality with a view to reinforcing country ownership and other Paris Declaration Principles by increasing emphasis on harmonized, results-based conditionality."

LIMITS OF KANBUR'S PROPOSAL

According to Buiter (2007), realized past outcome changes may not be a good measure of future aid productivity: "the aid could have been looted, diverted or wasted, that is, not even spent on any activity likely to boost the indicator, and the improvement in the indicator could have been produced by domestic or foreign factors that have nothing to do with the aid dispensed during the benchmark period, but never mind."[16] Hence the implicit assumption made by Kanbur that past output indicators are a good guide to future aid productivity is questionable.

Similarly, McGillivray (2004) underlines that Kanbur's proposal does not really provide an understanding of what makes aid work. This is why he argues in favor of more radical changes to the IDA formula than outlined in Kanbur's proposal. According to him, what is required is a better knowledge of what makes aid work, and the revisions to the aid allocation formula should be considered in this light.

THE NEED FOR AN AID PRODUCTIVITY MEASURE

What emerges clearly from the criticisms of both the CPIA and Kanbur's proposal—and more generally of any outcomes-based allocation—is that what is needed is an aid productivity measure. The CPIA is not an aid productivity measure, being excessively focused on a one-size-fits-all approach of development. An outcomes-based allocation would not overcome this difficulty. In order to overcome it, one needs to establish a clear statistical link between past outcomes and future aid productivity. This has never been done and seems hardly feasible. Indeed, this supposes first to evaluate the elasticity of this outcome variable with respect to aid (which can be interpreted as aid productivity). Second, this supposes to evaluate the elasticity of aid productivity with respect to past changes in this outcome variable. In both steps of the estimation, one would be faced with endogeneity and omitted variable concerns. Moreover, in case one would like to introduce not one but various measures of outcomes, the estimation would be even more complicated by the fact that these outcomes may be interdependent. And then it remains to determine the optimal weight to give to each of these outcomes.

Well aware of all these difficulties but at the same time aware of the real need for an aid productivity measure, I offer a new way to approach this issue. The idea is to directly use aid effectiveness as such a measure.

A NEW APPROACH: USING AID EFFECTIVENESS TO ALLOCATE AID EFFECTIVELY

Aid effectiveness has to be defined with respect to a given outcome, which has to be chosen by donors when they establish their selectivity criteria. This can be the growth rate of the economy, the reduction in the poverty rate, the rate of girls' enrollment, or other goals depending both on donors' priorities and recipient countries' specificities. Aid is said to be very effective if aid elasticity with respect to the outcome is very high. For example, if the outcome is the growth rate, the higher the aid elasticity with respect to growth—that is, the more the growth rate increases for each increase in the aid flows received—the more the aid is effective.

Generally, in order to compute aid effectiveness, one would like to estimate the following equation for each country i and year t:

$$\text{Outcome}_{it} = \alpha + \beta_{it}\frac{\text{Aid}}{\text{GDP}_{it}} + X'_{it}\,\gamma + \epsilon_{it} \qquad (2)$$

$$\text{where } \epsilon_{it} \sim N\left(0, \sigma_\epsilon^2\right)$$

β_{it} measures aid effectiveness. Outcome$_{it}$ is the outcome of interest (for example, the growth rate of per capita GDP), and Aid / GDP$_{it}$ are the aid flows normalized by GDP. X_{it} is a vector of control variables. ε_{it} is a year-country shock. All the coefficients in equation (2) are time varying, which is why I write β_{it} to denote the coefficient on aid in country i at year t.

The difficulty comes from the fact that with the econometric methods that are usually used, the equation one estimates is not (2) but:

$$\text{Outcome}_{it} = \alpha + \beta_i\frac{\text{Aid}}{\text{GDP}_{it}} + \gamma X_{it} + \epsilon_{it}$$
$$\text{where } \epsilon_{it} \sim N\left(0, \sigma_\epsilon^2\right) \qquad (3)$$

That is, one only computes one coefficient for each country i and the entire time period (β_{it}) and not one coefficient for each country i and year t (β_{it}). In other words, one cannot estimate aid effectiveness annually.

One way to estimate aid effectiveness annually—to implement the estimation of equation (2)—is to use the "local Gaussian-weighted ordinary least squares" method (Aghion and Marinescu 2007). The basic idea of this method—which is also called kernel-based nonparametric regression or local smoothing—is to put more weight on the most recent years. For each year, points that are closer in time are given more weight than points that are further away. More precisely, all the observations are weighted by a Gaussian centered at date t, but, because to estimate aid effectiveness in t one only wants to use the information available for the years preceding t, I put a zero weight on the years following t.

Under this method, jumps in the coefficient β are mainly due to changes in the immediate neighborhood of date t, as those observations in the immediate neighborhood of date t are given highest weight. Hence if there is a change in the aid effectiveness coefficient in t—say an increase—this comes from the fact that the country has improved its effective use of aid in t. And so in terms of aid allocation, it has to be rewarded for this improvement.

Using the local Gaussian-weighted ordinary least squares method, one could thus estimate an aid effectiveness coefficient for each country and each year. However, aid can be endogenous, which can lead to biased results.[17] In order to deal with these endogeneity problems, one can use Gaussian-weighted two-stage least squares instrumenting for aid. (The relevance of the method is totally independent of the instrument choice.)

Using Gaussian-weighted two-stage least squares, one could thus obtain a time-varying measure of aid effectiveness, with one coefficient per year and per country. These coefficients can be interpreted as an estimate of aid elasticity with respect to the outcome of interest, that is, a measure of the country performance with respect to aid effectiveness. This tool could thus be used to reward a good "aid performer." Doing so, it helps overcome one of the main weaknesses of the outcomes-based allocations that have been proposed until now in the literature: it does not reward good luck. Indeed, a country can have in one given year, for example, a very high growth rate and at the same time obtain a very low coefficient for aid effectiveness if it did not use aid in an effective way. In this case, its aid allocation decreases despite its good growth performance. The tool I propose only relies on the implicit assumption that past aid effectiveness is a good guide to future aid effectiveness. This is a less demanding and more relevant assumption than the one according to which past output indicators are a good guide to future aid effectiveness.

One can also choose to normalize the coefficients obtained using local Gaussian-weighted ordinary least squares by the "global" aid effectiveness coefficient obtained by performing equation (3) for all the countries of the sample taken together (cross-countries regression with country-fixed effects). Another possibility could be to take into account for each country the performance of its neighbors rather than to normalize by the cross-countries coefficient, for example using the geographical distance. Indeed, there may be some externalities created by an increase or a decrease in aid effectiveness in a country for its neighbors.

DISCUSSION

A possible caveat of such a measure is that it does not take into account how donors can have an impact on aid effectiveness. Implicit here is indeed the assumption that aid performance is only the consequence of decisions of the recipient country itself and not of somebody else. Aid effectiveness depends not only on the behavior of the recipient countries but also on the donor's behavior. Recipients should not suffer from the bad behavior of donors. One possibility would be to control for an index of donor performance.

Similarly, aid effectiveness can be affected by events not depending only on the recipient's economic policy, for example exogenous shocks like natural disasters. One would have to be very careful in controlling for these exogenous shocks.

Despite these caveats, the aid effectiveness coefficient I propose in this chapter appears to be a relevant tool to allocate aid. With such a tool, donors won't provide aid to the countries that are the best performers (for example, in the sense of having a higher rate of girls' enrollment), but to those where aid will be used in the most efficient way. That is to say, to the countries that have a sufficient absorptive capacity for receiving higher aid flows. Used together with other indicators, it could help in allocating a scarce resource in the most efficient way.

CONCLUSION

In this chapter I evaluate the pertinence of the CPIA and of the various alternatives that have been proposed in the literature.

Using a yearly panel dataset of over 146 countries between 1977 and 2008, I show that the CPIA is correlated with current growth rates but that it is not a good predictor for future economic growth. I thus argue in favor of other measures of policy performance for aid allocation. I show that performance-based measures, as opposed to measures implying ex-ante conditionality, are more accurate instruments for aid allocation. However, performance-based measures proposed in the literature do not help overcome the difficulty of estimating the elasticity of aid effectiveness with respect to outcomes-based performance indicators. They leave unsolved the question of whether, when a donor rewards a recipient for its good performance with respect to a given outcome variable, he or she is rewarding "luck" rather than providing an effective use of aid.

In order to allocate aid effectively, it is essential to evaluate the elasticity of aid effectiveness with respect to performance indicators. I therefore propose a new tool based on this elasticity. Using new econometric methods, I show that one could use a time-varying measure of aid effectiveness as an indicator of the performance of a country with respect to aid efficiency. This tool shares with an outcomes-based allocation the advantage of not relying on ex-ante conditionality. Moreover, it is an improvement upon this outcomes-based approach because it is a way to reward a good "aid performer" rather than good "luck."

Needless to say, more research on aid effectiveness indicators is necessary before they can be applied. The tool could indeed be used by different donors with different goals (growth, poverty, education). The downside is that aid effectiveness coefficients might be too volatile to be used as single indicators. The most promising avenue is to use them together with other key development indicators.

APPENDIX

DATA SOURCES AND DESCRIPTION

Aid: Net Aid Transfers (NAT). *Source*: DAC.

CPIA: Country Policy and Institutional Assessment. Annual performance assessment of its client countries' capacity to effectively absorb development assistance carried out by the World Bank since 1977. *Source*: World Bank.

CPIA Criteria (2008). *Source*: World Bank (2008).

A. Economic Management
  1. Macroeconomic Management
  2. Fiscal Policy
  3. Debt Policy

B. Structural Policies
    4. Policies and Institutions for Economic Cooperation, Regional
       Integration, and Trade
    5. Financial Sector
    6. Business Regulatory Environment

C. Policies for Social Inclusion/Equity
    7. Gender Equality
    8. Equity of Public Resource Use
    9. Building Human Resources
    10. Social Protection and Labor
    11. Environmental Policies and Regulations

D. Governance Rating: Public Sector Management
   and Institutions
    1. Property Rights and Rule-Based Governance
    2. Quality of Budgetary and Financial Management
    3. Efficiency of Revenue Mobilization
    4. Quality of Public Administration
    5. Transparency, Accountability, and Corruption in the Public Sector

Per capita GDP growth rate: Annual percentage growth rate of per capita GDP at market prices based on constant local currency. *Source*: WDI.

M2 (percent GDP): Money and quasi-money comprise the sum of currency outside banks, demand deposits other than those of the central government, and the time, savings, and foreign currency deposits of resident sectors other than the central government. *Source*: WDI.

Votes in the UNGA: Annual correlation of voting records in UNGA between recipient and the United States (–1 to 1). *Source*: Erik Voeten (United Nations General Assembly Voting Data).

NOTES

I am particularly thankful to Ravi Kanbur, Akbar Noman, Thomas Piketty, and Joseph Stiglitz for helpful comments and suggestions. Participants at the Initiative for Policy Dialogue Task Forces also provided valuable advice. The usual disclaimer applies.

   1. An exception is Stuckler, King, and Patton (2009) who show, using the EBRD's own data, that the EBRD's indices of progress in market reforms are biased in the direction of positive growth.

2. "From the little internal research that has been done, coupled with anecdotal evidence from Bank staff" (World Bank 2001, 16).

3. Indeed, according to the World Bank, the aim of the CPIA is to assess "how conducive [a country's policy and institutional] framework is to fostering poverty reduction, sustainable growth and the effective use of development assistance" (World Bank 2007).

4. More precisely, for each criterion, countries are rated on a scale of two (weak) to five (strong), and a country is rated a one if it is very weak for two years or more and a six if it is very strong for three years or more.

5. Similarly, Herman (2004) emphasizes that "although the index was substantially revised in 1998 (and again in 2001) and smaller revisions are made each year, neither the changes in the structure of the CPIA nor in the definitions of individual items seemed to cause significant changes in the rating scores, at least through 2000" (see also World Bank 2001).

6. For the description and the sources of the data in more detail, see the data appendix at the end of chapter 9.

7. NAT is a net transfer concept, net of both principle payments received on ODA loans and of interests received on such loans. Moreover, NAT excludes cancelation of old non-ODA loans because such cancelation generates little or no additional net transfers.

8. See, for example, World Bank (2001): "There is evidence that ratings may be unduly influenced by contemporaneous growth."

9. When I estimate my regressions using the two-step system GMM, I use the forward orthogonal deviations transform instead of first differencing because it maximizes the sample size in panel with gaps (Roodman 2006). The forward orthogonal deviations transform is an alternative to differencing proposed by Arellano and Bover (1995) that preserves sample size in panel with gaps. Indeed, instead of subtracting the previous observation from the contemporaneous—what does the first-difference transform that thus magnifies gaps in unbalanced panels—it subtracts the average of all future available observations of a variable. No matter how many gaps there are, it is computable for all observations except the last for each individual, so it minimizes data loss. (Because lagged observations do not enter the formula, they are valid instruments.)

10. Similarly, Glaeser et al. (2004) underline that indicators measuring the quality of institutions, supposed to explain economic growth, are in fact the result and not the cause of economic growth.

11. Angola in the 2005–2008 period; Azerbaijan in the 1993–1996 and 2005–2008 periods; Equatorial Guinea in the 1997–2000 and 2001–2004 periods; Liberia in the 1989–1992 and 1997–2000 periods; Tajikistan in the 1993–1996 period; and Ukraine in the 1993–1996 period.

12. A large instrument collection overfits endogenous variables even as it weakens the Hansen test of the instruments' joint validity.

13. In order to be eligible to the IDA resources, a country has to meet two criteria. First, its relative poverty defined as GNI per capita has to be below an established threshold that is updated annually (in fiscal year 2010: $1,135). Second, it has to lack creditworthiness to borrow on market terms and therefore to need concessional resources to finance its development program.

14. "While leaving the current IDA allocation methodology essentially intact, IDA should introduce one new category of scoring in the CPIA. This category should evaluate the evolution of an actual development outcome variable up to the present. The choice of variable is open."

15. The Paris Declaration on Aid Effectiveness and the Accra Agenda for Action are available at http://www.oecd.org/dac/effectiveness/34428351.pdf.

16. Similarly, Collier et al. (1997) acknowledge that "one disadvantage with switching from policies to outcomes is that it can reward good luck."

17. This endogeneity can come from (1) reverse causation: growth causes aid (for example, the higher its growth rate, the less aid a country receives because it does not need it); or (2) simultaneous causation: an omitted variable causes both aid and growth.

REFERENCES

Aghion, P., and I. Marinescu. 2007. "Productivity Growth and Countercyclical Budgetary Policy: What Do We Learn from OECD Panel Data?" *NBER Macroeconomic Annual* 22: 251–278.

Aizenman, J., and N. Marion. 1999. "Volatility and Investment: Interpreting Evidence from Developing Countries." *Economica* 66: 157–179.

Alesina, A., and D. Dollar. 2000. "Who Gives Foreign Aid to Whom and Why?" *Journal of Economic Growth* 5 (1): 3–63.

Alesina, A., and B. Weder. 2002. "Do Corrupt Governments Receive Less Foreign Aid?" *American Economic Review* 92 (4): 1126–1137.

Amprou, J., P. Guillaumont, and S. Guillaumont-Jeanneney. 2006. "Aid Selectivity According to Augmented Criteria" *CERDI Etudes et Documents, E 2006.16*.

Arellano, M., and O. Bover. 1995. "Another Look at the Instrumental Variables Estimation of Error Components Models." *Journal of Econometrics* 68: 29–51.

Barder, O., and N. Birdsall. 2006. "Payments for Progress: A Hands-Off Approach to Foreign Aid." Center for Global Development Working Paper No. 102.

Buiter, W. H. 2007. "No Bricks Without Straw: A Critique of Ravi Kanbur's 'Modest Proposal for Introducing Development Outcomes in IDA Allocation Procedures.'" Note prepared at the meeting for the Initiative for Policy Dialogue at Columbia University, New York, April 5.

Burnside, C., and D. Dollar. 2000. "Aid, Policies and Growth." *American Economic Review* 90 (4): 847–868.

Cogneau, D., and J.-D. Naudet. 2007. "Who Deserves Aid? Equality of Opportunity, International Aid, and Poverty Reduction." *World Development* 35 (1): 104–120.

Collier, P., and D. Dollar. 2001. "Can the World Cut Poverty in Half? How Policy Reform and Effective Aid Can Meet International Development Goals." *World Development* 29 (11): 1787–1802.

——. 2002. "Aid Allocation and Poverty Reduction." *European Economic Review* 45 (1): 1–26.

Collier, P., P. Guillaumont, S. Guillaumont, and J. W. Gunning. 1997. "Redesigning Conditionality." *World Development* 25 (9): 1399–1407.

Dollar, D., and L. Pritchett. 1998. *Assessing Aid—What Works, What Doesn't, and Why.* World Bank policy research report. Washington, DC: World Bank.

Gelb, A., B. Ngo, and X. Ye. 2004. "Implementing Performance-Based Aid in Africa: The Country Policy and Institutional Assessment." World Bank Africa Region Working Paper No. 77.

Glaeser, E., R. La Porta, F. Lopez-de Silanes, and A. Shleifer. 2004. "Do Institutions Cause Growth?" *Journal of Economic Growth* 9: 271–303.

Hadi, A. S. 1992. "A New Measure of Overall Potential Influence in Linear Regression." *Computational Statistics and Data Analysis* 14: 1–27.

Herman, B. 2004. "How Well Do Measurement of an Enabling Domestic Environment for Development Stand Up?" Paper draft XVII presented at Technical Group Meeting of the Group of 24, Geneva, Switzerland, March 8–9.

Independent Evaluation Group. 2009. "The World Bank's Country Policy and Institutional Assessment: An Evaluation." World Bank, June 30.

Kanbur, R. 2005. "Reforming the Formula: A Modest Proposal for Introducing Development Outcomes in IDA Allocation Procedures." Paper presented at the AFD-EUDN conference, Paris, France, November 25–27.

Kraay, A., and V. Nehru. 2004. "When Is External Debt Sustainable?" World Bank Policy Research Working Paper No. 3200.

Kurtz, M. J., and A. Schrank. 2007. "Growth and Governance: Models, Measures, and Mechanisms." *Journal of Politics* 2: 538–554.

Kuziemko, I., and Werker, E. 2006. "How Much Is a Seat on the Security Council Worth? Foreign Aid and Bribery at the United Nations." *Journal of Political Economy* 114: 905–930.

Levine, R., and D. Renelt. 1992. "A Sensitivity Analysis of Cross-Country Growth Regressions." *American Economic Review* 82 (4): 942–963.

Llavador, H. G., and J. E. Roemer. 2001. "An Equal-Opportunity Approach to the Allocation of International Aid." *Journal of Development Economics* 64: 147–171.

McGillivray, M. 2004. "Aid Effectiveness and Recipient Policy Regimes: A Comment on Ravi Kanbur's 'Reforming the Formula' Paper." Comment presented at the second AFD-EUDN Conference, Paris, France, November 25–27.

Ramey, G., and V. A. Ramey. 1995. "Cross-Country Evidence on the Link Between Volatility and Growth." *American Economic Review* 85 (5): 1138–1151.

Roodman, D. 2006. "An Index of Donor Performance." Center for Global Development Working Paper No. 67.

——. 2009a. "How to Do xtabond2: An Introduction to Difference and System GMM in Stata." *Stata Journal* 9 (1): 86–136.

——. 2009b. "Practitioners' Corner. A Note on the Theme of Too Many Instruments." *Oxford Bulletin of Economics and Statistics* 71 (1): 135–158.

Schraeder, P., S. Hook, and B. Taylor. 1998. "Clarifying the Foreign Aid Puzzle: A Comparison of American, Japanese, French, and Swedish Aid Flows." *World Politics* 50: 294–323.

Stiglitz, J. E. 1999. "The World Bank at the Millennium." *Economic Journal* 109 (459): F577–F597.

Stuckler, D., L. King, and G. Patton. 2009. "The Social Construction of Successful Market Reforms." Political Economy Research Institute working paper.

Van Waeyenberge, E. 2006. "The Missing Piece: Country Policy and Institutional Assessments at the Bank." University of Warwick.

Windmeijer, F. 2005. "A Finite Sample Correction for the Variance of Linear Efficient Two-Step GMM Estimators." *Journal of Econometrics* 126: 25–51.

Wood, A. 2007. "Looking Ahead Optimally in Allocating Aid." QEH Working Paper No. 137.

World Bank. 2001. "OED IDA Review: Review of the Performance Based Allocation System—IDA 10–12." Operations Evaluation Department (OED) Working Paper Series, IDA review 2001, World Bank, Washington, DC.

———. 2004. *Country Policy and Institutional Assessments: 2004 Assessment Questionnaire.* Operations Policy and Country Services. Washington, DC: World Bank.

———. 2005. *Economic Growth in the 1990s: Learning from a Decade of Reform.* Washington DC: The International Bank for Reconstruction and Development and World Bank.

———. 2007. *Country Policy and Institutional Assessments: 2007 Assessment Questionnaire.* Operations Policy and Country Services. Washington, DC: World Bank.

———. 2008. *Country Policy and Institutional Assessments: 2008 Assessment Questionnaire.* Operations Policy and Country Services. Washington, DC: World Bank.

Akbar Noman is at Columbia University, where he combines being a senior fellow at the Initiative for Policy Dialogue (IPD) with teaching as an adjunct at the School of International and Public Affairs. He is co-chair of IPD's Africa Task Force. Professor Noman's numerous publications include "Strategies for African Development" (jointly with Joseph Stiglitz) in *Good Growth and Governance in Africa: Rethinking Development Strategies* (Oxford University Press, 2012). He has wide-ranging experience of policy analysis and formulation in a variety of developing and transition economies, having worked extensively for the World Bank, as well as at the IMF and other international organizations and at senior levels of government. His other academic appointments have been at Oxford University (where he was also a student) and the Institute of Development Studies at the University of Sussex.

Joseph E. Stiglitz is university professor at Columbia University, the winner of the 2001 Nobel Memorial Prize in Economics, and a lead author of the 1995 IPCC report, which shared the 2007 Nobel Peace Prize. He was chairman of the U.S. Council of Economic Advisers under President Clinton and chief economist and senior vice president of the World Bank from 1997 to 2000. Stiglitz received the John Bates Clark Medal, awarded annually to the American economist under forty who has made the most significant contribution to the subject. He was a Fulbright Scholar at Cambridge University, held the Drummond Professorship at All Souls College Oxford, and has also taught at MIT, Yale, Stanford, and Princeton. He is the author most recently of *The Price of Inequality: How Today's Divided Society Endangers Our Future* (W. W. Norton & Co., 2012). In 2011, *Time* named him one of the world's one hundred most influential people.

Girum Abebe is a researcher at the Ethiopian Development Research Institute (EDRI). He obtained a PhD in Development Economics from the National Graduate Institute for Policy Studies (GRIPS) in Tokyo, Japan. He has been actively engaged in the study of issues in industrial development focusing mainly on mechanisms firms employ to learn new knowledge from technology leaders at home and abroad, and the roles human capital and agglomerations economies play in the learning process. He has also been working on field experiment designs, particularly in the implementations and impact evaluations of business and management skills training to young entrepreneurs and the impact evaluation of job search assistance schemes to young unemployed job seekers.

Julia Cagé is assistant professor in Economics at Sciences Po Paris. She received her Economics PhD from Harvard University in 2014. She specializes in Political Economy, Economic History, and International Economics. She is particularly interested in the media, especially the question of how media competition affects the provision of information and political attitudes. She is also working on international trade, studying the impact of trade liberalization on developing countries.

Ha-Joon Chang teaches economics at the University of Cambridge. In addition to numerous journal articles and book chapters, he has published fifteen authored books (four co-authored) and ten edited books. His main books include *The Political Economy of Industrial Policy* (Palgrave, 1994), *Kicking Away the Ladder* (Anthem Press, 2002), *Bad Samaritans* (Bloomsbury, 2010), *23 Things They Don't Tell You About Capitalism* (Bloomsbury, 2011), and *Economics: The User's Guide* (Bloomsbury, 2014). By the end of 2014, his writings will have been translated and published in thirty-six languages and thirty-nine countries. Worldwide, his books have sold around 1.8 million copies. He is the winner of the 2003 Gunnar Myrdal Prize and the 2005 Wassily Leontief Prize. He was ranked number nine in the *Prospect* magazine's World Thinkers 2014 poll.

Stephany Griffith-Jones is currently financial markets director at the Initiative for Policy Dialogue, based at Columbia University, and associate fellow at the Overseas Development Institute. Previously she was professorial fellow at the Institute of Development Studies at Sussex University, where she is now Emeritus. Her fields of research include reform of the international financial architecture, management of capital flows, the role of development banks, policies for restoring European growth, and the structure and regulation of the financial sector (with special focus on low-income countries, she is currently leading a project on this for ESRC and DfID). She held the position of Deputy Director of International Finance at the Commonwealth Secretariat and worked at the United Nations Department of Economic and Social Affairs and the Economic Commission for Latin America and the Caribbean, as well as advising numerous governments and international organizations. She has published over twenty books and written many scholarly and journalistic articles. One of her recent books, edited jointly with José Antonio Ocampo and Joseph Stiglitz, is *Time for the Visible Hand: Lessons from the 2008 World Financial Crisis* (Oxford University Press, 2012).

Akio Hosono is the current senior research adviser and former director (2011–2013) of Japan International Cooperation Agency (JICA) Research Institute. He holds a doctorate in economics from the University of Tokyo. After graduation he served in a variety of posts such as Vice-President at Tsukuba University in Tsukuba Science City, Japanese Ambassador to El Salvador, and Professor at the National Graduate Institute for Policy Studies (GRIPS) in Tokyo, Professor at the Research Institute of Economics and Business Administration at Kobe University to name a few. His publications include *Getting to Scale: How to Bring Development Solutions to Millions of Poor People* (with Chandy, Kharas, and Linn, Brookings Press, 2013); *Regional Integration and Economic Development* (with Saveedra, and Stallings, Palgrave, 2003); and *Development Strategies in East Asia and Latin America* (with Saveedra, Macmillan Press, 1998).

Ewa Karwowski is a lecturer in economics at Kingston University, London, and a PhD candidate at SOAS, London. Ewa Karwowski has worked as an economic consultant for government authorities in emerging economies and international organizations. She has published on macroeconomic stability, financial fragility, and Islamic banking.

Danny Leipziger is professor of International Business, George Washington University, and managing director, the Growth Dialogue. He is former vice president of the Poverty Reduction and Economic Management Network (2004–2009) at the World Bank. Over the course of his twenty-eight-year career at the World Bank, he held management positions in the East Asia Region and the Latin America and Caribbean Region, as well as in the World Bank Institute. Prior to joining the Bank, Dr. Leipziger served in senior positions at the U.S. Agency for International Development and the U.S. Department of State. He has also been a vice chair of the independent Commission on Growth and Development (2006–2010). He has published widely on topics of development economics and finance, industrial policy, and banking, including books on Korea, Chile, and East Asia and recent volumes *Globalization and Growth* (with Michael Spence, World Bank, 2010) and *Stuck in the Middle* (with Antonio Estache, Brookings Institution Press, 2009), and the most recent *Ascent after Decline: Regrowing Global Economies after the Great Recession* (with Otaviano Canuto, World Bank, 2012).

Annalisa Primi is senior economist at the OECD Development Centre in charge of analysis and policy advice on innovation and industrial development. She is the coordinator of the OECD Policy Dialogue Initiative on GVCs, Production Transformation and Development. She has been the lead economist for the OECD *Perspectives on Global Development 2013: Industrial Policies in a Changing World* (OECD, 2013). From 2003 to 2009 she worked at the United Nations Economic Commission for Latin America and the Caribbean (CEPAL). Her work focuses on the linkages among innovation, production development, and intellectual property and the role of the state in shaping development trajectories. She has extensive experience in targeted policy support and technical assistance in emerging and developing economies on innovation and industrial policies. She has a record of official and academic publications such as *Start-up Latin America: Promoting Innovation in the Region* (OECD, 2013); *Industrial Policies and Territorial Development: Lessons from Korea* (OECD, 2012); co-author of *Intellectual Property and Industrial Development: A Critical Assessment* (with Cimoli, Dosi, and Stiglitz, Oxford University Press, 2009); and *Industrial Policy and Development* (Oxford University Press, 2009). She holds a PhD in Economics from the School of Business and Economics of the University of Maastricht, an MA in

International Cooperation and Economic Development from the University of Pavia (Italy), and a degree *cum laude* in Economics of Institutions and Financial Markets at the University of Tor Vegata (Italy).

Florian Schaefer is research officer and PhD candidate in the Department of Development Studies at SOAS, University of London. He holds a BSc and an MSc from the University of Bristol and the London School of Economics, respectively. His PhD focuses on commercial agriculture and industrial policy in Ethiopia. Florian has spent several years living in Ethiopia, where he worked as an ODI fellow in the Ministry of Water and Energy and later as an independent researcher. He has published on industrial policy and the political economy of industrial policymaking in Ethiopia, as well as on power relations in defining how development is measured.

Go Shimada is Associate Professor of International Economics, Graduate School of International Relations, the University of Shizuoka, Visiting Scholar of Columbia University, Visiting Scholar of JICA Research Institute, Adjunct Researcher of Waseda University. Dr. Shimada joined JICA in 1992, where his past appointments have included Director, Trade and Investment Division, Department of Industrial Development, Special Assistance to the President, Office of the President, First Secretary, Permanent Mission of Japan to the United Nations, New York. He has a PhD in International Studies from Waseda University and an MA in Economics from the University of Manchester.

Shahid Yusuf is currently chief economist of the Growth Dialogue at the George Washington University School of Business in Washington, DC. He holds a PhD in Economics from Harvard University and a BA in Economics from Cambridge University. Prior to joining the Growth Dialogue, Dr. Yusuf was on the staff of the World Bank. During his thirty-five-year tenure at the World Bank, Dr. Yusuf was the team leader for the World Bank-Japan project on East Asia's Future Economy from 2000 to 2009. He was director of the *World Development Report 1999/2000, Entering the 21st Century*. Prior to that, he was economic adviser to the senior vice president and chief economist (1997–1998), lead economist for the East Africa Department (1995–1997), and lead economist for the China and Mongolia Department (1989–1993). Dr. Yusuf has also authored or edited twenty-six books on industrial and urban development, innovation systems, and tertiary education, which have been translated into a number of different languages. He has written extensively on development issues, with a special focus on East Asia, and has also published widely in academic journals.